A Critical Theory of Global Justice

A Critical Theory of Global Justice

The Frankfurt School and World Society

MALTE FRØSLEE IBSEN

Great Clarendon Street, Oxford, OX2 6DP,
United Kingdom

Oxford University Press is a department of the University of Oxford.
It furthers the University's objective of excellence in research, scholarship,
and education by publishing worldwide. Oxford is a registered trade mark of
Oxford University Press in the UK and in certain other countries

© Malte Frøslee Ibsen 2023

The moral rights of the author have been asserted

Impression: 1

All rights reserved. No part of this publication may be reproduced, stored in
a retrieval system, or transmitted, in any form or by any means, without the
prior permission in writing of Oxford University Press, or as expressly permitted
by law, by licence or under terms agreed with the appropriate reprographics
rights organization. Enquiries concerning reproduction outside the scope of the
above should be sent to the Rights Department, Oxford University Press, at the
address above

You must not circulate this work in any other form
and you must impose this same condition on any acquirer

Published in the United States of America by Oxford University Press
198 Madison Avenue, New York, NY 10016, United States of America

British Library Cataloguing in Publication Data
Data available

Library of Congress Control Number: 2022943174

ISBN 978–0–19–286412–3

DOI: 10.1093/oso/9780192864123.001.0001

Printed and bound by
CPI Group (UK) Ltd, Croydon, CR0 4YY

Links to third party websites are provided by Oxford in good faith and
for information only. Oxford disclaims any responsibility for the materials
contained in any third party website referenced in this work.

For Simone, with love

Acknowledgements

Writing this book has been a fantastic voyage. It has spanned ten years of my life, in which I have had the privilege of calling Frankfurt, Berlin, New York, and Copenhagen my intellectual and physical home. Looking back now, it is clear to me that the impetus for writing this book is ultimately rooted in the historical experience of the 2008 financial crisis, which not only sent shock waves through the global economy but also rattled me out my own dogmatic slumber, ripping off my personal veil of ignorance to expose the irrationality and unreasonableness of this world of financialized global capitalism. The book was finished amidst a new global crisis, the COVID-19 pandemic. To me, both of these global crisis experiences have only served to accentuate the acute relevance and importance of the book's undertaking. I hope others may feel the same way.

Many travel companions have joined me on this voyage, more than I can remember, and many of whom have contributed in crucial ways to my intellectual journey and the life of this book. The book began as a doctoral dissertation at the Goethe Universität Frankfurt, written under the supervision of Rainer Forst and Axel Honneth. Rainer has been a true *Doktorvater* in the emphatic sense of that German word. He believed in the project from the first time I met him at a conference in London, and he has offered invaluable intellectual guidance, friendship, and support throughout the whole process—as he has continued to do after I left Frankfurt in 2016. This expression of gratitude seems woefully insufficient, but I offer it nonetheless. Axel Honneth not only offered his unsurpassed knowledge into the Frankfurt School tradition of critical theory during supervision in Frankfurt, but also kindly extended an invitation to the Philosophy Faculty at Columbia University in the fall semester of 2016, where our long talks proved immensely helpful for the subsequent comprehensive reworking of the dissertation into a book manuscript. I also want to thank Jürgen Habermas, who on several occasions in Heidelberg and Frankfurt took time to discuss the dissertation with me—and offer anecdotes about Adorno. He remains, in many ways, my great intellectual hero, and I am grateful for the privilege of personally experiencing the magnetic aura of our greatest European thinker and intellectual, a living embodiment of the postwar history of Western philosophy.

I must extend a special debt of love and gratitude to three dear friends and intellectual travel companions, who have made an inestimable mark on my thinking since our Oxford days—Theresa Clasen, Jeffrey Howard, and Tobias Berger—as well as to Anders Dahl Sørensen, who has been the closest of friends, a non-metaphorical travel companion, and an intellectual interlocutor since high school. I am also grateful to the old Frankfurt crowd, especially Johannes Schulz, Dorothea Gädeke, Julian Culp, Arvi-Antti Särkelä, Casper Mölck, Esther Lea Neuhann, Marius Piwonka, Philipp Schink, Tamara Jugov, Federica Gregoratto, Darrel Mollendorf, Martin Saar, Thomas Biebricher, and Titus Stahl, for intellectual stimulus and friendship alike.

I thank Neal Carrier, Navid Pourgazi, Despina Potari, Matteo Garavoglia, Christian Schemmel, David Axelsen, Ditte Maria Brasso Sørensen, Rune Møller Stahl, Siri Ranva Hjelm Jacobsen, Tiago Rito, Poya Pakzad, and Emily Hertz for helping me, in various ways, along the way. I also thank Christian Rostbøll and Lars Tønder, who read and commented on parts of the book manuscript and offered helpful advice on publication. Emma Holten has become a dear friend and comrade, who read and commented on the entire manuscript—tak! Dominic Byatt at Oxford University Press has been the kind of editor you hope for but don't dare expect. I thank him for his enthusiastic support for the project and for his gracious and professional sheepherding of this book to publication. I also thank two anonymous referees for Oxford University Press, whose prescient criticisms vastly improved the manuscript.

I admit to sometimes having feared that this fantastic voyage would turn to erosion and never get old—to paraphrase the great David Bowie. The fact that it has come to life is no small part due to the unwavering love and support of my family: my sister Siri and my mum and dad, Anne-Mette and Bjarne. Along this book's journey, I experienced the secular miracle of becoming a father myself, first to my daughter Frida and subsequently to my son Finn. Frida's and Finn's presence in this world and future on the planet has given a concrete meaning to the fears and hopes embodied in this work. Finally, my greatest debt of gratitude: For your love and companionship in life and letters, for your unyielding support and sacrifice in allowing me the space to work endless hours on this project, for having gifted me our *to små muler*, for your forgiveness of my faults. This book is for you.

Contents

Introduction 1
  0.1 A Bourgeoning World Society 1
  0.2 The Contradictions of Critical Theory 3
  0.3 The Idea of a Critical Theory 6
    0.3.1 The Historical Dimension 7
    0.3.2 The Sociological Dimension 10
    0.3.3 The Normative Dimension 12
    0.3.4 The Practical Criterion of Validity 14
  0.4 An Outline of the Book 17

PART I. HORKHEIMER

1. Max Horkheimer and the Original Paradigm of Critical Theory 27
  1.1 Stages in the Project of a Critical Theory of Society ... 27
    1.1.1 Materialism and Ideologiekritik 30
    1.1.2 Traditional Theory and Critical Theory 35
  1.2 Marx, Lukács, and the Materialist Philosophy of History .. 40
    1.2.1 Historical Materialism 40
    1.2.2 Lukács and the Theory of Reification 42
    1.2.3 Lukács's Theory of Class Consciousness 45
    1.2.4 Class Consciousness as an Empirical Problem 46
  1.3 Structural Transformations in Capitalism and Class Consciousness 47
    1.3.1 Monopoly Capitalism 48
    1.3.2 Freudo-Marxism and the Rise of Fascism 51
  1.4 Critical Theory and Bourgeois Morality 56
    1.4.1 A Reasonable Society 56
    1.4.2 A Critical Theory of Justice 61

2. Horkheimer's Original Paradigm and the Idea of a Critical Theory of World Society 66
  2.1 'Existing capitalist society, which has spread all over the world from Europe and for which the theory is declared valid' 66

      2.1.1 Colonialism, Empire, and the Trappings of Historical
           Materialism   67
      2.1.2 Pluralism, Political Economy, and the Rise of
           Right-Wing Populism   72
      2.1.3 Emancipation, Ecology, and the Mastery of Nature   75
  2.2 Horkheimer in Exile   77

PART II. ADORNO

3. Theodor W. Adorno and the Negativist Paradigm
   of Critical Theory   85
  3.1 Reflections from a Damaged Life   85
      3.1.1 Philosophy as Interpretation   86
      3.1.2 Negative Dialektik   92
  3.2 The Dialectic of Enlightenment   99
      3.2.1 Enlightenment Reverts to Mythology   100
      3.2.2 Myth is already Enlightenment   102
  3.3 A Physiognomy of Late-Capitalist Society   104
      3.3.1 The Administered World   107
      3.3.2 Ego-Weakness and the Universal System of Delusion   110
  3.4 The Dialectic of Individual Autonomy   118
      3.4.1 Mündigkeit   118
      3.4.2 Mimesis and an Ethics of Resistance   122

4. Adorno's Negativist Paradigm and the Idea of a Critical
   Theory of World Society   127
  4.1 The Consummate Eurocentric   127
      4.1.1 Expressive Totality and the Vanishing of World
           Society   128
      4.1.2 Non-Identity at the End: An Ecological Dialectic
           of Enlightenment   132
      4.1.3 The 'Non-Identical' of Western Modernity   135
  4.2 Adorno and the Student Movement   142

PART III. HABERMAS

5. Jürgen Habermas and the Communicative Paradigm
   of Critical Theory   149
  5.1 'The Leading Systematic Philosopher of Our Time'   149
  5.2 Foundations of a Critical Theory of Society   151
      5.2.1 The Theory of Knowledge as Social Theory   151
      5.2.2 A Formal Pragmatics of Communicative Reason   155
      5.2.3 'A Social Life in Uncoerced Communication'   163
  5.3 The Theory of Social Evolution   172

5.3.1 A Reconstruction of Historical Materialism	172
5.3.2 The Rationalization of the Lifeworld	175
5.4 The Theory of Communicative Action	177
5.4.1 System and Lifeworld	177
5.4.2 The Colonization Thesis	184
5.5 The Normative Content of Modernity	187
5.5.1 Discourse Ethics	188
5.5.2 A Discourse Theory of Law and Democracy	192
6. Habermas's Communicative Paradigm and the Idea of Critical Theory of World Society	200
6.1 A Kantian Cosmopolitanism	200
6.1.1 The Postnational Constellation and a Multilevel Global Constitutional Framework	200
6.1.2 The Limits of Law	208
6.1.3 The Limit of Proceduralism	213
6.1.4 The Limits of Western Modernity	214
6.1.5 The Limits of Intersubjectivity	217
6.2 The Last Marxist?	219

PART IV. HONNETH

7. Axel Honneth and the Recognition Paradigm of Critical Theory	227
7.1 Introduction	227
7.2 Early Themes: Power, and the Recovery of the Social	228
7.2.1 The Critique of Power	228
7.2.2 Three Conceptions of Power	234
7.3 The Struggle for Recognition	239
7.3.1 The Original Programme	239
7.3.2 Innovations and Revisions	246
7.4 The Reality of Freedom as Democratic Ethical Life	250
7.4.1 The Turn to Hegel's Mature Political Philosophy	250
7.4.2 Communicative Freedom: An Excursus on Kant and Hegel	253
7.4.3 Das Recht der Freiheit	261
7.4.4 A Hegelian Account of Moral Normativity	278
8. Honneth's Recognition Paradigm and the Idea of a Critical Theory of World Society	283
8.1 Beyond Social Freedom?	283
8.1.1 A Western-European 'Culture of Freedom'	283
8.1.2 The Limits of Hegelianism	290
8.1.3 Natural Conditions of Autonomy	292

PART V. ALLEN AND FORST

9. Amy Allen's Contextualist Paradigm of Critical Theory	299
9.1 A New Synthesis with Poststructuralism	299
9.2 Power, Autonomy, and Allen's 'Contextualization of Habermas'	299
9.3 Decolonizing Critical Theory: The Idea of Self-Problematizing Critique	304
10. Rainer Forst's Justification Paradigm of Critical Theory	313
10.1 Reason, Power, and Justification	313
10.2 The Right to Justification	313
10.2.1 The Ground of Morality	316
10.3 A Critique of Relations of Justification	322
10.4 Beyond Proceduralism and Ethical Life	332
10.5 A Critical Theory of Transnational Justice	336
Conclusion: The Tasks of a Critical Theory of World Society	342
11.1 Kantian Constructivism and Self-Problematizing Critique: The Dialectic of Power and Autonomy	343
11.2 The Critique of Global Capitalist Modernity	348
11.3 Methodological Holism and the Planetary	351
Bibliography	353
Index	363

Introduction

> The only respectable form of philosophy in view of the desperation would be the attempt to regard all things as they appear from the standpoint of redemption. Knowledge has no light like that which the redemption shines upon the world: everything else disappears in reconstruction and remains a piece of technique. Perspectives must be constructed in which the world is equally displaced, unfamiliar, its cracks and tears revealed, as it will one day lay bare, needing and disfigured in the Messianic light. Without arbitrariness and violence, to win such perspectives fully out of empathy with the objects, that alone is what thinking comes down to.
>
> Theodor W. Adorno, *Minima Moralia*

0.1 A Bourgeoning World Society

These words are committed to paper at a time when the world is in the grip of a deadly pandemic virus. Scientists tell us that such outbreaks of infectious diseases are going to occur at greater frequency in the future, as a result of anthropogenic climate change. Coastal areas will be increasingly prone to flooding from rising ocean levels, while inland habitats and agriculture will be exposed to draughts and extreme weather events with increasing frequency and volatility. Due to global warming, ever greater parts of the Earth's land surface will become inhospitable to human life, which will produce millions of climate refugees, fleeing from the onslaught of natural ecosystems that have been fundamentally destabilized by human activity. In short, as a result of the combustion of fossil energy sources that power industrialized societies across the globe, the natural existential conditions for life on Earth will gradually worsen through the generations—in the worst-case long-term scenario, making our planetary home all-but 'unliveable'.

The human destabilization of age-old equilibria within the Earth system mirrors, in quite unsettling ways, the recent destabilization of equilibria within the heavily financialized and unfathomably unequal global economic system. In just over a decade, the world economy has experienced two shocks of a similar magnitude to the theretofore worst financial and economic crisis in human history, the first unleashed by endogenous forces within a pathologically bloated financial system, the second by an external shock from a pathogen that likely migrated from bats to humans somewhere in a Chinese province. Societies across the globe today experience dramatic repercussions of events that happen in distant lands, as the failure of a single investment bank on Wall Street can bring down the whole globally integrated economy and cast millions across the world into unemployment and destitution, while a virus can travel with hitherto unheard-of speed through a global network of commercial airline traffic, which again reflects a historically unprecedented level of global economic integration across finance, production, and trade.

The burgeoning *world society* that has emerged from these formidable forces of integration is shot through with contradictions. Power appears more dispersed through global networks than ever before, yet to many the powerful seem more remote and removed from the bread-and-butter concerns of ordinary people than at any time in living memory. We are told that globalized capitalism has lifted millions out of the scourge of poverty and drastically reduced global inequality through the rise of an Asian 'middle class', yet domestic economic inequality is approaching levels unseen since before the First World War. More people are uprooted and exiled from their homes, and more people are free to travel across borders than ever before in human history, yet new physical and mental barriers are erected to stave off 'hoards' of unwanted refugees and deny migrants the 'right to hospitality' that Kant saw as the only true cosmopolitan right. The global integration of economies, cultures, and digitalized public spheres and dense networks of global travel has brought us closer than ever before to far-away peoples, yet we seem to be fatally bereft of the kind of transnational or global institutional structures that might allow us to politically tame the disruptive forces of globalized capitalism and avert the permanent catastrophe of a drastically heated Earth system.

Global societal integration represents a formidable challenge to philosophy and social science, making a mockery of John Rawls's 'idealised assumption' of 'closed societies' that 'persons enter only by birth, and exit only by death'.[1] The notion of 'society' as a geographically, culturally, and politically demarcated entity was always an abstraction—and it was never an innocent one—trading on fragmented linguistic and cultural lifeworlds while ignoring cross-border economic relations and external relations of overt political domination. But decades of ever-intensifying globalization have rendered that assumption irrevocably indefensible, to the extent that 'methodological nationalism' has today become close to a meaningless fiction.

Many social theorists and philosophers have taken stock of this fundamental shift within the object of social-scientific study and normative thinking, while others still neglect or refuse to countenance its implications. Yet more than anything, what might ultimately force a perspective change from nationally demarcated societies to a world society of societies might be the disruptive and potentially

---

[1] John Rawls, *The Law of Peoples* (Cambridge MA: Harvard University Press, 1999).

catastrophic forces of climate change, which have already provoked a global scientific response that calls, with increasing desperation, for a globally coordinated political response. This emerging *planetary* perspective of human society as part of an integrated Earth system of ecological interchange between natural and social systems has even given rise to a new geo-historical classification of the present epoch in the planet's existence: the Anthropocene, where human civilization has itself become a geological force to be reckoned with.

This book is written on the assumption that critical theory has yet to come to terms with the implications of this novel historical constellation. What is the meaning of the idea of a 'critical theory of society' in a world in which so many of the bounds between states, cultures, and communities have all but eroded—in an emergent world society? What becomes of the left-Hegelian philosophical project of 'grasping its time in thought' when modernity is no longer conceived in terms of a temporal *and* spatial disjuncture between modern and pre-modern societies—at once historically differentiated, as well as culturally and geographically differentiated within a single moment in time—but as a truly global condition? From the point of view of critical theory, this philosophical problem has until now escaped systematic treatment. It is the purpose of this book to fill this *lacuna* in the literature.

0.2 The Contradictions of Critical Theory

The Frankfurt School tradition of critical theory today finds itself in a curious position. On the one hand, the Frankfurt School has achieved undisputed global fame, and critical theory is taught in departments and universities across the world. At the same time, however, critical theory is today rarely *practiced* in the sense intended by its founders. As originally conceived, critical theory was supposed to offer an interdisciplinary and cooperative theoretical vehicle for apprehending the injustices and pathologies of modern capitalist society, with the aim of allowing agents to overcome those injustices and pathologies in practice. In the contemporary academy, this distinctive methodological outlook—with its commitment to enabling large-scale practical emancipation through a comprehensive and interdisciplinary theory of society—has largely given way to rivalling currents of thought to an extent that the concept of 'critical theory' is today widely understood in a very different sense from its intended meaning when Max Horkheimer coined the term in 1937. Accordingly, any book on critical theory must today begin by clarifying exactly what is meant by this term.

One of the important tensions within the contemporary meaning of critical theory is that the *methodological holism* characteristic of the Frankfurt School sense of critical theory—which is what I will call a methodological orientation towards the 'totality' of society, or towards society as such, in the various senses of that term to be exemplified in the chapters of this book—has largely given way to a *methodological nominalism*—which is what I will call an orientation towards how social reality is discursively constituted through discrete forms of power, and which eschews the attempt to disclose a unified background structure or develop a general theoretical framework. A second and associated shift in meaning is a move away from the Frankfurt School's defining concern with *human emancipation* towards more ambiguous normative concerns with 'not being governed like that', the 'subversion of binary oppositions', etc. In Michel Foucault's affirmative summation of this transformation, 'the historical ontology of ourselves must turn away from all projects that claim to be *global* or *radical*'.[2]

These tensions and gradual shifts in meaning of the very concept of critical theory may to some extent reflect the great philosophical debate between 'modern' and so-called 'postmodern' currents of thought. Arising from developments in French philosophy in the 1980s, postmodernism is—insofar as it makes sense to speak of a coherent body of thought at all—characterized by its strong suspicion of 'grand narratives'. Jean-Francois Lyotard, a prominent harbinger of postmodernity, describes as modern 'any science that legitimates itself with reference to a metadiscourse of this kind making an explicit appeal to some grand narrative, such as the dialectics of Spirit, the hermeneutics of meaning, the emancipation of the rational or working subject, or the creation of wealth'.[3] The Frankfurt School tradition of critical theory unabashedly embraces such grand narratives, which may be one reason that its influence has faded in tandem with the rise of postmodern sentiments throughout the academy and the post-Marxist intellectual climate of the left after the fall of the Berlin Wall.

However, I want to suggest that something above and beyond grand philosophical shifts may also be at work here. The Frankfurt School's relative theoretical marginalization has not only taken place in parallel with the rise of 'postmodernism' but also, and perhaps just as importantly, in the course of the present wave of globalization, and in the course of a concomitant and acutely warranted decentring and even 'provincialization' of Western political consciousness. More specifically, the displacement of the Frankfurt School tradition of critical theory may have been midwifed in part by the remarkable silence of its historical standard bearer's on some of the central struggles of our day, such as struggles against sexism or racism, or against colonial, neocolonial, and imperial forms of domination, and in part by a growing recognition of the deeply *Eurocentric* assumptions of some of its main theoretical protagonists—as forcefully argued by Amy Allen in *The End of Progress: Decolonizing the Normative Foundations of Critical Theory* from 2016.

---

[2] Michel Foucault, 'What Is Enlightenment?', in *The Politics of Truth*, ed. by Sylvère Lotringer (Cambridge MA: Semiotext(e), 2007), p. 114 [emphases added].

[3] Jean-Francois Lyotard, *The Postmodern Condition: A Report on Knowledge*, transl. by Geoff Bennington et al. (Manchester: Manchester University Press, 1984), p. xxiii.

It is one of the working assumptions of the present book that the charge of Eurocentrism not only has merit but also helps to explain the gradual displacement of Frankfurt School critical theory from the contemporary academy. In each of the chapters of this book, I will thus be concerned with determining the extent to which the charge of Eurocentrism applies to the central philosophical protagonists of the Frankfurt School tradition. Although I will defend the tradition from some of Allen's specific criticisms and objections, I will also argue that a critical theory of world society must embrace and incorporate the sort of epistemic humility and problematizing critique of the blind spots and distortions of Western modernity propounded by postcolonial and feminist scholars, and Allen in particular.

Moreover, although the first generation of the Frankfurt School shared a deep concern with the relationship between human society and nature, more recent iterations of the Frankfurt School idea of a critical theory of society have had surprisingly little to say about this ecological relationship—and, specifically, about the devastating impact of fossil-fuelled capitalist expansion and economic development on the natural ecosystems that may ultimately threaten the natural conditions of existence for much of life on Earth, including human life. The fact that critical theorists in the Frankfurt School tradition have had little to say about anthropogenic climate change and its potentially catastrophic implications may be another reason for the tradition's relative marginalization in recent years. In this book, I will therefore also be concerned with reconstructing what they have actually had to say about ecological questions and with drawing out the implications for comprehending the relationship between society and nature that we find in the work of some of the tradition's central thinkers.

Yet the central project of this book is to expound and defend the *idea* of Frankfurt School critical theory in the context of an emergent world society and to argue that its animating theoretical aspirations are just as relevant and worthwhile as when originally conceived. I use the concept of 'world society' as what Jürgen Habermas has called a 'placeholder' concept: as an abstract philosophical concept 'standing in' for a *theory* of world society.[4] The purpose of this book is not to develop a full-fledged critical theory of world society, but rather to think about *what such a project might mean*, through a critical reconstructive engagement with the Frankfurt School tradition as a whole that combines the twin perspectives of the history of ideas with the systematic intentions of social and political theory. I pursue this aim through what Axel Honneth calls a 'history of theory with systemic intent': that is, through a reconstruction of a distinctive philosophical tradition

---

[4] Jürgen Habermas, 'Philosophy as Stand-In and Interpreter', in *Moral Consciousness and Communicative Action*, transl. by Christian Lenhardt and Shierry Weber Nicholson (Cambridge: Polity Press, 1990).

with the aim of uncovering in this tradition a *learning process* that culminates in a sketch of the foundations and elemental building blocks of a critical theory of world society. However, as Honneth remarks, 'The history of critical theory could be conceived as a learning process only if at least an indication of the standard was first specified by which insight or progress within that theoretical development was to be measured'.[5]

In the following third section, I thus want to provide a brief introductory account of the idea of a critical theory of society, which, I hope, will become clearer as this idea is given substantive content in the course of the book, before in the fourth section I present an outline of the book's central arguments and conclusions. Such an introductory account is also warranted in part because the idea of critical theory has *itself* been appropriated by diverse alternative currents in cultural and literary theory, and it is therefore decisive that we get a clear sense of what is so distinctive about this idea, as originally conceived by Horkheimer and the Frankfurt School. The account that I present here construes critical theory as defined by a commitment to *three core methodological dimensions*, as well as a distinctive *criterion of validity*, where an account of each of these three methodological dimensions represents a necessary condition for a theory to qualify as a critical theory of society, and only an account of all of them a sufficient set of conditions for qualifying as a comprehensive critical theory in the Frankfurt School sense of the term.

0.3 The Idea of a Critical Theory

As we shall see in Parts 1 to Parts 4, I reconstruct the Frankfurt School tradition of critical theory as *four paradigms of critical theory*: the original paradigm of the young Max Horkheimer, the negativist paradigm of Theodor W. Adorno, the communicative paradigm of Jürgen Habermas, and the recognition paradigm by Axel Honneth. In Part 5, I add two emerging paradigms to this reconstruction: the contextualist paradigm developed by Amy Allen, and the justification paradigm developed by Rainer Forst. Each of these paradigms of critical theory offers distinctive accounts of the three methodological dimensions with different accents and emphases arising from their respective substantive commitments. But they are nevertheless distinguished as paradigms *of critical theory* in virtue of sharing a *methodological commitment* to these three dimensions and a distinctive practical criterion of validity. I describe them as methodological dimensions in a broad sense: they are rooted in certain philosophical assumptions about the nature of social reality, the epistemology of social inquiry, and the relationship between

---

[5] Axel Honneth, *The Critique of Power: Reflective Stages in a Critical Social Theory*, transl. by Kenneth Baynes (Cambridge MA: The MIT Press, 1991).

social theory and practice. Although these assumptions are formulated at a fairly general and abstract level, they are not completely formal or vacuous, and some of them are quite controversial indeed.

In what follows, I provide a brief exposition of each dimension and the most important assumptions undergirding each of these core dimensions, and, finally, of critical theory's practical criterion of validity. It is of course possible for someone to be committed to the methodological idea of a critical theory while only providing an account of some of these three commitments. Indeed, given the extremely ambitious and demanding nature of that idea, it will often be the case that any individual person will focus his or her attention on one or more of these dimensions, while bearing in mind that such work only pertains to parts of the methodological framework that constitutes a comprehensive critical theory of society, which represents—as we shall see—an inherently cooperative and interdisciplinary theoretical endeavour. I call any theory that provides (or aspires to provide) an account of all three dimensions, and which submits to its practical criterion of validity, a *paradigm* of critical theory—or a *comprehensive* critical theory.

0.3.1 The Historical Dimension

The first dimension of a critical theory of society comprises a *historical account* of the theory's own context of origin, situating the theory within the historical evolution of society as a whole. However, this historical account of the theory's context of origin is not historiography in the ordinary sense. Rather, this dimension requires a diachronic account of *a socially embodied reason*, from which a critical theory can *reflexively reconstruct* itself, including its own normative standard. This latter claim represents the perhaps most ambitious and controversial assumption of Frankfurt School critical theory: namely, the Hegelian idea that reason should not be understood as a faculty of the human mind, but rather as an essentially social and historically evolved phenomenon. Axel Honneth describes this idea as follows:

> Critical Theory ... —and in a way that may be unique to it—insists on a mediation of theory and history in a concept of socially effective rationality. That is, the historical past should be understood from a practical point of view: as a process of development whose pathological deformation by capitalism may be overcome only by initiating a process of enlightenment among those involved. It is this working model of the intertwining of theory and history that grounds the unity of Critical Theory, despite its variety of voices. Whether in its positive form with the early Horkheimer, Marcuse, or Habermas or in its negative form with Theodor Adorno or Benjamin, one finds the same idea forming the

background of each of the different projects—namely, that social relationships distort the historical process of development in a way that one can only practically remedy.[6]

The basic thought here might be understood as follows. Any human society is ordered by certain normative rules that regulate interaction in various spheres of life, and the members of a society will have to master these rules if they are to be able to participate in social life. These rules are in turn the outcome of a long historical process, in which successive generations have learned to master and augment these rules according to various contextual considerations and changes in the social and natural environment. As we shall see in what follows, all four paradigms of Frankfurt School critical theory agree that, in the course of human history, these normative rules become gradually more differentiated and sophisticated, and that we can grasp the development of these rules as a process of *social rationalization*.

The historical dimension of a critical theory requires an account of this process of social rationalization—that is, of reason as a historically evolved set of normative rules embedded in social practice. Moreover, aside from first-order rules that govern social interaction, we also find in several paradigms an assumption that we can reconstruct certain *second-order rules*, which undergird the first-order rules in different social spheres by providing their underlying conditions of possibility. I will not go further into this issue here, but, as we shall see, candidates for such second-order rules in the Frankfurt School tradition include the rules that regulate communicative interaction, mutual recognition, and relations of justification.

To be sure, the assumption that it even makes sense to provide such an account of a socially embodied, historically evolved reason relies on a further premise: namely, that the dynamic historical process in which these rational rules of action unfold *itself* has some kind of rational structure that we can account for. Without such a rational developmental structure, historical development would simply be an anarchic and contingent process in which we would not be able to detect any pattern or sense of direction. The historical dimension of a critical theory assumes that we can and do find such patterns in social history, which we can reconstruct as following a certain rational pattern or 'developmental logic'.[7]

The assumptions undergirding the historical dimension of critical theory can thus be summarized as follows. First, the historical dimension of a critical theory

---

[6] Axel Honneth, 'A Social Pathology of Reason: On the Intellectual Legacy of Critical Theory', in *Pathologies of Reason: On the Legacy of Critical Theory*, transl. by James Ingram (New York: Columbia University Press, 2009), p. 21.

[7] Jürgen Habermas, *Zur Rekonstruktion des Historischen Materialismus* (Frankfurt: Suhrkamp, 1976), p. 155.

presupposes a conception of reason that refers to historically evolved rules governing social interaction within different spheres of social life. Second, the historical process in which these rules have developed exhibits a coherent structure. Third, this structure can be theoretically reconstructed. Of course, if such a historical account of socially embodied reason is to avoid the risk of complacency, licencing all existing rules of conduct as 'rational', a further assumption is needed. Indeed, it is a fourth and equally central assumption of the Frankfurt School tradition that historically evolved, socially embodied reason can *itself* serve a systematic function in the establishment and maintenance of relations of domination. The assumption here is that the historically evolved rational rules of action may enable some social groups to dominate others, or might *themselves* dominate individual subjects in virtue of the *kind* of structures of social interaction to which they give rise. Indeed, it is precisely this thought that animates the famous credo of the first generation of the Frankfurt School: namely, the idea of reason 'reverting into its opposite'.

Accordingly, the Frankfurt School ambition goes further than illuminating how a historically evolved and socially embodied reason might facilitate or become complicit in certain forms or structures of domination. Indeed, the aim is nothing less than the Kantian project of a *critique of reason through reason itself*: to reconstruct *through* the historical account of socially embodied reason a *normative* dimension that enables critical theory to analyse and illuminate relations and structures of domination as 'pathologies of reason'[8]—that is, where reason has reverted into domination—with the aim of *overcoming those pathologies in practice*. We might capture this double-sidedness in reason—with the idea of 'rational' rules of action that both facilitate domination as well as enable emancipation—in terms of the Kantian distinction between the *reasonable* and the *rational*, which has been popularized by John Rawls but which we also find in the work of the young Max Horkheimer. Indeed, Horkheimer explicitly argues that the 'idea of morality, as Kant has formulated it, contains the truth that the [rational] courses of action ... are not necessarily also the reasonable ones'.[9]

This points to a central category in the young Horkheimer's original paradigm, but which we find in some form or other in all paradigms of critical theory: namely, the normative idea of a 'reasonable society', which is understood precisely in terms of a *societal congruence between the reasonable and the rational*. The distinction between the reasonable and the rational thus allows us to appreciate how rules for action that can be rational at the individual level may nonetheless be unreasonable at the collective level, by allowing some social groups to dominate others, or by

---

[8] Honneth, 'A Social Pathology of Reason'.
[9] Max Horkheimer, 'Materialismus und Moral', in *Gesammelte Schriften Band 3: Schriften 1931–1936*, ed. by Alfred Schmidt (Frankfurt: Fischer, 2009), p. 118. For Rawls's account of the distinction, see John Rawls, 'Kantian Constructivism in Moral Theory', in *Collected Papers*, ed. by Samuel Freeman (Cambridge MA: Harvard University Press, 2001).

forming part of a basic structure of society which can itself in some sense dominate individual subjects. The historical account of socially embodied reason is thus also meant to allow a critical theory to reflexively reconstruct a normative standard, which can then be applied in a *sociological* account of relations and structures of domination within the basic structure of society, to which we now turn.

0.3.2 The Sociological Dimension

The second methodological dimension of a critical theory comprises a *sociological account* of the basic structure of society that illuminates and accounts for the relations and structures of domination that it enables or facilities. Note that I use 'sociological' in a broad sense that encompasses political economy, social psychology, and other associated social-scientific disciplines. Moreover, as we shall see, we can construe the Frankfurt School claim that both individual agents and social structures can dominate agents in virtue of the overarching criterion of *autonomy-impairment*, such that any agent, institution, or social structure which impairs the autonomy (or the development of the necessary social conditions of autonomy) of an individual agent is defined as dominating that agent. This second dimension rests on two crucial assumptions: first, that *society has a basic structure*, and, second, that this basic structure is *key to illuminating relations and structures of domination*.

The concept of the basic structure of society gained widespread credence in Anglophone political philosophy under the influence of Rawls's *A Theory of Justice*, but the Frankfurt School in fact employed the concept of the basic structure of society (*'die Grundstruktur der Gesellschaft'*[10]) long before Rawls. In critical theory, as in Rawls, the idea of the basic structure of society should be understood primarily as a *qualitative* notion. That is to say, the basic structure refers to *the way in which a given form of social life orders and arranges its various component parts and reproduces itself over time*. In other words, the concept of the basic structure of society tells us something about what *kind* of society we live in, in terms of the overall arrangement of its constituent elements into a more or less socially coherent and temporally continuous whole.

The content of the basic structure of society therefore changes through the epochs, and it is impossible to give a transhistorically valid conceptual criterion for demarcating the basic structure in abstraction from an account of present and bygone basic structures of society. To be sure, the basic structure of society is not something we can go out and measure in the sense that we can measure voter

---

[10] See, for example, Theodor W. Adorno, *Erziehung zur Mündigkeit* (Frankfurt: Suhrkamp, 1971), p. 88; or Hebert Marcuse, 'Der Kampf gegen den Liberalismus in der totalitären Staatsauffassung', in *Zeitschrift für Sozialforschung: Jahrgang 3/1934* (München: Kösel-Verlag, 1970), 161–195, p. 166.

attitudes; rather, we can only comprehend the basic structure of society through the conjunction of empirical analysis and a *theory* of society. Adorno suggests that this commitment to social theory as the *organon* for comprehending society is the decisive difference between his preferred 'dialectical' theory of society—by which he means critical theory—and positivist social science that only admits of observable social facts:

> What is decisive, in the case of wage satisfaction as in all others, is the power relations, the employers' command of the production apparatus, if only in an indirect manner. Without an explicit awareness thereof, no individual situation can be sufficiently comprehended without assigning to the part what really belongs to the whole, within which alone it has its meaning and importance. Just as little as the mediation of society would exist without that which is mediated, without the elements: individual humans, individual institutions, and individual situations; just as little do these elements exist without the mediation. When the details come to seem the strongest reality of all, on account of their tangible immediacy, they blind the eye to genuine perception.[11]

Importantly, this does not mean that a critical theory of society cannot be falsified through the derivation and testing of hypotheses—but it does mean that the explanatory power of these hypotheses partly stems from the theory of society from which they are derived.

This points to the second assumption undergirding the sociological dimension of critical theory: namely that the basic structure of society is key to making sense of relations and structures of domination. The central idea here is that relations and structures of domination can only ultimately be understood when they are placed within a comprehension of the structure of society as a whole.[12] As suggested above, this methodological holism is distinctly out of fashion; why, indeed, should we not be able to understand different forms of domination in abstraction from their larger social context?

To be sure, this is, again, ultimately not a question that we can answer in abstraction from an actual sociological account of the existing basic structure. However, what we can say for sure is that all the philosophers belonging to the Frankfurt School tradition share the conviction that part of what distinguishes the basic structure of modern capitalist society from previous kinds of basic societal structures is—in Adorno's words—that 'human domination is exercised through the

---

[11] Theodor W. Adorno, 'Gesellschaft', in *Soziologische Schriften I* (Frankfurt: Suhrkamp Verlag, 2003), pp. 10–11.
[12] For an argument to the same effect from the point of view of republicanism, see Dorothea Gädeke, 'Does a Mugger Dominate? Episodic Power and the Structural Dimension of Domination', *Journal of Political Philosophy* (28/2), 2020: pp. 199–221.

economic process'.[13] This means that in capitalist society, we will not be able to understand the predominant relations and structures of domination unless we place them within an understanding of the 'economic process'. This claim does not imply that *all* power is thus mediated; of course, domination can also be mediated by other social-structural processes, such as gender or racial norms or colonial or neocolonial relations—although, as we shall, the Frankfurt School has been much less concerned with these forms of domination. But it is clear, for example, that the power that transnational corporations' are able to exercise over democratically elected governments, and the egregious exploitation to which they are able to subject unskilled labour in many developing countries, are both forms of domination that could not be exercised but for the enabling structure of ownership within the global capitalist economy.

0.3.3 The Normative Dimension

The third dimension in a critical theory comprises a *normative account* of human freedom. It is this normative account that enables a critical theory to illuminate relations and structures of domination in the basic structure of society. Indeed, it follows logically that it is only in virtue of tacitly assuming or explicitly positing a positive conception of human freedom that a critical theory of society can disclose existing forms of unfreedom. As we saw above, this normative standard must be won from the historical account of a socially embodied reason, which identifies— in Axel Honneth's words—'a normative potential that reemerges in every new social reality because it is so tightly fused to the structure of human interests'.[14] In other words, a critical theory must reconstruct a conception of human freedom from the historically evolved normative rules of action in a way that enables us to see how this standard is at once operative in and frustrated by the present basic structure of society.

Moreover, the Frankfurt School tradition consistently conceptualizes freedom in terms of Kant's concept of *autonomy*. This shared commitment of course reflects the profound indebtedness of critical theory to Kant's critical philosophy, but this indebtedness extends to the connotations that freedom as autonomy received in the left-Hegelian tradition, of which Marx is the most prominent figure. In fact, in contrast to Kant, the Frankfurt School is not interested in autonomy solely as a property of individual practical cognition, or as a metaphysical idea of acting as an uncaused cause. Rather, as we shall see, the members of the Frankfurt School

---

[13] Theodor W. Adorno, 'Spätkapitalismus oder Industriegesellschaft', *Soziologische Schriften I* (Frankfurt: Suhrkamp Verlag, 2003), p. 360.

[14] Axel Honneth, 'The Point of Recognition', in *Redistribution or Recognition: A Political-Philosophical Exchange*, ed. by Axel Honneth and Nancy Fraser (New York: Verso Books, 2003), p. 244.

generally construe autonomy as what I will call—with inspiration from Honneth—a *communicative* conception of freedom.

This communicative conception of freedom conceives of individual autonomy as a *socially constituted capacity* and thus ultimately as a historical achievement resting on certain necessary social and psychological conditions, and that individual self-determination is therefore something that we can, in an important sense, only do *together*. In the Frankfurt School tradition, the possibility for individual self-determination is seen as a function of the structure of the relations in which we are situated, and no individual can be truly free if social reality is not organized such 'that autonomous human beings are able to live in it', as Adorno puts the point. In other words, human beings can only be truly free within a basic structure of society that situates individual subjects in communicative relationships that furnish each and every one with the necessary internal and external means for living an autonomous life.

Of course, the only kind of basic structure that allows self-determination is one that is *itself* amenable to being shaped by the subjects that inhabit it, and the only way in which we can determine the basic structure is ultimately through some form of collective or indeed *democratic* self-determination. However, such collective self-determination cannot fully overwrite individual self-determination, or some of us would then cease to be *self*-determining. As we shall see, in contrast with other prominent thinkers in the tradition of Western Marxism, the members of the Frankfurt School were quick to realize that the Soviet caricature of Marx's 'Realm of Freedom' is in fact merely domination with another face, precisely because it sacrifices individual autonomy at the altar of a misconceived (or deliberately misconstrued) form of collective self-determination.

Individuals can only be truly free within a basic structure that allows for *both* individual self-determination of one's own life *and* collective self-determination of the social conditions of each individual life. We cannot live autonomous lives in a society where we have no influence on the arrangement of its basic structure; if the basic structure merely assigns us a social position or role in a way that we have no effective capacity to influence or contest, then we are not self-determining: then we are unfree, and heteronomy is socially imposed upon us, whether this is done by the anarchic dynamics of the capitalist economy, the captains of industry, or the Politburo of the Central Committee.

These are the broad contours of the communicative conception of freedom as autonomy that runs through the whole Frankfurt School tradition. Moreover, I will also argue that the commitment to freedom as autonomy is not simply a contingent preference of the thinkers of the Frankfurt School, but is rather a *conceptually necessary part of any critical theory*. This is partly because, for any group of individuals, freedom can only be realized in the communicative process of working out what freedom means *for those individuals*. But it is also because the conception of freedom as autonomy is *built into* the conceptual structure of a critical theory though its very *criterion of validity*—a point to which I return below. Human autonomy is therefore the constitutive normative concern of *any* critical theory in the Frankfurt School tradition, which cannot simply be replaced with a different normative concept like utility, welfare, or some non-anthropocentric normative ideal, since then it would cease, I submit, to *be* a critical theory.

0.3.4 The Practical Criterion of Validity

Finally, in addition to comprising these three core methodological dimensions, any critical theory is subject to what I call a *practical criterion of validity*. This criterion states that a critical theory is valid if and only if its practical account of human emancipation actually enables dominated groups and individuals to emancipate themselves in practice. This distinctive notion of validity comprises both a necessary empirical condition (the theory must be descriptively and explanatorily correct) and a necessary normative condition (groups and individuals relying on the theory must be able to successfully *self*-emancipate according to a normative conception of human freedom), which are only together sufficient for redeeming a critical theory of society. The practical criterion of validity is thus the epistemological core that truly distinguishes Frankfurt School critical theory from not just positivist social science but also the alternative strands of 'critical theory' discussed above.

Together, the historical, the sociological, and the normative dimensions of critical theory are thus supposed to enable a *practical account* of the conditions for human emancipation. This account must comprise (or 'anticipate') theoretically derived recommendations for how dominated groups and individuals can overcome the relations and structures of domination to which they are subject and emancipate themselves in practice. These recommendations have an analogous status to hypotheses in positivist theories, and they are also falsifiable—although according to a more complex criterion than correspondence with observed facts. Of course, if a critical theory is to counsel dominated groups and individuals on how they can pursue practical emancipation, it must necessarily include an account of the courses of action that are *actually* open to the dominated groups and individuals in question. This is precisely what the first and second methodological dimensions are supposed to furnish. The practical account of emancipation is the directly *action-guiding* part of a critical theory, without which—in Raymond Geuss's words—'the critical theory of society would be no more than another utopian fantasy, a dream of an ideal state of which we could say neither whether it was possible nor how it might be realized'.[15]

---

[15] Raymond Geuss, *The Idea of a Critical Theory: Habermas and the Frankfurt School* (Cambridge: Cambridge University Press, 1981), p. 76.

As we shall see in this book, there is substantial disagreement among the four paradigms of critical theory concerning their recommendations for practical emancipation. Whereas the young Horkheimer still accepts the Marxian notion of a revolutionary overthrow of private ownership and the socialization of the means of production in a rationally planned economy, any such hopes have been purged from Adorno's negativist paradigm, where structural domination is conceived as so penetrating and pervasive that the aspiration for practical emancipation, while not ultimately relinquished, recedes firmly into the background. In Habermas's communicative paradigm, we find a renewed practical commitment to the pursuit of collective self-determination through democratic will-formation in the public sphere and the legal-political institutions of modern constitutional democracy. Finally, Honneth's recognition paradigm broadens the scope of the institutional conditions for individual autonomy to include *all* the major social and political institutions of modern Western society.

These shifts in the tradition's emancipatory recommendations can indeed be seen as following a general pattern, where a 'revolutionary' account of emancipation is gradually replaced with a 'reformist' one. But this abandonment of revolutionary aspirations is actually inaugurated by the young Horkheimer, for whom it is, in part, explicitly motivated by an appreciation of the normative constraints that the communicative conception of freedom as autonomy imposes on practical emancipation, as well as by Stalin's evident encroachment on these constraints during the politically engineered mass starvation of the kulaks and the subsequent Great Terror.

Notwithstanding this 'farewell to revolution', the Frankfurt School remains— even in its reformist guise—one of the few living, breathing traditions of social and political thought in which we still find a commitment to the *kind* of large-scale critique of capitalist society and practical emancipation that Marx inaugurated, and which left-wing intellectuals have largely abandoned in favour of the political moralism of liberal theories of justice or postmodern refusals to countenance any such grand narratives. In my view, however, the continued relevance of the Frankfurt School lies *precisely* in the fact that the tradition has maintained an unbroken commitment to the idea that the purpose of social and political theory is ultimately to enable such large-scale human emancipation in practice, while maintaining an equally firm yet undogmatic commitment to learn from history and grasp the social transformations of capitalist society that we can observe only if we continuously develop and refine our understanding of relations and structures of domination in view of the evolving nature of the basic structure as a whole.

Accordingly, the practical criterion of validity is ultimately met only if a critical theory represents a *correct* theory of society and succeeds in *guiding* dominated groups and individuals to emancipate themselves *through reasonable insight* into the truth of the critical theory's account of the relationships of domination to which they are subject. To be sure, I cannot provide anything like a full-blown epistemological defence of the practical criterion of validity here, which would require a book-length treatment of its own. Instead, I want to suggest what seems to me its most important implication: namely, that a critical theory of society effectively relinquishes authority over its own validity to the autonomous, reflective endorsement and enactment of those dominated subjects, whom it aspires to emancipate in practice.

The crucial point here is that it is the endorsement and 'praxis' of individuals and groups, who find themselves within relationships of domination, that is the final court of appeal for a critical theory, and no philosopher, expert, or revolutionary avant-garde has the authority to determine the content of emancipation for them. Indeed, the practical criterion of validity implies that a critical theory of society can only be seen as an input to a *process of enlightenment*, which aims at giving groups and individuals knowledge about their existing basic structure and the forms of domination to which they are subject, but which has no ultimate authority independently of their reflective endorsement of its content and pursuit of the practical emancipation that it counsels. In the Frankfurt School tradition, the philosophical aspiration of metaphysical certainty is thus replaced with the uncertainty of action-motivating, emancipatory insight; and, just as envisioned by the young Marx, it is only, ultimately, the *practical realization* of the emancipatory recommendations of a critical theory that can make a critical theory of society redundant. At the most basic conceptual level, a critical theory can therefore never become a blueprint for top-down social engineering or a clandestine manual for professional revolutionaries of a Leninist bend. In Habermas's famous phrase: 'in a process of enlightenment there can be only participants'.[16]

In this sense, too, the Frankfurt School remains committed to the left-Hegelian idea that emancipatory guidance must be rooted in a historical account of a socially embodied reason, such that a critical theory of society can *itself* be understood as a moment in social history that aspires to 'unleash' an unrealized emancipatory potential immanent in reason itself. Critical theory aims to contribute to dominated subjects' reflection on their shared experiences of socially compelled suffering by casting a 'light of redemption' through which the 'cracks and tears' of their world may be revealed, allowing them to formulate and struggle for reasonable demands in practice. Practical emancipation can thus be conceived as the *completion of a learning process*, and as the overcoming of a one-sided process of social rationalization, which reconciles the rational with the reasonable.

---

[16] Jürgen Habermas, *Theory and Practice*, transl. by John Viertel (Cambridge: Polity Press, 1988), p. 40.

0.4 An Outline of the Book

The purpose of this book's reconstruction of the Frankfurt School tradition as four paradigms of critical theory is not only to bring the central theoretical positions of that tradition before our eyes; it is also to identify the conceptual and methodological obstacles that prevent those paradigms from gaining a proper grasp of the injustices and pathologies of world society, and to appraise what we might nevertheless still learn from them in our present attempt to grapple with global capitalist modernity. Moreover, I will discuss the theoretical obstacles and resources within each paradigm for coming to terms with systematic questions concerning *the relationship between human society and nature* and *the postcolonial condition*. This gives the book the following structure.

The book is divided into five parts: one part for each of the four paradigms of critical theory, and a final part on the two emerging paradigms of critical theory, comprising ten chapters in total, excluding this introduction and a conclusion. Each part comprises a reconstructive chapter, which offers a comprehensive exposition of the paradigm in question, and a systematic chapter, which is structured along three thematic questions: (1) the systematic question concerning the methodology of a critical theory adequate to our bourgeoning world society and the nature and scale of global concerns; (2) the systematic question concerning the relationship and interchange between human society and nature and the impact of human activity on natural ecosystems within a critical theory of world society; and (3) the systematic question concerning the need for a critical theory of world society to overcome a Eurocentric view of modernity, including the normative, political, and epistemological implications of coming to terms with the postcolonial condition. In this way, the book aims to be able to serve both as a general and comprehensive *introduction* to the Frankfurt School tradition of critical theory (Chapters 1, 3, 5, and 7), and as a systematic contribution to the tradition's potential contribution to central debates and questions of contemporary social and political theory (Chapters 2, 4, 6, 8, 9, and 10).[17] In the rest of this section, I offer a brief outline of the book, along with its central arguments and conclusions.

In **Chapter 1**, I reconstruct the original paradigm of critical theory, largely conceived by the young Max Horkheimer as the head of a remarkable interdisciplinary group of philosophers, psychologists, economists, and literary scholars associated with the famed Frankfurt Institute for Social Research in the interwar Weimar Republic. The young Horkheimer maintained a firm yet undogmatic commitment to a fairly orthodox interpretation of historical materialism, while his perhaps most original contribution to social theory was his and Erich Fromm's synthesis

---

[17] In general, due to their aspiration for comprehensiveness in exposition, the reconstructive chapters are significantly longer than the systematic chapters.

of the Marxian critique of political economy and Freudian psychoanalysis in an account of the basic structure of monopoly capitalism and its deep-seated forces of reification and cultivation of authoritarian personality types.

However, his truly lasting philosophical contribution is the idea of critical theory itself, which was first formulated as an interdisciplinary programme of dialectical 'interpenetration' of philosophy and social inquiry and a materialist *Ideologiekritik* of the distorted expressions that the truth content of *bourgeois* concepts and moral ideas receive in *bourgeois* thought. This programme informed an ambitious empirical research project into the revolutionary 'readiness' of the German proletariat, which proved disappointing, however, and gradually transformed into the more defensive project of explaining the rise of National Socialism in Germany. Moreover, I argue that the most overlooked part of Horkheimer's original paradigm is his attractive but underdeveloped normative idea of a 'reasonable society' and his conception of critical theory as itself a kind of theory of justice, albeit distinct in important ways from *bourgeois* or traditional theories of justice that also predominate in the contemporary academy.

In **Chapter 2**, relying on recent postcolonial theory, I argue that Horkheimer's original paradigm was ultimately unable to redeem its global claim to validity, because its weddedness to historical materialism at the same time commits Horkheimer to a 'stagist' philosophy of history, which sees global variations as temporally coexisting stages of epochal development and thus threatens to collapse the sociological dimension of a critical theory of world society into its historical dimension. Moreover, I also argue that the young Horkheimer subscribed to a then-prevalent 'Promethean' interpretation of historical materialism, which sees ever-increasing human mastery over nature as an essential condition of human emancipation. Although this interpretation of Marx's thought has subsequently been disputed, there remains little room in the young Horkheimer's thought for ecological concerns about natural limits to human production. Nevertheless, I also argue that a critical theory of contemporary world society must salvage from Horkheimer's original paradigm not only the idea of a critical theory of justice but also the critical engagement with political economy, which has all but disappeared from recent paradigms of critical theory, rendering them blind to some of the constitutive injustices of global capitalist modernity.

In **Chapter 3**, I proceed with a reconstruction of Theodor W. Adorno's negativist paradigm of critical theory, which is methodologically grounded in his attempt to free dialectics from Hegel's affirmative and system-building embrace and unleash negative dialectics as an open-ended remembrance of suppressed non-identity. This method is put to practice in his and Horkheimer's dark masterpiece, the *Dialektik der Aufklärung*, which reconstructs human history and the enlightenment project as a long struggle to wrest power over human life from nature's hands that ultimately reverts into blind human domination of not only external nature but also inner human nature as well as other human beings, culminating in the collapse of enlightened civilization into fascist barbarism, total war, and the gas chambers of Auschwitz.

Moreover, Adorno also develops an exceedingly bleak sociological account of late-capitalist society, which sees individual subjects as in thrall to all-powerful and pervasive forces of social heteronomy through the administered world and a universal system of delusion—maintained, in part, by the culture industry's reduction of art to the manipulation of needs. Animating Adorno's work is, I argue, a firm (yet dialectical) normative commitment to a conception of freedom as autonomy and *Mündigkeit*, which calls for an individual ethics of resistance to social heteronomy and a mimetic reconciliation with nature that can only, however, be grasped at in our present, comprehensively reified form of life.

In **Chapter 4**, I argue that Adorno's negativist paradigm rests on two fundamentally flawed assumptions: first, the idea of late-capitalism as an 'expressive totality', in whose abstractions the concrete global context of application vanishes, and, second, the notion that economic and political power has fused in an all-pervasive system of administration and delusion, which renders his paradigm unable to grasp the asymmetrical power that globalized market forces wield over fragmented states in contemporary world society. But I also maintain that Adorno's central concern with non-identity is acutely relevant for a critical theory of world society in at least two ways: in terms of the relationship between reason and nature and the 'ecological dialectic of enlightenment' actualized by the prospect of catastrophic anthropogenic climate change, and in terms of the postcolonial concern with empowering the 'non-identical' of Western modernity. Both of these concerns must be integrated into a critical theory of world society, I argue, without embracing the theoretical *cul-de-sacs* and practical impasse of Adorno's negativist paradigm. Finally, I insist on Adorno's insight that the reconciliation with nature, which today has become an existential imperative, cannot be achieved in theory, as some 'new materialist' philosophers may seem to suggest, but ultimately only in practice.

Chapter 5 reconstructs Jürgen Habermas's communicative paradigm of critical theory, which responds to the limitations of Adorno's negativist paradigm and seeks to grasp the emancipatory potential of the new-founded constitutional-democratic order of post-war Europe. In order to do so, Habermas undertakes a turn to an intersubjective paradigm of reason and pursues a philosophical foundation for a critical theory of society in a pragmatic reconstruction of the universal rational infrastructure that he finds in ordinary language communication. This reconstruction of communicative reason enables Habermas to develop a sophisticated theory of social evolution and an ambitious social theory that sees modern capitalist society as both a cultural lifeworld and a system of functional subsystems. This two-concept theory of communicative action in turn allows Habermas to reconceptualize the concept of reification as a pervasive social pathology of modern democratic capitalism: namely, as the colonization of the lifeworld by system imperatives, which undercuts the social and psychological conditions of individual autonomy.

Habermas's reconstruction of communicative reason also grounds the normative dimension of his critical theory, which comprises an account of the moral point of view in terms of a theory of discourse ethics and a reconstruction of the 'self-understanding' of modern constitutional democracy. He construes the latter in terms of a system of rights and a two-track theory of deliberative politics that charts how processes of democratic will-formation in the public sphere are channelled through an elected parliament, which submits the functional subsystems of the capitalist market and the public administration to democratically enacted law.

Moreover, as we shall see in **Chapter 6**, Habermas has in recent years sought to apply his communicative paradigm to world society in response to his increasing appreciation of the disruptive forces of economic globalization, developing a proposal for a multilevel global constitutional framework, which can re-establish the necessary legal and political conditions for democratic self-determination in the post-national constellation of powerful globalized market forces and fragmented states. Yet I argue that this concern with the legal and political conditions of autonomy is too restrictive, and that Habermas's proceduralism ultimately blinds his theoretical gaze to profound injustices in contemporary world society.

Furthermore, I argue that Habermas's distinction between communicative, strategic, and instrumental action (where the latter refers to human relations with the natural world) renders Habermas's social theory incapable of accommodating ecological concerns actualized by anthropogenic climate change, and, in this sense, that his communicative paradigm falls behind Adorno's advances into the Promethean limitations of Horkheimer's original paradigm. I also discuss Amy Allen's recent critique that Habermas's theory of social evolution commits him to a pernicious view of non-Western societies as developmentally inferior to modern Western societies. In response, I argue that although the global application of Habermas's communicative paradigm leaves many questions unanswered, contrary to Allen's claim he explicitly understands modernity as a truly global condition, in which no completely pre-modern societies remain.

In **Chapter 7**, I reconstruct Axel Honneth's recognition paradigm of critical theory. His defining concern with recognition is motivated by a critique of Habermas's power-free account of the lifeworld and a concomitant aspiration to eschew systems theory and develop a monistic social theory that conceives of power relations as struggles for recognition within the lifeworld, where moral consciousness and individual identity are forged in the heat of social conflict. Honneth develops this idea into a theory of three spheres of recognition as a formal conception of the good life, which, in his later work, is explicitly construed as a communicative conception of the necessary social and psychological conditions of individual autonomy. Building on this theory, Honneth's mature work undertakes a reformulation of Hegel's *Rechtsphilosophie* as a 'theory of justice as social analysis', which reconstructs and criticizes the major institutions of social freedom in modern Western society across the domains of personal relationships, the market economy, and the democratic constitutional state.

In **Chapter 8**, I argue that the phenomenon of globalization is strikingly absent from Honneth's work and appears only in his mature theory as a mysterious external force that undercuts the promise of social freedom embodied in the institutional structure of modern Western society from without. This lack of attention to existing forces of global integration—as well as concerns distinctive to the emerging world society such as climate change and the postcolonial condition—attests, I argue, to the limits of Honneth's Hegelian method of normative reconstruction, which presupposes the existence of already-if-imperfectly-realized institutions of social freedom. Such an encompassing 'culture of freedom' is conspicuously absent from contemporary world society, where the nature of globalized market forces seems better captured by Habermas's systems-theoretical construal than by Honneth's interpretation of the capitalist market as a genuine institution of social freedom.

Although Honneth thus offers a sophisticated instantiation of the young Horkheimer's idea of a critical theory of justice, which—in contrast to Habermas—is able to conceptualize structural autonomy-impairment across all the major social institutions of modern Western society, I argue that his Hegelian reconstructive methodology ultimately precludes the application of his recognition paradigm to world society. Finally, although Honneth has largely remained silent on the relationship between society and nature, I argue that Honneth's recognition paradigm actually offers the conceptual resources for reconceiving the communicative conception of freedom so as to make room not only for social and psychological conditions but also natural conditions of individual autonomy.

In **Chapter 9**, I introduce the first of two emerging paradigms of critical theory, through which the shape of a critical theory of world society begins to take form: namely, the emerging contextualist paradigm of Amy Allen. First, I argue that Allen is right to foreground the concept of subjection and that the Frankfurt School has generally been complacent about the extent to which subordinating racial and gender norms are introduced into the very formation of the subject. Moreover, given the extent to which power and resources in contemporary world society are still ordered along formally disestablished colonial and imperial lines, I argue, with Allen, that a critical theory of world society must integrate the reflexive check of problematizing critique. However, I also maintain that this self-problematizing mode of critique is by itself insufficient and that Allen's principled contextualism is unable to ground a critical theory of world society, since what she offers is ultimately a limited framework for the self-interrogation of Western capitalist modernity.

In **Chapter 10**, I reconstruct Rainer Forst's emerging justification paradigm and his account of the basic right to justification. Starting from this foundational moral right, Forst develops a critical theory of society conceived as multiple contexts of justice and relations of justification, which is developed from the beginning with a view to the global context of application. I argue that the Kantian constructivism at the heart of Forst's justification paradigm enables a critical theory of world society to escape the two dead-ends posed by Habermas's and Honneth's respective paradigms. Eschewing both the formality of Habermas's proceduralism and the strictures of Honneth's Hegelian method of normative reconstruction and critique, a Kantian-constructivist approach is able to embrace both a reconstructive approach to existing institutions of social freedom and an imaginative political construction of the transnational or even global institutions necessary for submitting global capitalism to democratic control and averting a planetary disaster.

In the conclusion, I offer a sketch of the tasks of a critical theory of world society, which summarizes the systematic findings of the book. I argue that a critical theory of world society must combine and integrate the epistemic humility of Allen's problematizing critique with the Kantian constructivism of Forst's right to justification. Indeed, I argue that we can understand both of these modes of critique as moments in a moral learning process rooted in the dialectic between power and autonomy, which represents a central and continuously evolving insight throughout the whole Frankfurt School tradition of critical theory. Finally, I end the book by arguing that, in the context of the Anthropocene, critical theory's methodological holism commits the tradition to go beyond the traditionally self-imposed confines of social theory to include an ecological analysis of the planetary relationship between the Earth system of natural ecosystems and the social totality of world society.

A note on selection and language: I have omitted several philosophers that might, for various reasons, otherwise warrant inclusion in a comprehensive reconstruction of the Frankfurt School tradition as a whole. Most notable among these is, arguably, Herbert Marcuse. I have chosen to omit Marcuse not because I believe that no insights can be reaped from his work, but because of the degree of overlap between Marcuse's work and the first two paradigms. In the first two chapters, I have mostly relied on the German texts, since many translations are of questionable quality, and all quotes in the text are translated by me from the original German except when noted. In the remaining chapters, I have relied on the English translations, except where none exist.

Let me finish this outline of the book with a more general observation. Since, as we have seen, a critical theory is always a theory of society at a particular historical moment, what we find in our reconstruction of four successive paradigms of critical theory is not only four different ways of substantiating their shared methodological commitments, as expounded in Section 3: it is also an unbroken *history of Western capitalist modernity* as seen through the prism of Frankfurt School critical theory. To be sure, as I have argued, this is far from historiography in the traditional sense. Rather, the reconstruction of the tradition offered in this book represents a historical account of the changing faces of societal relations of freedom and domination through the dramatic events, ruptures, and violent ups-and-downs that marked Western societies during the first half of the twentieth century, as well as the post-war achievements that Western societies managed to erect upon the moral and physical rubble of the European continent. And as I will try to show, this critical history also bears an imprint of the blind spots and distortions of Western modernity vis-à-vis both the non-Western social world and the natural world.

Moreover, this is a critical history of Western capitalist modernity that culminates in and has practical implications for the *present*: whereas some of the concrete social analysis of 'monopoly capitalism' and 'state capitalism' that we find in the paradigms of the young Horkheimer and Adorno are partly of historical interest, the diagnoses and analyses that we find in the paradigms of Habermas and Honneth are of more immediate contemporary relevance. In Habermas's and Honneth's work, we ultimately find both philosophers grappling with the disruptive consequences of globalization. As we shall see, any critical theory that limits its focus to a domestically circumscribed context of application will today be bound to blindly countenance these increasingly powerful dynamics of global integration as external forces that assault domestic society from the outside. This demonstrates, I submit, that in the present historical moment, *any attempt to reinvigorate the project of critical theory must ultimately take the form of a critical theory of world society*. The great challenge faced by the Frankfurt School tradition of critical theory today is thus to learn from both the strengths and blind spots of its critique of Western capitalist modernity in the singularly daunting task of mounting a critique of global capitalist modernity, which may enable and guide emancipation in practice within *and* across borders. With this book, I hope to have made some small contribution to this project.

PART I
HORKHEIMER

Max Horkheimer's early work arguably represents the most underappreciated and overlooked contribution to the Frankfurt School tradition. However, in the course of his intellectual development during the 1930s, as we shall see in Chapter 1's reconstruction of his thought, Horkheimer developed an attractive 'materialist' conception of an interdisciplinary and cooperative form of social inquiry, in which philosophy serves the integrative function of weaving findings across empirical social sciences into a coherent theory of society as a unified object of study, which he would later refine into his famous idea of a critical theory of society.

As the director of the *Institut für Sozialforschung*, Horkheimer led an intimate circle of philosophers, political economists, literary theorists, and psychologists in their attempt to make sense of, first, the fact that a proletarian revolution did not occur despite Marx's predictions, and later, the rise of fascism across the European continent, developing a theory of monopoly capitalism and its associated conditions of personality formation, which provided the social-psychological support structure for fascism. Moreover, Horkheimer developed an attractive normative ideal of a 'reasonable society' as a social condition in which autonomous subjects democratically govern society's social and economic life, and an original account of a critical theory of society as a novel kind of theory of justice, which curiously remains largely unacknowledged in the secondary literature on his work.

However, in Chapter 2, I will also argue that Horkheimer's original paradigm of critical theory is marked by an inextricable contradiction between his critical theory's explicit global claim to validity and his commitment to historical materialism, the teleological structure of which prevented Horkheimer from truly developing a critical theory of *global justice*. Indeed, its stagist view of history confines anyone who has not yet been integrated into the industrial proletariat to what Dipesh Chakrabarty has called an 'imaginary waiting room of history', rendering a critical theory wedded to historical materialism not only unable to offer any meaningful emancipatory guidance but positively detrimental to anyone outside the industrialized West. Moreover, I will also argue that the young Horkheimer remained committed to a 'Promethean' view of human emancipation as in part given by the unbridled exploitation of nature, which has become wholly untenable in the face of global warming and contemporary ecological destruction.

Nevertheless, I will maintain that a critical theory of world society can also find important resources in the young Horkheimer's original paradigm of critical theory. While more recent paradigms of critical theory have all but given up on political economy, Horkheimer's work points to the need for a critical theory of a present-day world society characterized by a vast concentration of wealth and power to reintegrate the crucial disciplinary perspective of political economy—and, indeed, to offer an *immanent critique* of contemporary neoclassical economy. Finally, I argue that the Horkheimer circle's attempt to account for the rise of fascism in the 1930s through an original synthesis of Marx's and Freud's work has been re-actualized by the recent surge of right-wing populism across and beyond the West and may offer valuable lessons for how we confront those who would use democratic politics to destroy democracy in our present day and age.

1
Max Horkheimer and the Original Paradigm of Critical Theory

1.1 Stages in the Project of a Critical Theory of Society

In October 1930, Max Horkheimer became director of the *Institut für Sozialforschung* (IfS) in Frankfurt am Main.[1] The merely 35-year-old philosopher, who had only recently been appointed Professor of Social Philosophy at the university in Frankfurt, assumed the directorship at the wealthy and privately funded institute at a time when Europe was once again verging on disaster. Barely over a decade had passed since the German Empire had fallen prey to the November Revolution in 1918, which simultaneously ended the bloody mayhem of the First World War and ushered in the constitutionally progressive but politically volatile Weimar Republic. And less than three years would pass before Adolf Hitler was to assume dictatorial powers over the German state and set Europe on the disastrous path towards the Holocaust and another world war.

However, even before its fatal dissolution into the *Third Reich*, the short-lived Weimar Republic was chronically troubled by political instability, severe economic depression, hyperinflation, and widespread social destitution. The interwar experience of devastating social crisis–which only intensified with the crash on the New York Stock Exchange in 1929, the German financial collapse in 1931, and the austerity policies pursued by the German government[2]–led many German socialists to interpret the 1920s and 1930s as the final transitory stage in the capitalist epoch. According to Marx, this is the stage in which the capitalist mode of production is ripped apart by crises insurmountable within itself, provoking ever more violent class struggles that eventually rouse the proletariat to overthrow capitalist production relations and realize a new and superior mode of production. Fuelled by expectations of imminent revolution, this electric atmosphere sparked sectarian struggles among left-wing political fractions propagating different courses of

---

[1] The following remarks draw on Ralf Wiggershaus, *Die Frankfurter Schule: Geschichte, Theoretische Entwicklung, Politische Bedeutung* (München: Deutscher Taschenbuch Verlag, 1998); Martin Jay, *The Dialectical Imagination: A History of the Frankfurt School and the Institute for Social Research 1923–1950* (London: Heinemann, 1973).

[2] Adam Tooze, *The Wages of Destruction: The Making and Breaking of the Nazi Economy* (London: Penguin Books, 2007); Tobias Straumann, *1931: Debt, Crisis, and the Rise of Hitler* (Oxford: Oxford University Press, 2020).

action in this final reckoning with capitalism, while also animating a generation of socialist intellectuals, who set out to contribute to capitalism's demise by reinvigorating and refining the Marxian philosophy of history and critique of political economy.

Recognized today as a distinctive tradition of Western Marxism, these prolific thinkers include Karl Korsch, Ernst Bloch, Bertolt Brecht, and Georg Lukács, as well as the group of scholars who would subsequently come to be known as the first generation of the Frankfurt School. Spearheaded by the young Horkheimer, this diverse circle counted psychoanalyst Erich Fromm, economist Friedrich Pollock, sociologist Karl August Wittfogel, literary theorists Walter Benjamin and Leo Löwenthal, and philosophers Herbert Marcuse and Theodor W. Adorno. When the Nazis assumed power in 1933, these predominantly Jewish-Marxist intellectuals were forced to flee their homeland from political and anti-Semitic persecution. Horkheimer left for Switzerland in 1933 and then New York in 1934, after spending his last weeks in Frankfurt spontaneously lecturing on the concept of freedom. One important if more loosely connected member of the group never made it to safety: Walter Benjamin committed suicide during a failed attempt to escape Europe through Spain and Portugal in 1940.

However, even in involuntary exile, and as their homeland was overrun by fascism, a powerful if steadily dwindling remnant of the revolutionary optimism of the days of the Weimar Republic would remain in Horkheimer's thought throughout the 1930s, until it took a strongly pessimistic turn in tone and outlook around the outbreak of the war in 1940. It is the young Horkheimer's original vision of a materialist or critical theory of society, as formulated in his contributions to the IfS's house journal, the *Zeitschrift für Sozialforschung* (ZfS)—around which the first generation of the Frankfurt School rallied—which represents the first distinct paradigm of critical theory in this book's reconstruction of the Frankfurt School tradition.

Born in Stuttgart in 1895 as the only son of a wealthy Jewish industrialist, Horkheimer's life was profoundly shaped by the dramatic events of the first half of the twentieth century. Drafted into military service in 1917, he was spared an early death in the trenches after failing a medical exam, and he experienced the end of the Great War and the fall of the German Empire from a hospital bed in Munich. He enrolled at the university in Munich during the failed attempt to establish a Bavarian council republic (*Räterepublik*) on the model of the Russian revolution, but after the Weimar Constitution was adopted—and Horkheimer came to fear for his life in Munich, having been mistaken for a prominent revolutionary leader—he relocated to Frankfurt to study psychology and philosophy under the supervision of neo-Kantian philosopher Hans Cornelius. To the great disappointment of his father, who also disparaged Max's relationship and later marriage with his father's former secretary Rose Riekher—a gentile, eight years Max's senior—Horkheimer decided to pursue a career in academic philosophy. He wrote his doctoral dissertation and *Habilitation* on Kant's epistemology and critique of judgement, while maintaining a growing interest in Schopenhauer, Hegel, and Marx on the side—an interest mostly explored through a series of aphorisms published in Switzerland in 1934 with the title 'Dawn and Decline: Notes in Germany' (*Dämmerung: Notitzen in Deutschland*) under the pseudonym of Heinrich Regius.

As a comparative novelty in Marxian theory, Horkheimer's appointment as director of the IfS must have come as something of a surprise to many of his contemporaries—a testament to his increasingly apparent skilfulness as a political operator in the academic world. Founded in 1923 by the wealthy Marxist Felix Weil, the IfS had in the years prior to Horkheimer's appointment pursued an openly socialist research agenda under the leadership of Austro-Marxist Carl Grünberg, with a strong emphasis on the history of the labour movement. After assuming the directorship, however, Horkheimer quickly refocused the IfS's resources on his own, highly distinctive research programme. As Helmut Dubiel argues, the work of the IfS in the 1930s can be distinguished into two phases, which partly reflect changes in the social and political environment, and partly the corresponding changes in Horkheimer's views on the nature of their intellectual activity.

The first phase, from Horkheimer's appointment in 1930 until 1936/1937, is characterized by a commitment to a *materialist programme of interdisciplinary social research,* in which philosophy is assigned the mediating role of integrating insights won in the fragmented social-scientific disciplines. The second phase, inaugurated in 1937 with Horkheimer's coinage of the term *critical theory* and lasting until 1940, is characterized by an effective abandonment of the programme of interdisciplinary social research and a narrower 'philosophical' focus on clarifying the distinctive epistemological assumptions and cognitive structure that Horkheimer identifies in Marx's philosophy of history and critique of political economy.[3]

In this chapter, I subsume both of these phases under Horkheimer's original paradigm of critical theory, but I also seek to account for the most important differences and the concerns driving the evolution of his thinking. However, before expounding the historical, sociological, and normative dimensions of this paradigm, I want to first sketch the nature of Horkheimer's evolving and deeply original epistemological reflections on the IfS circle's intellectual activity and the innovative programme of *Ideologiekritik* that he pursued through the first and second phases of his thinking, as these contain some of his most enduring insights and a crucial backdrop for subsequent chapters.

---

[3] Helmut Dubiel, *Wissenschaftsorganisation und politische Erfahrung: Studien zur frühen Kritischen Theorie* (Frankfurt: Suhrkamp, 1978). The third phase, which Dubiel charts from 1940 until 1945, will be discussed in Chapter 3 with a focus on Adorno's work, due to his increasingly decisive influence.

1.1.1 Materialism and Ideologiekritik

In his inaugural lecture from 1931, 'The Present State of Social Philosophy and the Tasks of an Institute for Social Research' (*Die gegenwärtige Lage der Sozialphilosophie und die Aufgaben eines Instituts für Sozialforschung*), Horkheimer presents the research programme to which the IfS's resources would be devoted under his directorship, and which would characterize the first phase of his intellectual development. Horkheimer envisions the basic task of the IfS as the development of a comprehensive theory of society, in which social philosophy and individual social-scientific disciplines complement and inform each other on a continuous and open-ended basis. This complementary relationship is supposed to safeguard social inquiry from deteriorating into either of the twin pitfalls of philosophical arrogance towards empirical knowledge or a restricted scientific focus on discrete empirical facts with no concern for the overall picture. Horkheimer plans to steer clear of these two vices through a 'continuous dialectical interpenetration and development of philosophical theory and scientific practice' and by harnessing 'the ability of philosophy, as a theoretical intention oriented towards the general perspective, that which is truly important, to give the specific [scientific] inquiries inspiring impulses while remaining sufficiently open-minded to let itself be impressed and transformed by the progress of the concrete studies'.[4]

The relationship between philosophy and the social sciences in the early phase is thus one in which philosophy serves an *integrative epistemic function*, weaving insights from the fragmented scientific inquiries into an overall picture that is more appropriate to its object of study: namely, 'society as a whole'.[5] In more specific terms, Horkheimer's early programme involves a commitment

> to organise inquiries on the basis of pressing philosophical questions, in which philosophers, sociologists, economists, historians, and psychologists can unite in a permanent working community and together do that which in other areas can be done alone in the laboratory, and what all true researchers have always done, namely to pursue great philosophical questions on the basis of the finest scientific methods; to modify and improve the precision of questions in the course of working on the object of research; to invent new methods—and yet not to let the overall picture fall from view.[6]

---

[4] Max Horkheimer, 'Die gegenwärtige Lage der Sozialphilosophie und die Aufgaben eines Instituts für Sozialforschung', in *Gesammelte Schriften Band 3: 1931–1936*, ed. by Alfred Schmidt (Frankfurt: S. Fischer Verlag, 1988, p. 29.

[5] Max Horkheimer, 'Vorwort [zu Heft ½ des 1. Jahrgangs des Zeitschrift für Sozialforschung]', in *Gesammelte Schriften Band 3*, p. 36.

[6] Horkheimer, 'Die gegenwärtige Lage der Sozialphilosophie', pp. 29–30.

Horkheimer thus envisions a truly interdisciplinary and cooperative form of social research, 'which no single person has the capacity to realise' alone, and which employs the knowledge of specialists under the director's 'dictatorship of planned work'.[7] This scientific vision of a cooperative and interdisciplinary mode of social inquiry represents the *positive side* of Horkheimer's early research programme, which would come to fruition in the major collective study undertaken by the IfS in the 1930s, the 'Studies in Authority and Family' (*Studien über Autorität und Familie*), to which almost all of its resources were devoted in that decade (and which I will discuss in Section 3 of this chapter).

However, if we wish to understand the underlying concerns that animate Horkheimer's interdisciplinary programme, we must turn to the *negative side* of his research programme—that of *Ideologiekritik*, as developed in his philosophical essays published in the ZfS. In these highly innovative and sophisticated treatments of classical and contemporaneous philosophical literature, Horkheimer consistently refers to the interdisciplinary programme of the IfS as grounded in a commitment to a view that he simply calls 'materialism', as the 'present content' of materialism is 'the theory of society' and 'materialism requires the unity of philosophy and science'.[8]

Horkheimer's description of his view as 'materialist' is key to understanding his project in this early stage, which he clarifies in two important essays from 1933, 'Materialism and Metaphysics' (*Materialismus und Metaphysik*) and 'Materialism and Morality' (*Materialismus und Moral*), by way of a critical engagement with idealist metaphysics and morality. According to Horkheimer, idealism has always aspired to establish the truth of certain claims as independent of any possible changes in the physical world, and to develop these truths into a system of absolute and eternally valid knowledge. Such eternal metaphysical truths are in turn supposed to have normative consequences for human practical life—a structure that idealism shares with religious belief systems: 'the metaphysical faith that the organisation of individual existence is justifiable with reference to a discoverable [metaphysical] reality is most clearly expressed in immediately theological systems'.[9] To be sure, in its secular idealist instantiation, the will of God is replaced with metaphysical postulates such as 'pure reason' or the 'absolute idea', but the structure of such religious and secular varieties of metaphysics—and the contemplative, inward-looking philosophical method through which metaphysical speculation is pursued—remains largely the same.

Horkheimer insists that materialism does not oppose idealism as a rival metaphysical doctrine. Rather, in its most general sense, materialism simply represents

---

[7] Horkheimer, 'Die gegenwärtige Lage der Sozialphilosophie', p. 31.
[8] Max Horkheimer, 'Materialismus und Metaphysik', in *Gesammelte Schriften Band 3*, pp. 84, 94.
[9] Horkheimer, 'Materialismus und Metaphysik', p. 78.

the meta-philosophical insight that human thought is always conditioned by the social and historical context from within which it emerges. However, even if certain historically conditioned forms of thought may be false in a strict sense, they may also express certain legitimate human concerns or interests in a form that is epistemically constrained and distorted by their historical context. From this premise follows the possibility of reconstructing and preserving that which is true in historically constrained and distorted forms of thought, simultaneously accounting for the roots of the ideological form in which it is expressed.

This sophisticated model of *Ideologiekritik*, to which many of Horkheimer's essays from the first phase are devoted, is applied in a series of materialist critiques of the Western philosophical canon, idealism in particular. From the point of view of materialism, idealism 'serves the function of couching human, historical, and particular ends in the appearances of eternity, and to relate these ends to an unconditioned reference point exempt from historical change'.[10] Furthermore, the task of materialist *Ideologiekritik* is to understand *why* the idealist is driven to express these legitimate human ends as unconditioned, supra-historical truths.

In 'On the Problem of Truth' (*Zum Problem der Wahrheit*) from 1935, Horkheimer develops an account of truth that attempts to steer a middle path between the absolutism of traditional metaphysics and the relativism of the 'anti-rationalism' of his day.[11] According to Horkheimer, anti-rationalists are right to deny that there is an *a priori* or absolute truth of the matter in the sense imagined by Kant and Hegel, but they are wrong to argue that this qualification requires one to give up on the very concept of truth. In Thomas McCarthy's apt restatement of Horkheimer's critique, their 'fallacy of disappointed expectations' derives from the mistaken 'equation of fallibility with relativity'.[12] For Horkheimer, the fact that truth has lost its metaphysical purchase does not warrant giving up on the distinction between truth and falsity *within* the historically developed state of our knowledge:

> For the materialist, the abstract qualification that one's own state of knowledge will once be falsified by warranted criticism—that it is subject to correction—does not imply complete liberality towards contradictory opinions or sceptical paralysation of judgment; rather, it implies vigilance towards one's own mistakes, and represents the changeability of thought as such ... Since this supra-historical and thus [metaphysically] overcharged conception of truth—which derives from

---

[10] Horkheimer, 'Materialismus und Metaphysik', p. 81.
[11] On the latter topic, see also Max Horkheimer, 'Zum Rationalismusstreit in der gegenwärtigen Philosophie', in *Gesammelte Schriften Band 3*, pp. 163–122.
[12] Thomas McCarthy, 'On The Idea of a Critical Theory and its Relation to Philosophy', in Thomas McCarthy and David Couzens Hoy, *Critical Theory* (Oxford: Blackwell Publishers, 1994), p. 10.

the belief in a pure and eternal *Geist*, and ultimately from the concept of God—is impossible, it is senseless to orient the state of our knowledge towards this impossibility, and in this sense calling it relative.[13]

Moreover, in response to Nietzsche's polemics against the concept of truth, Horkheimer maintains that critique would be impossible without presupposing and orienting oneself towards the concept of truth: 'critique does not merely include the negative, sceptical moment, but equally the inner independence not to loose sight of that which is true; to remain firm in its application, even though it might one day change'.[14] Horkheimer's materialism thus amounts to a *post-metaphysical* philosophical programme, which repudiates any metaphysically grounded authority of philosophy and instead seeks to establish the objectivity of philosophical thought with reference to its integrative function in furthering knowledge about society as a whole.[15]

Horkheimer's claim that there is no extra-historical point of view from which reality can be observed and comprehended—that all observations carry the stamp of the beholder and the particularities of their historical, social, and personal situation—also has implications in the philosophy of the social sciences. Although 'materialism recognises unconditional respect for the truth as a necessary but also insufficient condition for true science', it also 'knows that research is co-determined by socially and personally conditioned interests, whether or not the scientist is aware of this fact'.[16] This claim about the *subjective* impossibility of scientific value-freedom implies that there can be no strictly value-free social research, because research is always codetermined by extra-scientific concerns that may well escape the attention of the researcher. Indeed, in a society inescapably beset by conflicting interests, the crucial question is instead *whose side* the researcher chooses to be on, and on *what grounds*.

From Horkheimer's earliest writings, a central animating concern of his thought is the status and place of negative human experiences such as misery, privation, and suffering in philosophy and science, as in ordinary human life.[17] Indeed, he argues that it is the unbearable experience of *human suffering* that ultimately drives the idealist to seek refuge in metaphysical systems of thought, and which ignites the hope, shared by religious believers and idealists philosophers alike, that the promise of a better world is enshrined in an eternal order beyond our mundane existence:

[13] Max Horkheimer, 'Zum Problem der Wahrheit', in *Gesammelte Schriften Band 3*, pp. 295–296.
[14] Horkheimer, 'Zum Problem der Wahrheit', p. 319.
[15] See also Jürgen Habermas, 'Notes on the Developmental History of Horkheimer's Work', *Theory Culture Society* (10/61) (1993): pp. 61–77.
[16] Horkheimer, 'Materialismus und Moral', p. 148.
[17] See, for example, the aphorism 'Monadologie' in 'Dämmerung: Notizen in Deutschland', in *Gesammelte Schrriften Band 2: Philosophische Frühschriften 1922–1932* (Frankfurt: Fischer Verlag, 1987).

> The life of most human beings is so miserable, the instances of deprivation and humiliation so numerous, effort and success are often so crassly disproportionate that the hope that this worldly order is not the only one is only too understandable. By striving to rationalise rather than to explain this hope for what it really is, idealism becomes an instrument of misrepresentation for the privation caused by nature and the relations of society.[18]

In fact, Horkheimer seems at times to observe this ideological function in philosophy *as such*—or, at least, in all those 'theodic' philosophical doctrines that attempt to reconcile subjects with a fundamentally irreconcilable world:

> On the other hand, these individuals have learned to demand reasons for the societal forms of life—i.e. for the distribution of work functions, for the kind of goods produced, for the property relations, legal forms and international relations—which they uphold and, if necessary, protect through their everyday actions. They want to know why they should act in such and such a way and not differently, and they demand some kind of guidance. Philosophy attempts to manage this helplessness through the metaphysical provision of meaning. Instead of answering the demand of individuals for meaning to their actions in terms of a clarification of the contradictions of society and how they can be practically overcome, [philosophy] distorts the understanding of the present by choosing the themes of a possible 'true' life or even 'true' death and by attempting to introduce some deeper meaning to mere existence.[19]

In contrast to the philosophical complacency and false reconciliation of idealism, the defining feature of Horkheimer's materialism is its aspiration to be fully conscious and take account of its own relation to human suffering, by explicitly allying itself with those for whom misery is a constant fact of everyday existence. In that capacity, Horkheimer insists, 'materialism ... understands itself as *the theoretical side of the struggle to rid the world of existing misery*'.[20] This allegiance is motivated not only by moral but also by epistemic reasons, since 'the groups that bear knowledge of the roots of evil and the ends on which their emancipation depends are those that experience privation as a consequence of their position in the reproductive process of society'.[21]

Indeed, Horkheimer claims that in a modern capitalist society this task can only be pursued through the development of a *theory of society*, which is able to grasp

---

[18] Horkheimer, 'Materialismus und Metaphysik', p. 83.
[19] Max Horkheimer, 'Bemerkungen zur philosophischen Anthropologie', in *Gesammelte Schriften Band 3*, p. 252–253.
[20] Horkheimer, 'Materialismus und Moral', p. 131 [emphasis added].
[21] Max Horkheimer, 'Anfänge der bürgerlichen Geschichtsphilosophie', in *Gesammelte Schriften Band 2*, p. 247. As we shall see in Section 2, this sentiment clearly echoes the work of Georg Lukács.

the relationship between existing suffering and the basic structure of society: 'Contemporary misery is tied to the societal structure. Therefore, the theory of society represents the content of contemporary materialism'.[22] The specific 'theory of society' that Horkheimer has in mind here is—with some important reservations and modifications—Marx's philosophy of history and critique of political economy, and, following Marx, it is the *proletariat* to which Horkheimer pledges his allegiance.[23] However, before turning to an exposition of Horkheimer's distinctive interpretation of Marx's work, we must account for the second stage in the young Horkheimer's intellectual development and the term that would come to define his philosophical legacy.

1.1.2 Traditional Theory and Critical Theory

In 1937, Horkheimer published his most famous essay, 'Traditional and Critical Theory' (*Traditionelle und kritische Theorie*), which inaugurates the second phase in his early thought. In this second phase, Horkheimer effectively abandons the attempt to organize a cooperative programme of interdisciplinary social research and instead focuses his attention on an epistemological clarification of the idea of a critical theory of society. The worry is no longer merely the methodological fragmentation of the social sciences and the resulting inability to comprehend society as a unified object of research; rather, the problem is now seen as the whole paradigm of the philosophy of science within which modern social-scientific research is framed, what Horkheimer calls 'traditional theory'.

From the point of view of traditional theory, science represents a library of knowledge, and its ultimate goal is a complete and internally coherent system of descriptive and explanatory propositions about the world. Traditional theory regards itself as causally isolated and logically independent from its subject matter—in the social sciences, from facts about society. It thus subscribes to a fundamental 'dualism' of 'thought and existence, understanding and observation', and scientific inquiry is cast as the 'establishment of a relation between mere observation or reporting of a fact and the conceptual structure of our knowledge'.[24] To be sure, traditional theory also sees scientific knowledge as a *practical tool-kit*, as a system of means that can be utilized to understand and master the natural world in pursuit of human ends, which are nevertheless always understood as *extra-scientific*. That is to say, traditional theory sees the ends for which scientific knowledge is utilized as logically independent of scientific inquiry, as

---

[22] Horkheimer, 'Materialismus und Metaphysik', p. 84.
[23] On this, see Helmut Dubiel, *Wissenschaftsorganisation und politische Erfahrung*, p. 37.
[24] Max Horkheimer, 'Traditionelle und kritische Theorie', in *Gesammelte Schriften Band 4: 1936–1941*, ed. by Alfred Schmidt (Frankfurt: S. Fischer Verlag, 1988), pp. 167–171.

paradigmatically expressed in Max Weber's famous methodological principle that the scientist should strive to rid herself of all value judgements.[25]

Now, Horkheimer does not in any way deny that human mastery of nature and the ordering of economic and social relations presupposes a 'structuring of knowledge in the form of a body of hypotheses' and that 'the technical progress of the *bourgeois* age is inseparable from this function of the scientific profession'. But, he maintains, insofar 'as the concept of theory is hypostatized, as if it were justifiable with reference to the inner essence of cognition or in another ahistorical way, it is transformed into a reified, ideological category'.[26] His strategy for bringing out the fundamentally ideological character of traditional theory is to clarify the discrepancy between the traditional scientific self-understanding and the social function of science in modern capitalist society as a whole, identified against the background of Marx's materialist philosophy of history and critique of political economy.

Accordingly, what accounts for the unavoidable social and political partiality of scientific research is no longer simply the *subjective impossibility* of the scientist ridding herself and her research of personal interests—as Horkheimer maintained during the earlier phase—but also the *objective function*, the systematic consequences of science *as a social institution* within the structure of interests and division of labour in modern capitalist society. That is to say, the sciences fulfil their carefully circumscribed role in the capitalist mode of production ultimately as productive forces in service of the capitalist class. By refusing to reflect on the nature of this social function, traditional theory in effect leads the sciences into blind service at the hands of a propertied minority against the interests of the great majority, supplying knowledge and technical means that enable the present and future reproduction of the *status quo*, to the detriment of the suffering masses.

As we shall see in greater detail in Section 3 of this chapter, Horkheimer believes that the capitalist process of production and exchange disempowers individual subjects by submitting them to unpredictable and crisis-ridden economic dynamics and class domination. Accordingly, the social circumstances of individuals living in a capitalist society are largely constituted through a blind, unjust, and irrational organization of economic activity, which is unable to harness the full productive potential inherent in the forces of production, and which leaves untold masses in an avoidably deprived and miserable condition. Moreover, depending on their social position, individuals caught up in this process are blindly assigned a role in the division of labour in a way that takes little or no account of individual need or potential but simply treats them as just another unit of labour to be exploited for the capitalist's gain. However, there is also a silver lining in

---

[25] Max Weber, 'Science as Vocation', in *From Max Weber*, ed. by H.H. Gerth and C. Wright Mills (New York: Oxford University Press, 1946).
[26] Horkheimer, 'Traditionelle und kritische Theorie', p. 168.

this gloomy story, which is that by producing, collecting, and rationally ordering human knowledge, the sciences also contain a productive potential that can be reaped by a future, superior mode of production and reasonable organization of society. The crucial question is thus: how can a society ever attain knowledge of this possibility and the transformation necessary to transition to such a superior mode of production, if its collective apparatus of epistemic production is completely in thrall to traditional theory and has blindly submitted to servicing the class benefitting from maintaining the *status quo*?

The answer is given by an alternative understanding of the significance and social function of social science that Horkheimer finds in Marx, and which he refers to as *critical theory*. Like the materialist programme, critical theory 'has society itself as its object'.[27] That is, critical theory does not concern itself simply with amassing knowledge, nor even with piecemeal improvement or solving problems encountered within the existing organization of society; rather, it is concerned with understanding the basic structure of society *as a whole*, in its historical genesis, present, and possible future form. However, the difference between critical theory and traditional theory is not only given by how they conceive of their respective objects of study, but also by their different social functions. In contrast to traditional theory, critical theory actively aspires to fulfil a self-consciously normative social function in social reality: it is 'aimed at ... emancipation, and has the transformation of the whole as its end'.[28] Eschewing the forlorn ideological commitment to scientific value-freedom, critical theory is thus driven by 'an interest in a reasonably organised future society'[29], and it strives towards 'a condition without exploitation or repression, in which an actual embracing subject—self-conscious humanity—exists'.[30]

Critical theory thus recognizes that 'like the influence of the material on the theory, the application of the theory on the material is not an intra-scientific process, but also a societal one'. That is to say, in contrast to traditional theory's dualisms of reality and perception, fact and value, critical theory sees itself as the theoretical expression of a historically emergent claim to human emancipation, and it sees its own value as a theory as fully dependent on its ability to fulfil this emancipatory social function, and it must thus be able to reflexively account for its own historical origins and societal implications. An understanding of its historical enabling conditions and the effects of its practical realization is thus part and parcel of a critical theory of society, which must, accordingly, provide an account both of its *context of emergence* and its *context of application*.

Critical theory's recognition of its own historical conditionedness, the situated point of view from which it emerges, is predicated on Horkheimer's insight that

---

[27] Horkheimer, 'Traditionelle und kritische Theorie', p. 180.
[28] Horkheimer, 'Traditionelle und kritische Theorie', p. 182.
[29] Horkheimer, 'Traditionelle und kritische Theorie', p. 207.
[30] Horkheimer, 'Traditionelle und kritische Theorie', p. 214.

> [t]he facts that our senses supply are preformed in a two-fold way: through the historical character of the object of perception and the historical character of the organ of perception. Neither is simply natural, but formed through human activity, although the individual perceives himself in the act of perception as receptive and passive.[31]

In other words, Horkheimer holds that both the *object* of knowledge, society, as well as the knowing *subject* are socially constituted through a historical process of human activity. This has profound implications for how we understand our practical situation: 'insofar as the facts given in perception are grasped as products, which are fundamentally subject to human control and in any case ought to be in the future, they lose their character of mere facticity'.[32] In other words, once we understand that both society and our own subjectivity are ultimately social and historical products of human activity, the misery and suffering affected by the basic structure loses its appearance of givenness and inevitability and becomes amenable to critique and the possibility of practical transformation.

Horkheimer's account of the cognitive structure of critical theory is the direct result of his reflections on the epistemological presuppositions of Marx's work:

> The Marxian categories of class, exploitation, surplus value, profit, immiseration, collapse are moments of a conceptual whole, the meaning of which should not be sought in the reproduction of contemporary society, but in the transformation of this society into the correct one.[33]

However, while Horkheimer more openly and explicitly aligns himself with the epistemological underpinnings of Marx's critique of the capitalist mode of production than in the earlier stage, he simultaneously distances himself from the claim—to which a great many Marxists of his day subscribed—that the inherent contradictions of capitalism will on their own accord bring forth the proletarian consciousness necessary for the reorganization of society:

> [T]he idea of a reasonable organisation of society that can meet the needs of the whole community [is] immanent in human labour but not presently grasped by individuals or the public spirit. A specific interest is required to understand and observe these tendencies. Marx and Engels taught us that such an interest will necessarily be generated in the proletariat ... But in this society, not even the situation of the proletariat is a guarantee for the correct understanding. No matter how much the proletariat experiences the senselessness and continued growth of privation and injustice on itself, this consciousness is prevented from becoming

---

[31] Horkheimer, 'Traditionelle und kritische Theorie', p. 174.
[32] Horkheimer, 'Traditionelle und kritische Theorie', p. 183.
[33] Horkheimer, 'Traditionelle und kritische Theorie', p. 192.

a general social force by the differentiations in its social structure advanced from above and the personal and class-based interests whose oppositional nature only breaks through in extraordinary circumstances.[34]

That is to say, whereas Horkheimer saw his earlier materialist programme as the theoretical dimension of the proletariat's struggle to rid itself of the misery imposed upon it by the basic structure of capitalist society, in the second phase he does not believe that critical theory can lay claim to that same privilege, since Horkheimer has in the meantime all but lost his confidence in the ability of the proletariat to effect the emancipation of human kind. In place of the proletariat, Horkheimer thus argues that critical theory is addressed towards anyone exhibiting what he calls a 'critical attitude', where critical, as Horkheimer specifies in a footnote, is 'meant not so much in the sense of the idealistic critique of pure reason as in the sense of the dialectical critique of political economy'.[35] To be sure, the claim that critical theory addresses whoever displays the requisite critical attitude irrespective of their class position is of course a commitment to a much more indeterminate addressee than the industrial proletariat, and it thus reflects Horkheimer's dwindling hopes for the prospects of an emancipatory transformation of society.

However, Horkheimer's most important innovation in the second stage of his intellectual development lies in his epistemological claim that Marx's work is in fact distinguished from traditional scientific theory by being a wholly *novel form of knowledge*. As I argued above, critical theory distinguishes itself from traditional theory by not only being a hypothesis or observation of reported facts, but by also being a *practical recommendation* to certain agents, whose claims to emancipation it aspires to inform. The issue is that if a critical theory were measured on the criterion advanced by traditional theory, simple correspondence between hypothesis and observed reality, it would obviously be false, since its aim of a reasonable organization of society does not have the status of a predicted occurrence issuing from an observation of things as they are.

Rather, critical theory issues *counsel* for existing or potential agents to transform the way things are *out of insight* into the unacceptable nature of the *status quo*, as revealed by the critical theory. According to Horkheimer, 'the historical meaning of [the theorist's] contribution does not speak for itself; rather, *it depends on whether human beings speak and act on its behalf*. It does not belong to an already finished historical form'.[36] The defining epistemological feature of a critical theory is thus what I have called its practical criterion of validity, according to which a critical theory is valid only if it actually enables human emancipation in practice:

---

[34] Horkheimer, 'Traditionelle und kritische Theorie', pp. 186–188.
[35] This 'kritisches Verhalten' can also be translated as 'critical conduct' or even 'critical activity'.
[36] Horkheimer, 'Traditionelle und kritische Theorie', p. 194 [emphasis added].

> Cognition in this traditional sense, including every kind of experience, is included in critical theory and practice. But the corresponding concrete observation of the important transformation toward which the latter is oriented is lacking before it actually happens. If the eating is the proof of the pudding, then that proof still lies in the future.[37]

Now, in this account of the two phases in Horkheimer's original paradigm of critical theory, I have only briefly touched upon the underlying reasons that motivate these revisions in the young Horkheimer's thought. However, these reasons will surface in the course of the next two sections, in which I take a closer and more systematic look at the historical and sociological dimensions of Horkheimer's original paradigm of critical theory. The historical dimension, to which I will first turn, is above all characterized by an undogmatic but unrelenting commitment to Marx's materialist philosophy of history, as well as a critical reception of the Hegelian Marxism of George Lukács. As I will argue in Chapter 2, it is ultimately Horkheimer's commitment to Marx's materialist philosophy of history which prevents him from doing justice to the global scope of critical theory's claim to validity.

1.2 Marx, Lukács, and the Materialist Philosophy of History

Unlike in subsequent paradigms of critical theory that we will encounter in this book, the young Horkheimer never develops an independent account of the historical dimension of his original paradigm of critical theory. Instead, as we have seen, he largely commits himself to a pre-existing view: namely, the materialist philosophy of history developed in the Left-Hegelian, Marxian tradition—and he thus inherits both the insights and disadvantages of this view, as I will argue in Chapter 2. Accordingly, this section will first expound the materialist philosophy of history developed in this tradition of Western Marxism and subsequently clarify Horkheimer's distinctive interpretation of this view.

1.2.1 Historical Materialism

In the preface to his book *Contribution to the Critique of Political Economy* from 1859, Marx offers a famously succinct statement of the basic claims and structure of historical materialism:

> In the social production of their life, men enter into definite relations that are indispensable and independent of their will, relations of production which

---

[37] Horkheimer, 'Traditionelle und kritische Theorie', p. 195.

correspond to a definite stage of development of their material productive forces. The sum total of these relations of production constitutes the economic structure of society, the real foundation, on which rises a legal and political superstructure and to which correspond definite forms of social consciousness. The mode of production of material life conditions the social, political and intellectual life process in general. It is not the consciousness of men that determines their being, but, on the contrary, their social being that determines their consciousness. At a certain stage of their development, the material productive forces of society come in conflict with the existing relations of production, or—what is but a legal expression for the same thing—with the property relations within which they have been at work hitherto. From forms of development of the productive forces these relations turn into their fetters. Then begins an epoch of social revolution.[38]

The central claim of historical materialism is that different production relations and their attendant forms of society rise and fall depending on whether they further or fetter human productive power. Production relations are 'the relations of ownership by persons of productive forces or persons or relations presupposing such relations of ownership'.[39] The relations of production represent the 'base' or economic structure of society, while its 'superstructure' is comprised of legal, political, religious, cultural, and other 'non-economic' institutions.[40] To this superstructure then correspond certain forms of social consciousness, including political and moral consciousness.

On a widespread interpretation of the passage quoted above, historical materialism assumes an explanatory hierarchy between these phenomena, such that the existence of certain forms of social consciousness can be explained with reference to the existence of a certain superstructure, the existence of a certain superstructure can be explained with reference to the existence of certain relations of production, and the existence of certain relations of production can be explained with reference to whether they fetter or further the continued development of the production forces. As long as they further productive power, a given set of production relations will continue to exist along with their corresponding superstructure and forms of consciousness. But once they begin to fetter the development of the productive forces, a revolution ensues that overthrows the now-antiquated production relations and replaces them with superior relations that can once again further human productive power.

---

[38] Karl Marx, 'Marx on the History of his Opinions [Preface to a Contribution to the Critique of Political Economy]', in *The Marx-Engels Reader. Second Edition* (New York: W.W. Norton & Company, 1978), pp. 4–5.
[39] G.A. Cohen, *Karl Marx's Theory of History: A Defence* (Princeton: Princeton University Press, 2000), pp. 34–35.
[40] G.A. Cohen, *Karl Marx's Theory of History*, p. 45.

To be sure, a social revolution does not come about all of itself, and Marx both expected and encouraged the industrial proletariat to execute the death sentence that he issued over capitalist production relations, once the conditions for revolution were ripe. However, many subsequent Marxists have interpreted Marx as suggesting that the proletariat would more or less automatically come to recognize and step up to its role as the designated executioner of capitalism. Horkheimer denies any such historical guarantees for the future emancipatory success of the proletariat; in fact, he makes the very question of the proletariat's ripeness for revolution the centrepiece of his early empirical research programme. In order to account for this construal of proletarian class-consciousness, not as some certain future fate, but, ultimately, as an *empirical problem* worthy of interdisciplinary study, we must, however, first familiarize ourselves with two important innovations that George Lukács brings to the framework of historical materialism: namely, his work on reification and class consciousness.

1.2.2 Lukács and the Theory of Reification

In his highly influential collection 'History and Class Consciousness' (*Geschichte und Klassenbewußtsein*) from 1923, Lukács develops a distinctive interpretation of historical materialism that draws extensively on Weber's theory of social rationalization and Hegel's dialectics. In particular, the essay 'Reification and the Consciousness of the Proletariat' exercised an enormous influence not just on the young Horkheimer but on the Frankfurt School tradition as a whole.[41] Lukács's crucial significance for the Frankfurt School lies first and foremost in his theory of *reification*, which he understands in terms of the commodity form and the rationalization of modern capitalist society. The original model for the theory of reification derives from Marx, specifically the famous section of the first chapter of *Capital* on 'commodity fetishism'. Marx defines this religious metaphor as 'a definite social relation between men, that assumes, in their eyes, the fantastic form of a relation between things'.[42] Fetishism in general implies that one mistakenly perceives an attributed quality as an inherent quality, and the more specific phenomenon of *commodity fetishism* implies that one mistakenly perceives the exchange-value of a commodity as inherent in, rather than as attributed to, the commodity form.[43]

In Marx's account, the explanation of this epistemic mistake relies on his basic distinction between use-value and exchange-value and the labour theory of value.

---

[41] See Hauke Brunkhorst and Peter Krockenberger, 'Paradigm-core and theory-dynamics in critical social theory: people and programs', *Philosophy & Social Criticism* (24/6), 1998: pp. 67–110.
[42] Karl Marx, 'Capital. Vol. I', in *The Marx-Engels Reader*, p. 321.
[43] For an illuminating exposition of fetishism in capitalism on which this paragraph draws, see G.A. Cohen, *Karl Marx's Theory of History*, Ch. 5.

The use-value of a commodity represents the immediate utility derived from consumption of the commodity, whereas the exchange-value of a commodity represents its market price. The labour theory of value, which Marx in large part inherited from classical political economy, holds that the value of a product is equal to the socially necessary labour time expended on it through the process of its production. A commodity is the product of labour and its value is equal to the labour invested in it. But the commodity nonetheless *appears*, even to those who have produced it, as if it only has value because it can be sold on the market, and as if it possesses such exchange-value as an inherent property. However, this perceptual mistake is not simply the effect of the worker's slow wit or lack of education; rather, the fact that commodities appear as having value only in virtue of possessing exchange-value derives from their crucial *integrative role* in the capitalist mode of production.

Indeed, it is a distinctive feature of the capitalist mode of production that the products of labour only gain what Marx calls a 'social character' through the process of exchange.[44] That is, labourers do not relate to one another and the products of their labour in a direct or unmediated sense, but only through the institutional mediation of the capitalist market. It is thus because of market mediation that the value of products—including the value of labour power—seems determined by market exchange, rather than by the labour invested in them. Marx's more general claim is thus that in the capitalist mode of production, exchange-value becomes the central medium for integrating relations between workers and their products, obfuscating their own labour as the true source of the value of those products.[45]

It is from this premise that Lukács's argument takes its departure. Lukács understands commodity fetishism as a *form* of reification, but reification refers to a much more general and all-pervasive kind of social phenomenon. As he remarks in the beginning of his essay on reification, 'at this stage in the history of mankind there is no problem that does not ultimately lead back to that question and there is no solution that could not be found in the solution to the riddle of *commodity-structure*'.[46] However, this remark actually obscures that Lukács is only able to generalize the concept of reification to the status of the central and all-defining problem of capitalist society by complementing Marx's analysis of the commodity form with Weber's theory of social rationalization. That is, Lukács's account of reification does not only rely on the integrative function of markets, but also on the

---

[44] Marx, 'Capital: Vol. I', in *The Marx-Engels Reader*, p. 320.
[45] Titus Stahl, *Immanente Kritik: Elemente einer Theorie sozialer Praktiken* (Frankfurt: Campus, 2013), p. 433.
[46] Georg Lukács, 'Reification and Consciousness of the Proletariat', in *History and Class Consciousness: Studies in Marxist Dialectics*, transl. by Rodney Livingstone (Cambridge, MA: The MIT Press, 1971), p. 83.

more comprehensive Weberian conception of the history of Western modernity as a gradual unfolding of instrumental reason.

Weber understands rationalization as the qualitative impact on society of increasingly widespread measures of specialization and calculability in social spheres such as the economy, bureaucracy, and law.[47] According to Lukács, social rationalization has both an objective and a subjective dimension, exercising a profound impact on both the objective process of production and the psychology of human subjects:

> In consequence of the rationalisation of the work-process the human qualities and idiosyncrasies of the worker appear increasingly as *mere sources of error* when contrasted with these abstract special laws functioning according to rational predictions. Neither objectively nor in his relation to his work does man appear as the authentic master of the process; on the contrary, he is a mechanical part incorporated into a mechanical system. He finds it already pre-existing and self-sufficient, it functions independently of him and he has to conform to its laws whether he likes it or not.[48]

Etymologically, the word 'reification' derives from the Latin word *res*, meaning 'thing'. In Lukács's view, the objective and subjective sides of reification are both consequences of social rationalization, as the individual human being is *treated as* and comes to *regard herself* as a mere thing—as little more than a cog in the machine of an increasingly fine-tuned productive apparatus operating according to its own laws. From the point of view of rational calculability and prediction, which orders the modern system of capitalist production, all unpredictable idiosyncrasies and forms of human spontaneity are thus reduced to mere disturbances, and individuals who sell part of their physical and mental activity—their labour power—as a commodity thereby come to see and comport themselves merely as objects of rational control.

Individual subjects under capitalism are thus comprehensively *objectified*; they are both socially reduced to and understand themselves as things in a rationalized process over which they have no power of their own. The worker finds himself within 'a specialised process that has been rationalised and mechanised, a process that he discovers already existing, complete and able to function without him and in which he is no more than a cipher reduced to an abstract quantity, a mechanised and rationalised tool'.[49] This is the basic form of Lukács's theory of reification, which, as we shall see in chapters to come, is one of the central animating themes of the Frankfurt School tradition as a whole.

---

[47] Max Weber, *The Protestant Ethic and the Spirit of Capitalism*, transl. by Talcott Parsons (London: Routledge, 2001).
[48] Lukács, 'Reification and Consciousness of the Proletariat', p. 89.
[49] Lukács, 'Reification and the Consciousness of the Proletariat', p. 166.

1.2.3 Lukács's Theory of Class Consciousness

We are now in a position to account for Lukács's second innovation and its influence on the young Horkheimer: namely his Hegelian interpretation of the relationship between socialist theory and practice as the proletarian class subject's coming to self-consciousness. Lukács's basic problem is how to grasp the objective possibility for the proletariat to develop a consciousness of itself as a class, which can engage in revolutionary action. However, whereas Marx invested his hopes in structural transformations like the falling rate of profit and the increasing immiseration of the working class to induce the requisite consciousness of a shared proletarian class interest in overthrowing capitalist production relations, Lukács believes that it is possible to derive this possibility directly from his account of the *reified form* of the worker's self-consciousness. To be sure, as Lukács makes clear in the essay 'Class Consciousness', a distinction must be made between 'the *actual*, psychological state of consciousness of proletarians' and the '*true*, practical class consciousness' of the proletariat.[50] Since the former is thoroughly reified, we cannot simply assume that the proletariat will gain true self-consciousness of itself as a class, but we nevertheless have to clarify how this might be possible. And this is possible, Lukács argues, because the proletariat is in the unique position of being *both the subject and the object of history*.

At this point, Lukács relies on a distinction between two kinds of subjects and objects, namely individuals and classes, along with a crucial distinction between *conscious* and *unconscious* production. As we saw above, the individual subject is completely negated as a subject by the process of capitalist production, which reduces him to a mere object of rationalized planning and control. However, the great trick of reification is of course that it only *treats* and makes subjects *appear* as objects to themselves, whereas underneath the reified and objectified deception, the (self-misperceiving) subject is still present. Under the objective compulsion of the capitalist production process, the subject has been *objectified*, but he remains a subject nonetheless. Even under the spell of reification, the worker therefore still has a repository sense of the practical category mistake to which he is subject:

> [O]n the one hand, in his social existence the worker is immediately placed *wholly* on the side of the object: he appears to himself immediately as an object and not as the active part of the social process of labour. On the other hand, however, the role of object is no longer purely immediate. That is to say, it is true that the worker is objectively transformed into a mere object of the process of production by the methods of capitalist production (in contrast to those of slavery and servitude) i.e. by the fact that the worker is forced to objectify his labour-power over against his total personality and to sell it as a commodity. But because of the

---

[50] Georg Lukács, 'Class Consciousness', in *History and Class Consciousness*, p. 74 [emphasis added].

split between subjectivity and objectivity induced in man by the compulsion to objectify himself as a commodity, the situation becomes one that can be made conscious.[51]

Now, the way that Lukács believes that this category mistake can be 'made conscious' is precisely through theory—or, more specifically, through Marx's critique of political economy, which exposes the reification of the worker through its analysis of the commodity form. In Lukács's words, 'Inasmuch as [the worker] is incapable in practice of raising himself above the role of object his consciousness is the *self-consciousness of the commodity*'.[52] By thus recognizing himself as reified under capitalist production relations, the worker glimpses the *beating heart* of the capitalist mode of production: namely, that it lives off and can only exist through the mass objectification and exploitation of workers as commodities.

However, by seeing through the systematic veil of reification, the worker also recognizes that he and all the other workers are in fact the *subjects* that produce history, but that this crucial historical role has so far remained fully *unconscious* to the proletariat under the reifying spell of capitalist production relations. In the final step in this self-reflective process of coming to class consciousness, the proletariat thus comes to realize that—as the subject class that unconsciously produces history—it alone has the power to free itself from its reified condition and introduce a *conscious* mode of production. By thus knowing itself as what Lukács, with inspiration from Fichte, calls the 'identical subject-object of history', the proletariat is finally motivated to overthrow capitalism and replace it with a mode of production according to a rational plan. To be sure, this can only happen when theory has brought the proletariat to class-consciousness and thus helped jump-start revolutionary action in practice.

1.2.4 Class Consciousness as an Empirical Problem

As much as the young Horkheimer remains firm in his commitment to historical materialism, he characteristically subscribes to a non-dogmatic and *fallibilistic* interpretation of Marx's philosophy of history. In Horkheimer's view, Marx's philosophy of history is troubled by certain scientifically ungrounded assumptions:

> The theory's claim that the historical behaviour of human beings and groups of human beings is determined through the economic process can only be understood, at the individual level, through the scientific clarification of their own independent ways of reacting [to the economic process] in a given historical

---

[51] Lukács, 'Class Consciousness', pp. 167–168.
[52] Lukács, 'Class Consciousness', p. 168.

period. As long as we still haven't understood how structural transformations in economic life affect transformations of the whole form of life of the members of different social groups through the psychological constitution of those members at any given moment, then a doctrine which maintains the dependence of these forms of life upon the economic structure will contain dogmatic elements that severely limit its hypothetical value for an explanatory account of the present.[53]

In other words, since Marx neglected to clarify the nature of the process through which transformations in the basic economic structure affect transformations in the superstructure of society and the attendant forms of consciousness, the scientific status and usefulness of historical materialism has been greatly compromised. Moreover, while Horkheimer is immensely inspired by Lukács's Weberian construal of the concept of reification and his emphasis on theory as a decisive element in the formation of proletarian class-consciousness, he transforms Lukács's Hegelian derivation of the proletariat's coming-to-class-consciousness into an *empirical problem*: namely, as a problem of *social psychology*.

As we shall see in the next section, it is precisely this empirical construal of the formation of proletarian class-consciousness that would—in the course of the IfS's empirical studies—lead Horkheimer to lose confidence in the proletariat as the revolutionary subject of history. Indeed, the more empirical material the IfS gathered, the more Horkheimer lost confidence in the proletariat's ability to act as the conscious subject of history, and the more he turned away from the proletariat as the sole addressee of the materialist theory of society of his early phase, sliding instead towards the more indeterminate 'critical attitude' of the second phase. In order to further explore Horkheimer's original paradigm of critical theory—and to ascertain the empirical reasons for the young Horkheimer's loss of confidence in the proletariat as the world-historical subject of revolutionary emancipation—we must now turn to his sociological account of monopoly capitalism and the vast concentration of capital and power that it enables and sustains.

1.3 Structural Transformations in Capitalism and Class Consciousness

In contrast to his reliance on a fairly orthodox interpretation of historical materialism, the synchronic dimension of Horkheimer's original paradigm of critical theory offers a novel sociological account of the regime of capitalist society and its attendant relations of domination that Horkheimer saw himself confronted with in his day, which combines Marx and Freud in a highly distinctive and theoretically innovative way. I will first expound Horkheimer's

---

[53] Max Horkheimer, 'Geschichte und Psychologie', in *Gesammelte Schriften Band 3*, p. 58.

political-economic account of the transformations that the basic structure of capitalist society had undergone since the Industrial Revolution, and then proceed to sketch his social-psychological account of the systematic hindrances that this transformation imposes on the formation of proletarian class consciousness, and, indeed, of the authoritarian personality types that it instead engenders.

1.3.1 Monopoly Capitalism

Horkheimer's account of 'monopoly capitalism' is both premised on and goes beyond Marx's account of the inner workings of the capitalist mode of production. In *Capital*, Marx identifies exploitation of labour as the necessary condition for capital accumulation and the hidden source of surplus value under capitalist production relations. In his complex analysis, Marx begins from an exposition of the commodity form and proceeds through the sphere of exchange into the 'hidden abode' of production, in order to chart the process by which surplus value is created, which he identifies as the extraction of value from labour over and above the socially necessary costs of its subsistence.

To be sure, the production of surplus value through the exploitation of labour is possible only because of the great trick of capitalist production, which is that labour power is the only commodity able to produce more value than its market price, since its use-value (actually performed labour) is higher than its exchange value (labour power). Consequently, the creation of surplus value through the exploitation of labour does not violate the legally enshrined rules of the capitalist labour market, since workers do in fact receive the full exchange value of their labour power:

> The circumstance, that on the one hand the daily sustenance of labour-power costs only half a day's labour, while on the other hand the very same labour-power can work during a whole day, that consequently the value which its use during one day creates, is double what he pays for that use, this circumstance is, without doubt, a piece of good luck for the buyer, but by no means an injury to the seller.[54]

Marx did not moralistically condemn the capitalist mode of production on account of its necessary reliance on the exploitation of labour; rather, he held that capitalism serves the important and necessary historical purpose of developing human productive power up until the point where the material conditions for a communist mode of production are realized. However, he also maintained that the huge increase in productive power effected by the capitalist mode of production is ultimately the roots of its own undoing.

---

[54] Marx, 'Capital: Vol. I', p. 358.

This argument—known as the argument from the falling-rate-of-profit—rests on two premises. Firstly, capitalism creates a vast increase in productivity through technological innovation and development, and in this process capitalists will recalibrate what Marx called the 'organic composition of capital' by increasing the ratio of constant capital (roughly: technology) to variable capital (labour), in order to reap the short-term profits of technological productivity gains and survive in competition with other capitalists. As a consequence, an ever-greater part of labour is replaced with ever-more efficient machinery, creating what Marx calls an unemployed 'reserve army' of the proletariat. Second, since Marx assumes that all surplus value ultimately derives from the exploitation of labour, this structural tendency for constant capital to crowd out variable capital in the organic composition of capital will steadily undermine the extraction of surplus value, and the capitalist mode of production will, as a consequence, end up in a condition where it has been rendered systemically unable to utilize the immense productive potential of the forces of production that it has itself effected.

In other words, capitalist production relations will begin to fetter the continued development of the productive forces. This is what Marxists refer to as one of capitalism's inherent *contradictions*. Since it will simultaneously create an ever-greater gulf between the living standards of capitalists (who, given the lower labour costs, still accumulate capital for themselves, notwithstanding the falling rate of profit) and the permanently unemployed proletarians (who will also, in virtue of their number, exert a constant downward pressure on wages), the proletariat will ultimately deem such conditions intolerable, overthrow their shackles, and replace capitalism with a productively superior mode of production that caters to actual human need.

The IfS members all believed that this analysis—including the argument from the falling-rate-of-profit—was essentially correct of capitalism *in Marx's day*, or what they call '*bourgeois*-liberal capitalism'. However, they also believed that in the years since Marx's death, capitalism had undergone a fundamental structural transformation and morphed into what Horkheimer's circle (and many other contemporaneous Marxists, including Lenin) called 'monopoly capitalism'. This structural transformation, which was fuelled by the Great War and interwar economic crises, was laid out by Friedrich Pollock in his article 'The Present Condition of Capitalism and the Prospects of a New Order of Economic Planning' (*Die gegenwärtige Lage des Kapitalismus und die Aussichten einer planwirtschaftlichen Neuordnung*) from 1932:

> The growth of the economic units [i.e. corporations] gives their leaders increasing economic and political power. Thus arises the much discussed 'solidification' of the economy, where the prices of many important commodities are no longer determined by the 'free play of the [market] forces' but through monopolistic constraints. These constrained prices are enabled by the fact that a customs policy

has been enacted through the political influence of the great economic powers, which excludes foreign competition from internal markets, or allows the great conglomerates to divide the markets between them and the foreign competition.[55]

According to Pollock, the protectionistic and monopolistic interwar economy amounted to a suspension of the fierce competition between individual capitalists, which drives investment in technological innovation in the hunt for short-term profit, and which in turn causes the long-term change in the organic composition of capital in favour of constant capital. The chaotic and decentralized forces of the market have thus been partly replaced by a limited and selective form of centralized economic planning in order that industrial tyrants may reap monopoly rents without the constant risk of bankruptcy that they faced under *bourgeois-liberal* capitalism. Monopoly capitalism has therefore effectively suspended the structural dynamic that fuels the falling rate of profit, without, however, transcending the basic economic structure of the capitalist mode of production, which is still maintained in virtue of the existence of a propertied capitalist class and a toiling proletariat. Pollock's objective in the article is to ascertain the prospects of a truly rationally planned economy, and he readily concludes that 'all the economic conditions for its realisation are fulfilled'.[56] Nevertheless, prospects for revolution are grim:

> In this constrained capitalism, much speaks for the claims that the [economic] depressions will be longer, the upswing phases will be shorter, and the crises will be more destructive than in the time of 'free competition', but its 'automatic' collapse is not to be expected. Economically speaking, there is no inescapable compulsion to replace [monopoly capitalism] with a different economic system.[57]

Along with Pollock, Horkheimer and the rest of the IfS circle assumed that a rationally planned economy is vastly more efficient than monopoly capitalism, and that economic planning therefore holds the potential to raise the suffering masses out of their misery by utilizing the full potential contained in the productive forces. Horkheimer further agrees that the capitalism of their day is 'to a large extent dominated by monopolies, but still chaotic and disorganised in a global perspective,

---

[55] Friedrich Pollock, 'Die gegenwärtige Lage des Kapitalismus und die Aussichten einer planwirtschaftlichen Neuordnung', in *Zeitschrift für Sozialforschung, Vol. 1* (München: Kösel-Verlag, 1970), pp. 8–27, p. 12.

[56] Pollock, 'Die gegenwärtige Lage des Kapitalismus', p. 27. These conditions include that 'the weight of industrial production lies in large scale mass manufacture', that the 'process of centralisation has reached a certain level, that the technical and organisational means for mastering the tasks of centrally controlled economy are known', and, most importantly, 'that a considerable productivity reserve is at hand, which can be exploited through the application of the methods of economic planning'.

[57] Pollock, 'Die gegenwärtige Lage des Kapitalismus', p. 16.

richer than ever before and nevertheless unable to eliminate misery'.[58] However, for Horkheimer, this analysis is in fact only the back-story; in accordance with his aspiration to scientifically bolster historical materialism, he is more interested in the empirical question of why the proletariat does *not* take the revolutionary leap out of their economically unnecessary misery.

In an aphorism in 'Dawn and Decline' called 'The Powerlessness of the German Working Class' (*Die Ohnmacht der deutschen Arbeiterklasse*), Horkheimer speculates that part of the explanation might be found in a structural transformation of the German proletariat that occurred in the interwar years, and which gained momentum during the Great Depression, where a relative improvement in the social conditions of workers with long-term employment went hand in hand with a considerable growth in the truly miserable, permanently unemployed *Lumpenproletariat*.[59] Moreover, within the group of long-term employed workers, yet another split occurred between blue-collar industrial workers and white-collar employees (so-called *Angestellte*). Since Horkheimer regards the pivotal question of proletarian class-consciousness ultimately as an empirical problem, these developments naturally gave rise to considerable concern. Indeed, they held the potential to severely compromise the formation of proletarian class-consciousness and the political coherence of the proletariat, many of whom had gained so many privileges within the existing system that the prospects of a revolution seemed too much of a short-term risk, even if they still in principle stood to gain from a reorganization of the system as a whole.

1.3.2 Freudo-Marxism and the Rise of Fascism

It is this potentially fatal incongruence between the objective interests of workers in a revolutionary overthrow of productivity-fettering monopoly capitalism and the structurally induced fragmentation of their class-consciousness that hinders them from grasping and acting on these objective interests, which is the central theme of the first empirical investigation of the IfS: the so-called 'Worker and Employee Survey' (*Arbeiter- und Angestellten-Erhebung*) undertaken in 1930/31. In order to investigate the empirical problem of proletarian class-consciousness, Horkheimer relies heavily on Erich Fromm—the psychologist who must, next to Horkheimer, be regarded as the leading light of the IfS in its first, materialist phase. Their highly innovative common project of merging two prominent social-scientific traditions of their day—Marx's critique of capitalism and Freud's psychoanalysis—was absolutely central to the first generation of the Frankfurt

---

[58] Max Horkheimer, 'Bemerkungen über Wissenschaft und Krise', in *Gesammelte Schriften Band 3*, p. 45.
[59] Horkheimer, 'Dämmerung', p. 373.

School, and, as we shall see in subsequent chapters, set a precedent for the tradition as a whole. The background problem of the 'Worker and Employee Survey' was formulated by Horkheimer in his first essay in the ZfS, 'History and Psychology' (*Geschichte und Psychologie*), from 1932:

> That human beings uphold economic relations, beyond which their powers and needs have already grown, instead of replacing these with a higher and more rational form of organisation, is only possible because the actions of numerically significant social classes is determined not through knowledge and understanding, but through a system of [psychological] drives that results in false consciousness.[60]

Horkheimer thus proposes an explanation of the lack of proletarian class-consciousness with reference to the conjunction of economic and psychological factors. The individual questions of the survey and the categorial apparatus for interpreting its results were based on Fromm's social psychology, which the latter had set out in an important article in the first issue of the ZfS:

> The social-psychological appearances should be understood as processes of active and passive adaption of the drive complex to the socioeconomic situation. The drive complex is—in some of its fundamental aspects—biologically given but considerably modifiable; the economic conditions serve the role as the primary modifying factors ... Social psychology must explain the common, socially relevant spiritual attitudes and ideologies—and, in particular, their subconscious roots—from the influence of the economic conditions on the libidinal strivings.[61]

The highly ambitious survey (3300 questionnaires with 271 questions were sent out, of which 1150 were returned) was largely devised by and executed under the leadership of Fromm. Its central objective was an investigation into the 'psychological structure' of workers and employees, which was subsequently analysed and categorized in terms of Fromm's tripartite character typology of 'revolutionary personality', 'ambivalent personality', and 'authoritarian personality'.[62] However, the results of the survey proved disappointing, if not outright alarming: only 15% of the respondents could be classified as exhibiting a revolutionary personality, and thus as possessing the requisite class-consciousness for joint revolutionary action, while 75% displayed an ambivalent personality and 10% an authoritarian

---

[60] Horkheimer, 'Geschichte und Psychologie', p. 59.
[61] Erich Fromm, 'Über die Methode und Aufgabe einer analytischen Sozialpsychologie', in *Zeitschrift für Sozialforschung: Jahrgang 1/1932* (München: Kösel-Verlag, 1970), p. 40.
[62] Max Horkheimer (ed.), *Studien über Authorität und Familie: Forschungsberichte aus dem Institut für Sozialforschung* (Lüneburg: Dietrich zu Klampen Verlag, 1987), pp. 239–271.

personality. The survey results thus delivered a severe blow to Horkheimer's hopes on behalf of the proletariat to serve as the revolutionary agent in overthrowing monopoly capitalism, and, perhaps because of its depressing results, it was never published in his lifetime.[63]

Now, the account of monopoly capitalism developed by Horkheimer and his associates expounds a transformation not only in the political-economic structure of capitalism relative to Marx's day, but also in the way that power is ordered and exercised within capitalist society, in the *relations of power and domination* enabled and sustained by monopoly capitalism. Whereas *bourgeois*-liberal capitalism was characterized by capitalist class domination over the proletariat, the distribution of power *within* the capitalist class was more fragmented, since its members were locked in a permanent condition of intense competition. Monopoly capitalism, on the other hand, involves a much more centralized distribution of power among economic and political elites, which have all but merged into one class. This analysis was elaborated from a different perspective in the subsequent empirical study of the IfS, the 'Studies on Authority and Family' (*Studien über Authorität und Familie*), which was written and published in 1936 after Horkheimer and the IfS circle had already fled to New York. In this study, which was the most encompassing—and, as it happens, also the last—interdisciplinary effort of the IfS to combine theoretical and empirical work during the early phase, the focus changed from an assessment of the revolutionary potential of the proletariat to the more defensive project of explaining the rise of National Socialism in Germany.

It was once again Fromm who provided the central social-psychological framework, relying heavily on Freud's theory of individual character formation. In his essay 'The I and the Id' (*Das Ich und das Es*) from 1923, Freud had developed his 'structural model' of the psyche, distinguishing three parts of the psychological apparatus: the ego, the super-ego, and the id. The id is the subconscious centre of drives and instincts, the super-ego is the moral and critical faculty (the conscience), and the ego exercises control over the other parts and mediates between outer reality and inner instinctual life.[64] According to Freud, the relative weight of the component parts of the psychic personality is partly determined by biological factors and partly by external reality. However, since he was convinced that any form of culture implies a necessary restriction of the satisfaction of both sexual and aggressive instinctual drives, Freud regarded the prospects for progress in culture

---

[63] Although a short report on the state of the survey was published as part of the larger study on authority and the family. The whole study was later published as Erich Fromm, *Arbeiter und Angestellte am Vorabend des Dritten Reiches. Eine sozialpsychologische Untersuchung*, ed. by Wolfgang Bonß (Stuttgart: Deutsche Verlags-Anstalt, 1980).

[64] Sigmund Freud, 'Das Ich und das Es', in *Werkausgabe in Zwei Bänden. Band 1: Elemente der Psychoanalyse*, ed. by Anna Freud and Ilse Grubrich-Simitis (Frankfurt: Fischer Verlag, 2006), 369–401.

with the utmost pessimism, noting gloomily: 'the intention that the human being should be "happy" is not part of "creation"'.[65] By contrast, Fromm and Horkheimer share the historical-materialist conviction that the inner constitution of the psychic personality is heavily conditioned by historically variant factors, chiefly the organization of the basic structure of society and one's place within that structure. Accordingly, Fromm believed that a rationally planned economy would be able to procure resources for a more immediate and general gratification of needs, which would in turn enable the development of less inhibited, less pathological personality types.

The study's explanation of the rise of National Socialism—which is offered from different points of view by Horkheimer and Fromm in their respective contributions—relies in part on Freud's account of the formation of the ego and superego from the subconscious libidinal energies of the id through the young child's overcoming of the Oedipus complex. According to this account, the young boy in the phallic stage develops libidinal desires for his mother, as well as an aggressive jealousy and hatred of his father. However, he is eventually forced to submit to the overpowering authority of his father, after which he renounces the sexual desire for his mother and learns to transform his hatred of his father into love. In the repressive achievement of overcoming the Oedipus complex, a faculty of self-control is born, in order to mediate between inner and outer demands: namely, the ego. Moreover, the authority of the all-powerful father is internalized into an inner authority—the superego—that eventually comes to function as the moral conscience. Indeed, in implicit appeal to Kant, Freud uses the term 'categorical imperatives' to describe the mode of the superego's operation.[66]

In their contributions to the study, Horkheimer and Fromm both emphasize the historical contextuality of this account, which corresponds to the family structure in *bourgeois*-liberal capitalism and the *bourgeois* circles of Freud's native Vienna. In this context, the authority of the father ultimately derives from his family role as breadwinner, which gives him a superior status as head of the family. This is true even to some extent of the proletarian father, notwithstanding the domination and exploitation to which he is subjected in economic life. However, with the transition to monopoly capitalism and its frequent and profound crisis, mass unemployment, and extreme concentration of wealth and power, the relative independence of the family as a social institution is undermined and its members seamlessly integrated into society's steeply hierarchical power structure.[67] Due to mass unemployment, the proletarian boy is deprived of the awesome father figure,

---

[65] Sigmund Freud, 'Das Unbehagen in der Kultur', in *Werkausgabe in Zwei Bänden. Band 2*, p. 376.
[66] Freud, 'Das Ich und das Es'.
[67] Horkheimer, 'Allgemeiner Teil', in *Studien über Autorität und Familie*, p. 3.

who derives his authority in part from his ability to support his family, and he risks developing what Fromm calls a 'sadomasochistic personality' with a weakened ego that leads the young man in search for external authorities—a *Führer*. Such a personality type is a perfect fit in the hierarchical power structure of a fascist society: he takes pleasure in dominating and punishing his perceived inferiors, he idolizes his superiors and revels in his own punishment, and he blindly submits to authority whatever its justification.[68]

This political-economic-*cum*-social-psychoanalytic theory is arguably the principal reason why Horkheimer came to believe that, functionally speaking, fascism is quite simply the most appropriate political superstructure for monopoly capitalism. As the IfS circle had already glimpsed in the 'Worker and Employee Survey', given the disconcertingly high number of proletarians exhibiting ambivalent and outright authoritarian tendencies, the precarious economic situation in which monopoly capitalism places a significant part of the proletariat systematically nurtures, through intra-family psychodynamics, an authoritarian personality type that is exceedingly easy prey for fascist strong-men and demagogues. Coupled with the vast economic and political centralization arising in support of the great industrial conglomerates, monopoly capitalism thus contains forces that pull towards an authoritarian and fascist form of government from both top and bottom. Horkheimer subsequently captured the gist of this materialist account of the growth of fascism from the womb of monopoly capitalism in his famous claim, 'he who does not want to talk about capitalism, he should also keep silent about fascism.'[69]

The relations of domination in monopoly capitalism have therefore become more steeply hierarchical and unmediated, since corporate and political elites enjoy a form of centralized and unconstrained domination over the majority population that *bourgeois*-liberal capitalism did not allow. However, even though the fundamental economic structure remains largely unchanged, the underlying class conflict has been obscured by psychological misdevelopments within the proletariat (some of whom come to take pleasure in the domination to which they are subjected and direct their anger at 'aliens', such as Jews), and as a result, the more centralized relations of domination of monopoly capitalism have become *even more opaque* from the perspective of the proletarians. The combined effect of this increasingly obscure but much more centralized and cohesive form of elite domination is to further worsen the prospects for the proletariat's escape from the economically unnecessary misery and suffering to which monopoly capitalism inevitably gives rise.

---

[68] Erich Fromm, 'Sozialpsychologischer Teil', in *Studien über Autorität und Familie*, p. 110.
[69] Max Horkheimer, 'Die Juden und Europa', in *Gesammelte Schriften Band 4*, pp. 308–309.

1.4 Critical Theory and Bourgeois Morality

One of the most underappreciated aspects of Horkheimer's original paradigm of critical theory is the sophisticated normative dimension that informs the above analysis, which, I will argue, also plays a central and widely unacknowledged role in Horkheimer's methodological account of the very idea of a critical theory of society. I will begin the exposition of the normative dimension of Horkheimer's original paradigm of critical theory by sketching the account of human freedom that we find in the young Horkheimer's work—in the form of the idea of a 'reasonable society'—and then proceed to clarify the conception of justice which he espouses, and, in particular, the relation between the concept of justice and the idea of a critical theory of society.

1.4.1 A Reasonable Society

We have seen that Horkheimer understands critical theory as allied with those struggling to rid the world of existing suffering. However, the normative core of Horkheimer's original paradigm of critical theory is in fact a highly distinctive conception of *freedom*, which guides the theoretical and empirical work of the IfS in their efforts to illuminate relations of domination in monopoly capitalism. The conception of freedom at the heart of Horkheimer's thought exhibits the influence that not only Marx, Lukács, and Freud but also Kant exercises upon his though, and these strands all come together in the normative ideal of a 'reasonable society'. In this account of the necessary conditions of human freedom—which, as we shall see in Chapter 7, represents a form of what Axel Honneth calls 'communicative freedom'—we find elements of the Marxian conception of freedom as mastery over nature, of Lukács's theory of reification, and, not least, of Kant's conception of freedom as autonomy.

Horkheimer follows Marx's materialist view of the possibility of the 'realm of freedom' as depending on the full development of the productive forces, and as the ideal of 'socialised man, the associated producers, rationally regulating their interchange with Nature, bringing it under their common control, instead of being ruled by it as by the blind forces of Nature; and achieving this with the least expenditure of energy and under conditions most favourable to, and worthy of, their human nature'.[70] Horkheimer thus understands sufficient technological 'mastery of nature' as a necessary historical condition for a reasonable society and a rationally organized economy, and the assumed productive superiority of the latter is ultimately supposed to enable humanity to escape the fatal condition of material scarcity that has beset the human condition since the dawn of human kind.

---

[70] Karl Marx, 'Capital: Vol. III', in *The Marx-Engels Reader*, p. 441.

Horkheimer sometimes seems to speak as if the principal meaning of a reasonable society is simply that of a *planned economy*, of subjecting society's economic life to a rational plan. However, it would be wrong to suggest that the mere concept of rational economic planning exhausts the normative content of his ideal of a reasonable society. To begin with, Horkheimer is increasingly cognizant of the fact that economic planning can also be used for irrational and deeply pernicious ends, but even a rationally planned economy would not be sufficient for achieving a reasonable society, since this idea is compatible with a form of technocratic management of economic affairs which is wholly anathema to Horkheimer's view. Indeed, if economic planning is to serve the cause of human freedom, certain further necessary conditions must be fulfilled, and in order to clarify these we must first return to Lukács's theory of reification.

Recall the central claim of that theory: namely, that the basic structure of capitalist society not only treats individual subjects as objects of rational control, but also makes subjects self-identify as objects. Horkheimer's normative ideal of a reasonable society can to some extent be understood as the *positive inversion* of a society integrated through reification; it is a society in which individuals are both empowered as subjects by the basic structure of society *and* in which subjects reflectively self-identify as such. However, in some of Horkheimer's remarks, the idea of reasonable society also seems to involve the somewhat more fanciful notion of society or even human kind *as itself* a conscious subject:

> In the transition from the present to a future form of society, human kind ought to *constitute itself as a conscious subject* and actively determine its own form of life. Even if the elements of the culture of the future are already at hand, this will still require a conscious and novel construction of economic relations.[71]

Note that the perhaps most striking aspect of Horkheimer's claim that humanity must constitute itself as a conscious subject is the evident *moral universalism*, which it presupposes. The subject in question in this passage is not any particular society, or even the proletariat as a class, but rather every single human being across the world when considered as a universal human community. This indicates that the scope of the validity that Horkheimer claims for his original paradigm of critical theory is indeed truly *global*—or, in his own words: it takes as its object 'existing capitalist society, which has *spread all over the world* from Europe and *for which the theory is declared valid*'.[72] I shall unpack the implications of this claim in Chapter 2.

---

[71] Horkheimer, 'Traditionelle und kritische Theorie', p. 207 [emphasis added].
[72] Horkheimer, 'Traditionelle und kritische Theorie', pp. 226–227 [emphases added].

However, it may also be difficult to escape the sense that Horkheimer's idea of human kind as such constituting itself as a 'conscious subject' has a somewhat menacing or even totalitarian ring to it. For example, Thomas McCarthy argues in this vein that Horkheimer has a tendency to 'conceptualize society as at least potentially a unified subject with a unified will and, hence, to marginalize considerations of social, cultural, and political pluralism'.[73] This worry is not without merit, but it also overlooks the fact that the young Horkheimer demonstrates a clear appreciation of the irreducible value of the individual subject, the importance of free reflection and autonomous individual judgement, and the necessity of a democratic organization of political life. In contrast to Lukács, individual subjects are never simply merged into an undifferentiated proletariat, nor do they simply dissolve into the unified macro-subject of conscious humanity, as McCarthy suggests.

Rather, Horkheimer uses the idea of humanity as a conscious subject as shorthand for the *collective self-rule of conscious individual subjects*, who govern themselves democratically. This democratic interpretation of his conception of a reasonable society finds its clearest expression in a short 'Postscript' that Horkheimer wrote for 'Traditional and Critical Theory':

> If [economic] socialisation [*Vergesellschaftung*] is also socialisation in the sense that critical theory intends, i.e. if a higher principle is realised in that process, it depends not only on the transformation of certain property relations or on an increase in productivity in new forms of societal labour processes, but just as much on the nature and development of the society in which all this takes place ... To the content of the concept of socialisation also belong the problems of ... the active relationship of the individual to the government, the relation between administrative decrees and the will and knowledge of affected individuals, the dependence of all humanly mastered states of affairs on actual mutual understanding—in short, the significant moments of true democracy and association.[74]

To be sure, this is in no way meant to suggest that Horkheimer has a very clear idea about what such a 'true democracy' is supposed to involve in institutional terms; indeed, he only ever describes this normative ideal of a free and reasonable society in highly abstract and indeterminate terms. As we shall in the next subsection, this lacuna in Horkheimer's original paradigm can in fact be seen as a failure on the terms of his own account of what a critical theory is supposed to offer. But there is little doubt that Horkheimer believes that the normative ideal of a reasonable

---

[73] McCarthy, 'On the Idea of a Critical Theory and its Relation to Philosophy', p. 13.
[74] Max Horkheimer, 'Nachtrag', in *Gesammelte Schriften Band 4*, pp. 223–224.

society is understood as involving the free consent and participation of the affected individuals, and that any society which technocratically determines the fates of its subjects from above can never qualify as a reasonable society in Horkheimer's sense.[75]

According to Horkheimer, however, it is Kant who provides the most sublime expression of *bourgeois* morality, with his conception of human freedom as autonomy. To be sure, Kant's doctrine of transcendental idealism is also a central target of Horkheimer's materialist critique—but as we saw in Section 1, the point of such materialist *Ideologiekritik* is precisely 'to clarify those existing relations from which the problem of morality arises and which are reflected in moral-philosophical doctrines, if in a distorted form.'[76] In Horkheimer's view, Kant correctly identifies the irreducible conflict between what is rational and what is reasonable in *bourgeois* society. Moreover, Kant correctly understands this conflict as one between natural causation and the autonomous will, but he misinterprets the conflict in metaphysical terms and thereby fails to grasp its *historical* character:

> In this epoch, economic advantage is the natural law under which individual life stands. The categorical imperative holds the "universal law of nature" up against this individual natural law as a normative standard—as the law of life of human society. This would be senseless if the particular interest and universal needs were perfectly and necessarily congruent. The fact that they are not is the great defect of the *bourgeois* economic model: there exists no reasonable relationship between the medium, the free competition amongst individuals, and that which is mediated, the existence of society as a whole.[77]

According to Horkheimer, it speaks to Kant's greatness that his two-world metaphysics inadvertently captured the paradoxical structure of capitalist society so early in its inception: Kant conceived of the conception of freedom as autonomy as an internal matter of individual moral motivation, while he claimed that the external world must be accepted as determined by natural forces wholly beyond

---

[75] This central concern with individual autonomy and the 'independence of thought' is also expressed in Horkheimer's objection to the totalitarian tendencies of socialism as practiced in the Soviet Union: 'Among those who at present appeal to critical theory, some knowingly degrade it to a mere rationalisation of their given actions; others stick to flattened concepts whose very meaning has become alien, and of which they make a levelling ideology, which everyone understands because he thinks nothing of it. But ever since its origins, dialectical thinking has described the most progressive state of knowledge ... As long as that thinking has not triumphed, it can never feel safe in the shadow of power. *It demands independence*. But even if its concepts, which originate in social struggles, sound vain today, since little stands behind dialectical thinking but its persecutors, the truth will nonetheless become clear; because the goal of a reasonable society, which, to be sure, today seems to be supplanted into mere phantasy, is actually inherent in every human being [*in jedem Menschen wirklich angelegt*]'. Horkheimer, 'Nachtrag', p. 224 [emphasis added].
[76] Horkheimer, 'Materialismus und Moral', p. 118.
[77] Horkheimer, 'Materialismus und Moral', pp. 116–117.

the individual's control—an antinomy that he could only systematically accommodate with the metaphysical distinction between *noumena* and *phenomena*. Yet while Horkheimer very much agrees that human life is in thrall to heteronomous forces, it is not the laws of nature but rather the anarchic and unconscious (and thus *nature-like*) forces of capitalist production and exchange that determine the fates of individual subjects:

> The [societal] process is realised as a natural occurrence and not under the control of a conscious will. The life of society in general is the blind, random, and bad result of the chaotic hustle and bustle of individuals, industry, and the states. This irrationality finds expression in the misery of the great majority of human beings … In the *bourgeois* epoch, this problem [i.e. the incongruence between particular and universal interests], which can only be reasonably solved through the planned integration of all human beings into a consciously guided labour process, appears as a conflict in the inner life of individual subjects.[78]

As long as the basic economic structure of capitalism and its great fault line between capitalists and proletariat endures, unfreedom and suffering for the great majority will inevitably persist. Owing to his limiting historical point of view, Kant was blind to the constitutive injustices of the capitalist social order, and he therefore wrongly construed his otherwise essentially correct insight into the nature of morality *in foro interno*—displacing autonomy into the individual as a matter of moral motivation. The materialist solution to this problem is therefore to reconstrue the 'moral law' not as a categorical imperative for individual moral action, but rather as a *political imperative* to reorganize society in *a reasonable form*:

> The idea of morality, as Kant has formulated it, contains the truth that the courses of action corresponding to the law of economic advantage are not necessarily also the reasonable ones. This idea does not simply juxtapose the interest of the individual with emotion or even regression to blind obedience; neither interest nor reason is slandered or derided, but reason rather recognises that it need not merely serve the natural law of individual advantage—namely in the case where it integrates the universal law of nature into its will. To be sure, the individual cannot realise the demand for a reasonable organisation of society as a whole. Human mastery over the societal process as a whole is only complete when humanity has overcome its anarchic form and constituted itself as a real subject—that is, through a historical act. Such an act does not arise from the individual alone, but through a constellation of social groups. To be sure, in this dynamic, the individual conscience plays a very important role.[79]

---

[78] Horkheimer, 'Materialismus und Moral', pp. 116–117.
[79] Horkheimer, 'Materialismus und Moral', p. 118.

Horkheimer thus recasts Kant's conception of freedom as autonomy as a social and historical *achievement*, which we have *yet* to truly achieve, rather than as a metaphysical claim about the rational person. In his hands, freedom as autonomy requires the practical reorganization of society into a reasonable form, in which individuals are empowered by the basic structure of society to self-identify as subjects with the actual power to govern their collective social and economic life democratically.

Finally, Horkheimer's ideal of a reasonable society also integrates Freudian or even Nietzschean themes in a way that anticipates some of the central concerns of Adorno's negativist paradigm. As we saw in the previous subsection, Horkheimer was convinced that the 'drive complex' is heavily conditioned by the basic structure of society, and that life under capitalist social relations installed in people a denial or even contempt of one's own as well as other's basic needs and desire for happiness. This structurally compelled psychic repression tended towards a kind of nihilism, 'which has expressed itself again and again in the history of the modern age as the practical destruction of everything joyful and happy, as barbarity and destruction'.[80] By contrast, a reasonable society is also implicitly conceived as a social condition, which—in virtue of the superior productive potential of a democratically planned economy—would dismantle structural obstacles in the way of needs gratification and gradually lead to a much less inhibited and pathological development of the inner drive complex and its expressions.

1.4.2 A Critical Theory of Justice

The normative dimension in Horkheimer's original paradigm is remarkable not only for its distinctive account of freedom as a reasonable society democratically governed by autonomous subjects, but also for the way that Horkheimer explains the *epistemic function* of this central normative ideal in the construction of his critical theory of society. We can glean a first estimation of this function from an important remark on the difference between theory construction in traditional and critical theory:

> The development of theories in the traditional sense represents an occupation delimitated from other scientific and related activities, which need not know anything about the historical objectives and tendencies in which such scientific business is always entangled. By contrast, both in the construction of its categories and in all phases of its development, a critical theory fully consciously follows the

---

[80] Max Horkheimer, 'Egoismus und Freiheitsbewegung', in *Gesammelte Schriften Band 4*; see also the discussion in David Owen, 'Nietzsche and the Frankfurt School', in *The Routledge Companion to the Frankfurt School*, ed. by Peter E. Gordon, Espen Hammer and Axel Honneth (New York: Routledge, 2019), whom I would also like to thank for pressing me to clarify this point.

interest in the reasonable organisation of human activity, the *illumination* and *legitimation* of which is also part of its task.[81]

In this remark—I want to argue—we see the sense in which a critical theory can in fact be understood *as a kind of theory of justice*, although a highly distinctive kind, which is very different from the predominant understanding of what a theory of justice is supposed to be and offer in contemporary normative political theory. The sense in which we can think of critical theory as kind of theory of justice is that Horkheimer sees critical theory as a methodological vehicle for the *correct instantiation* of the *bourgeois* idea of justice:

> The demand for a universal realisation of the *bourgeois* idea of justice must also lead to a critique and practical transformation of the society of free exchange, in whose self-conception this idea originally won its content. The demonstration of a contradiction between the principle of *bourgeois* society and its actual existence brings the one-sided determination of justice through freedom and the one-sided determination of freedom through mere negation [i.e. negative freedom] into consciousness and defines justice in a positive sense, through the outline of a reasonable society.[82]

As is clear in this important passage, critical theory does not reject the idea of justice out of hand as simply a piece of *bourgeois* ideology, as many other Marxists have done, and perhaps even Marx himself tended to do.[83] Rather, in critical theory, the normative content of the *bourgeois* concept of justice is integrated into a critical account of the basic structure of capitalist society that illuminates the *injustices* to which individuals are subject within that structure, and the idea of a reasonable society is extrapolated from this account as a characterization of a society that transcends the structural roots of existing injustices. In other words, the critique of existing injustice *precedes* and is *presupposed* by the positive account of a just society. Indeed, critical theory is the methodological instrument for developing such a positive account of a just society, and in this way a critical theory can itself be understood as a distinctive kind of theory of justice.

This intrinsic connection between the young Horkheimer's idea of a critical theory of society and the concept of justice seems to me to pass almost unnoticed in the literature on the Frankfurt School tradition, and on Horkheimer's early work in particular.[84] It also raises the equally underappreciated, but in this light very

---

[81] Horkheimer, 'Nachtrag', p. 218 [emphasis added].
[82] Horkheimer, 'Materialismus und Metaphysik', p. 82.
[83] Allan W. Wood, 'The Marxian Critique of Justice', *Philosophy & Public Affairs* (1/3), 1972: pp. 244–282.
[84] In John Abromeit's impressive and insightful recent book on Horkheimer's thought, for example, this implication is unmentioned. John Abromeit, *Max Horkheimer and the Foundations of the Frankfurt School* (Cambridge: Cambridge University Press, 2011).

important, question of how Horkheimer thought about the concept of justice in a more general sense. To begin with, it seems clear to me that Horkheimer does not subscribe to a *distributive* view of justice, but rather to a view of justice couched in the conceptual register of freedom and power, autonomy, and domination. To be sure, this claim may seem to conflict with some of his explicit remarks on the concept of justice, where he suggests that 'the general content of the concept of justice' is that 'the social inequality existing at any given time requires a rational justification. This inequality is no longer perceived as good, but as something that must be overcome'. However, immediately after this passage, he adds that equality must always be understood in relation to the concept of *freedom*: 'With the idea of equality, one also necessarily assumes the idea of freedom. If, to begin with, no individual has less of a claim to realise and satisfy itself than another, then the use of *coercion* by one human group against another is also thereby understood as an evil. The concept of justice can just as little be separated from the concept of freedom as it can from the concept of equality'.[85]

Another way to phrase this point is that although Horkheimer explicitly associates the concept of justice with equality, he does not understand equality in a distributive sense, but rather in terms of what contemporary political theorists such as Elizabeth Anderson and Samuel Scheffler refer to as a 'relational' conception of justice—or in the sense of Philip Pettit's status conception of freedom as nondomination.[86] The animating normative idea in Horkheimer's work is that human beings have an equal moral claim to freedom from domination; that freedom from domination presupposes autonomy, or that human beings relate to each other in a way that treats them and enables them to self-identify as subjects; and that they will only be able to enjoy this status in a reasonable society, in which individuals' social and economic circumstances are determined not by arbitrary market forces and the captains of industry, but by their own democratic self-government.

Interestingly, Horkheimer intimates that, from a materialist point of view, the concept of justice can be understood as the historical result of certain systematic experiences of misery, suffering, and privation, for which human beings have 'learned to demand reasons'.[87] We might thus say that it is this practice of *demanding justifications*—which is itself the result of a historical learning process—that

---

[85] Horkheimer, 'Materialismus und Moral', p. 141 [emphasis added].
[86] Elizabeth Anderson, 'What Is The Point of Equality?', *Ethics* (109/2), 1999: pp. 287–337; Samuel Scheffler, 'What is Egalitarianism?', *Philosophy and Public Affairs* (31/1), 2003: pp. 5–39; Philip Pettit, *On the Peoples Terms: A Republican Theory and Model of Democracy* (Cambridge: Cambridge University Press, 2014).
[87] Horkheimer, 'Materialismus und Metaphysik', p. 83; Horkheimer, 'Bemerkungen zur philosophischen Anthropologie', pp. 252–253.

provides the bridge between the experience of suffering and the normative concepts of freedom as autonomy and justice as equal freedom from domination in Horkheimer's original paradigm of critical theory.

However, as we have seen, monopoly capitalism systematically obscures the structural roots of the pervasive suffering and misery to which the vast majority in society is subject, and *bourgeois* morality offers principles only from the point of view of the isolated and atomised individual. With Lukács, Horkheimer thus sees the *epistemic function* of critical theory as that of furthering this collective learning process by enlightening subjects about the underlying structural roots of these injustices, thereby enabling emancipation through collective action. In fact, under the impression of the rise of totalitarian fascism, Horkheimer maintains that a critical theory is the only way to *safeguard* the normative content of *bourgeois* morality and the intellectual legacy of the Enlightenment from the increasingly brutal realities of *bourgeois* society:

> Some claim that the *bourgeois* ideas of freedom, equality and justice have turned out to be corrupt. However, it is not the ideas of the propertied class, but the conditions that violate them, which have demonstrated their inadequacy. The solutions of the Enlightenment and the French revolution are *more correct than ever before*: the dialectical critique of society, which takes these ideas under its protection, consists precisely in the demonstration of their continued relevance, and that their urgency has not been undermined by reality. *These ideas are nothing other than the individual elements of a reasonable society, as that society is anticipated in morality.* A politics appropriate to morality must therefore not abandon its demands, but rather realise them—not, to be sure, by sticking to historically conditioned definitions in a utopian manner, but in accordance with their present meaning. The content of these ideas is not eternal but rather subject to historical change ... since the human impulses, which demand a better world, are given a new form in the given historical material in which they play out. The unity of these concepts is less a result of the constancy of their elements than of the historical development of the conditions of those for whom their realisation is necessary.[88]

In effect, Horkheimer thus reconstructs *bourgeois* morality as the revolutionary imperative to establish a society *beyond* the need for *bourgeois* morality, and critical theory as the methodological vehicle through which this command can come to inform and guide collective action. We might restate this point by saying that the young Horkheimer does not develop a *traditional* theory of justice,

---

[88] Horkheimer, 'Materialismus und Moral', pp. 136–137 [emphasis added].

such as we might expect from the *bourgeois* tradition of political philosophy, but rather a *critical* theory of justice.[89] In Chapter 2, we shall explore the implications of this idea—and of Horkheimer's original paradigm of critical theory more generally—for a critical theory of contemporary world society.

---

[89] To be sure, Horkheimer is adamant in his insistence that morality, or what he calls the 'moral feeling', cannot be justified with reference to any otherworldly authority—indeed, that 'morality does not admit of justification, neither through intuition nor argument. It rather represents a psychological phenomenon, which is a task of psychology to describe and to understand in terms of its personal conditions and mechanisms of transmission from one generation to the next.' Max Horkheimer, 'Materialismus und Moral', p. 133.

2
Horkheimer's Original Paradigm and the Idea of a Critical Theory of World Society

2.1 'Existing capitalist society, which has spread all over the world from Europe and for which the theory is declared valid'

As I noted in the beginning of Chapter 1, the young Horkheimer's original paradigm of critical theory is arguably the least well known and least understood of all the paradigms of critical theory reconstructed in this book. Although his term 'critical theory' has found its way into mainstream academic discussion across the world, it has also changed its meaning to such an extent that often very little if anything at all remains of the distinctive meaning that Horkheimer originally gave to this concept. All too often, the Horkheimer with which people are familiar is not the radical and practically engaged thinker of his earlier life; it is rather the gloomy and pessimistic figure appearing alongside (and arguably overshadowed by) Adorno in the 'Dialectic of Enlightenment'. But as we shall see, that work belongs squarely in the negativist paradigm of critical theory, which is above all associated with Adorno, and which differs in important ways from the more hopeful and action-oriented paradigm of critical theory that I reconstructed in the previous chapter, of which the young Horkheimer was the principal intellectual architect.

Hoping to remedy some of these gaps and misunderstandings, I have sought to demonstrate in Chapter 1 that Horkheimer's early work contains: first, an innovative vision for a materialist programme of interdisciplinary social inquiry, which gradually transforms into the sophisticated methodological idea of a critical theory of society; second, a compelling account of the monopoly-capitalist society of his day and its distinctive relations of domination, including a path-breaking synthesis of Marx's and Freud's work to account for the rise of National Socialism; third, an attractive normative account of the necessary conditions of human freedom in the ideal of a reasonable society, in which subjects are empowered by the basic structure of society to self-identify as subjects with the claim and power to govern their social and economic life democratically, and; fourth, a widely unacknowledged methodological construal of critical theory as itself a kind of theory of justice—a critical theory of justice, as it were.

In this second chapter, I explore the contradiction between the young Horkheimer's explicit conviction that his original paradigm of critical theory was, in an important sense, applicable to the world at large, and his almost complete disregard for not just societies outside the European (and, later, North-American) context, but also for the imperially ordered world society of his day. I argue that this indifference is ultimately grounded in the robustly teleological structure of Marx's philosophy of history, to which the young Horkheimer remained firmly committed until the late-1930s, which implies a 'stagist' view of history that tends to collapse the sociological dimension into the historical dimension of his critical theory when applied to the world at large. Moreover, I also argue that the young Horkheimer was firmly steeped in a 'Promethean' view of human emancipation as complete human mastery over nature, until his view of the relationship between human reason and nature would undergo a profound transformation around the outbreak of World War II. Finally, I discuss the relevance of Horkheimer's original paradigm for making sense of contemporary globalized capitalism and the recent surge of right-wing populism across the world.

2.1.1 Colonialism, Empire, and the Trappings of Historical Materialism

I want to argue that, when we look back on Horkheimer's early work from the point of view of the present, we are immediately confronted with a glaring contradiction in the young Horkheimer's original paradigm of critical theory. This is a contradiction between the claim to universal, indeed *global* validity that Horkheimer explicitly raises on behalf of his critical theory, and the parochial and arguably deeply Eurocentric focus of both the materialist programme of interdisciplinary social inquiry undertaken by the members of the IfS circle and Horkheimer's theoretical interests more narrowly conceived.

On the one hand, as we have seen, Horkheimer explicitly maintains that his historical and sociological account of monopoly capitalism is global in scope: that it pertains to 'the existing capitalist society, which has spread all over the world from Europe and for which the theory is declared valid'.[1] On the other hand, he hardly demonstrates any direct theoretical interest in societies outside the Western context, let alone in the genuinely global context of application of his day.[2] One searches in vain for a critique of contemporaneous forms of imperial rule, or for a more sustained critical analysis of the developing Stalinist nightmare in the Soviet Union, or indeed for any kind of reflection on the contribution that critical theory might offer the suffering masses beyond the industrialized West. To some extent, this confinement of his theoretical interests to Western Europe is arguably due to Horkheimer's increasing appreciation of the threat to the continent from National

---

[1] Horkheimer, 'Traditionelle und kritische Theorie', pp. 226–227.
[2] Absent a largely unenthusiastic willingness to fund Karl August Wittfogel's research on China.

Socialism in the course of the 1930s. But it can also be explained with reference to certain systematic reasons intrinsic to historical materialism, which have been criticized from both outside and inside the Frankfurt School tradition of critical theory.

As the historian and postcolonial scholar Dipesh Chakrabarty has argued, historical materialism represents a version of what Edward Said has called 'historicism', which entails what he calls a 'stagist' view of history, where political-economic differences and cultural variations within the global context are understood and treated as different developmental stages on the royal road towards the end-state of communism.[3] This implication ultimately derives from the robustly teleological structure of historical materialism, which views history as a continuous process of expansion of capitalist production relations in both intensity and extensity, along with those inner tensions that ultimately threaten to rip capitalism apart at the seams.

The teleological structure of historical materialism effectively confines anyone who lives in a society categorized by the theory as feudal or pre-capitalist to what Chakrabarty calls an 'imaginary waiting room of history'.[4] Although rural peasants in India and Sub-Saharan Africa may be subject to certain peripheral consequences of the capitalist mode of production—in particular, to the forms of violent conquest, expropriation, and dispossession associated with what Marx called 'primitive accumulation'—they have *not yet* been integrated into the industrial proletariat, and therefore they do not yet count among the subjects that a critical theory wedded to historical materialism aspires to enlighten and emancipate. Evidently, this implication not only severely restricts the scope of the emancipatory potential of critical theory, but also risks actively contributing to the plight of 'the wretched of the Earth', in Franz Fanon's famous phrase.[5] Horkheimer's abandonment of the industrial proletariat as the addressee of his materialism and turn to the more elusive 'critical attitude' might seem to mitigate this worry, but the problem goes deeper than this revision is able to amend, precisely because it issues from the *conceptual structure* of historical materialism to which the young Horkheimer remained committed.

When the theory is applied outside the industrialized Western context or the world at large, the robustly teleological structure of historical materialism implies that critical theory's sociological dimension recedes into the background, and, indeed, threatens to *collapse* into the diachronic point of view of Marx's philosophy of history. This means that global synchronic variations are construed simply as temporally coexisting stages of epochal development, and this is—I believe—what ultimately explains Horkheimer's silence on all things non-Western

---

[3] Dipesh Chakrabarty, *Provincializing Europe: Post-Colonial Thought and Historical Difference* (Princeton: Princeton University Press, 2000).
[4] Dipesh Chakrabarty, *Provincializing Europe*, p. 65.
[5] Frantz Fanon, *The Wretched of the Earth*, transl. by Richard Philcox (London: Grove Press, 2005).

and global. Accordingly, Horkheimer understands the analysis of social relations in the 'Third World' as *categorially implicit* in any investigation of economic, psychological, and cultural phenomena in the more developed Western context, since such phenomena are ultimately understood as structurally emergent elements of the capitalist mode of production in its higher developmental stages, to which the less developed areas of the world will eventually catch up.

That Horkheimer subscribed to such a stagist view of history is evident, for example, in his reflections on history in his contribution to the 'Studies on Authority and Family' from 1936—as expressed here in a revealing passage:

> We spoke earlier of how the great Asiatic societies, China and India, have managed to resist the invasion of Western European ways of life. This should in no way be taken to mean that no very real conflicts of interest are involved, *which must end with the victorious penetration of the superior capitalist mode of production or of some still more progressive economic principle*. But the capacity of these cultures for resistance does not find its real expression in their members' belief (a distorted belief for the great majority) that the specifically Chinese or Indian form of production is the most advantageous. Rather, when great masses of people have, against their interests, held fast to their modes of production, a great role has been played by a crippling fear of moving out of the old world of beliefs and ideas which had taken such deep hold on the individual psyche. The culture's specific way of experiencing the world had been built up through simple and recurring tasks and over the centuries had become a necessary element in the life of a society.[6]

What comes to the fore in this passage—and in other passages throughout Horkheimer's work—is belief that it is only a matter of time before the outdated modes of production, still clinging to life in places like India and China, will be surpassed by the superior capitalist mode of production, along with the 'old world of beliefs and ideas' that resist this transformation.

This tendency to collapse the synchronic dimension into the diachronic point of view explains why research into the seemingly parochial attitudes of German workers and employees can in an important sense be seen as an undertaking with an implicit global scope. And this is also why Horkheimer can claim that the European experience with fascism is in fact representative of an emergent political superstructure *inherent in monopoly capitalism as such*—and thus as not just a European, but, ultimately, truly global phenomenon. He can make this claim only because he understands the significance of these categories in strongly

---

[6] Max Horkheimer, 'Authority and the Family', in *Critical Theory: Selected Essays*, p. 82 [emphasis added].

teleological terms, which assume that developing societies beyond the Western context will eventually assimilate to the latter, at which point the analysis undertaken in present-day Europe will then apply to them in equal measure. On these presuppositions, if critical theory is able to answer the question as to why interwar German workers do not exhibit the requisite revolutionary consciousness and instead tend towards a sadomasochistic or authoritarian personality, the significance of that answer is by no means limited to the German context, since that answer may also eventually hold true for future developmental stages of the less developed areas of the world.

This assumption—that the basic structure of industrialized Western societies represents an emergent and latently global model of modern capitalist societies across the world—has been subject to forceful critique by the Subaltern Studies Group, a group of historians of the South Asian subcontinent. In his influential work, Ranajit Guha has argued that 'the colonial state in South Asia was very unlike and indeed fundamentally different from the metropolitan bourgeois state which had sired it'.[7] The central structural difference between the colonial and the metropolitan state was, according to Guha, that the Indian *bourgeoisie*—unlike the *bourgeois* class in Britain—never succeeded in establishing *hegemony* over Indian society, but had to rely on coercive power to maintain their dominance. This failure of the Indian *bourgeoisie* to impose hegemony on Indian society implied that there were 'vast areas in the life and consciousness of the people which were never integrated into their hegemony', most notably the Indian peasantry, which remained part of a heterogeneous plethora of *subaltern classes* persisting outside the official structure of the Indian colonial state. In contrast with the orientation towards British-style parliamentary politics and constitutionalism of the colonial elite, Guha maintains, there therefore existed an 'autonomous' domain of 'subaltern politics' or 'politics of the people', which found expression in peasant revolts against elite domination organized around kinship and territoriality.[8]

Guha's argument is, in part, explicitly developed as a refutation of traditional Marxian historiography, which imposes the teleological structure of historical materialism upon Indian modernity. The upshot of his analysis, and of the work of the Subaltern Studies Group more generally, is that a fundamental heterogeneity persists between the metropolitan and the colonial or postcolonial state—between European modernity and South Asian modernity, that is—and that the attempt to make sense of politics and the state on the South Asian subcontinent with a conceptual framework developed within and for making sense of politics and

---

[7] Ranajit Guha, *Dominance Without Hegemony: History and Power in Colonial India* (Cambridge MA: Harvard University Press, 1997), p. xii.
[8] Ranajit Guha, *Elementary Aspects of Peasant Insurgency in Colonial India* (Delhi: Oxford University Press, 1983). See also Dipesh Chakrabarty, 'A Small History of *Subaltern Studies*', in *Habitations of Modernity: Essays in the Wake of Subaltern Studies* (Chicago: Chicago University Press, 2002).

the state in Europe fundamentally misconstrues crucial aspects of non-European modernity.[9]

Guha's argument has been criticized in recent years—most notably, perhaps, by Vivek Chibber[10]—and I will return to some of its wider implications in Chapter 6. But as an indication of the conceptual trappings of historical materialism, it does not seem to me to have lost any plausibility. In my view, the only way out of this collapse of the synchronic dimension of critical theory into its diachronic dimension when applied to the global context is to loosen up on the teleological structure of historical materialism—which of course would mean abandoning Marx's philosophy of history altogether, or reconstructing it in a very different form.

Owing to its constitutive dependence on historical materialism, Horkheimer's original paradigm of critical theory is thus caught in a contradiction: while he understands its claim to enable and further human emancipation as truly universal in scope, and its account of the basic structure of capitalist society as potentially applicable to world society, he is unable to offer any meaningful guidance to anyone who happens to find themselves outside the industrialized Western context—other than to simply wait for the emergence of capitalist production relations, which are bound to impose themselves on their societies at some future point. It seems clear to me that this is not a feature of Horkheimer's theoretical framework that he was even remotely aware of—nor did he likely pose himself the question of what his critical theory might have to offer anyone outside the Western context—but it is a feature with momentous implications for the idea of a critical theory of world society. The stagist view of history is so deeply entrenched into the theory of historical materialism that anyone operating under its presuppositions risks getting caught in this contradiction and must either ignore such questions altogether or give up or seek to transform that framework.

To be sure, Horkheimer's disinterest in contexts beyond Europe was not shared by contemporaneous Marxist writers such as Lenin and Rosa Luxemburg, who sought to update and rethink the Marxian framework in a global account of the relationship between capitalism and the imperialist order of the world society of their day.[11] Lenin's classic work *Imperialism, the Highest Stage of Capitalism* from 1917 shares with Horkheimer the analysis of a structural transformation in capitalism from its *bourgeois*-liberal form to monopoly capitalism, but he sees the global expansion of monopoly capitalism as driven by the financialization of

---

[9] This latter point is emphasized by Chakrabarty in *Provincializing Europe*.
[10] Vivek Chibber, *Postcolonial Theory and the Specter of Capital* (London: Verso Books, 2013). See also Rosie Warren (ed.), *The Debate on* Postcolonial Theory and the Specter of Capital (London: Verso Books, 2017).
[11] Vladimir Lenin, 'Imperialism, the Highest Stage of Capitalism', in *Essential Works of Lenin*, ed. by Henry M. Christman (New York: Dover Publications, 1987); Rosa Luxemburg, *The Accumulation of Capital*, transl. by Agnes Schwarzschild (London: Routledge, 2003).

capital—the 'merging of bank capital and industrial capital, and the creation, on the basis of "finance capital", of a financial oligarchy'—and the partition of the world into empires, where competing international monopolies in imperial creditor nations reap immense profits through the exploitation of debtor nations. In contrast to the young Horkheimer, Lenin thus sees the rise of monopoly capitalism as intrinsically connected with imperial conquest and partition of the world. Although this theory does not escape the stagist view of history—as it still conceives of world society as characterized by temporally coexisting forms of epochal development—it nonetheless expands the framework of historical materialism in a form that enables Lenin, in contrast to the young Horkheimer, to develop an incipient theory of the world society of his day.

2.1.2 Pluralism, Political Economy, and the Rise of Right-Wing Populism

To be sure, even such an expanded version of historical materialism does not remedy the limited scope of the forms of domination captured by Marx's theoretical framework. Seyla Benhabib has argued that the 'model of work activity', which informs Marx's philosophy of history and critique of political economy, 'results in a denial of human *plurality*'. By plurality, Benhabib means that 'our embodied identity, and the narrative history that constitutes our selves, give us a unique perspective on the world', and it is 'essential to the condition described as plurality that one reaches one's perspective only as a result of the cognitive and moral process which teaches one also to recognize the presence of other perspectives in the world'.[12]

As Sally Haslanger has argued, such narrative histories and socially situated perspectives are structured in terms of social categories such as gender, race, or ethnicity and religion, and those categories are themselves 'defined in terms of how one is socially positioned, where this is a function of, for example, how one is viewed, how one is treated, and how one's life is structured socially, legally, and economically'.[13] In Benhabib's words, 'Marx's concept of class tends to deny the condition of plurality'. Another way of phrasing this point is that Marx's focus on relations of class domination captures but *one form* of domination in modern society, but is blind to a host of other forms that operate through or in conjunction with social categories such as race, ethnicity, and gender.

This is an important—and often rehearsed—critique of Marx. However, there is also an important flipside to these objections, which apply in equal measure to

---

[12] Seyla Benhabib, *Critique, Norm, and Utopia. A Study of the Foundations of Critical Theory* (New York: Columbia University Press, 1986), p. 140.
[13] Sally Haslanger, *Resisting Reality: Social Construction and Social Critique* (Oxford: Oxford University Press, 2012), p. 229.

Horkheimer's original paradigm of critical theory, wedded to Marx's philosophy of history as it is. Since the fall of the Berlin Wall and the collapse of the Soviet Union, Marxism has to a large extent been declared dead and gone across the world—and in the self-congratulatory ruse of the capitalist West, so has, perhaps until recently, the very idea of class domination that Marx sought to expose. Indeed, as we shall see in later chapters, very little remains of Marx's critique of political economy in the most recent paradigms of Frankfurt School critical theory. But once critical theory is applied to the contemporary global context, we are compelled to recognize the dangers not only of reductive economism, but also of *purging* the perspective of political economy from a critical theory of world society.

As the French economist Thomas Piketty has argued in his *Capital in the Twenty-first Century* from 2014, wealth and wage inequality are tending towards extremes unseen since the pre-war era of *bourgeois*-liberal capitalism. Moreover, as Piketty suggests, the mainstream neoclassical model of marginal productivity is fundamentally unable to account for the recent dramatic rise in wage inequality, which, in his view, is in part a function of the tectonic shift in the relative bargaining power between capital and labour affected by economic globalization.[14] In Piketty's view, the forces that drive rising inequality in the distribution of wealth and power across and beyond the West thus represent a vicious circle of increasing class domination and conflict.

A critical theory of world society requires a categorial framework to address this vicious circle of ever-worsening inequality and class domination. Indeed, such a theory should be just as concerned with reintroducing certain Marxian themes into its conceptual framework as with resisting the reduction of domination to the economic domain alone—with *bringing political economy back in*, as it were— which, of course, cannot rely on historical materialism or his critique of political economy in unreconstructed form. But a research programme true to Marx's original intentions would not today be an anachronistic critique of classical political economy and the *bourgeois*-liberal capitalism that it once served to justify, but rather a critique of *neoclassical* political economy and the globalized capitalism that it serves to justify in the present day and age.

The final point I want to make in this context is that, in recent years, political developments across and beyond the West have also re-actualized the Horkheimer circle's interdisciplinary attempt to account for the rise of fascism in the 1930s. Events such as Donald J. Trump's ascendancy to the highest political office in the US in 2016, the United Kingdom's decision by referendum in 2015 to leave the European Union, and the rise of right-wing populism across the European continent and the world at large cry out for an explanation, which is able to connect more long-term developments in the socioeconomic structure of contemporary

---

[14] Thomas Piketty, *Capital in the Twenty-first Century* (Cambridge MA: Harvard University Press, 2014), Ch. 9.

capitalist society with the political earthquakes that have recently rattled the established political order across the West.[15]

These political campaigns, movements, and parties are often characterized not only by charismatic leaders and strongman figures with authoritarian predispositions, but also by various xenophobic orientations ranging from anti-Muslim sentiments to open racism and anti-Semitism. It is just such an explanation for a crisis of democracy that the IfS circle's synthesis of Marx's and Freud's work sought to offer, although in a different historical context faced with more openly anti-democratic and militant political organizations. Although this synthesis arguably relies too heavily on Freud's theory of the Oedipus complex, the explanatory model developed by Horkheimer and Fromm can be reconstructed in a way that does not depend on these, today, controversial Freudian assumptions.

The central idea of this explanatory model is that personality formation depends on developments in the larger sociostructural environment, and, specifically, on the extent of concentration of wealth and power in society and the possibility of social mobility. In the context of *bourgeois*-liberal capitalism, where certain individuals within the lower ranks of society (in the *petite bourgeoisie*, and even in parts of the industrial proletariat) actually faced a limited but real possibility of rising up the social ladder to the capital-owning class through entrepreneurship, ingenuity, and hard work, the *bourgeois* meritocratic ideal still maintained some surface credibility. Accordingly, the psychodynamics of the development of the personality structure within families belonging to those ranks could meaningfully foster predispositions appropriate to that ideal, such as autonomy, self-efficacy, and a 'protestant' work ethic in Weber's sense.

However, with the transition to monopoly capitalism's intensified concentration of wealth and power and much steeper social and political hierarchy, in which economic and political power is monopolized by a tiny integrated class, the credibility of the meritocratic ideal breaks down. This beats the path for what Fromm calls a sadomasochistic personality, who idolizes all-powerful rulers separated from him by an ever-growing abyss, and who finds enjoyment in his own suppression of and aggression towards others who find themselves further down the social hierarchy, or minorities deemed 'alien', 'foreign', 'parasites', and the like.[16]

I offer this highly tentative reconstruction only as a candidate explanation at least worthy of consideration. The explanatory model developed by the Horkheimer circle in the 1930s to account for the rise of fascism compels us to theorize the relationship between rising inequality, the intensifying concentration of wealth and power, the psychodynamics of personality development, and the political predispositions that result from this economic-psychological matrix

---

[15] See Malte Frøslee Ibsen, 'The Populist Conjuncture: Legitimation Crisis in the Age of Globalized Capitalism', *Political Studies* (67/3), 2019, 795–811.

[16] See also Arno J Mayer, 'The Lower Middle Class as Historical Problem', *The Journal of Modern History*, (47/3), 1975: 409–436.

in a way that might seem to offer a promising account of the rise of contemporary right-wing populism and associated political forces. To paraphrase Horkheimer's famous words: he who does not want to talk about capitalism, he should also keep silent about right-wing populism.

2.1.3 Emancipation, Ecology, and the Mastery of Nature

The concept of nature in Marx's work has been hotly debated in recent decades. Marx has often been criticized by ecologists and eco-socialists for subscribing to a 'productivist' or 'Promethean' view of human emancipation and progress as ever-greater mastery of nature and industrial development of the productive forces—as expressed here by Michael Löwy:

> there is a tendency in Marx (pronounced in the Marxism after Marx) to consider the development of the forces of production as the principal vector of progress, to adopt a fairly uncritical attitude toward industrial civilization, particularly its destructive relationship to nature ... Marx does not possess an integrated ecological perspective. His optimistic, 'promethean' conception of the limitless development of the productive forces once the limits of capitalist relations of production are removed is today indefensible. This is so not only from a strictly economic standpoint—incorporating ecological costs in calculating value—but above all from the standpoint of the threat to the ecological balance of the planet represented by the productivist logic of capital.[17]

In a similar vein, Ted Benton has argued that Marx recognizes no natural limits to the development of human productive power, and that 'the possibility of human emancipation is premissed upon the potential for the transformative, productive powers of associated human beings to transcend apparent natural limits, and to widen the field of play for human intentionality'.[18] From a contemporary point of view, such a Promethean belief in the limitless exploitation of nature seems not just indefensible but indeed positively detrimental to humanity's future prospects on Earth, as it is precisely the uninhibited human exploitation of natural resources that has wreaked havoc on natural ecosystems, and which threatens to catastrophically worsen the natural conditions for the existence of human life and that of many other species.

However, in recent years this line of critique has been met with compelling refutations from Marxist thinkers such as John Bellamy Foster, Paul Burkett, and Kohei Saito, who have unearthed an evolving but deeply integrated ecological dimension

---

[17] Michael Löwy, 'For a Critical Marxism', *Against the Current* (12/5), 1997: 31–35.
[18] Ted Benton, 'Marxism and Natural Limits: An Ecological Critique and Reconstruction', *New Left Review* (1/178), 1989: 51–86, p. 76.

in Marx's thought.[19] Although Marx died before he was able to present a systematic historical-materialist account of the relationship between human society and nature, his evolving ecological thinking is scattered across manuscripts and notes written around and after the 1867 publication of Volume I of *Capital*. According to Saito, the mature Marx approaches 'the relationship between humans and nature using the physiological concept of "metabolism" to criticize the degradation of the natural environment as a manifestation of the contradictions of capitalism'.[20] Accordingly, these thinkers argue, rather than being a proponent of a naïve productivism that unconditionally embraces uninhibited industrialization and the human mastery of nature, Marx can be said to anticipate—and may today help us navigate—the environmental destruction wrought by capitalism in our time.

Unfortunately, like many other Marxists of his day, the young Horkheimer remained wholly unaware of the ecological dimension in Marx's thought, and it would not be an exaggeration to say that, even if it may be unfair to level this critique at the work of the mature Marx, Horkheimer's early thinking assumes precisely the Promethean view of the relationship between humanity and nature as a progressive developmental process of ever-greater conscious human mastery over natural processes that has been so forcefully criticized by contemporary ecological thinkers. We see a clear expression of the young Horkheimer's Promethean commitments in the following passage from 'Traditional and Critical Theory':

> Unemployment, economic crises, militarisation, terrorist governments—the whole condition of the masses is not grounded, for example, in limited technological possibilities, as might have been the case in earlier periods, but in relations of production which are no longer suitable for our time. The application of all intellectual and physical means for the mastery of nature is hindered under the prevailing relations, because these means are entrusted to particular, mutually struggling interests.[21]

Indeed, as we saw in Chapter 1, it is an integral part of Horkheimer's account of human emancipation and the normative ideal of a 'reasonable society' that humanity is able to escape the fateful condition of material scarcity through a conscious, democratically planned economy that is able to unleash the full productive potential inherent in the forces of production under monopoly capitalism.

All the more remarkable, then, that ten years later, the very same philosopher would pen—in his 1947 book 'The Eclipse of Reason'—lines such as 'The more

---

[19] Paul Burkett, *Marx and Nature: A Red and Green Perspective* (New York: St. Martin's Press, 1999; John Bellamy Foster, *Marx's Ecology: Materialism and Nature* (New York: Monthly Review Press, 2000); Kohei Saito, *Karl Marx's Ecosocialism: Capitalism, Nature, and the Unfinished Critique of Political Economy* (New York: Monthly Review Press, 2017).
[20] Saito, *Karl Marx's Ecosocialism*, pp. 14–15.
[21] Horkheimer, 'Traditionelle und kritische Theorie', p. 187.

devices we invent for dominating nature, the more must we serve them if we are to survive', and the 'total transformation of each and every realm of being into a field of means leads to the liquidation of the subject who is supposed to use them', giving 'modern industrialist society its nihilistic aspect'.[22] One significant change in Horkheimer's view of the relationship between reason and nature is that, in his early work, he seems to only have the domination of external nature in mind, whereas in his later work the fateful mastery of *internal*, libidinal nature of human beings plays an ever greater theoretical role. We shall explore this dramatic change in Horkheimer's view of this relationship, including its implications for how we might conceptualize contemporary global warming as an ecological 'dialectic of enlightenment' with regard to external nature, in Chapters 3 and 4, as this much more sobering appraisal of the theme of human mastery of nature comes to fruition in Adorno's negativist paradigm of critical theory.

2.2 Horkheimer in Exile

As we have seen, the young Horkheimer nurtured a non-dogmatic but robust commitment to Marx's materialist philosophy of history and critique of political economy, and a concomitant if failing hope that a reasonable society might yet be achieved through the concerted revolutionary action of the proletariat, or, later, whoever exhibits the necessary critical attitude. However, his continued exile in America and the outbreak of World War II eventually eradicated the last traces of revolutionary optimism from his thought. To some extent, this pessimistic turn can probably be explained by the grim nature of his personal circumstances: having already fled his native Germany from anti-Semitic and political persecution, Horkheimer eventually had to part with the newfound home-in-exile of the IfS at Columbia University for the personally alienating context of southern California, owing to the New York climate's disagreeable effects on his worsening heart condition. However, a purely psychological explanation for his change of mind would miss the mark; rather, the most important reason for his descent into pessimism is arguably to be found in the IfS's assessment of certain further structural developments in monopoly capitalism on the eve of World War II.

As we have seen, the members of the IfS shared a belief from early on that capitalism had undergone a dramatic change in the years that had passed since Marx offered his critique of *bourgeois*-liberal capitalism. Most importantly, they had come to believe that capitalist society was no longer predominantly integrated through the classical-liberal principle of free exchange. Rather, economic centralization and increasing state power had given way to monopoly capitalism, in which prices were predominantly fixed by alliances of private conglomerates and political

---

[22] Max Horkheimer, *Eclipse of Reason* (New York: Oxford University Press, 1947), p. 93, p. 97.

elites in order to stabilize profit extraction without the burdens of competition. By selectively incorporating elements of economic planning, these forces of monopolization and centralization undercut both the decentralized market mechanism and Marx's thesis of the falling rate of profit. Moreover, Pollock had sounded a cautionary note that monopoly capitalism's suspension of this tendency worsened the prospects for revolution; in its new and more centralized form, monopoly capitalism might last much longer than suggested by Marx's predictions, which were based on *bourgeois*-liberal capitalism's more manifest and self-destructive contradictions.

However, nine years later—from the IfS's New York exile—Pollock revised his hypothesis in an even more pessimistic direction. According to Pollock, Hitler's fascist command economy and Roosevelt's New Deal had both taken a decisive step *beyond* monopoly capitalism, in the direction of what he now called *state capitalism*. In state capitalism, politics has completely displaced the market mechanism as the structuring principle of capitalist society.[23] Power was now fully in the hands of political and socioeconomic elites—or *rackets*, as Horkheimer called them—and the working-classes had been fully integrated into the false social unity of a totalitarian political system or incipient democratic welfare-states (notwithstanding the highly significant political differences between these regime types, of which Pollock was very much aware), which all but completely obscured the great fault line between capitalist and proletariat without overcoming its underlying socioeconomic basis. State capitalism thus had the effect of shifting the principal engine of human history from the *profit motive* in the economic sphere towards the *power motive* in the political sphere, thereby conclusively undermining the ultimately progressive tension between the productive forces and the productive relations that Marx had diagnosed as the fatal construction flaw of *bourgeois*-liberal capitalism.[24]

Although superior in productive power to monopoly capitalism, state capitalism reproduced the basic fault line between capitalists and proletariat in an even more stable opposition between the reigning elite and the dominated masses, but with sufficient ideological manipulation and redistribution to permanently avoid large-scale social unrest.[25] The ideologically deluded working classes were thereby left blindly at the mercy of a political-economic elite, who—in the form of National Socialism—would reveal themselves as one of the most inhumane and murderous

---

[23] This definition begs the question, of course, of whether such a society can still meaningfully be called 'capitalist'. This question was the subject of much controversy between the members of the New York branch of the IfS.

[24] Friedrich Pollock, 'State Capitalism' and 'Is National Socialism a New Order?', in *Zeitschrift für Sozialforschung/Studies in Philosophy and Social Science*, Vol. 9 (München: Kösel-Verlag, 1970).

[25] The 'currency' of redistribution in state capitalism need not be purely monetary; indeed, as Pollock notes, Hitler's command economy was partly supported by allowing certain ethical and moral strictures to dissolve—such as traditional sexual morality and the 'social check' on open manifestations of anti-Semitism.

political forces in all of human history. However, Pollock suggested that both the democratic and fascist variants would eventually give way to a completely rationalized form of state capitalism closer to the full integration of state and society found in the Soviet model, thus putting an end to 'all the remnants of a world not yet totally administered'.[26] In other words, as if monopoly capitalism wasn't bad enough, its successor model of state capitalism marked the final imprisonment of humanity in an inhumane society, with little or no hope for the practical realization of the reasonable society, which was the whole *raison d'être* of Horkheimer's original paradigm of critical theory. It is this profoundly depressing conviction, which represents the starting point for Adorno's negativist paradigm of critical theory, to which we now turn.

[26] Jürgen Habermas, 'Notes on the Developmental History of Horkheimer's Work', *Theory Culture Society* (10/61), 1993, 61–77, p. 65.

PART II
ADORNO

In the early 1960s, George Lukács scathingly quipped that Adorno had 'taken up residence at the "Grand Hotel Abyss" ... a beautiful hotel, equipped with every comfort, on the edge of an abyss, of nothingness, of absurdity. And the daily contemplation of the abyss between excellent meals or artistic entertainments, can only heighten the enjoyment of the subtle comforts offered'.[1] This less than subtle charge of hypocrisy should not be taken at face value. In fact, as Adorno himself suggests, one might suspect this damning judgement to reflect Lukács's need to justify his own practice of heeding communist party doctrine—which lead to his scandalous self-repudiation of *History and Class Consciousness* after the work had been decreed heresy by Moscow—just as much as any deeper insight into Adorno's much more independent, but also more practically disengaged theoretical position.[2]

This is not to deny that Adorno very much lived and embodied the personal contradiction of relentlessly propagating a life-long condemnation of late-capitalist society as 'radically evil' in theory, while not being averse to indulging in some of the higher pleasures that this society offers an established university professor in practice. However, as Adorno might have argued, this seeming contradiction in personal ethics can perhaps be understood, if not thereby resolved, as in part a reflection of the aspiration to gain a critical grasp of the very real contradictions of late-capitalist society, and the fact that it is precisely the higher pleasures—in particular, art and music—which hold the greatest potential for illuminating and resisting its radically evil nature. Of course, whether one is willing to accept *this* line of defence depends on one's attitude towards Adorno's negativist paradigm of critical theory, which undergirds it; and what our attitude to this paradigm should be—specifically concerning its implications for a critical theory of world society—is what the two chapters in Part II aim to explore.

---

[1] George Lukács, 'Preface', in *The Theory of the Novel: A Historico-philosophical Essay on the Forms of Great Epic Literature* (London: Merlin Books, 1974), p. 22.

[2] For Adorno's subtle retort on the impact of servility to party doctrine on Lukács's part, see Theodor W. Adorno, 'Ad Lukács', in *Gesammelte Schriften Band 20:1. Vermischte Schriften I* (Frankfurt: Suhrkamp Verlag, 1986).

Much like Adorno's own life and person, his negativist philosophy resists straightforward classification according to general criteria, including the methodological dimensions of the Frankfurt School idea of a critical theory, as I have reconstructed them in the Introduction. This may seem odd, since many arguably associate the Frankfurt School above all with Adorno, who rose to fame and prominence as not just a leading philosopher but also one of the leading public intellectuals of the post-war German Federal Republic until his death in 1969, and whose work has experienced a justified renaissance in recent years. However, Adorno nevertheless remains something of an outsider in the present reconstruction of the Frankfurt School tradition, not because he does not belong in that tradition—he most certainly does—but because his thought represents the strongest challenge to the claim that this tradition exhibits the kind of *methodological* coherence that I have argued it does. Indeed, there is no way around the fact that any attempt to present Adorno as subscribing to a systematic methodological framework in the way that I have proposed to construe critical theory is in considerable tension with some of the core commitments of his thought.

In marked contrast to the other three paradigms of critical theory reconstructed in this book, Adorno's thought is characterized by a thoroughgoing rejection of the system-building aspirations of the whole Western philosophical canon. Moreover, he explicitly disavows traditional forms of philosophical presentation, such as linearity in the structure of argument and deduction from premises to conclusions, not to speak of analytical philosophy's requirements of rigour and clarity—at least as these requirements are most often understood in the Anglophone world. To be sure, this does not mean that it is impossible to distinguish a historical, a sociological, and a normative dimension in Adorno's negativist paradigm of critical theory. But it does mean that Adorno would probably have resisted such a reading of his work. Indeed, he would likely take issue with the very attempt to give a systematic account of his thought, once going so far as to claim that 'philosophy is not reproducible [*referierbar*]'.[3] In all of his major published works, he aspired to 'beat the system' by writing in a style that is condensed, extremely demanding on the reader's erudition, and seemingly without form or structure—which obviously complicates any attempt to give a concise account of his thought. However, Adorno's thinking also reveals an exceptional sense of aesthetic beauty, moral fervour, and human fragility, and if one is willing to engage with his work on its own terms, it can be a deeply rewarding—if not exactly cheerful—experience.

In spite of these qualms, Chapter 3 aims to reconstruct Adorno's negativist philosophy as a genuine and self-standing paradigm of Frankfurt School critical theory. The justification for this approach is that it seems to me both possible and valuable to interpret his work as part of a coherent philosophical tradition that begins with the young Horkheimer and continues through Habermas's and

---

[3] Theodor W. Adorno, *Negative Dialektik* (Frankfurt: Suhrkamp Verlag, 1966), p. 44.

Honneth's work, where the coherence of the tradition is largely (but not only) given by their shared commitment to the methodological framework of critical theory. In other words, even if this overtly systematic intention and schematic reconstruction sits uneasily with the spirit of Adorno's thought, I maintain that the prism offered by the methodological framework of critical theory is at the very least a *fruitful* way of interpreting his philosophy.

Moreover, as we shall see, his negativist paradigm of critical theory can helpfully be understood as an integral part of a historical learning process initiated by the young Horkheimer and subsequently carried forth in the later generations of the Frankfurt School, and, indeed, I will argue that we cannot make sense of this learning process without him. Finally, as I shall argue in Chapter 4, even if we have reason to resist some of Adorno's central premises and claims, I also want to argue that we can draw important lessons for a critical theory of contemporary world society from Adorno's central concern with 'the nonidentical', in our attempt to grapple with such crucial global concerns as neocolonial forms of domination and the prospect of catastrophic climate change as an 'ecological dialectic of enlightenment'. So, with no suggestion that the reconstruction of the following chapter represents an exhaustive or completely faithful account of Adorno's negativist philosophy as a whole, let us nonetheless see what Adorno, *the critical theorist*, has to teach us, the denizens of twenty-first century globalized capitalism.

3
Theodor W. Adorno and the Negativist Paradigm of Critical Theory

3.1 Reflections from a Damaged Life

Theodor Wiesengrund Adorno was born in 1903 and raised in the comfortable surroundings of Frankfurt's liberal and cultivated bourgeoisie.[4] His father was a successful Jewish wine salesman (hence the name Wiesengrund), while his mother and aunt—whom he referred to as his 'second mother'—were both gifted musicians of Italian origin (hence the name Adorno). It was soon clear that the bright and delicate son took after his maternal side, and after finishing his doctorate in philosophy at the University of Frankfurt, the multitalented 'Teddy' travelled to Vienna—a city bustling with genius and creativity during the 1920s—to study musical composition with Alban Berg.

A prominent representative of the so-called *Neue Wiener Schule*, Berg was renowned for his mastery of the atonal compositional style that was spearheaded above all by the charismatic Austrian maestro Arnold Schönberg, in whose work Adorno saw a veritable 'break-through in consciousness'.[5] Unfortunately, Schönberg was rather unimpressed with Adorno's skill and originality as a composer, and the aspiring musician never succeeded in fulfilling his youth's dream of becoming a professional practitioner of '*die neue Musik*'. He would, however, go on to become its most prominent musical *theorist*. Notwithstanding his personal disappointment, Adorno remained a lifelong admirer of Schönberg to an extent that has led some commentators to suggest that Adorno's work might even be understood as an attempt to translate Schönberg's musical genius into philosophical form.[6]

With his musical ambitions thwarted, Adorno returned to Frankfurt to pursue a career in philosophy, quickly associating himself with the slightly older Horkheimer. Although their early relationship was not always uncomplicated, Adorno found much to admire in Horkheimer, who would eventually become

---

[4] The following biographical remarks draw on Stefan Müller-Doohm, *Adorno: Eine Biographie* (Frankfurt: Suhrkamp Verlag, 2003).
[5] Theodor W. Adorno, 'Zur gesellschaftlichen Lage der Musik', in *Zeitschrift für Sozialforschung*, Vol. 1, 1932 (München: Kösel-Verlag, 1970), p. 110.
[6] Martin Jay, *Marxism and Totality. The Adventures of a Concept from Lukács to Habermas* (Berkeley: University of California Press, 1984), p. 252.

a lifelong intellectual comrade and close personal friend. However, although Adorno remained part of the director's circle of confidents in the early 1930s, he wasn't formally accepted as a full member of the IfS until the outbreak of the war, and he had to endure several years of rather unhappy exile in Oxford—where he, perhaps unsurprisingly, felt misplaced and misunderstood—while the other members had long since reassembled in New York.

On the other hand, this distance from Horkheimer probably also allowed him to remain somewhat impervious to the latter's charismatic influence and in relative intellectual freedom to develop his own distinct interpretation of their shared ideas. This considerably more gloomy interpretation is inspired to a larger extent by Hegel, Walter Benjamin, Siegfried Kracauer, and—even more profoundly than Horkheimer—George Lukács. Moreover, when Horkheimer and Adorno finally did reach the intellectual consensus that culminated in their most famous collaboration, the 'Dialectic of Enlightenment' (*Dialektik der Aufklärung*), it was Horkheimer who gave up the last vestiges of his interdisciplinary programme for a materialist theory of society and adopted Adorno's more negativist philosophical stance.[7]

The chapter is structured as follows. In Section 3.2, I will expound Adorno and Horkheimer's dark masterpiece, the *Dialektik der Aufklärung*—which sees the rise of totalitarian fascism as a consequence of a world-historical reversion of enlightenment into blind domination—as the historical dimension of Adorno's negativist paradigm. In Section 3.3, I will account for what I reconstruct as the two guiding ideas of the sociological dimension in Adorno's paradigm: namely, the ideas of the 'administered world' and the 'system of delusion'. In Section 3.4, I reconstruct the normative dimension of his critical theory in terms of the Kantian concept of *Mündigkeit* and the negative concept of social heteronomy. In the remainder of this introductory section, Subsection 3.1.1 will account for Adorno's early programme of philosophy as interpretation, before Subsection 3.1.2 turns to a brief exposition of the *magnum opus* of his mature thought, the imposing 'Negative Dialectics' (*Negative Dialektik*), as the methodological basis for his negativist paradigm.

3.1.1 Philosophy as Interpretation

As we saw in Chapter 1, Horkheimer's thought underwent substantial shifts from his inauguration as director of the IfS to the outbreak of World War II. By contrast,

---

[7] Although Adorno and Horkheimer in fact formulated parts of this second paradigm of critical theory in close cooperation, I have chosen to focus the exposition on the former, since Adorno seems to be the driving force behind Horkheimer's change of mind, and he continued to develop the presuppositions and implications of the negativist paradigm after Horkheimer had largely ceased publishing.

Adorno's work exhibits a remarkable consistency throughout his intellectual life. Indeed, much of his later work is contained *in nuce* in the early programmatic lecture 'The Present Relevance of Philosophy' (*Die Aktualität der Philosophie*), delivered upon the assumption of a teaching position in Frankfurt in 1931. In fact, the opening sentences of this lecture contain what might be described as the central animating impulse of Adorno's thought as a whole:

> He who chooses philosophy as a profession today must from the beginning renounce the illusion with which earlier philosophical projects began: that it is possible to capture the totality of reality in the power of thought. No justifying reason could find itself in a reality, whose order and form strikes down every demand of reason. Only in a polemical sense does reality as a whole offer itself to the knowing subject, while it only meets the hope for a future right and just reality in the form of residues and traces. Philosophy, which pretends to be able to do this [i.e. capture the totality of reality in thought], serves no other purpose than to cover up reality and eternalise its present condition.[8]

What Adorno expresses here is his belief that social reality resists genuine rational comprehension, because it is so fundamentally irrational. This belief amounts, in a way reminiscent of the young Marx's call for a 'ruthless criticism of all that exists', to an inversion of Hegel's famous dictum that 'what is rational is real, and what is real is rational'.[9] As Adorno suggests, this has dramatic implications for philosophy, whose central task has been understood since Plato as that of disclosing the eternal truths at the foundations of reality. If the world is fundamentally irrational, if it exhibits no overall transparency or meaningful and rational order, then the project of trying to understand our world in terms of certain foundational laws that would be true in any possible world is nonsensical. Even if such laws do exist, their present form is such that we cannot rely on them to make sense of the world as a rational whole.

Moreover, this thesis also largely accounts for Adorno's animosity towards philosophical systems: a genuine philosophical system is possible only if its parts are related in a rational or sufficiently harmonious manner, and although Adorno does believe that the different component parts and spheres of social reality are systematically related, he thinks that they are related in deeply inharmonious, antagonistic, and contradictory ways. In short, although social reality presents itself as a 'social totality', it does not present itself as the kind of totality that we can accurately represent or capture in a rational philosophical system. To the contrary, the fundamental irrationality and epistemic opacity of present social reality

---

[8] Theodor W. Adorno, 'Die Aktualität der Philosophie', in *Gesammelte Schriften Band 1: Philosophische Frühschriften* (Frankfurt: Suhrkamp Verlag, 2003), p. 326.

[9] G.W.F. Hegel, *Grundlinien der Philosophie des Recht: Werke 7* (Frankfurt: Suhrkamp Verlag, 1986), p. 24.

can only find theoretical representation in a form that *mirrors* its antagonistic and contradictory form.

A second aspect of the passage worth highlighting is that Adorno contrasts the fundamental irrationality of social reality with a future *right* [*richtig*] and *just* society, of which we find glimpses in our own. On the one hand, this highlights the *historicity* of Adorno's thesis that social reality is fundamentally irrational: this thesis is not a metaphysical claim about reality as such, but a diagnostic claim about the actual, historically evolved social reality. Moreover, the combination of predicates such as right and just is characteristic for Adorno, who believes this is warranted because these are inseparable in the *real* phenomena they describe. When Adorno talks about the rightness (or correctness) and wrongness of reality, he has a specific kind of wrongness in mind, namely, in part, that the social reality of the existing human form of life *contradicts* the beliefs and expectations that it leads individuals to form about it—it means that reality is not what it makes itself out to be.[10]

But reality is wrong (*falsch*), not only because it claims to be something it is not, empirically speaking, but also because it falsely claims to be justified, in normative terms. A right and just society would be a fundamentally reasonable and transparent form of human existence that—so to speak—is what it purports to be, and which lives up to its own normative ideals. Although he maintains the impossibility of a 'justifying reason' being able to find itself in *this* social reality, the passage also suggests the possibility of a future society in which it might do so. Indeed, throughout his work, Adorno never tires of emphasizing that even if our fundamentally irrational reality presents formidable subjective and objective obstacles to the practical realization of a reasonable society, the fact that our reality contains such glimpses of a right and just condition is testament to its real possibility. Adorno maintains that it is the very purpose of philosophy to insist on this possibility, and to nurture the hope of realizing a reasonable society, in spite of the immense practical obstacles and forces of delusion that presently obstruct its realization. As he would later write in the essay, 'Why still Philosophy' (*Wozu noch Philosophie*):

> If philosophy is still necessary, then it is—as it has been since time immemorial—as critique, as resistance towards the unfolding heteronomy, as what might be the powerless attempt of thought to remain its own master, and to convict as untrue by their own criteria both a fabricated mythology and a conniving, resigned conformism ... However, if both heteronomies are untrue and this can be irrefutably demonstrated, then this does not merely add another link to the comfortless

---

[10] Adorno, *Negative Dialektik*, p. 190.

chain of philosophy, but it also announces a trace of hope that unfreedom and subjugation—the evil that requires as little philosophical proof as does its existence—shall not have the last word.[11]

The inaugural lecture also contains an early account of Adorno's epistemological assumptions and philosophical method, which must be understood against the background of his thesis concerning the fundamental irrationality of social reality. With inspiration from Walter Benjamin, Adorno argues that philosophy must gather the dispersed and meaningless elements of reality, as these elements are ascertained in the individual sciences, into meaningful and coherent *constellations*—a view that undergirds his early specification of 'philosophy as interpretation' (*Deutung*).[12] On this account, philosophy is assigned the task of constructing and assigning meaning to particular phenomena, without, however, interpreting these phenomena as representative of a greater meaning or universal truth.

In contrast to Benjamin, who understands ideas as 'timeless constellations'[13]—a view that Adorno would later describe as 'metaphysical'[14]—Adorno regards constellations as 'composed of individual elements derived from historical reality'.[15] Constellations are thus relations between concepts that are historical through and through. Moreover, constellations are developed in explicit contrast to Kantian epistemology, in which cognition of empirical reality is construed as classificatory subsumption of particular phenomena under general concepts—in short, by *identifying* phenomena with certain concepts. For Adorno, constellations are a way of constructing meaning that does not make sense of particulars *in terms* of such general concepts—the hallmark of what Adorno calls 'classificatory' or 'identity thinking'—but which rather 'illuminate that which is specific to the object ... in terms of the relation in which they place concepts, centred around a subject-matter'.[16] As we shall see below, this critique of identity thinking is an absolutely central concern in Adorno's thought, and the aspiration to respect that which is specific to particular phenomena, rather than understanding them as putative instantiations of conceptual genera, is one of the foundational themes of his work.

[11] Theodor W. Adorno, 'Wozu noch Philosophie', in *Kulturkritik und Gesellschaft II: Eingriffe und Stichwrote. Gesammelte Schriften Band 10.2* (Frankfurt: Suhrkamp Verlag, 2003), pp. 464–465.
[12] Adorno, 'Die Aktualität der Philosophie', p. 326.
[13] Walter Benjamin, 'Ursprung des deutschen Trauerspiels', in *Gesammelte Schriften I:I*, ed. by Rolf Tiedemann and Hermann Schweppenhäuser (Frankfurt: Suhrkamp Verlag, 1991) p. 215.
[14] Adorno, *Negative Dialektik*, p. 166.
[15] Adorno, *Negative Dialektik*, p. 167.
[16] Adorno, *Negative Dialektik*, p. 164.

Moreover, these assumptions further suggest that philosophy is often better positioned to reach insights from subjecting mundane, everyday phenomena to critical scrutiny, rather than the perennial 'big questions' that have traditionally preoccupied philosophical thinking:

> At its present historical state, philosophy has its true interest where Hegel, in accordance with the tradition, announced his disinterest: in the non-conceptual, the individual, and the particular; in that which since Plato has been discarded as the transient and negligible and to which Hegel attached the etiquette of 'lazy existence'.[17]

The arguably most sublime expression of this focus on the non-conceptual, individual, and particular is Adorno's masterpiece *Minima Moralia*, published in 1951 with the aptly phrased subtitle *Reflections From the Damaged Life*. In a number of aphorisms and reflections that Adorno wrote during and after World War II, he discusses everything from doorknobs, cars, marriage, divorce, prehistoric fossils, room service, the functional separation of hotels and restaurants, and the experience of high-speed train travel. However, in these short texts Adorno's intention is always to illuminate the more general significance of such everyday, minutiae phenomena: how their meaning is conditioned by and expressive of the antagonistic and contradictory totality of late-capitalist society, and how this totality determines our understanding of ourselves and the world around us. That is to say, these everyday phenomena serve as *heuristics* through which Adorno illuminates the irrational and antagonistic societal background, by showing how even our most intimate experiences and supposedly innocuous habits and patterns of behaviour and thought reflect and fulfil their function in a larger social context that is as unjust as it is delusionary.

The title *Minima Moralia* is a pun on the *Magna Moralia*, a treatise on ethics attributed to Aristotle concerned with positively establishing the conditions for living a good or virtuous life. By contrast, the most famous claim of *Minima Moralia* is that 'there can be no right life in a wrong [life]' (*es gibt kein richtiges Leben im Falschen*).[18] As we have seen, Adorno insists that the present human form of life is wrong, implying that we who live it are unable to live a right life. However, what we can do—and what Adorno sets out to do in *Minima Moralia*, with great eloquence and moral sensitivity—is to illuminate *that* and *how* our lives are distorted and damaged; the myriad ways in which 'life does not live', as the epigraph of the book notes. As such, the book expresses the basic *negativistic* presuppositions of

---

[17] Adorno, *Negative Dialektik*, pp. 19–20.
[18] Theodor W. Adorno, *Minima Moralia: Reflexionen aus dem beschädigten Leben* (Frankfurt: Suhrkamp Verlag, 2003), p. 43.

Adorno's thought, which are perhaps most clearly explicated in his lectures on moral philosophy from 1963:

> We may not know what the absolute good is or the absolute norm is, we may not even know what the human being, the human, or humanity is, but we know very well what the inhumane is. And, I would say that the place of moral philosophy today should be sought more in the concrete denunciation of the inhumane than in the elusive and abstract attempt to situate the human being in its existence.[19]

It is precisely the pervasive wrongness and falsity of social reality that makes it impossible for us to know how to live a right life, to know that which is humane or absolutely good. We can make sense of this negativistic view as having two sides, one practical and one epistemic, with the first side corresponding to an *empirical* and *practical negativism*, and the other to an *epistemic* and *methodological negativism*.[20] Adorno's empirical-practical negativism holds that our present form of life is substantially unjust and untrue—that the world is made into what it is through real 'forces of negativity'—and that this makes a mockery of the notion that an individual human being may live a right or virtuous life, since this life has to be lived through an unjust and wrong form of existence. His epistemic negativism holds that the injustice and wrongness of the world prohibits us from *knowing* what a just and right form of life would be, since we have to rely on the distorted cognitive resources of a wrong form of existence. This stands in marked contrast to the young Horkheimer, who considered the task of illuminating and guiding the practical path towards a reasonable society the very purpose of a critical theory.

This epistemic negativism is perhaps the most radical and unusual element of Adorno's distinctive paradigm of critical theory—and, in a sense, it is the claim that distinguishes his paradigm as truly negativistic. This claim implies that *epistemic access* to knowledge of the right and just *also presupposes certain social conditions*, and when these social conditions are not realized, we simply *cannot know* these things. It thus follows that in our present form of life we cannot know what reality really is, and what a just reality would be like. By thus undercutting the traditional project of philosophy of ascertaining knowledge of the true and the just, Adorno's epistemic negativism has the dramatic methodological implications to which Adorno's philosophy gives such consistent expression. In other words, if Adorno's epistemic negativism is warranted, philosophy in its traditional form is simply impossible given our present, fundamentally wrong form of life.

---

[19] Theodor W. Adorno, *Probleme der Moralphilosophie* (Frankfurt: Suhrkamp Verlag, 2010), p. 261.
[20] The distinctions roughly trail Fabian Freyenhagen's distinctions in *Adorno's Practical Philosophy: Living Less Wrongly* (Cambridge: Cambridge University Press, 2013), introduction.

However, as suggested above, the silver lining—if one can indeed call it that—is that even if philosophy cannot under present social conditions hope to ascertain knowledge of the true and the just, it can nevertheless disclose the pervasive wrongness of the world by revealing the ways in which our present human existence—both in social life as in forms of thought—contradicts its own claims to be right, just, and rational in concrete instances. This, essentially, is Adorno's distinctive take on the methodological procedure of *immanent critique*, and it is this perspective that Adorno has in mind when he claims that philosophy has its true interest in the non-conceptual, the individual, and the particular, and that moral philosophy has its place in the concrete denunciation of the inhumane. Moreover, as we shall see, the philosophical perspective of immanent critique is consistent with the only kind of practical orientation that Adorno thinks possible in our unjust world, namely individual *resistance* towards the wrong form of life.

3.1.2 Negative Dialektik

Evidently, Adorno's epistemic negativism requires further argument than the diagnostic claim that the world is substantially wrong and unjust. This argument is ultimately provided in Adorno's *magnum opus*, the dense and inaccessible *Negative Dialektik* from 1966, which represents the most encompassing statement of his philosophical method and the basic presuppositions of his thought. Adorno describes the task of *Negative Dialektik* as freeing 'dialectics from its affirmative character'[21]—as dialectics has been understood and practiced since Plato—and from the system-building function that it is accorded in Hegel's idealism. To this effect, Adorno undertakes nothing less than a wholesale immanent critique of philosophical idealism, with Kant and Hegel as his central antagonists.[22] Accordingly, to understand the basic idea of negative dialectics, it is necessary to backtrack a bit and get a clearer view of what is both Adorno's central target and source of inspiration: Hegel's idealist dialectics.

For Hegel, dialectics represents a three-step cognitive movement or procedure. Dialectics starts from an *abstract* thought, which, in a second step, is *negated* by another abstract thought, before, in the third and final step, this contradiction is *sublated* (*aufgehoben*) in a *concrete* thought, which reconciles the contradiction by reintegrating its component parts into what Hegel calls a *determinate negation*.[23] A determinate negation is both the positive outcome of Hegel's affirmative dialectics

---

[21] Adorno, *Negative Dialektik*, p. 9.
[22] The book also contains an immanent critique of Martin Heidegger's fundamental ontology, which is less relevant for our present purposes.
[23] Hegel does not understand the word 'concrete' in its common language sense, as the opposite of 'abstract' (i.e. 'stone' as opposed to 'matter'), but rather as 'mediated' thought—that is, as thought which has passed through and included the negation within itself.

as well as the basic building block of his idealist system.[24] For Hegel, dialectics is not only a philosophical method but also the structure of the movement of thought itself. This can be brought out with an example from his *Logic*, where he begins the dialectical unfolding of his all-encompassing system of ideas with the idea of 'simple immediacy'—or what, according to Hegel, amounts to the same thing: namely, *pure being*.

Upon reflection, we come to realize that the thought of pure being is without any determinate content; it is completely empty and void—it is *nothing*. The claim that being and nothingness are identical is clearly a contradiction, but it is a 'dialectical contraction', since nothing is merely the abstract negation of being. Upon further reflection, however, we see that what has in fact happened is that being has cognitively 'passed over' into nothingness: 'Their truth is therefore this *movement* of the immediate vanishing of one into the other: *becoming*, a movement in which the two are distinguished, but by a distinction which has just as immediately dissolved itself'.[25] The concept of becoming is thus the dialectical reconciliation of the abstract contradiction between being and nothingness; the sublation of both into a more concrete thought that mediates and contains both being and nothingness as 'moments' within itself. Moreover, the example is itself of far-reaching substantial importance, since it expresses Hegel's conviction that existence is a dynamic rather than a static category—that everything exists in a state of becoming, either coming-to-be or ceasing-to-be—and it undergirds his philosophical insistence on the importance of process and history, which Adorno shares.

According to Hegel, dialectics also represents the structure of the developmental process in which *Geist* (Spirit) comes to self-consciousness through the vehicle of subjective human knowledge, as well as the historical process in which *Geist* unfolds in the objective structures and social institutions of human society.[26] In doing so, *Geist* continually proceeds through a dialectical movement of contradiction and sublation, relentlessly pressing onwards towards total reconciliation. Along the way, new contradictions continuously arise that are resolved by integrating them as moments in an ever larger and more differentiated whole. Hegel's speculative philosophy follows and reconstructs this process in its continuous expansion towards the fully differentiated and reconciled totality, the 'concrete universal' of the 'absolute idea'—the complete system, which contains the process of its realization and all the attendant differentiations within itself. The absolute idea—or fully unfolded, internally differentiated, and self-conscious *Geist*—thus represents both the historical culmination of the complete subjective realization of reason in human knowledge and the objective realization of reason in human society.

---

[24] G.W.F. Hegel, *The Science of Logic* (Cambridge: Cambridge University Press, 2010), pp. 33–34.
[25] Hegel, *The Science of Logic*, p. 60.
[26] G.W.F. Hegel, *Phänomenologie des Geistes. Werke III* (Frankfurt: Suhrkamp Verlag, 1970); *Grundlinien der Philosophie des Rechts*, §341–460.

Just as in thought, we therefore encounter dialectical contradictions in human history, in which peoples or nations (*Völker*) rise and fall in order to pave the way for more internally differentiated and encompassing forms of social and political life. At the apex of history—as described in Hegel's *Rechtsphilosophie*—these contradictions are finally reconciled in the concrete universal of a constitutional monarchy. In such a truly modern society, the different social spheres and classes are each assigned their rightful place in an all-encompassing social and political context, in which—as we shall discuss more extensively in Chapter 7—Hegel also believes, all the relevant aspects of human freedom are realized. For Hegel, dialectics thus ultimately serve the twin functions of realizing the system of human knowledge and as a means of social and political *reconciliation*.

It would not be quite right to say that negative dialectics is simply an inversion of Hegel's affirmative dialectics, although Adorno would seem to suggest this interpretation with his famous counter-proposition, '*Das Ganze ist das Unwahre*' (the whole is the untrue).[27] Rather, Adorno charges Hegel with losing his nerve in drawing the implications of his insight into the 'tremendous power of the negative'. In the preface to the *Phänomenologie des Geistes*, Hegel famously remarks:

> the life of Spirit is not the life that shrinks from death and keeps itself untouched by devastation, but rather the life that endures it and maintains itself in it. It wins its truth only when, in utter dismemberment, it finds itself. It is this power, not as something positive, which closes its eyes to the negative, as when we say of something that it is nothing or is false, and then, having done with it, turn away and pass on to something else; on the contrary, Spirit is this power only by looking the negative in the face, and tarrying with it. This tarrying with the negative is the magical power that converts it into being. This power is identical with what we earlier called the Subject.[28]

Through this 'tarrying with the negative' (*bei dem Negativen verweilen*), dialectics blows life into *Geist* through its destructive operations, utter dismemberment, and subsequent reconciliation. However, according to Adorno, this appreciation of the negative aspect of dialectics dissipates in Hegel's insistence that the dynamic, processual, and open-ended character of dialectics is ultimately reconcilable with the static notion of *Geist* as a putatively all-encompassing, positive system. As a result, Adorno effectively accuses Hegel of resting his whole philosophical system on a

---

[27] Raymond Geuss does see an inversion in the sense that Adorno constructs an *anti-theodicy* to counter Hegel's more traditional theodicy—theodicy being the old Christian expression for a description of the world, which, in spite of its apparent evils, reconciles us with its essential nature. Raymond Geuss, 'Art and Theodicy', in *Morality, Culture and History: Essays on German Philosophy* (Cambridge: Cambridge University Press, 1999).

[28] G.W.F. Hegel, *Phenomenology of Spirit*, transl. by A.V. Miller (Oxford: Oxford University Press, 1977), p. 19.

petitio principii: 'Hegelian philosophy was never truly in a state of *becoming*, but was, implicitly, already assumed in every single determination'.[29]

According to Adorno, this loss of nerve also explains Hegel's affirmative 'scurrilities', such as his suggestion that 'world history has culminated in the Prussian state'.[30] However, if one disavows the static, apologetic notion of a positive and all-encompassing system, 'dialectics undergoes a qualitative change. Systematic unanimity disintegrates', since the 'thought that must not posit anything positive beyond the dialectical procedure shoots above and beyond the object with which it no longer pretends to be identical'.[31] Freed from the tendentious system and its reassurance of ultimate identity and reconciliation, focus is instead shifted to the negative element in dialectics—the *non-identical*—which can no longer be seen as reconciled into a larger whole, but which appears instead like a trail of destruction in the wake of an incessant process of identification. Without the systemic *telos* of an all-encompassing, coherent totality, dialectics becomes an essentially *open-ended* process, and without its affirmative bias towards 'the identity of identity and non-identity', 'dialectics is the unrelenting consciousness of non-identity'.[32]

To be sure, Adorno's disagreements with Hegel do not stop here. The arguably central idea of idealism is that of the *constitutive subject*, which in Kant's transcendental idealism takes the form of the 'I think' of transcendental apperception, and in Hegel's absolute idealism, the world-historical form of self-positing *Geist*. In Kant's thought, it is the subjectively projected experiential filter through which empirical reality must pass to reach the understanding that ensures correspondence between the subject and object of knowledge. In Hegel's thought, the constitutive subject is understood as positing the social world through its coming to self-knowledge, ensuring identity between subject and object. The primacy of the subject also undergirds the idealist idea of freedom, which on Kant's account implies that human beings can understand themselves as autonomous even while immersed in a natural order of causal determination, while, on Hegel's account, it is evident in the apologetic embrace of *bourgeois* 'constitutional monarchy' as the concrete universal that realizes the freedom of all. From the idealist point of view, subjects can therefore in an important sense always regard themselves as self-determining 'authors' of their lives, irrespective of the particular social and political circumstances they actually find themselves in.

Against idealism's primacy of the subject, Adorno posits the *primacy of the object*, and in support of this reversal he mounts both conceptual and phenomenological arguments. On the one hand, Adorno argues that the object must be primary, because we are able to think the object in abstraction from the subject, but not *vice-versa*. The self-reflecting subject is necessarily also an object of thought,

---

[29] Adorno, *Negative Dialektik*, p. 38 [emphasis added].
[30] Adorno, *Negative Dialektik*, p. 38.
[31] Adorno, *Negative Dialektik*, p. 39.
[32] Adorno, *Negative Dialektik*, p. 17.

but the object has no similar conceptual connection with a subject: 'It belongs to the meaning of subjectivity also to be an object; it does not in the same way belong to objectivity also to be subject'.[33] Furthermore, Adorno also supports this conceptual claim with an observation about the putative experience and reality of the relationship between subject and object in late-capitalist society: 'The powerlessness of *Geist* [the subject] in all its judgements and in the organisation of reality is an index of the primacy of the object'.[34]

In Adorno's view, the primacy of the constitutive subject is thus the great illusion of idealism; it represents the philosophical justification of the *bourgeois* ideology that the objective world of late-capitalism answers to the subject and its 'justifying reason'.[35] In Adorno's thesis of the primacy of the object, we thus find a clear echo of Lukács's claim that modern capitalist society is pervasively reified. In the final analysis, the object holds primacy *because* human beings find themselves within a basic societal structure over which they have no power, but which rather subjects them to anonymous forces of structural heteronomy and domination that deprive them of their very ability to think and act as subjects. As we saw in the discussion of Lukács' theory of reification in Chapter 1, the Hungarian philosopher held that capitalist society both treats subjects as objects and leads them to misapprehend and comport themselves as objects. It makes them into something they are not, both at a subjective and an objective level, *identifying* them with, and making them *self-identify* as, commodities: 'In the thing-like, each is contained in the other: the un-identity of the object and the subjection of human beings to the ruling relations of production, their own, unrecognisable functional system'.[36]

The primacy of the object also entails that dialectics cuts its umbilical cord to idealism and must become a *materialist* dialectics. This implies that the impetus for dialectics does not issue from the movement of *Geist's* coming-to-self-consciousness—as in Hegel's idealism—but rather from the nature and organization of existing social reality, which in turn accounts for Adorno's description of one of the central aims of *Negative Dialektik* as the 'exposition of the concept of philosophical experience'.[37] The idea of 'philosophical experience' refers to Adorno's thesis that *all concepts are sedimented experience*, and that, accordingly, there can be no such thing as Kantian pure categories or a priori knowledge: 'thought, itself a form of conduct, contains the need—in the first instance, the most vitally necessary needs—within itself. Thinking is thought out of need, even where this is dismissed as "wishful thinking"'.[38]

---

[33] Adorno, *Negative Dialektik*, p. 184.
[34] Adorno, *Negative Dialektik*, p. 187.
[35] Adorno, *Negative Dialektik*, p. 211.
[36] Adorno, *Negative Dialektik*, p. 192.
[37] Adorno, *Negative Dialektik*, p. 10.
[38] Adorno, *Negative Dialektik*, p. 399.

The point here, which echoes an insight of the young Horkheimer, is that thought always contains and expresses the lived experience from which it emerges. This is why idealism and its stress on constitutive subjectivity is not wholly false, but is in fact, in the work of its greatest masters, a remarkable philosophical testament to the lived experience of the social and historical context from which it has emerged. For example, 'the exchangeable end-product [of the capitalist production process] is similar to the Kantian object, which is subjectively made but accepted as objectivity'.[39] It is because concepts are ultimately sedimented experience that the process which makes negative dialectics necessary—to wit: the objective compulsion towards identification of the non-identical; the universal subsumption of particularity under general concepts—does not ultimately derive from the structure of thought, as Hegel claims, but is ultimately predicated on the antagonistic and contradictory reality of society:

> The totality of the contradiction is nothing less than the untruth of total identification, as the former manifests itself in the latter. Contradiction is non-identity under the spell of the law [of value], which also influences the nonidentical. This law, however, is not one of thinking, but real.[40]

Adorno's claim here is that identification has two sides, one subjective and one objective, but that the latter side must be understood as predominating over the former. At the subjective level, identity thinking dominates all forms of thought in late-capitalist society, leading us to misapprehend particular phenomena—including ourselves—as exemplars of *genera* rather than as what they (and we) truly are. But identification also has a real and objective side, from which, in accordance with the nature of late-capitalist society, it gains its all-powerful dominance. Adorno thus suggests that even if we were to try our best to *think* differently, we would still ultimately find ourselves under the spell of identification, as long as the objective identity-principle is in force.

As we shall explore further in Section 3.3, Adorno claims that this objective side is the Marxian exchange-principle, according to which the value of commodities is made equivalent and quantifiable through the socially necessary labour time expended on them, enabling their standardized exchange on the market. Again echoing Lukács, Adorno argues that the exchange-principle orders society in a totalizing, reifying manner, much in the same way as the identity-principle orders our cognition through cognitive subsumption of particular phenomena under general categories. Both principles reduce all particularity to general standards (exchange value and concepts) and annihilate or supress all that is non-identical—all aspects of objects and thoughts that do not fit into pre-established schemata.

---

[39] Adorno, *Negative Dialektik*, p. 380.
[40] Adorno, *Negative Dialektik*, p. 18.

As we shall see, these principles are not merely what ultimately account for the profound and pervasive wrongness of social reality; they also produce a universal system of delusion and ideological conceptual schemes that prevent us from seeing reality for what it truly is. The task of negative dialectics is thus to lay bare the moments of this irrational totality by demonstrating, through the construction of meaning in constellations, how both thought and reality contradict their own claims to identity—i.e. the contradiction between how objects and thoughts are classified, and what they actually are. Only by revealing glimpses of the all-pervasive distortion and domination of the non-identical, by dialectically backtracking to clarify and maintain the reality of the contradictions and the unsublated particularity of the non-identical that Hegel's idealist dialectics sought to affirm as moments within a rational totality, is negative dialectics able to momentarily penetrate the system of delusion, and thus disclose—however fleetingly—the wrongness and injustice of our whole form of life.

It should be clear from this introduction and methodological overview that Adorno's judgement of modern capitalist society is extremely bleak, to say the least. In Adorno's view, as we have seen, the wrongness and injustice of our existing form of human existence is so pervasive that not only can we not *live* a right life, but we cannot even *know* what living a right life in this false form of existence would mean. Many contemporary readers will likely find this unrelenting negativism unpersuasive and even hyperbolic. They might also take issue with the apparent elitism of Adorno's claim that ordinary folks suffer from an all-encompassing false consciousness that only the critical philosopher is able to see through.

However, before Adorno is discarded as an arrogant but extremely erudite and articulate misanthrope, it is worth recalling the nature of his historical experience. Along with the few other lucky Jews (whether assimilated, as the Wiesengrund-Adornos, or not) that got away, Adorno was forced into exile by a murderous fascist regime, which was out to get people of his kind on both political *and* racist grounds. Moreover, while he lingered in the deeply alienating but relatively safe environment of wartime USA, his home country was, after having first projected its military might all over Europe and beyond, subsequently engulfed from all sides by the most destructive military campaign ever launched in the history of human warfare. When he returned to Germany in 1953 to participate in the intellectual reconstruction of the Federal Republic, he was confronted with a country that had not only experienced the complete physical destruction of its cities and industrial infrastructure, but which had also vaporized what was left of its moral integrity, along with the bodies of the European Jews and thousands of Roma, Sinti, homosexuals, and political prisoners.

Perhaps more than anything else, it is ultimately the great historical schism of the Holocaust that undergirds the profound bleakness of Adorno's account of late-capitalist society. Indeed, it would not be an overestimation—and only slightly anachronistic—to describe Auschwitz as the central problem of Adorno's negativist philosophy. The question, Adorno asks himself, is what conditions must truly operate under the surface of a seemingly civilized society capable of such hitherto unimaginable horror. In *Negative Dialektik*, Adorno insists that it is indeed the Holocaust, which has made any kind of metaphysics impossible:

> The feeling, which after Auschwitz resists every claim to positivity of existence as sanctimonious rubbish, as an injustice to the victims; that feeling, which recoils against squeezing any meaning—be it ever so diluted—out of their fate, has its objective moment after events, which condemn the construction of an immanent meaning as radiating from an affirmatively posited transcendence to a mockery. Such a construction would affirm the absolute negativity and ideologically contribute to its continued existence, which, in any case, really lies in the principle of existing society unto its self-destruction.[41]

Adorno here argues that Auschwitz was the extreme and horrific instantiation of an immanent tendency in late-capitalist society—'in the camps, it was no longer the individual that died, but the exemplar'[42]—and that its very historical facticity has permanently undermined any possibility of seeking solace in the transcendent meaning of metaphysics. This is so not only because it would serve to obscure the continued existence of the conditions that enabled the genocide of the European Jews, but also because the claim that reality exhibits such higher meaning and purpose would be an affront to the millions who succumbed to the death squads and the gas chambers. Accordingly, the Holocaust was not merely a contingent and atypical relapse into a form of barbarism that is unlikely to repeat itself, as many prefer to think. Rather, it was made possible by—*and* brought to murderous expression—the very structure of late-capitalist society that persists to this day. It is the task of Adorno's negativist critical theory to disclose this structure and thereby confront the question of how a man-made catastrophe like the Holocaust could ever have happened, and whether it could happen again.

3.2 The Dialectic of Enlightenment

Horkheimer and Adorno's original account of the historical enabling conditions of totalitarian fascism and the Holocaust is developed in their coauthored book, *Dialektik der Aufklärung*, first published in 1944. This book is beyond any doubt the most famous and influential work of the Frankfurt School tradition. It is a book of breathtaking scope and ambition, and no less demanding on the reader than *Negative Dialektik*. The *Dialektik der Aufklärung* wrestles with one overarching

---

[41] Adorno, *Negative Dialektik*, p. 355.
[42] Adorno, *Negative Dialektik*, p. 355.

paradox described in its opening pages: 'Enlightenment, understood in the widest sense as the advance of thought, has always aimed at liberating human beings from fear and installing them as masters. Yet the wholly enlightened earth is radiant with triumphant calamity'.[43] In other words, the task of the book is to explain how an ostensibly civilized and enlightened society can revert back into the barbarity and brutality of fascism, murderous racism, and total warfare. It attempts to understand why human kind have utilized their immense productive power to wreak destruction upon themselves, and to erect the gas chambers of Auschwitz, when the Earth, 'right here and now, could be paradise'—as Adorno would later phrase the point.[44] The explanation offered is, quite simply, the dialectic of enlightenment itself: the fatal disfigurement of an emancipatory project through the process of its historical realization. The nature of the dialectic is summed up in the book's preface: 'Myth is already enlightenment, and enlightenment reverts to mythology'.[45] Let us look at each of these puzzling propositions in turn.

3.2.1 Enlightenment Reverts to Mythology

The basic idea behind the claim that 'enlightenment reverts to mythology' should be understood as follows. The enlightenment project has always been defined by its commitment to the rule of human reason over the merely given—that is, as the aspiration to place human existence on no other pillars than those sanctioned by reason. Kant aptly captured this ambition in the famous rallying-cry for the Enlightenment: *Sapere Aude!*—have the courage to think for yourself. The *Dialektik der Aufklärung* deliberately gives this programme a political edge by cashing it out in conceptual terms of *power*: 'In the most general sense of progressive thought, the Enlightenment has always aimed at liberating men from fear and establishing their *sovereignty*'.[46] To be sure, in an important sense Adorno and Horkheimer see themselves as *continuing* this project—as adhering to Kant's programmatic claim that 'reason should take on the most difficult of all its tasks, namely, that of self-knowledge, and to institute a court of justice, by which reason may secure its rightful claims while dismissing all its groundless pretensions.'[47] However, at the same time, they locate the phantom menace in Kant's programme precisely in its stated intention to let reason *reign* supreme.

In the relationship between humanity and nature, the enlightenment aspiration for self-knowledge has been cashed out in the form of human mastery over nature's

---

[43] Theodor W. Adorno and Max Horkheimer, *Dialectic of Enlightenment: Philosophical Fragments*, transl. by Edmund Jephcott (Stanford: Stanford University Press, 2002).
[44] Theodor W. Adorno, *Ästhetische Theorie* (Frankfurt: Suhrkamp Verlag, 1970), p. 55.
[45] Adorno and Horkheimer, *Dialectic of Enlightenment*, p. xvi.
[46] Adorno and Horkheimer, *Dialectic of Enlightenment*, p. 3 [emphasis added].
[47] Immanuel Kant, *The Critique of Pure Reason*, trans. by Paul Guyer and Allen W. Wood (Cambridge: Cambridge University Press, 1998), p. 101.

'groundless pretensions': the overcoming of human life's subjection to the contingencies of natural forces and the power of myth over the human mind. However, in this process, reason has become purely *instrumentalized*—it has been reduced to an instrument solely for classifying, arranging, preparing, and administering nature for human ends. Instrumental reason is itself a form of identification: the unremitting conversion of natural objects into commodities, means for human consumption and profit, to the universal detriment of particularity and the non-identical. However, at the same time, reason has ruthlessly destroyed all traditional belief-systems and allowed nothing in their place—an echo of Weber's famous claim that rationalization has 'disenchanted' the world—leaving humanity with an immense technical apparatus for mastering nature but without any substantive ends left to pursue. In its self-reduced, purely instrumental form, reason thus reverts back into myth as meaningless human power over nature, replacing the givenness of natural causation with a world of thoroughgoing contingency bereft of all substantial normativity and experienced as wholly without meaning or purpose. Humanity's own means of survival have come to reign over them; they have become akin to a mythical force of nature.[48]

Moreover, in this process it is not only external nature—such as rocks, iron ore, and the other animals—that has been subjected to human control and exploitation. Rather, human nature—including our inner, *psychological* nature, our needs, wants, and cognitive processes—has also been shaped and disciplined by a social order integrated through instrumental reason. As a result, the distinction between human and non-human has been all-but obliterated and both categories have come to be regarded as equally contingent and disposable objects of planning and control. In this way, the instrumentalization of nature has had a qualitative recoil effect on the organization of the psyche and social relations. These have increasingly become characterized by brute and naked power, while experienced less and less as a normative order resting on a—however diluted—*bourgeois* promise of individual freedom. For Adorno and Horkheimer, the rise of fascism and predatory imperialism all over the world in the 1930s and 1940s provided apt corroboration of this bleakest of diagnoses.

This account of how enlightenment reverts into its opposite appeals in part to the different connotations of the German words *Beherrschung* and *Herrschaft*. Human *mastery over nature* (*Naturbeherrschung*) and the human self (*Selbstbeherrschung*) reverts into the *domination* (*Beherrschung/Herrschaft*) of humans over humans, and the anonymous *structural domination* of human subjects by the very structure of late-capitalist society. In this way, 'the self-mastering [*selbstherrliche*] subject's subjugation of everything natural at the end culminates precisely

---

[48] This claim clearly picks up on Marx's theme that in the capitalist mode of production, dead labour dominates living labour, as well as Weber's metaphor of the 'iron cage' of rationalization.

in the domination [*Herrschaft*] of the blindly objective and natural'[49]—including the objectified human subject. Totalitarian fascism and the Holocaust can thus be understood as enabled by—and, to some extent, as giving horrendous expression to—a more general historical tendency towards the objectification, quantification, classification, administration, and control of all that exists, including human nature itself. When subjects have been reduced to mere objects of administration, when all ends have lost their value and thus in an important sense ceased to be ends—including Kant's 'end in itself', humanity as such—those in power no longer face any socially recognized normative restrictions on their treatment of those whom prejudice, fear, and opportunism would single out as scapegoats, or as an alien presence in the ethnically homogenous *Volk*.

Moreover, the claim that human mastery of nature includes inner nature is expounded in Adorno's Freudian thesis that the 'history of civilization is the history of the introversion of sacrifice—in other words, the history of renunciation.'[50] Adorno substantializes this sweeping diagnosis in an original rereading of a classic text in the canon of Western civilization: the *Odyssey*. In this paradigm epic of ancient Greek mythology, Odysseus faces a number of trials during his voyage back to Ithaca and his beloved Penelope, such as, famously, escaping the fatal lure of the Sirens' song by letting his crew tie him to the mast of his ship and blocking their hearing. In Adorno's eyes, this signifies nothing less than the inception of the enlightenment subject and an ancient anticipation of the form of subjectivity constitutive of the individual in modern capitalist society: the ability to repress gratification of one's needs for the possibility of future gain.

However, in the age of totalitarian fascism, even this individual capacity for self-mastery is made redundant by the omnipresent societal machinery of administration and control. In the hero's progressively refined skill in subjugating the needs and inclinations of his inner nature to the instrumental rule of his rational will (*Seblstbeherrschung*), Adorno thus sees the history of Western civilization condensed, including the fatal reversion of the enlightenment programme into the pure domination of fascist barbarity: 'The antireason of totalitarian capitalism, whose technique of satisfying needs, in their objectified form determined by domination, makes the satisfaction of needs impossible and tends towards the extermination of humanity—this antireason appears prototypically in the hero who escapes the sacrifice by sacrificing himself'.[51]

3.2.2 Myth is already Enlightenment

According to Horkheimer and Adorno, totalizing enlightenment reason will only find rest from its ceaseless destruction of everything experienced as outside its

---

[49] Adorno and Horkheimer, *Dialectic of Enlightenment*, p. xviii (translation amended).
[50] Adorno and Horkheimer, *Dialectic of Enlightenment*, p. 43.
[51] Adorno and Horkheimer, *Dialectic of Enlightenment*, p. 43.

reach when it recognizes its own limits: its own entanglement with myth and nature, with the merely given. Moreover, myth—the ostensible opposite of enlightenment reason—was never merely blind submission to the given; it was always also an attempt to explain and justify the power of nature over human life with reference to spiritual or otherworldly influence. This accounts for the second proposition in the dialectic of enlightenment: namely, that 'myth is already enlightenment'. Accordingly, the supposed other of reason is in fact a 'forgotten' part of reason itself, just as instrumental reason has today become a form of myth.

Horkheimer and Adorno thus reject the Marxian conception of human freedom as total mastery over nature, which was still very much presumed in Horkheimer's original paradigm of critical theory—as we have seen—but which he came to doubt partly through witnessing the descent of Europe into fascism and the failure of Soviet collectivization. Rather, they argue, true human freedom must be understood in terms of a *non-dominating* attitude towards nature, as an attitude *beyond* instrumental manipulation, conceptual classification, and identification. Adorno captures this attitude in the important concept of *mimesis*, which denotes an empathic act of imitation that does not try to manipulate or make sense of an object as something other than itself—and to which we shall return in Section 3.4.

The *Dialektik der Aufklärung* is not a traditional work of history, nor a philosophy of history in the sense familiar from Condorcet, Kant, Hegel, and Marx. The philosophical project of *Universalgeschichte* (universal history), which discloses a general meaning in world history, relies on the assumption that a 'total continuity' runs through all of history. This assumption also implies that the suffering and sacrifices offered by generation after generation of wretched humanity serve some greater purpose. It is precisely this kind of affirmative reading of history that the book is meant to undermine. As Adorno writes in *Negative Dialektik*:

> Universal history should be constructed and denied. After the catastrophes, and in view of the ones to come, it would be cynical to claim that a global unifying plan towards a better world manifests itself in history. However, this does not imply the denial of the unity that forges the discontinuous, chaotically splintered moments and phases of history together—that of human mastery over nature progressing into its domination over human beings, and ultimately over internal nature. No universal history runs from savagery to humanity, but there is indeed one leading from the slingshot to the megaton bomb. It ends in the total menace that organised humanity poses to organised human beings, in the epitome of discontinuity.[52]

The *Dialektik der Aufklärung* should thus be read as an immanent critique of the enlightenment project, which sublates the abstract contradiction between myth and enlightenment in the determinate negation that the two opposites converge

---

[52] Adorno, *Negative Dialektik*, p. 314.

and revert into one another in the horrific reality of the concentration camps. In a word: it is a work of negative dialectics in operation. True to the open-ended nature of negative dialectics, the *Dialektik der Aufklärung* does not terminate in a positive vision for a society *beyond* the dialectic of enlightenment, but attempts instead to disclose the historical conditions of possibility for civilization's relapse into utter barbarity that they witnessed in horror from their American exile.

This ominous diachronic account of how reason has unfolded in human history carries the pessimistic gist of Pollock's analysis of state capitalism to a more general philosophical and world-historical level of abstraction. By generalizing the central thesis of Pollock's political-economic argument, it maintains that Marx's analysis of *bourgeois*-liberal capitalism represents but one moment in a human history characterized by the struggle to wrest power over human life from the grip of blind natural causation.[53] It discloses how the profit motive at the heart of Marx's critique of political economy is in fact a particular instantiation of the more general power motive at work in the world-historical realization of the enlightenment project as instrumental reason, which has broken out in full force in the totalitarianism and industrialized genocide of the fascist state. After the traumatic memory of Auschwitz has been brutally carved into the annals of human history— the *Dialektik der Aufklärung* insists—critical theory can never again return to even the cautious Marxian optimism of Horkheimer's original paradigm.

3.3 A Physiognomy of Late-Capitalist Society

The diachronic account of reason's reversion into barbarism offered in the *Dialektik der Aufklärung* represents the historical background for Adorno's sociological account of late-capitalist society. The core of this account is the exchange principle's objective domination over social life in what Adorno calls the *administered world* and the identity principle's subjective domination over the human mind in what he calls the *universal system of delusion* (*der universelle Verblendungszusammenhang*). However, let us first look at Adorno's methodological approach to social inquiry and then address these subjective and objective sides of domination in turn. In a number of essays on social theory and social-scientific method from the 1960s, Adorno advances a dialectic and holistic approach to society, understood as a *process* in which particular social phenomena are 'mediated' by the societal structure as a whole.

In his 1962 confrontation with Karl Popper over the 'logic of the social sciences'—subsequently dubbed *der Positivismusstreit*—Adorno defends his dialectical approach against Popper's critical rationalism. True to his falsificationist

---

[53] Theodor W. Adorno, 'Reflexionen zur Klassentheorie', *Soziologische Schriften I*, (Frankfurt: Suhrkamp Verlag, 2003), pp. 380–381.

view of the scientific method, Popper's account of social-scientific method sees the objectivity of the social sciences as given by their commitment to falsify hypotheses deduced from theory in response to 'a discovery of an inner contradiction between our supposed knowledge and the supposed facts'.[54] The central task of sociology, Popper argues, is to seek a non-contradictory and non-falsifiable account of 'situational logic'—an explanation of action with reference to objective factors in the actor's practical situation—and of social traditions, institutions, and the unintended aggregate consequences of individual purposive action.

Somewhat uncharitably, Adorno consistently refers to this approach as 'positivist'. This pools Popper's account together with more crudely empiricist approaches, which begin from immediate 'social facts' such as opinions, attitudes, and the self-understanding of individual subjects and construes 'society' simply as the 'average consciousness'.[55] However, what in Adorno's view nevertheless justifies the moniker—which is equally disliked by Popper—is that Popper remains committed to an understanding of scientific practice in terms of the scientist's 'problematizing observation' of social reality: observation of theoretically problematic social facts and subsequent theory construction and deduction of explanatory hypotheses, even if Popper has a fairly inclusive view of what counts as social facts.

Against this approach, Adorno emphasizes both (echoing Horkheimer's *Traditionelle und kritische Theorie*) the intertwinement of social-scientific knowledge and social practice, and (echoing Lukács's *Geschichte und Klassenbewusstsein*) the concept of *totality* and the distinction between essence and appearance. The emphasis on the concept of totality reflects Adorno's holistic conviction that it is impossible to understand particular social phenomena without understanding the overall societal context from which they emerge, and of which, in some way or another, they are always to some extent an expression. Echoing Durkheim, however, Adorno claims that the totality does not itself appear as a social fact, but must rather be theoretically comprehended through the particular social facts that give expression to it:

> That society cannot be pinned down as a fact reflects the practical circumstance of mediation: that the facts are not final and impenetrable in the manner in which the predominant sociology construes them, according to the pattern of sensual data associated with traditional epistemology. In the facts, something appears, which they are not. It is far from the slightest difference between the positivist and the dialectical conception that the positivist ... only allows appearances whereas dialectics insists on the distinction between essence and

---

[54] Karl Popper, 'Die Logik der Sozialwissenschaften', in *Der Positivismusstreit in der deutschen Soziologie*, ed. by Theodor W. Adorno et al. (Berlin: Luchterhand, 1971).
[55] Theodor W. Adorno, 'Einleitung zum "Positivismusstreit in der deutschen Soziologie"', *Soziologische Schriften I*, (Frankfurt: Suhrkamp Verlag, 2003), p. 278.

appearance. According to the latter, it is a law of society that decisive structures of the social process—like the inequality of the apparent equivalents, which are exchanged—are incomprehensible without the intervention of theory.[56]

A similar argument is made in the essay 'Society' (*Gesellschaft*) from 1965, in which Adorno maintains that 'society is essentially a process' and that 'only a fully developed [theory] is able to account for society'.[57] A theory of society is necessary, because individual social facts can only be understood in terms of the societal context that continuously enables and conditions them as social facts: 'society appears in actual social situations'.[58] For the same reason, social conflicts are incomprehensible if they are not understood with reference to the *kind* of society in which they appear; they are 'the masks of deeper antagonisms':

> What is decisive, in the case of wage satisfaction as in all others, is the power relations, the employers' command of the production apparatus, if only in an indirect manner. Without an explicit awareness thereof, no individual situation can be sufficiently comprehended without assigning to the part what really belongs to the whole, within which alone it has its meaning and importance. Just as little as the mediation of society would exist without that which is mediated, without the elements: individual human beings, individual institutions, and individual situations; just as little do these elements exist without the mediation. When the details come to seem the strongest reality of all on account of their tangible immediacy, they blind the eye to genuine perception.[59]

Adorno's attitude towards mainstream social-scientific methods of quantitative and qualitative research is somewhat ambiguous, but he insists that the outcome of such research methods will remain incomprehensible if they are not understood in terms of a theory of society, which aspires not to rid itself of all contradictions, but rather accepts certain contradictions as reflections of the actual contradictions and antagonisms that pervade the social reality of late-capitalist society. In other words, Adorno argues that *critique*—a concept to which Popper and Adorno are both committed—cannot simply denote the aspiration to rid scientific knowledge of all contradictions, but must take account of the objective contradictions of social reality: between what society claims to be and what it is not; between what is individually and collectively rational; between its promise of freedom, equality, and prosperity, and its reality of unfreedom, inequality, and privation.[60] To simply rid the theory of these contradictions between ideal and reality would be to miss

---

[56] Adorno, 'Einleitung zum "Positivismusstreit in der deutschen Soziologie"', p. 291.
[57] Adorno, 'Gesellschaft', pp. 9–11.
[58] Adorno, 'Gesellschaft', p. 10.
[59] Adorno, 'Gesellschaft', pp. 10–11.
[60] Adorno, 'Einleitung zum "Positivismusstreit in der deutschen Soziologie"', p. 304.

the essence of late-capitalist society, which presupposes some form of widespread belief in and adherence to its ideals for its continued existence, and, consequently, to misjudge the very nature of the object of social-scientific research.

3.3.1 The Administered World

Adorno's concept for the condition of late-capitalist society, coined not for the purpose of describing the totalitarian Nazi state but the more subtly technocratic postwar society, is the highly suggestive but rather elusive notion of the 'administered world'—a society freed from fascist barbarism but still fully in the grip of instrumental reason. The term first appeared in a radio conversation with Horkheimer and the sociologist and Holocaust-survivor Eugen Kogon from 1950, where Adorno gives an intuitive account of his idea of the administered world that is worth quoting at length:

> The great majority of humanity has long since been reduced to mere functions within the monstrous societal machinery in which we are all embedded. Perhaps one can even put in such extreme terms and say that genuine living, in the sense that the word living has for all of us, no longer exists. More or less, as formulated by the important 19th century author Ferdinand Kürnberger: 'Life does not live'. And the phenomenon that I thereby seek to describe seems to me the most meaningful expression of that which we are speaking today, namely the transition of the whole world—all of life—into a system of administration: a particular kind of management from above ... Human beings are allowed an ever-narrower room for straying from those forms, the societally obligatory forms in which they exist. And through these forms, the pressure, the compulsion to adapt has become ever greater, and the possibility for living a life independently of this societal mechanism has become ever smaller. There are, accordingly, no possibilities for standing out any longer, and human beings therefore tend on their own account to repeat all these processes of administration that are inflicted upon them from without in themselves. In a sense, every individual becomes an administrative functionary of his or her own self.[61]

What Adorno describes here is a society in which instrumental reason has become so all-encompassing and social reality reified, objectified, commodified, and homogenized to such an extent that every individual being living in that society faces an extremely narrow space for the kind of actions that they are able to perform and the kind of people they are able to be. When everything has been paved

---

[61] Theodor W. Adorno, Max Horkheimer, Eugen Kogon, 'Die verwaltete Welt oder: Die Krisis des Individuums', in Max Horkheimer, *Gesammelte Schriften Band 13: Nachgelassene Schriften 1949–1972* (Frankfurt: Fisher Verlag, 1989), pp. 122–124.

over and prepared for integration into a total system of administration, living a life in which one resists *mitspielen*—'playing along', which is a notion that Adorno often invokes—in the established order of things has become next to impossible.

The sense of the predicate 'administered' that Adorno has in mind is not only its ordinary language-sense, in which administration suggests a form of top-down management—although he explicitly invokes that connotation as well. It is also meant to suggest an impersonal and anonymous form of structural normalization at work through the rules and norms—the 'societal machinery'—that govern our practices and through which we govern ourselves: 'the web of society has become so dense, the growing concentration of the economy, the executive and the bureaucracy has advanced to such an extent that people are reduced more and more to the status of functions'.[62] 'Administration' thus means for Adorno a kind of radical extension of Lukács's concept of reification, in which the objectification, commodification, and regimentation experienced by the worker in the production process has been extended to encompass virtually all spheres of social life.

Evidently, much in Adorno's striking claim that life in this kind of society 'does not live' depends on the sense of 'living' that he has in mind. Adorno's point here, I believe, should be understood in the sense that the activity of living means something particular *for us*—the children of the Enlightenment—namely living according to our own judgement, determining our own affairs, pursuing our own ends according to our own reasons. When these affairs, ends, and reasons have become predefined by an all-pervasive 'societal machinery' to have meaning and significance only in strictly limited and circumscribed terms, a mockery is made of the connotations that the world 'living'—for *us*—shares with the word 'autonomy'. In the administered world of late-capitalist society, life itself is damaged because our possibilities for straying from the societally preordained path, for standing out from the crowd, for relating to one another in a non-dominating way, have been all but obliterated, and we are therefore reduced, by society, to living a *heteronomous* life. Adorno's claim is thus that we find ourselves in a societal context of pervasive *social heteronomy*, which narrows, homogenizes, and restricts the practical content of our lives to such an extent that the very idea of living has all but lost its meaning.

Adorno shares with the rest of the IfS circle the Marxian assumption that the forces of production have been developed to such an extent that it would actually be possible to organize society beyond the imperatives of survival (Marx's 'realm of necessity') by enabling material abundance (undercutting the need for exchange) and the drastic reduction of the length of the working day (undercutting the reduction of human beings to their societal functions). Moreover, as in Pollock's concept of state capitalism, Adorno assumes that central parts of the basic

---

[62] Theodor W. Adorno, *Zur Lehre von der Geschichte und der Freiheit* (Frankfurt: Suhrkamp Verlag, 2006), pp. 11–12.

structure of *bourgeois*-liberal capitalism remain fundamentally unchanged in late-capitalist society, in the sense that the means of production still serve the extraction of surplus value and accumulation of capital for a small minority, rather than the gratification of the needs of humanity at large. Particular interests still hold sway over the production process, although the power of government officials and captains of industry have largely merged into one. Because the material conditions for organizing society beyond structurally produced suffering and generalized reification are thus at hand, Adorno's claim that we are all in thrall to all-powerful forces of social heteronomy does not appeal to a purely abstract ideal or far-fetched utopia, but criticizes society's mode of organization for its continued obstruction of a real possibility of constituting a social world in which human beings can live truly autonomous lives.

As we have seen, Adorno understands the exchange-principle as the principal medium of instrumental reason operative in late-capitalist society—as the valuative standardization and commodification of nature and human relations writ large. This unrelenting process of material identification, categorization, and instrumentalization is the all-pervasive integrative principle of social reality, which determines social institutions as much as, ultimately, human subjectivity:

> Insofar as this ['ether of society'] seems abstract, its abstractness does not stem from high-minded, idiosyncratic, and fact-obstinate thinking, but rather from the exchange relation, the real abstraction, which the societal life-process obeys. The power of this *Abstractum* is more tangible than that of every single institution, which taciturnly constitutes itself according to this schema and induces it into human beings. The powerlessness that every single individual experiences vis-à-vis the whole is its drastic expression.[63]

However, in contrast to Marx, the exchange-principle is primarily of *qualitative* significance for Adorno, since he does not believe that the labour theory of value survives the transformation of society from *bourgeois*-liberal to late capitalism as an exact economic basis for determining the rate of exploitation. In other words, Adorno's construal of Marx's value theory does not imply a technical, quantitative economic notion, which explains the production of surplus value in the capitalist mode of production, but rather is invoked in support of the social-theoretical and psychological theses of a pervasive reification and commodification of subjects and social relations. Although crucial structural aspects of *bourgeois*-liberal capitalism persist in late-capitalist society—and some of them even in amplified form—these different elements do not form a coherent, rationally penetrable whole, as they once did.

---

[63] Theodor W. Adorno, 'Spätkapitalismus oder Industriegesellschaft', in *Soziologische Schriften I*, pp. 364–365.

In other words, it is still very much the case that 'rule over human beings is exercised through the economic process', but according to Adorno the *modus operandi* of the system has become much less transparent than in Marx's day, since the boundaries between the economy and state power have increasingly become blurred:

> Marx had an easier task, since he was already confronted with the comprehensively developed system of liberalism in the [economic] science. He only had to ask if capitalism corresponded to this model in its own dynamic categories in order to develop an accurate theory of the system as a determinate negation of the received theoretical system [of classical political economy]. In the meantime, the market economy has become so diluted that no such confrontation is possible. The irrationality of the present structure of society obstructs its rational comprehension in theory.[64]

However, even if late-capitalist society cannot be rationally comprehended as a system or social totality in the same way as the more transparent *bourgeois*-liberal capitalism that Marx subjected to critical analysis in *Capital*, it remains the case, as we have seen, that certain general features of late capitalism can nonetheless be clearly grasped in their concrete wrongness:

> Even if the theory of immiseration [*Verelendungstheorie*] was not corroborated *à la lettre*, it has nonetheless come true in the no less alarming sense of the universal diffusion of the unfreedom of human beings, their dependence upon a machinery that flows from the consciousness of those who use it. The universally derided immaturity [*Unmündigkeit*] of the masses is only a reflection of the fact that they are less masters of their own lives than ever before; just as in myth, their lives are inflicted upon them as a destiny.[65]

3.3.2 Ego-Weakness and the Universal System of Delusion

The total administration of human life characteristic of late capitalism represents a formidable obstacle to escaping the social heteronomy of our present existence, in Adorno's view, but it is not alone in doing so. In addition, individuals living in late-capitalist society are subject to powerful forces of inner, subjective domination and self-control. Adorno develops a Freudian account of the bridge between objective and subjective domination—or, rather, of the subjective internalization of outer, objective domination. As we saw in Chapter 1, Freud maintains that the

---

[64] Adorno, 'Spätkapitalismus oder Industriegesellschaft', p. 359.
[65] Adorno, 'Spätkapitalismus oder Industriegesellschaft', p. 360.

ego is produced through the attempt of the subject, beginning in early childhood, to balance libidinal energies and the requirements of the external world, in particular through its struggle to overcome the Oedipus complex. In doing so, the ego becomes the 'administrator' of the self, adapting the individual psyche to external circumstance by imposing a delay of gratification.

Moreover, as we saw in his discussion of the Odyssey in Section 3.2, Adorno thinks that the ego is *itself* a historical achievement—the result of a dialectical, historical process of enlightenment. In line with Horkheimer, Adorno thinks that one of the advances of *bourgeois*-liberal capitalism was that, among certain classes, it provided the social conditions for the development of a strong ego, with the ability to appropriately mediate between the competing demands issuing from the id, the superego, and reality. This 'ego-strength' is a necessary condition for autonomous reflection and self-control, but it is a mixed blessing, since it does so only at the expense of subjecting inner nature to the ego's commands. The resulting split between nature and culture, body and mind within the human being paves the way for a subjective dialectic of enlightenment, implying that the possibility of human autonomy has come only at the price of objectifying self-mastery (*Selbstbeherrschung*) and the subjection of inner, libidinal nature to instrumental reason. In other words, freedom and domination have been bequeathed to us hand in hand:

> [C]haracter or will, which has become objectified in human beings from and against their reflexes, is the potential organ of freedom and at the same time undermines it. The reason is that it embodies the principle of domination, to which human beings progressively subject themselves. Identity of the self and self-alienation go together from the beginning ... In this way, they become juxtaposed to themselves ... as something external, according to the model of the outer world of things subject to causality.[66]

Adorno follows Horkheimer in his diagnosis that, in late-capitalist society, even the positive side of this mixed blessing is lost: namely, the precarious possibility of autonomous thought and action. Indeed, in the administered world, the ego is weakened to such an extent that the psychological basis for autonomy is all but undermined. Instead, the individual integrates external social compulsion and unreflectively allows social expectations to usurp the superego's function as the individual's conscience, undermining the ego's ability to reflect on or resist the demands and pressures of the social context. The weakened ego thus becomes the organ of social heteronomy in the individual psyche, ensuring that individual thought and action conforms to the 'reality principle': the ever-narrower

---

[66] Adorno, *Negative Dialektik*, p. 216.

constraints and limitations imposed on individual thought and action by the administered world.[67]

Moreover, the ego-weakness characteristic of the individual in the administered world is reinforced by what Adorno often refers to as *the universal system of delusion* (*der universelle Verblendungszusammenhang*). The universal system of delusion is Adorno's term of art for the belief system characteristic of late-capitalism—the spell that must be broken by negative dialectics, which Adorno at one point describes as 'at once imprint of the universal system of delusion and its critique'.[68] In Adorno's work, the universal system of delusion is intimately connected with the concepts of ideology and false consciousness, and unpacking these the latter two concepts will therefore help us account for the former.

In Adorno's terms, the concept of false consciousness refers, quite simply, to false beliefs about society and the world, about oneself and one's needs and situation, and about other human beings. However, the key to understanding Adorno's conception of ideology is to see that it does not simply denote false belief, nor even a kind of false consciousness leading an individual to serve another against his or her own interests, but rather what Adorno calls 'societally necessary illusion' (*gesellschaftlich notwendiger Schein*)[69]—or 'objectively necessary and likewise false consciousness'.[70] Ideology in this sense is a distinctively modern phenomenon, which can perhaps best be explained with reference to the claim that late-capitalist society is inherently contradictory.

As we saw in Chapter 1's discussion of the model of immanent critique developed by the young Horkheimer, the normative contradiction of capitalist society is the gulf between the normative promises of *bourgeois* morality and the history and reality of actual capitalist society. This gulf implies that members of modern society, who believe in the reality of its promises, have false beliefs about the society they live in: they believe that society offers them something that in fact it does not—freedom, equality, opportunity, etc. However, what renders these beliefs *ideological* is the more specific circumstance that such beliefs at once *derive from* and *feed back into* the basic structure of capitalist society itself: they are 'necessary' in the twin sense that they are inevitably produced by the structure of social life and fulfil a crucial function in its reproduction.[71]

In a society integrated through the exchange-principle, individuals encounter each other as free and equal on the market, and as long as they remain oblivious to the unfreedom and inequality to which they are subject in the sphere of

---

[67] Theodor W. Adorno, 'Bemerkungen über Politik und Neurose', in *Soziologische Schriften I*; Theodor W. Adorno, *Studien zum autoritären Charakter* (Frankfurt: Suhrkamp Verlag, 1995).
[68] Adorno, *Negative Dialektik*, p. 379.
[69] Adorno, *Negative Dialektik*, p. 44.
[70] Theodor W. Adorno, 'Beitrag zur Ideologienlehre', *Soziologische Schriften I*, p. 465.
[71] Theodor W. Adorno, 'Kulturkritik und Gesellschaft', in *Kulturkritik und Gesellschaft I: Prismen. Ohne Leitbild. Gesammelte Schriften Band 10.1* (Frankfurt: Suhrkamp Verlag, 2003), p. 21.

production, they mistakenly believe themselves to *be* free and equal. Moreover, the continued existence of capitalist society presupposes that a sufficiently large number of workers entertain such false beliefs; that workers misunderstand their true condition. However, because ideologies are intimately connected with the constitutive contradictions of capitalist society in this way, they also have a *truth content* in virtue of their explication of the unredeemed promises of the social order. Just as the young Horkheimer, Adorno believes that immanent critique can bring this truth content to bear on ideologies, and the numbing reality of the social order of late capitalism that they complacently serve to justify, by disclosing the wrongness of reality through what Adorno calls 'a physiognomy of society'.[72]

> In the end, the material process of production as such is revealed to be what it, besides the means for the preservation of life, always already was: ideology; the counterparts' false consciousness of one another, deriving from the exchange-relation.[73]

The notion of ideology as societally necessary false consciousness represents the conceptual core of the universal system of delusion, but Adorno broadens and extrapolates this (objectively compelled) subjective misperception to a much wider scope of social relations. Although he never explicitly defines the system of delusion, we may think of it—in accordance with his thesis of the primacy of the object—simply as the forms of thought and self-consciousness engendered by and supportive of the administrative world.

The connection between ideology and the system of delusion can be seen in Adorno's invocation of the German word *Verblendung* (which I have translated as 'delusion', but which might also be translated as 'blindness' or 'veneer') and its play on the double meaning of the word *Schein*, which can refer both to the shining of light and the (misleading) appearance of something. *Verblendung* can mean 'blinded' in a sensory sense as well as 'deluded' in a cognitive sense, as in, on the one hand, having one's sight blinded by a flashing of light, and, on the other, being deluded by the appearance of something, mistaking this appearance for what it really is. The term *Verblendungszusammenhang* (system of delusion) thus invokes both the kind of sensory confusion that the experience of being blinded by the obfuscating mechanisms of late-capitalist society evokes—its complete lack of transparency as a social form—as well as the cognitive mistake involved in its members' misapprehension of the appearance of society for its essential nature. The system of delusion represents those forms of thought that emanate from and provide cognitive and motivational support for the basic structure of late-capitalist society, but which also prevent individuals from seeing through its appearance

---

[72] Adorno, 'Beitrag zur Ideologienlehre', p. 465.
[73] Adorno, 'Kulturkritik und Gesellschaft', p. 25.

and grasping its true nature. Through their reified self-understanding as objects of exchange and administration, individual subjects reproduce a system that can only maintain itself on pains of stunting their subjectivity—but because they are blinded and deluded by the societally necessary illusion of late-capitalist society as rational, free, and equal, they fail to grasp the wrongness of their own form of life, and thus their state of socially engendered heteronomy.

Of particular moment in the system of delusion is what Adorno famously calls the *culture industry*. This suggestive term refers to the regression of culture—with all the evocative connotations of the German word *Kultur*—into a form of mere consumption and entertainment:

> In all divisions of the culture industry, products are more or less methodically produced, which are oriented towards consumption by masses and which to a large extent determines this consumption ... The customer is not king, as the culture industry would have us believe, not its subject, but its object.[74]

Adorno's highly sceptical view of modern culture contrasts sharply with that of his old friend Walter Benjamin. In the essay 'The Work of Art in the Age of Mechanical Reproduction', (*Das Kunstwerk im Zeitalter seiner technischen Reproduzierbarkeit*) first published in the ZfS in 1936, Benjamin argued that the mechanical reproduction of art changes the very nature of the work of art itself. On the one hand, by being reproducible and reproduced, the work of art loses its singular quality; it loses what Benjamin calls its '*aura*'—the peculiar perceptual quality of existing in the here and now. On the other hand, with new mass-produced forms of art such as photography, movies, and music, art itself is transformed, by cutting its last ties to rituals and myth and gaining in what Benjamin calls 'exhibition value'. According to Benjamin, the mechanical reproduction of art has the potential both for providing access to new forms of much more detailed and sensitive collective perception, as well as a potential for mass *politicization*, since 'every human being today has a claim to being filmed'[75] and this claim implicitly challenges the monopolization of 'film capital' of the means of (art) production.

For Adorno, the hopes that Benjamin invested in the mechanical reproduction of art could not be more misplaced. Indeed, Adorno sees precisely the opposite tendency at work in mechanically reproduced forms of art: namely, a means of duplicity and mass manipulation and the reduction of the receiving agent—the

---

[74] Theodor W. Adorno, 'Résumé über Kulturindustrie', in *Kulturkritik und Gesellschaft I: Prismen. Ohne Leitbild. Gesammelte Schriften Band 10.1* (Frankfurt: Suhrkamp Verlag, 2003), p. 337.

[75] Walter Benjamin, 'Das Kunstwerk im Zeitalter seiner technischen Reproduzierbarkeit', in *Gesammelte Schriften I:I*, p. 455.

movie-goer or the pop-music listener—to a mere consumer, whose experience has been carefully engineered:

> At its core, culture never merely deferred to the will of human beings, but also always objected to the petrified relations under which they live, and in doing so, it honoured human beings. However, by completely mimicking the humans, culture becomes entirely incorporated into the petrified relations and thereby degrades humans once more. Cultural [*geistige*] artefacts of a culture-industrial kind are no longer *also* commodities, but are commodities through and through.[76]

These remarks point to Adorno's high opinion of modern 'autonomous art', which aims at giving expression to the non-identical and all that which doesn't fit into a world in which everything supposedly fits. Autonomous art has value precisely by *not* being determined by its exchange value, by *not* being directed towards the gratification of the customer's needs, but rather by bringing forth the underlying antagonistic and unreconciled reality in an aesthetic reconciliation, which testifies to the wrongness of the world precisely by showing this reconciliation to be merely aesthetic and unreal.[77] In Adorno's view, the culture industry thus assaults the very nature of autonomous art precisely by engineering its own reception, and by catering to existing demand rather than posing a challenge to the society that fashions it. To be sure, the culture industry may *appear* to produce singular 'works of art', but its products are in fact mere exemplars of standardized forms and 'genres' that never surprise or challenge but merely gratify existing tastes, which the culture industry has largely itself defined. Adorno even goes so far as to formulate a 'categorical imperative of the culture industry', which states that 'you must adapt, without specifying to what; blend into whatever exists, and into that which everyone already thinks, as a reflex to its power and omnipresence'.[78]

Adorno suggestively compares the function of the culture industry with Kant's notion of the schematism of the imagination—this 'hidden art in the depths of the human soul'[79]—which mediates between the pure concepts of the understanding and empirical intuitions, enabling the subsumption of objects under concepts. Adorno claims that in late-capitalist society, this schematic function—a cornerstone of Kant's transcendental idealism—is increasingly fulfilled by the culture industry, which fits and narrows the conceptual schemes of its customers to a

---

[76] Adorno, 'Résumé über Kulturindustrie', p. 338.
[77] Adorno, *Ästhetische Theorie*.
[78] Adorno, 'Résumé über Kulturindustrie', p. 343.
[79] Immanuel Kant, *The Critique of Pure Reason*, p. 271.

natural and social reality reduced to commodities by the capitalist productive apparatus.[80] The culture industry is thus the systemically organized pre-emption of autonomy through the 'industrialised' manipulative determination of the content of consciousness and the 'stunting of the imagination and spontaneity of the cultural consumers'.[81] In the culture industry, enlightenment as technical mastery of nature is utilized for the manipulation of needs; it is, as the title of the chapter on the culture industry in *Dialektik der Aufklärung* suggests, 'enlightenment as mass-deception':

> The total effect of the culture industry is one of anti-enlightenment; in the culture industry, as Horkheimer and I defined it, enlightenment, as the continuous technical mastery of nature, becomes a means for the fettering of consciousness. The culture industry obstructs the formation of autonomous, independent, consciously judging and deciding individuals.[82]

This analysis connects with Adorno's remarks in *Negative Dialektik* on the failure of culture to prevent Auschwitz. In Adorno's view, 'After Auschwitz, all culture is garbage, including its urgent criticism'.[83] Since culture so readily 'restored itself after what occurred in its landscape, it has entirely become ideology'.[84] However, not only by simply carrying on after the fact, by continuing to produce poetry and music,[85] but also by being unable to prevent the extinction of the European Jews, modern culture—and, in particular, modern German culture—was complicit in their murder. Culture has always played the ideological function of sugar coating the suffering of everyday material life, by offering the rationalized consolation of a higher meaning. However, the ovens of the concentration camps, in which so many human bodies evaporated, also 'burned without consolation all assuaging aspects of *Geist* and its objectification, culture'.[86]

In a more general sense, Adorno thinks that it is the human catastrophe of Auschwitz that ultimately testifies to the inherent radial evil of late-capitalist society, and its potential for turning the amassed technical apparatus of humanity against human beings themselves. As such, Auschwitz serves for Adorno the inverse theoretical function of what the French Revolution served for Kant, who, in *The Conflict of the Faculties* from 1798, pointed to the occurrence of the French

---

[80] Horkheimer and Adorno, *Dialektik der Aufklärung*, p. 149.
[81] Horkheimer Adorno, *Dialektik der Aufklärung*, p. 151.
[82] Adorno, 'Résumé über Kulturindustrie', p. 345.
[83] Adorno, *Negative Dialektik*, p. 359.
[84] Adorno, *Negative Dialektik*, p. 359.
[85] Cf. Adorno's famous remark, 'to write a poem after Auscwitz is barbaric', in 'Kulturkritik und Gesellschaft', p. 30
[86] Adorno, *Negative Dialektik*, p. 358.

Revolution and the generally sympathetic public reactions it elicited from ordinary people as evidence for the 'moral progress of the human race'.[87]

By contrast, Adorno thinks that the occurrence of Auschwitz is evidence for the hitherto-unimaginable scale of the destructive potential inherent in the dialectic of enlightenment—a potential that was far from effaced through the Allied victory over Nazi Germany. Indeed, although Hitler's murderous fascism was ultimately defeated, Adorno is convinced that the 'objective societal presuppositions' that enabled it 'continue to exist', primarily in virtue of the underlying 'economic order', which 'still submits the majority to dependence on given factors over which they have no control, and to a state of intellectual immaturity [*Unmündigkeit*]'.[88] As long as human beings continue to live in a state of social heteronomy and suffer from ego-weakness and subjective delusion, which ensure their loyalty to even the most destructive and immoral social order, the fundamentally irrational nature of late-capitalist society risks reverting into human catastrophes of unimaginably destructive potential. Adorno found ample post-war evidence for this fear in the two super-powers' development of ever more destructive thermonuclear weapons, and in how breathtakingly near they came to deploying this species-exterminating technology during the 1962 Cuban missile crisis.

To be sure, the claim that Auschwitz has disclosed human civilization's inherent potential for self-destruction may seem somewhat far-fetched today, with seventy years separating us from the defeat of Hitler's armies, and even the Cold War a thing of the past. Moreover, Adorno's holistic approach to society as a dialectical process in which individual actions mediate the societal totality is arguably deeply at odds with the methodological individualism predominant in contemporary social science, as he was very much aware. Accordingly, to many contemporary social scientists the claim that particular phenomena express certain features of the social totality within which they appear may seem like a remnant of speculative philosophy in Adorno's thought, for which there is no place in modern science.

However, one might argue in response that even today we do not seem to lack examples that testify to the precarious character of human existence in a way that seems to reflect uncomfortable truths about the social system as a whole: as the extent of anthropogenic climate change becomes ever more evident, along with the glaring collective irrationality of the fact that human civilization may very well be on its way to making our planet uninhabitable in pursuit of wealth still overwhelmingly benefitting a small minority, Adorno's fears of the immense destructive potential inherent in the productive apparatus of late-capitalist society

---

[87] Immanuel Kant, 'The Conflict of the Faculties', in *Religion and Rational Theology*, transl. by Allen Wood (Cambridge: Cambridge University Press, 1996), p. 301.
[88] Theodor W. Adorno, *Erziehung zur Mündigkeit* (Frankfurt: Suhrkamp Verlag, 2013), p. 22.

may prove to be of no little relevance still. I will return to the question of Adorno's contemporary relevance in the shadow of the prospect of catastrophic climate change—as an 'ecological dialectic of enlightenment'—in Chapter 4.

3.4 The Dialectic of Individual Autonomy

Having accounted for the historical dimension of Adorno's negativist paradigm in Section 3.2 and its sociological dimension in Section 3.3, I now turn to its normative dimension—the conception of human freedom that informs Adorno's account of the forms of domination that the basic structure of late-capitalist society enables and sustains. Notwithstanding his dialectical treatment of the concept, the concept of freedom in Adorno's thought means—above all—freedom as autonomy. However, he offers a highly distinctive account of the social presuppositions of the possibility of living an autonomous life that, once again, places the concept of the 'non-identical' at its centre.

3.4.1 Mündigkeit

In a short but compelling essay on the concept of 'Critique' (*Kritik*) published only a month before his death, Adorno defines autonomy in a straightforwardly Kantian sense as 'judgement according to one's own insight, in contrast to heteronomy as obedience to the recommendations of others'.[89] However, in contrast to Kant, who understood autonomy as a belonging to every rational being in virtue of their noumenal selves, Adorno, much like the young Horkheimer, conceives of autonomy wholly as a *social and historical achievement*: as a potential in human beings that requires certain historical, social, and psychological conditions for its full development. For Adorno, freedom is seen 'not only as concept but also as experiential content', which 'whole epochs, whole societies lacked', and which 'could be wholly extinguished again, perhaps without leaving even a trace'.[90]

This appreciation of the social and historical conditions of autonomy links with the intimate connection, for Kant as well as for Adorno, between the concept of autonomy and the German word *Mündigkeit*. *Mündigkeit* is not an easy word to translate, but its closest English equivalent may be the somewhat convoluted 'state of intellectual maturity'. In the *Kritik* essay, and in the radio conversation 'Education towards *Mündigkeit*' (*Erziehung zur Mündigkeit*) recorded in the same year, Adorno explicitly aligns himself with Kant's conception of *Mündigkeit*, as this concept is developed in Kant's programmatic essay 'An Answer to the Question:

---

[89] Adorno, 'Kritik', in *Kulturkritik und Gesellschaft II*, p. 786.
[90] Adorno, *Negative Dialektik*, pp. 217–218.

What is Enlightenment?' from 1784. In that essay's opening lines, Kant provides his famous definition of enlightenment as

> *the human being's emergence [Ausgang] from his self-incurred immaturity [Unmündigkeit].* Immaturity is inability to make use of one's own understanding without direction from another. This immaturity is *self-incurred* when its cause lies not in lack of understanding but in lack of resolution and courage to use it without direction from another. *Sapere aude!* Have courage to make use of your *own* understanding! is thus the motto of enlightenment.[91]

Adorno refers to Kant's programme as 'extraordinarily relevant for our times [*außerordentlich aktuell*]', but he downplays Kant's emphasis on individual courage and volitional resolution in favour of a focus on the *social conditions* of autonomy and *Mündigkeit*. To be sure, this is not because he thinks the volitional dimension of *Mündigkeit* is irrelevant. However, he is convinced that under the social conditions of late-capitalist society it makes no sense to hold individuals responsible for their intellectual immaturity, since they are in the grip of such powerful forces of social heteronomy, which make a right life—*ein mündiges Leben*—impossible:

> He who speaks for himself, because he has thought for himself and doesn't just blindly accept the advice of others; he who is not patronised [*bevormundet wird*]—he is *mündig*. This shows itself in the power to resist pre-given opinions, and in unison with this, also to resist merely given institutions, *to resist all that is merely given*, which justifies itself with reference to its mere existence. Such resistance, as the capacity to distinguish between insight and the merely conventionally accepted, or that which is accepted under the coercion of authority, is one with critique—a concept that derives from the Greek *krino*, deciding. It would not be a gross exaggeration to regard the modern concept of reason as one with the concept of critique.[92]

It is hardly surprising that Adorno should choose to single out 'What is Enlightenment?' as the locus of his own commitment to Kant's programme. As Michel Foucault has later argued, Kant's approach in this text is both remarkably original and in some contrast to the more systematic parts of his oeuvre, in that his intention is to reflect on the historical claim that his is an 'age of enlightenment'. However, he pursues this intention not as a defence of his time as an 'enlightened age', or in terms of a philosophy of history that situates his age in the totality of a history moving towards perfect enlightenment. Rather, Kant

---

[91] Immanuel Kant, 'An answer to the question: What is enlightenment?', in *Practical Philosophy*, transl. by Mary J. Gregor (Cambridge: Cambridge University Press, 1999), p. 17 [translation amended].
[92] Adorno, 'Kritik', pp. 786–787 [emphasis added].

here provides a purely *negative* definition of enlightenment as the *Ausgang*—the 'emergence' or 'departure'—of human beings from their self-incurred immaturity, *Unmündigkeit*.[93] Although Adorno maintains that the most pertinent modern-day challenge to Kant's programme is less individual lack of courage than the administered world and the universal system of delusion, his own answer to the question 'what is enlightenment?' is nevertheless remarkably similar to Kant's in both substantive content and the negative character of its definition—even if, as we shall see, Adorno transforms the optimistically progressive aspects of Kant's programme into a more defensive notion of 'resistance'.

The commitment to *Mündigkeit* represents, I want to suggest, the normative core of Adorno's negativist paradigm of critical theory. As he notes in a different context, 'I understand an autonomous [*mündigen*] human being as one, who has the actual ability to determine his own fate in reality, and that implies an arrangement, an organisation of reality such that autonomous [*mündigen*] human beings are able to live in it.'[94] However, true to his negativistic philosophical commitments, Adorno never provides a comprehensive elaboration on what such a society—a society fit for autonomous human beings—would look like. Since we have no epistemic access to what a right society would be from our own reified and delusional form of life, we could only hope to advance towards a society fit for autonomous human beings through the determinate negation of present wrongness, in thought as well as in practice.

Moreover, Adorno's account of the dialectical origins of autonomy substantially complicates this picture. It is worth recapitulating this dialectic by quoting a rather lengthy passage from the *Dialektik der Aufklärung*, which weaves together a number of the central themes from Adorno's thought discussed in this chapter:

> In its confrontations with the superego, the ego, the agency of social control within the individual, keeps the drives within the limits set by self-preservation ... [and] this complex psychic apparatus enabled the relatively free interplay of subjects, which constituted the market economy. In the era of large conglomerates and world wars, however, the mediation of the social process by innumerable monads is proving obsolete. The subjects of the drive economy become psychologically expropriated, and the drive economy is more rationally operated by society itself. The individual is no longer forced to decide what he or she is supposed to do in a given situation in a painful inner dialogue between conscience, self-preservation, and drives. For the human being as a wage earner, the decision is taken by a hierarchy extending from trade associations to the national

---

[93] Michel Foucault, 'What is Enlightenment?', in *The Politics of Truth* (Cambridge MA: Semiotext(e), 2007).
[94] Adorno makes this statement in a television appearance reproduced in the documentary 'Der Bürger Als Revolutionär', by Meinhard Prill and Kurt Schneider, SWR Fernsehen BW. Unfortunately, I have not been able to find a transcribed version of the original television appearance.

administration; in the private sphere, it is taken by the schema of mass culture, which appropriates even the most intimate impulses of its forced consumers. The committees and [movie] stars function as ego and superego, and the masses, stripped of even the semblance of personality, are molded far more compliantly by catchwords and models than ever the instincts were by the internal censor. If, in liberalism, the individuation of part of the population was necessary for the adaptation of society as a whole to the state of technology, today the functioning of the economic apparatus demands that the masses be directed without the hindrance of individuation. The economically determined direction of the whole society, which has always governed the mental and physical constitution of human beings, is stunting the organs that enabled individuals to manage their lives autonomously. Now that thinking has become a mere sector of the division of labor, the plans of the authorized experts and leaders have made individuals who plan their own happiness redundant. The irrationality of the unresisting and eager adaptation to reality becomes, for the individual, more reasonable than reason. If, previously, the bourgeois had introjected the compulsions as a duty of conscience into themselves and the workers, now the entirety of the human being has become the subject-object of repression. In the progress of industrial society, which is supposed to have conjured away the law of increasing misery, which it itself had brought into being, the concept which justified the whole—the human being as person, as the bearer of reason—is going under. Objectively, the dialectic of enlightenment reverts into madness.[95]

The dialectic described in these lines is that *the social conditions for autonomy*, which were painstakingly established in the long history of enlightenment and culminated in the precarious individual autonomy made possible by *bourgeois-liberal capitalism*, have been eclipsed by the human struggle to achieve mastery of nature, from which these conditions originally emerged. Accordingly, the weakening of the ego that occurs in the administered world of late-capitalism is not merely a contingent historical outcome; it rather issues from the logic of the very process that enabled it to begin with: 'Individuals, in having to fend for themselves, develop the ego as the agency of reflective foresight and overview; over successive generations it expands and contracts with the individual's prospects of economic autonomy and productive ownership.'[96] In the end, however, the combination of the level of development of the productive forces and the production relations characteristic of late capitalism makes the mind's autonomous mastery of inner nature objectively redundant, since human beings are smoothly integrated into an all-encompassing network of administration. The human quest for freedom from natural determination thus culminates in the annihilation of human freedom itself.

[95] Adorno and Horkheimer, *Dialectic of Enlightenment*, pp. 168–169 [translation amended].
[96] Adorno and Horkheimer, *Dialectic of Enlightenment*, p. 68.

3.4.2 Mimesis and an Ethics of Resistance

The normative dimension of human freedom as autonomy and *Mündigkeit* in Adorno's work is thus of an exceedingly complicated nature. The question is: how can we imagine a form of autonomy—and, further, a society fit for *mündigen Menschen*—that does not carry within itself the seeds of its own destruction? In other words, how can we hope to escape the dialectic of enlightenment? Adorno has two answers: one fairly abstract and elusive answer concerning the relationship between reason and nature, as well a more concrete response that takes the form of a negativistic personal ethics. The first answer—which we have already touched upon in previous sections—is that reason must recognize its own origins in and entanglement with both outer and inner nature; it must cease its incessant identification, subsumption, and classification, and instead recognize and respect the non-conceptual, the nonidentical, and the particular as and for what they truly are. This does not mean that thinking must give up on classification and subsumption altogether—indeed, this would be impossible—or that there can be no element of identification in practice. However, it does mean that rational thought and action must accept their own limitations and give up on the *totalitarian* aspiration to capture the whole in thought and reduce nature to human means.

To be sure, these two sides of reconciliation with nature cannot be disentangled. In *Negative Dialektik*, Adorno remarks, 'The utopia of cognition would be to gain access to the non-conceptual with concepts, without making it equal to them'.[97] But this could only ultimately occur in a society in which the objective basis for totalitarian identification—the exchange-relation—has been overcome, and where there would no longer be an objective need for the critical self-reflection of negative dialectics:

> That the non-identifiable—the use value, according to Marxian terminology—is nevertheless needed for life to sustain itself, even under the ruling relations of production, is the ineffable of utopia. The latter reaches deep into that, which is determined that it should not be realised. In view of the concrete possibility of utopia, dialectics is the ontology of the wrong state of affairs. A right condition would be freed from dialectics, neither system nor contradiction.[98]

This recognition of the natural moment in reason—the part of reason that is not itself reason, so to speak—extends, in fact, also to that most 'metaphysical' of questions: namely, freedom of the will. Adorno develops this argument through an immanent critique of Kant's account of free volition, which construes willing as purely a matter of practical reason adopting a maxim or principle. In drawing his

---

[97] Adorno, *Negative Dialektik*, p. 21.
[98] Adorno, *Negative Dialektik*, p. 22.

basic distinction between free willing and natural causation, in 'solving' the third antinomy between the practical assumption of freedom and the world as causally determined system by ascribing them to the different worlds of *noumena* and *phenomena*, and in the moral juxtaposition between duty and inclination, Kant took up his place in the dialectic of enlightenment by positing reason and freedom in opposition to nature. Kant's account of freedom of the will thus provides an influential philosophical statement of the general enlightenment project of human emancipation as total human mastery over nature.

Adorno's attempt to show that Kant's juxtaposition of freedom and nature is misguided culminates in an original account of freedom of the will, which holds that just as concepts are sedimented experience, just as all thinking originates in a somatic element of basic human needs, and just as reason ultimately derives from libidinal energies,[99] so too does the very act of willing include both a discursive and a somatic aspect. Adorno supports this claim with a phenomenology of willing in practical deliberation, according to which all willing involves a 'jolt'—a rupture in practical reasoning, its 'active' element, which prompts us to pick out one consideration as the ground of action—which does not derive from reason itself or from consciousness. This 'addendum' (*das Hinzutretende*) is spontaneity, a central concept for Adorno, which Kant had assigned to the pure understanding, but which, in Adorno's view, is actually the *somatic moment* of willing; the echo of our biological nature in the act of willing.[100]

It is clear from this account of freedom of the will that the subjection of inner nature to instrumental reason is likewise, for Adorno, a frontal assault on human spontaneity, and thus on free will itself. Social heteronomy, construed as the administration of the inner human nature of deluded subjects with weakened egos, thus undermines autonomy in a very physical sense by *stunting the natural moment in volition*—the somatic origins of spontaneity. True autonomous action is only made possible by recognizing this somatic moment in practical deliberation; by reconciling reason with nature in inner human life. These highly abstract reflections are therefore all part of Adorno's more general materialist project of enlightenment: in order to do battle with the dialectic of enlightenment, we must reconcile ourselves to our own, ineliminable nature—that nature is part and parcel of its received opposite: human agency and reason. In humanity's feverish attempt to escape nature's rule over human life, modern society has in fact become ever more akin to nature-like forces, as our immense productive apparatus for mastering nature has turned against human beings in a quasi-necessary manner, and we have ourselves become enslaved by our own means of production.[101] Only by

---

[99] Adorno, *Negative Dialektik*, p. 227.
[100] For Adorno's account of free willing, see *Negative Dialektik*, pp. 226–230. For an admirably clear reconstruction, see the appendix of Fabian Freyenhagen, *Adorno's Practical Philosophy* (Cambridge: Cambridge University Press, 2013).
[101] Adorno and Horkheimer, *Dialectic of Enlightenment*, p. 57.

recognizing our own entanglement with nature in thought and practice—through reflective insight into the entanglement of reason, will and nature—can we nurture the hope of realizing a society fit for autonomous human beings, which is at once an objective possibility at the present state of technological development, and yet so far removed that it seems a mere chimera.

The second and more immediately practical answer to how we can defy the dialectic of enlightenment is given by Adorno's negativistic personal ethics: an ethics of resistance against social heteronomy. Of course, in accordance with his negativistic assumptions, Adorno does not think that such resistance can hope to achieve any change on a societal scale, which would require a kind of collective rupture that the administered beings of late-capitalist society are in no conceivable sense capable of. The aim of resistance is the more modest one of struggling against the forces of social heteronomy at a more local and personal level. In his lectures on moral philosophy from 1963, subsequently published as 'Problems of Moral Philosophy' (*Probleme der Moralphilosophie*) in 1983, Adorno provides his most extensive reflections on this ethics of resistance:

> The only thing that can perhaps be said is that the right life today would consist in a resistance to those forms of wrong life, which have been seen through and critically dissected by the most progressive minds. Besides this negative prescription, no guidance can really be envisaged. I may add that, negative although this assertion is, it can hardly be much more formal than the Kantian injunction we have been discussing this semester. So what I have in mind is the determinate negation of everything that has been seen through, and thus the ability to focus the power of resistance on all the things imposed on us, to everything the world has made of us, and intends to make of us, to a vastly greater degree.[102]

It is clear from these remarks that Adorno does not think that we, in our wrong form of life, can achieve the kind of robust autonomy that human beings would be able to develop in a society fit for *mündigen Menschen*. However, what he thinks we *can* hope to develop is the more limited *Mündigkeit* necessary for an ad hoc resistance against the forces of social heteronomy. This resistance is not conceived of as a political resistance against external domination, to which we must largely adapt if we wish to survive, but rather a resistance 'against all that in ourselves, in which we tend to play along'.[103] Adorno even goes so far as to say, 'the moment of self-criticism, of self-reflection today has become the true legacy of that which once was called moral categories'.[104]

---

[102] Adorno, *Probleme der Moralphilosophie*, pp. 248–249.
[103] Adorno, *Probleme der Moralphilosophie*, p. 249.
[104] Adorno, *Probleme der Moralphilosophie*, p. 251.

To be sure, this scrutiny of one's own conditionedness is a highly restricted form of resistance to social heteronomy, but Adorno insists that reflecting on the utter wrongness of life, and making conscious what it does to us, is as much as we can hope for in our present societal condition. The only practical form of resistance available to us is thus the *mimetic* attitude to inner and outer nature, which resists social heteronomy simply in virtue of not 'playing along' in the scheme of *Naturbeherrschung*. The concept of *mimesis*—an attitude to others and to inner and outer nature, which Horkheimer and Adorno describe as the subject making 'itself resemble its surroundings', rather than making 'its surroundings resemble itself'"[105]—is as central to Adorno's negativist paradigm as it remains exceedingly elusive. The basic idea is that in assuming a mimetic attitude, we refrain from imposing identity or instrumentalization and instead aspire to a kind of undistorted relation to nature and 'others'—in a word: we nurture a sensitivity towards the non-identical.

As Axel Honneth has suggested, the concept of mimesis may ultimately point back towards an 'affect of loving care', in which 'we learn by gradually envisioning others' intentions to relate to their perspectives on the world'.[106] However, this construal of *mimesis* restricts the attitude to interpersonal relations and fashions the mimetic attitude as a kind of undistorted intersubjectivity, which it is surely, but not only, meant to cover in Adorno's thought. To be sure, he never explicitly reflects on what it means to assume a mimetic attitude towards others in interpersonal relations as opposed to inner, libidinal, and outer nature, although these hardly seem to be similar relations. As we shall see in the following chapters, this unwillingness or inability to flesh out the normative concept at the core of his thinking may reflect a deeper philosophical tension within Adorno's negativist paradigm of critical theory: namely, his keen sense of the limitations of the 'philosophy of the subject'—the paradigm of reason that he inherits from German idealism—and simultaneous inability to truly push beyond it. Hence, as Seyla Benhabib argues, the concept of mimesis may at once sit at the heart of Adorno's thought, while also pointing beyond it.[107]

Beyond *mimesis*, we may interpret Adorno's practical ethics of resistance as a requirement to engage in critical thinking about society and its effects on the subject—to not merely accept that which is handed to us, and to critically scrutinize the myriad ways in which the present social world cripples our autonomy, in order to keep the hope alive that this world need not 'have the last word'. As we have seen in Section 3.3, Adorno thinks that we can only truly hope to grasp the

---

[105] Adorno and Horkheimer, *Dialectic of Enlightenment*, p. 154.
[106] Axel Honneth, *Pathology of Reason: On the Legacy of Critical Theory*, transl. by James Ingram (New York: Columbia University Press, 2009), p. 61.
[107] Seyla Benhabib, *Critique, Norm, and Utopia* (New York: Columbia University Press, 1986), p. 219.

sources of social heterogeneity though a critical theory of society. In other words, Adorno's ethics of resistance can also in part be construed as an imperative *to engage in critical theory*.[108] In the following chapter, we shall explore the implications of this injunction—and of Adorno's negativist paradigm more generally—for our contemporary predicament and the idea of a critical theory of world society.

---

[108] To be sure, as Adorno well realized, few people have the means or privilege to live a life of critical contemplation of society and our selves and to develop a mimetic attitude of nondomination over nature, and these seemingly elitist implications of Adorno's negativist paradigm have often drawn criticism from otherwise sympathetic readers. See, for example, Judith Butler, *Giving an Account of Oneself* (New York: Fordham University Press, 2005).

4
Adorno's Negativist Paradigm and the Idea of a Critical Theory of World Society

4.1 The Consummate Eurocentric

Our world seems at once far removed and eerily similar in certain respects to the physiognomy of a societal totality conjured up by Adorno's negativist paradigm of critical theory. In this chapter, I explore the limitations and resources that Adorno's negativist paradigm holds for a critical theory of contemporary world society. Of course, in accordance with Adorno's thoroughgoing epistemic and practical negativism, we should expect no such thing as an attempt to offer practical guidance for human emancipation on a global scale. In Adorno's thought, as we have seen, such a positive account of human emancipation is firmly beyond reach, owing to the crippling wrongness of late-capitalist society, which undercuts any hope of ascertaining knowledge of the practical path to a society beyond existing injustice, and, indeed, of what such a society would even look like. The negativist instantiation of Horkheimer's idea of a critical theory of society thus abdicates the ambition of sketching the contours of, and practical path to, a reasonable world society.

Instead, it orients itself towards the illumination of injustices and social pathologies for the vastly more defensive purpose of mounting individual resistance towards socially imposed heteronomy, in order to keep hope alive that a different form of life might one day be possible. A critical theory of world society grounded in Adorno's negativist paradigm would have to be conceived of as a determinate negation of existing wrong forms of life in the globally integrated totality of late-capitalist society. Although I will argue that there are forceful reasons to be sceptical of Adorno's radical practical and epistemic negativism, his negativist paradigm nonetheless compels us to theorize the 'non-identical' in the present, globally integrated capitalist world society, which is also a central concern of contemporary postcolonial theory. Moreover, nowhere does a fateful dialectic of enlightenment appear with greater consequence today than in the potentially disastrous climactic consequences of industrial society's attempt to master and instrumentalize nature for human ends. Indeed, although I will argue that there are strong reasons to reject certain basic assumptions undergirding Adorno's negativist paradigm, I will also argue that it is effectively impossible to escape the

A Critical Theory of Global Justice. Malte Frøslee Ibsen, Oxford University Press.
© Malte Frøslee Ibsen (2023). DOI: 10.1093/oso/9780192864123.003.0005

inference that some of his driving concerns are borne out precisely in the 'permanent catastrophe' inflicted by the long-term impact of humanity's fossil-fuelled productive apparatus on the Earth system as a whole.

4.1.1 Expressive Totality and the Vanishing of World Society

Let us first take a look at Adorno's own reflections on the global context of application. Although it is impossible to claim that Adorno paid much focused attention to this context, he nonetheless made occasional remarks suggestive of the global implications of his thought. Consider the following three passages, the first from *Negative Dialektik* and the second and third from Adorno's lectures on metaphysics from 1965:

> Darkness covers a condition of freedom, which would need no repression and no morality, because the drive would no longer have to express itself in a destructive manner. Moral questions are succinct, not in their dreadful parody of sexual repression, but in sentences like: torture ought to be abolished; concentration camps ought not to exist, while all of this continues in Africa and Asia and is only repressed because civilized humanity is as inhuman as ever against those it has shamelessly branded as uncivilized.[1]

> As long as culture lives on in a world arranged like ours, in which, whether in South Africa or Vietnam, things happen of which we know and only with difficulty repress the knowledge that they happen—in such a world culture and all the noble and sublime things in which we take delight are like a lid over refuse.[2]

> Through Auschwitz—and by that I mean not only Auschwitz but the world of torture which has continued to exist after Auschwitz and of which we are receiving the most horrifying reports from Vietnam—through all this the concept of metaphysics has been changed to its innermost core. Those who continue to engage in old-style metaphysics, without concerning themselves with what has happened, keeping it at arm's length and regarding it as beneath metaphysics, like everything merely earthly and human, thereby prove themselves inhuman.[3]

What Adorno expresses in these lines (and in others like them) is the quite remarkable conviction, first, that the radically evil forces that came to the fore in Auschwitz are not merely *latent* in postwar European societies, but are *manifest*

---

[1] Adorno, *Negative Dialektik*, p. 281.
[2] Theodor W. Adorno, *Metaphysics: Concept and Problems*, transl. by Edmund Jephcott (Stanford: Stanford University Press, 2001), p. 130.
[3] Adorno, *Metaphysics: Concept and Problems*, p. 101.

and in full view in other parts of the world; and, second, that the fact that these forces are at work in other parts of the world has the *same* implications for our thought and action as when these crimes were committed on European soil. For Adorno, the atrocities that took place during the Vietnam War and in apartheid South Africa are reminders that the kind of mechanized torture and industrialized murder committed in Auschwitz is an ever-present potential of our 'form of life' in a truly global sense—that so-called 'civilized humanity is as inhuman as ever against those it has shamelessly branded as uncivilized', beyond Europe's borders as much as within them. To be sure, in its breathtaking scale and industrial murderous efficiency, Auschwitz is arguably the most sublimely evil expression of those forces, but the point is not to morally relativize Holocaust; it is, rather, that the *function* of Auschwitz in Adorno's thought, as a negative sign in history providing evidence of the radically evil nature of late-capitalist society, is no solitary occurrence. This suggests that it is as much the global prevalence of these signs as it is the singularly evil quality of Auschwitz, which ultimately undergirds Adorno's negativism.

The fact that Adorno evidently thought of his negativist paradigm of critical theory as straightforwardly globally applicable may seem to conflict with the view of Adorno expressed by those like Espen Hammer, who deride his 'blunt Eurocentrism, focused as [he] was on Germany and Austria'.[4] In terms of Adorno's philosophical interests and concerns, this charge of Eurocentrism cannot be denied. Adorno's philosophical worldview was unashamedly steeped in and wholly limited to not merely the Western but arguably the German tradition of philosophy, and he gave little if any systematic thought to the theoretical implications that the global extension of his theory might have. But why didn't he? To be sure, the fact that Adorno personally did not take much interest in matters beyond Germany and the United States does not necessarily imply that his negativist paradigm cannot serve as a foundation for a critical theory of world society—especially as his thought speaks to some of the crucial issues of our day and age. And as we shall see, it is—perhaps somewhat surprisingly—precisely to Adorno that Amy Allen turns in her efforts to 'decolonize' Frankfurt School critical theory.

I want to argue, however, that the global context of application does not arise as a distinct theoretical problem for Adorno because he, much like the young Horkheimer, and in spite of his anti-systemic predilections, assumes from the beginning that the philosophical categories of his theory are universally applicable in a world in which the Enlightenment constitutes a totalitarian project and instrumental reason recognizes no bounds. For Adorno, the concept of 'totality' is intended not only in a qualitative sense—as referring to the whole societal context—but also, *implicitly*, in terms of geographical scope, even if this remains only indirectly acknowledged by Adorno.

---

[4] Espen Hammer, *Adorno and the Political* (London: Routledge, 2006), p. 5.

Accordingly, the concrete *global* context of application—along with the distinctive economic and institutional structures, philosophical challenges, and normative concerns that come clearly into view only once critical theory is applied to world society—simply vanishes in the abstractions of the 'expressive totality' of the late-capitalist form of life.[5] Unsurprisingly, Adorno never justifies any assumption that his physiognomy of late-capitalist life in Europe and the US can be extrapolated to the rest of the world—and in light of Europe's colonial and imperial history, such provincialism is far from innocent. In this sense, not only are Adorno's personal interests and concerns unabashedly Eurocentric—so is his negativist paradigm of critical theory. In effect, 'the world' is silently collapsed into Europe. Moreover, as we shall see, this effective theoretical effacement of Europe's 'Other' can be problematized with appeal to Adorno's own central concern with non-identity.

Notwithstanding his Eurocentric assumptions, might Adorno's physiognomy of late-capitalist society nonetheless *be* applicable in today's world? There are weighty reasons to doubt that this is the case. Indeed, I want to argue that an absolutely central assumption undergirding Adorno's account of late-capitalist society has not stood the test of time, and that this accounts in large part for the sense of estrangement that many of us today may feel when confronted with Adorno's uncompromising negativism and his gloomy physiognomy of the administered world and the system of delusion.

Recall that one of the background assumptions of *Dialektik der Aufklärung* was Pollock's theory that monopoly capitalism has been replaced by the regime of state capitalism, and that the profit motive still predominant in the former had in the course of this structural transformation been replaced by the power motive. As we have seen, Adorno and Horkheimer generalize this claim in arguing that the power motive—as expressed in the struggle for human mastery over nature, reverting into human domination over the self and others—is the real continuity in world history, and that the complete synthesis between economic and state power that we find in state capitalism is its present-day culmination. This argument in turn provides the background for Adorno's claim that we live in a pervasively administered world, which has structurally rendered individual autonomy superfluous, and that we are subject to a system of delusion that prevents us from seeing through this all-encompassing spell.

The crucial problem here is that the assumption at the beginning of this line of reasoning—i.e., that *bourgeois*-liberal and monopoly capitalism has been irrevocably replaced by state capitalism, in which market and state power has all but merged—appears much less intuitively plausible from our contemporary point of view. If anything, this assumption is singularly unhelpful as a starting point

---

[5] Martin Jay, *Marxism and Totality. The Adventures of a Concept from Lukács to Habermas* (Berkeley, CA: University of California Press, 1984).

for making sense of the injustices and pathologies that arise from the relationship between states and markets in the present context of globalized capitalism. The claim that the state and the economy have been seamlessly integrated into a total system of administration simply does not stand up to scrutiny in a world in which large sectors of the economy have been fully globalized, while the administrative apparatus of many states has in turn been subject to ever-greater pressure to conform to global economic imperatives (this claim will be substantiated in the coming chapters).

Moreover, although institutions of global and transnational governance such as the United Nations, the World Bank, and the World Trade Organization do exist, these institutions do not wield anything like the kind of power that the modern state has wielded within its dominion for centuries. Rather than being seamlessly integrated, we seem to face a situation today in which what matters is precisely the *asymmetry* between market and state power, as even some of the most powerful states are increasingly constrained in their attempt to fulfil basic state functions—such as financing expenditures through increases in taxation or public debt—because they face such powerful structural restrictions on policy-making in the globalized economy. In other words, state capitalism, even if such a synthesis actually ever transpired, increasingly seems like a proposition debunked by contemporary historical reality.

To be sure, this is not to deny that the proposition must have seemed much more pertinent for most of the second half of the twentieth century, where many agreed that Marx had hopelessly underestimated the importance of the state and that, as a consequence, his analysis of *bourgeois*-liberal capitalism had little purchase in the post-war Western World.[6] However, it is no little irony that Marx's prophetic, rhetorical question from *The German Ideology* in some ways seems less exaggerated today than do Adorno's fears of totalitarian administration:

> [H]ow is it that trade, which after all is nothing more than the exchange of products of various individuals and countries, rules the whole world through the relation of supply and demand—a relation which, as an English economist says, hovers over the earth like the fate of the ancients, and with invisible hand allots fortune and misfortune to men, sets up empires and overthrows empires, causes nations to rise and to disappear.[7]

In my view, this fundamental problem alone implies that it makes little sense to assume that we can simply apply Adorno's negativist paradigm of critical theory to our present world society in unreconstructed form. However, the fact that Adorno's negativist paradigm might not be applicable *tout court*, since some of its

---

[6] See, paradigmatically, Peter B. Evans, Dietrich Rueschemeyer, and Theda Skocpol (eds), *Bringing the State Back In* (Cambridge: Cambridge University Press, 1985).
[7] Marx, 'The German Ideology', in *The Marx-Engels Reader*, p. 162.

undergirding assumptions no longer seem credible, does not imply that central aspects of his negativist paradigm have lost all relevance.

4.1.2 Non-Identity at the End: An Ecological Dialectic of Enlightenment

There is an undeniable enduring relevance to Adorno's insight that the continuing occurrence of certain negative signs in history should not only lead us to question societies that engender or allow even the potential of such catastrophes but also to ponder the bewildering fact that these signs often do not translate into mass political opposition or even a mere wish to better understand their origins. The fact that we can stomach millions of human deaths each year from easily preventable diseases; the fact that half of humanity still faces a deeply precarious daily struggle to subsist while ever-more enormous mountains of wealth are amassed by a minority so tiny that you could fit them into a few buses; the fact that we can go about our daily business in a relatively undisturbed fashion while the exhaust fumes of humanity's amassed machinery of production and consumption are plunging us at ever greater speed towards a global environmental disaster that may render the planet increasingly hostile to human life in a few generations: all of this testifies to a shocking lack of responsiveness to the immense suffering and irrationality engendered by our present form of life on a global scale, which is so overwhelming that expressing our present predicament in terms of a 'universal system of delusion' might seem more like an appropriate exaggeration than unwarranted hyperbole.[8]

Moreover, a critical theory of contemporary world society must certainly face up to one of Adorno's most central themes: namely, his concern with the nonidentical. Two dimensions of this concern are of immediate relevance for a critical theory of world society: namely, the relationship between humanity and nature, and the 'other' of Western Modernity (I discuss this second theme in the section below). Firstly, we find in Adorno's thought a sustained attempt to grapple with the relationship between human beings and nature, and it is a basic theme of his thought that the human struggle to wrest power over human life from natural contingency has not only culminated in the nature-like domination of instrumental reason over human life, but also in what he calls 'permanent catastrophe':

> History is the unity of continuity and discontinuity. Society does not reproduce itself in spite of its antagonisms, but through them; the profit motive, and thereby the class relationship, are objectively the motor of the process of production, on which everyone's life depends and whose primacy has its vanishing-point in the death of all. This also implies that which is reconciling in the irreconcilable;

---

[8] Adorno famously quipped: 'In psychoanalysis, nothing is true but the exaggerations'. Adorno, *Minima Moralia*, p. 54.

because this alone allows human beings to live, there would not even be the possibility of a different life without it. That which historically created that possibility can destroy it just as easily. The world-spirit, a worthy object of definition, could be defined as permanent catastrophe.[9]

The concept of permanent catastrophe does not only refer to that which society has become, but also, and more dramatically, to the threat of human self-annihilation as a species, which is the 'vanishing point' of the primacy of the 'process of production'. Although Adorno was first and foremost concerned with the risk of nuclear war, in our present historical context it is above all the prospect of catastrophic climate change that stubbornly reactualizes some of the central concerns of *Dialektik der Aufklärung*.

A critique of global ecological destruction might seek its bearings from a close critical engagement with Adorno's thought, in which we find a concern with the potentially catastrophic consequences of human exploitation of nature that does not go beyond anthropocentric premises—as in much contemporary ecological thought—but rather sees the need for our learning to assume a mimetic attitude towards nature in the aspiration to redeem the emancipatory promises of the enlightenment. The radical evil of an already unfolding, humanly engendered mass extinction event on our planet is indicative of a fossil-fuelled global productive apparatus run amok, and Adorno's injunction that we can only hope to escape such a catastrophe through a fundamental reorientation in our attitude towards nature is as relevant and urgent as ever—even if his response to this problem, the mimetic attitude and the individual ethics of resistance, is perhaps not equally compelling.

The idea that anthropogenic climate change requires a fundamental reorientation towards nature has more recently been taken up by philosophers and political theorists alike. 'New materialist' philosophers such as Bruno Latour and Jane Bennett, who have drawn the implication that we should relinquish the sharp distinction between intentional human agency and nature and allow for non-human 'actants' or 'vibrant matter'[10]—and normative political theorists, such as Peter Singer, Sue Donaldson, and Will Kymlicka—renounce moral anthropocentrism and argue that we should accord moral standing or rights to the other animals, even political rights.[11] These efforts might be understood as attempts to dissolve the distinction between humanity and nature (nature means: the non-human) in order to reconcile humanity with nature by theoretical fiat.

---

[9] Adorno, *Negative Dialektik*, p. 314.
[10] Bruno Latour, *Facing Gaia: Eight Lectures on the Climatic Regime*, transl. by Catherine Porter (Cambridge: Polity Press, 2017); Jane Bennett, *Vibrant Matter: A Political Ecology of Things* (Durham: Duke University Press, 2010).
[11] Peter Singer, *Animal Liberation: A New Ethics for our Treatment of Animals* (New York: Harper Collins, 1975; Will Kymlicka and Sue Donaldson, *Zoopolis: A Political Theory of Animal Rights* (Oxford: Oxford University Press, 2011).

Latour and Bennett share with Adorno the aim of recasting the relationship between subject and object, but they pursue this aim ontologically by rethinking the applicability of concepts such as agency, power and matter. Bennett expresses the aspiration animating this rethinking clearly in her response to the self-posed question, 'Why advocate the vitality of matter?'

> Because my hunch is that the image of dead or thoroughly instrumentalized matter feeds human hubris and our earth-destroying fantasies of conquest and consumption. It does so by preventing us from detecting (seeing, hearing, smelling, tasting, feeling) a fuller range of the nonhuman powers that circulating within and around human bodies. These material powers, which can aid or destroy, enrich or disable, ennoble or degrade us, in any case call for our attentiveness, or even 'respect' (provided that the term be stretched beyond its Kantian sense). The figure of intrinsically inanimate matter may be one of the impediments to the emergence of more ecological and more materially sustainable modes of production and consumption.[12]

Animating these lines is a clear desire for a human reconciliation with nature, yet it is one that—even as it mirrors Adorno's concerns (as Bennett recognizes)—contrasts sharply with Adorno's approach to the problem. For Adorno, reconciliation with nature cannot be achieved by rethinking *nature*—rather, what must be done is not only rethink but also *practically reorient* our relationship to nature in a mode beyond instrumentalization.

Adorno's reflections on the relationship between reason and nature point in a different direction than the theoretical reconciliation attempted by new materialists such as Latour and Bennett. Rather than reconceptualizing nature as itself infused with agency in terms of, say, self-reinforcing climatic feedback processes such as the melting of the ice caps or the slowing down of the Gulf Stream, as Latour suggests, or with myriad non-human powers of matter as Bennett suggests, Adorno focuses our attention on the 'natural in the human', to put it in the form of a slogan. This is precisely not an aspiration to see the identical in natural processes or matter, but a remembrance of that which is *non*-identical; that which instrumental reason has negated, cast away, and reduced.

Recall Adorno's argument, as discussed in the previous chapter, that nature is not only a condition of possibility for reason and the will, but that an unrecognized natural element remains in reason and human volition. Just as reason ultimately derives from libidinal energies, so too does the act of willing include both a discursive and a somatic aspect—it encompasses a somatic 'jolt', which is its 'active' and spontaneous element. What Adorno wants to remind us with this argument is of course that reason is not ultimately only opposed to nature but also *arises from*

---

[12] Bennett, *Vibrant Matter*, p. ix.

and *expresses* nature, both within the individual subject and in the more encompassing sense of natural history. And yet he also maintains that reason has become socially reified into the nature-like compulsion of totalizing instrumental reason, which today threatens to destroy the natural conditions of human existence by ceaselessly instrumentalizing and exploiting nature 'until the last ton of fossilized coal is burnt', as Weber famously remarked.[13]

Yet this also makes clear that the reconciliation we need is not a *theoretical* reconciliation. In fact, we need precisely the opposite: to relentlessly remind ourselves, through theory, of our *fundamentally irreconciled* relationship with nature. We do not reconcile with the non-identical through theorizing it as identical—not even in the face of ultimate non-identity at the end of life, as it were. Rather, as Adorno would maintain, a true reconciliation between reason and nature is possible only in a world society where the human relationship with nature is freed from the blindly instrumentalizing and exploitative attitude that threatens to undermine the natural conditions of possibility for 'a liveable life'. That is to say, reconciling with nature is not ultimately a matter for theory. It is a *practical* task—by far the most important practical task of our lives.

4.1.3 The 'Non-Identical' of Western Modernity

Adorno's consistent aspiration to give expression to that which doesn't fit into the ruling schemes of classification is shared by many contemporary scholars in post- and decolonial theory. In spite of his 'blunt Eurocentrism', the intellectual-historical links between Adorno and postcolonial theory are hardly difficult to establish. The academic field of postcolonial studies was founded by social theorists such as Frantz Fanon, who was strongly influenced by Hegel, and literary scholars and philosophers such as Edward W. Said and Gayatri Spivak, who are deeply inspired by poststructuralists such as Michel Foucault and Jacques Derrida. Moreover, as Foucault realized towards the end of his life, some of the central concerns and ideas of his work were in fact anticipated by the first generation of the Frankfurt School—not least by Adorno.[14] Accordingly, it makes sense to explore these links a little further, before looking more closely at certain themes in Adorno's thought as a pivot for a postcolonial research agenda in a critical theory of world society.

Although there are many parallels between Foucault's and Adorno's thinking, there are also very important differences. Both see themselves as heirs to the 'critical attitude' of the enlightenment; both critically align themselves with Kant's

---

[13] Max Weber, *The Protestant Ethic and the Spirit of Capitalism*, transl. by Talcott Parsons (London: Routledge, 1992), p. 123.
[14] See, Michel Foucault, 'What is Critique?', in *The Politics of Truth*, ed. by Sylvère Lotringer (Cambridge MA: Semiotext(e), 2007).

definition of the enlightenment and his project of understanding the present (and both take some inspiration from Nietzsche); both see our present as decipherable only with reference to the historical trajectory of forms of rationality; and both sought to break with the myth of constitutive subjectivity.[15] Moreover, both sought to reap general insights about forms of power between individual subjects and social structures in terms of the practices in which these relations are expressed—and, in particular, the way in which such forms of power 'identify' or 'normalize'.[16] However, whereas Adorno was in many ways the philosopher par excellence, spending most of his adult years pouring over the Western (or German) philosophical canon in order to state his case, Foucault spent his life in archives, perusing thousands of historical documents to construct his genealogies of the subject.

It is clear that some of Foucault's central ideas, such as the claim that 'power ... makes individuals subjects',[17] and that power operates cognitively through what Foucault calls 'regimes of truth',[18] are highly germane to Adorno's thinking. Indeed, it is no coincidence that Foucault's concept of 'governmentality' and Adorno's concept of 'administration' sometimes seem almost equivalent in the meaning they are intended to convey, both referring to certain omnipresent practices and techniques for the management and self-management of individuals.[19]

In his immensely influential book *Orientalism* from 1978, Edward W. Said brings central Foucauldian ideas to bear on the old European colonial powers' relationship to their Middle-Eastern subject populations. Said's argument is that Orientalism constitutes a regime of truth, which is inextricably connected with the old Western powers' colonial domination of the Middle East, providing an academic, institutional, imaginative, and inherently political construction of the 'Orient' as the great Other of the West (the Occident), in which the Oriental is characterized as 'irrational, depraved (fallen), childlike, "different"', and the European as 'rational, virtuous, mature [*mündig!*], "normal"'.[20] In Said's treatment,

> Orientalism can be discussed and analyzed as the corporate institution for dealing with the Orient—dealing with it by making statements about it, authorizing views of it, describing it, by teaching it, settling it, ruling over it: in short, Orientalism

---

[15] For Foucault's reflections on his relationship to Kant, see Foucault, *The Politics of Truth*, and for his reflections on the need to dispense with 'constituent subjectivity', see Michel Foucault, 'Truth and Power', in *Power/Knowledge: Selected Interviews and other Writings 1972–1977*, ed. by Colin Gordon (New York: Pantheon Books, 1980).
[16] Michel Foucault, *Discipline and Punish: The Birth of the Prison*, transl. by Alan Sheridan (London: Penguin, 1991), pp. 177–184.
[17] Focault, 'The Subject and Power', p. 781.
[18] Foucault, 'Truth and Power', p. 131.
[19] For Foucault's use of the concept 'governmentality', see Michel Foucault, *Security, Territory, Population. Lectures at the College de France 1977–1978*, transl. by Graham Burchell (New York: Picador, 2007).
[20] Edward W. Said, *Orientalism* (London: Penguin Books, 2003), p. 40.

as a Western style for dominating, restructuring, and having authority over the Orient ... My contention is that without examining Orientalism as a discourse one cannot possibly understand the enormously systematic discipline by which European culture was able to manage—and even produce—the Orient politically, sociologically, militarily, ideologically, scientifically, and imaginatively during the post-Enlightenment period.[21]

In light of Adorno's Eurocentrism, Said's characterization of the West and the Orient as a great discursive opposition perhaps doesn't immediately seem to mirror the central concerns of Adorno's negativist paradigm of critical theory. However, on closer examination, they clearly do.

First, Said is interested in Orientalism not simply as an 'invented' discourse; rather, he regards Orientalist discourse as a complex of concepts, descriptions, and normative judgements—in short, a kind of 'second nature'—more or less unwittingly constructed and imposed by the European powers' throughout their years of colonial conquest to furnish a superstructure in support of their domination, but also adopted and practiced by Arab colonial elites, who thereby facilitated their own subjection by living the stereotypes that their European masters invoked to justify their rule. Orientalism is, in other words, a function of the underlying power structure; it is indeed something like a universal system of delusion, which prevented Orientals from even perceiving their own bondage.

Second, Orientalism displays another decisive feature clearly aligning it with Adorno's concerns, namely that it is a classificatory scheme imposing an alien identity on its object, which neglects the object's particularity and reduces the object—the region and people designated as the Orient and Orientals—to something they are not.[22] However, this imposition of a false identity should not be seen as deliberate (Said does not claim that it is), but rather ultimately as a consequence of the industrial and scientific revolutions that enabled Europe to conquer the world throughout the nineteenth century. Orientalism is, in other words, inextricably bound up with the dialectic of enlightenment and how the drive to impose human mastery over nature reverts into domination over human beings—in this case, the subject populations, who were explicitly regarded as uncivilized and 'closer to nature' than their civilized European masters.

As noted above, *Orientalism* is one of the founding texts of post- and decolonial theory, and many scholars have since taken up the baton from Said's subversive counter-history and written still new counter-histories for other of Europe's former (and present) subject populations. Many postcolonial theorists pursue a general motive of trying to wrest history and identity from the grip of the narratives

---

[21] Said, *Orientalism*, p. 3.
[22] As we have seen, Adorno can—in his tacit collapse of 'the world' into Europe—*himself* be charged with the imposition of this false identity on Europe's Other.

and imaginary of the former colonial masters, by criticizing the subjugating discourses once tailored to ease and justify colonial rule, but in which both former colonial masters and subjects remain caught up. Dipesh Chakrabarty has argued that the Indian subject is caught in a 'mimetic ... mode of self-representation' vis-à-vis a metanarrative of 'Europe constructed by the tales that both imperialism and nationalism have told the colonized' and is therefore 'bound to represent a sad figure of lack and failure'.[23] In Gayatri Chakravorty Spivak's seminal essay 'Can the Subaltern Speak?', she takes up the same motive from a feminist and deconstructionist point of view and argues that the voice of 'the subaltern female' is systematically silenced as a political subject, caught between the twin forces of 'subject-constitution' and 'object-formation' of 'patriarchy and imperialism'.[24] As the Other or nonidentical of the 'masculine-imperialist ideological formation', there 'is no space from which the sexed subaltern subject can speak', according to Spivak, and therefore her voice cannot be heard.

A critical theory of world society must offer a vantage point, from which it is able to engage, learn from, and contribute to debates on such crucial postcolonial concerns, which we might understand—in Adorno's terms—as an imperative to grapple with the non-identical of Western or European thought.[25] Such a vantage point should be able to countenance, for example, the notion of *global epistemic injustice* in a postcolonial perspective, which 'occurs when the concepts and categories by which a people understand themselves and their world are replaced or adversely effected by the concepts and categories of the colonizers'.[26] As such, some of the core animating concerns of Adorno's thought must be carried over into a critical theory of world society, which must not only be able to capture and illuminate different aspects of colonial and postcolonial forms of domination, but also interrogate *its own* entanglements in colonial narratives and assumptions (I will return to these questions in Chapter 9).

However, there are also important differences between Adorno and the Frankfurt School on one side, and Foucault, Said, Spivak, and much of the work done in postcolonial theory on the other, which bear repeated emphasis. The perhaps most important of these differences derives from what I have called the methodological holism of the Frankfurt School tradition and the methodological nominalism of the latter camp. Whereas Adorno was convinced that enlightenment has become

---

[23] Dipesh Chakrabarty, Provincializing Europe: *Post-Colonical Thought and Historial Difference* (Princeton: Princeton University Press, 2000), p. 40

[24] Gayatri Chakravorty Spivak, 'Can the Subaltern Speak?', in *Marxism and the Interpretation of Culture*, ed. by Cary Nelson and Lawrence Grossberg (London: MacMillan, 1988).

[25] For a somewhat exaggerated account of Adorno *as* a post-colonial theorist, see Robert Spencer, 'Thoughts from Abroad: Theodor Adorno as Post-Colonial Theorist', *Culture, Theory and Critique*, (51/3), 2010: 207–221.

[26] Rajeev Bhargava, 'Overcoming the Epistemic Injustice of Colonialism', *Global Policy* (4/4), November 2013: pp. 413–417, p. 414. For a systematic account of the concept of epistemic injustice, see Miranda Fricker, *Epistemic Injustice: Power and the Ethics of Knowing* (Oxford: Oxford University Press, 2007).

totalitarian, Foucault was committed to an anti-holistic or 'nominalist' view of reason—in a word, his focus was not on Reason, but on rationalities.[27] Reflecting on his own work, Foucault remarks that

> together with this sense of instability and this amazing efficacy of discontinuous, particular and local criticism, one in fact also discovers something that perhaps was not initially foreseen, something one might describe as precisely the inhibiting effect of global, *totalitarian theories* ... Let us give the term *genealogy* to the union of erudite knowledge and local memories which allows us to establish a historical knowledge of struggles and to make use of this knowledge tactically today.[28]

Foucault's consistent emphasis on the disaggregated character of reason and the localized character of genealogical critique echoes Lyotard's scepticism towards 'grand narratives'—as discussed in the Introduction—and this methodological nominalism is also characteristic of Said's work and much postcolonial theory. The target of criticism is often Marx's thought, which is explicitly singled out by Foucault along with psychoanalysis as an exemplar of such 'global, totalitarian theories'. This methodological nominalism pits Foucault and his heirs not only against the methodological holism of Marx, but also that of Adorno and the rest of the left-Hegelian tradition of the Frankfurt School.

Against such methodological nominalism, Adorno would no doubt maintain that although it would indeed be woefully mistaken to aspire to an unambiguously *affirmative* grand narrative—a positive theodicy, we might say—we will profoundly misunderstand the nature of late-capitalist society if we do not attempt to grasp it as a *negative totality*, and we can only do so through a critical theory of society. This seems to me to be the point on which the whole Frankfurt School tradition remains most firmly and inexorably in opposition to 'postmodern' critics and theorists, who abandon the attempt to understand modern capitalist society in holistic terms as a social totality. With Adorno, I shall maintain throughout this book that the holistic concern is not a methodological mistake on the part of critical theorists, who are stuck in an obsolete and metaphysically overwrought left-Hegelian worldview. Rather, that concern emanates from a substantive insight into the *kind* of social formation that capitalism is—a formation that today can only be grasped through a critical theory of *globalized* capitalism, or global capitalist modernity.

---

[27] Michel Focault, 'The Subject and Power', *Critical Inquiry*, (8/4), summer 1982: pp. 777–795. See also Michel Foucault, *The Birth of Biopolitics. Lectures at the College de France 1978–1979*, transl. by Graham Burchell (New York: Picador, 2008), Lecture I.

[28] Michel Foucault, 'Two Lectures', in *Power/Knowledge: Selected Interviews and other Writings 1972–1977*, pp. 80–83.

Adorno's concern with totality has yet another source. In the final aphorism of *Minima Moralia* called 'At the End', Adorno invokes the religious metaphor of 'redemption' to make a crucial epistemic point:

> The only respectable form of philosophy in view of the desperation would be the attempt to regard all things as they appear from the standpoint of redemption. Knowledge has no light like that which the redemption shines upon the world: everything else disappears in reconstruction and remains a piece of technique. Perspectives must be constructed in which the world is equally displaced, unfamiliar, its cracks and tears revealed, as it will one day lay bare, needing and disfigured in the Messianic light. Without arbitrariness and violence, to win such perspectives fully out of empathy with the objects, that alone is what thinking comes down to.[29]

In my view, this beautiful, even moving passage contains one of Adorno's most profound and enduring insights. This is the insight that true knowledge of society in a sense *requires* and presupposes a holistic, utopian perspective from which all suffering and injustice *is no more*. This perspective is the point of view of redemption: we can only truly perceive the brutally disfigured and irrational nature of our social world, if we—even if only implicitly—observe it in the 'Messianic light' of a society *beyond* suffering and injustice.

In other words, what is wrong with positivist social science, according to Adorno, is not just that it takes observable 'facts' as the only and final say in the matter without any regard for the mediating societal structure, but also that it profoundly misunderstands the nature of its object, because it refuses to countenance a normative perspective from which the devastating extent of present injustice can be grasped. Such suffering and injustice are no less part of our world than are doorknobs, symphonies, and hydrogen-bombs, but they do not register themselves to the disinterested observer in the same way as do the latter kinds of phenomena—partly because we have been conditioned by society to blind ourselves to them, but also because *seeing* and *hearing* them requires that we assume a perspective of 'empathy with the objects', with the *kind* of objects that they are.

Of course, Adorno's remark that 'our world' will 'one day' lay exposed in the Messianic light should not be interpreted to mean that he nurtures any hopes for divine intervention. Rather, it is meant to metaphorically express the immense distance that we would have to travel from our present predicament to reach such a social form, and to invoke in the imagination an image of ultimate salvation from humanity's miserable present existence here on Earth. The enduring lesson from this insight is that a critical theory of world society must not make any compromises with expedience or our own epistemic imperfection. If all thinking starts with need, it is only in the practical redemption of all human suffering that

[29] Adorno, *Minima Moralia*, p. 283.

thought ultimately comes into its own. And the acknowledgement that we are so far removed from such a state is not an error of thought, but rather a ruthless indictment of the wrongness of our world.

However, in an important sense, Adorno's own thinking was never really true to this crucial insight. For as we have seen, notwithstanding the occasional remark, he was never willing or able to break free from the parochial Eurocentric perspective that he so consummately embodied. We might be tempted to excuse this inconsistency between his avowed methodological holism and his Eurocentrism with reference to the constrained horizon of Adorno's historical context—but this would do him a disservice. To be sure, it is true that in today's globalized world, where the Promethean forces of capital have finally penetrated all corners of the globe, this inconsistency has become impossible to ignore, because the manifest global integration of societies makes it evident that a critical theory of society must today take the form of a critical theory of *world* society. But as I have argued in this chapter, Adorno's Eurocentrism is rooted in the very core of his negativist paradigm—in the idea of late-capitalist society as a negative, expressive totality, in which the *concrete* global context of application vanishes almost without a trace. Nonetheless, it is a measure of the vitality of Adorno's thought that his own central concern with the non-identical makes plain that 'the world' cannot be tacitly collapsed into 'Europe' without doing violence to its object.

As we shall see in Chapter 9, Amy Allen has recently argued that, along with Foucault's work, Adorno's thought contains crucial resources for 'decolonizing critical theory', and, in particular, that Adorno's paradoxical claim that 'progress occurs when it comes to an end' contains the seeds for a conception of 'critique as historical problematization' that Allen unfolds and defends. The aim of such a conception of critique is a critical, genealogically executed self-problematization of 'our own point of view' and the 'normative inheritance of Western modernity', and its upshot is a stance of 'epistemic modesty' towards our own normative commitments. Allen approvingly quotes Adorno's remark that it is precisely 'by reflecting on our own limitations (that) we can learn to do justice to those who are different'.

> By allowing us to reflexively critique the social institutions and practices, the patterns of cultural meaning and subject formation, and the normative commitments that have made us who we are, problematizing critique opens up a space of critical distance on those institutions, practices, and so forth, thereby freeing us up on relation to them, and thus also in relation to ourselves.[30]

I agree with Allen that 'problematizing critique' is a crucial task of a critical theory of world society, which must face up to its own entanglements with colonial and neocolonial forms of domination in a world society still ordered along formally

---

[30] Amy Allen, *The End of Progress: Decolonizing the Normative Foundations of Critical Theory* (New York: Columbia University Press, 2017), p. 197.

bygone imperial lines. However, as I shall also maintain, problematizing critique cannot be an *exhaustive* account of the tasks of a critical theory of world society, which must also go beyond Allen—and, indeed, beyond Adorno—in offering the kind of practical guidance for human emancipation that the young Horkheimer considered the very *raison d'être* of critical theory. Indeed, although preventing a climate catastrophe is perhaps the paramount practical task of humanity today, and, perforce, of a critical theory of world society, the methodological limitation of critical theory to the self-problematization of Western normative commitments unduly restricts critical theory from offering such practical emancipatory guidance, which is—I shall argue later in this book—a kind of methodological self-effacement that risks effectively abandoning the very idea of Frankfurt School critical theory.

4.2 Adorno and the Student Movement

Adorno's life and philosophical practice has a curious but oddly fitting epilogue. Sometime after Horkheimer and Adorno returned to the postwar Federal Republic to reopen the IfS and contribute to the moral and intellectual rebuilding of Germany, Adorno's belief in the administered world's resistance to any kind of practical challenge was itself challenged from an unexpected side. In the latter half of the 1960s, the German student movement—along with its other European, American, and Third-World counterparts—became increasingly radicalized and outspoken in its opposition to the status quo. However, the German students were not like the others, in that they were motivated not only by certain Marxist concerns and a desire for self-realization, but also by their frustration with what was widely perceived as previous generations' complacency and active participation in Nazi atrocities, and their refusal to open up the past to free and public discussion. Naturally, the student movement found a towering source of inspiration in the eccentric, neo-Marxist, impeccably anti-Nazi, previously-exiled philosophy professor in their midst: read in every study group and taught in every teach-in, the Frankfurt School, and especially Adorno, had finally found an appreciative audience.

Adorno had by then succeeded Horkheimer as director of the IfS, and he had devoted himself to writing the posthumously published companion volume to *Negative Dialektik*, 'Aesthetic Theory' (*Ästhetische Theorie*). When the student protests first began to gain traction, Adorno maintained an ambivalent but mostly positive attitude towards his students' challenges to the established order of things. However, as the student movement became ever more radicalized and vocal in its demands and even went so far as to call for a nationwide socialist revolution, Adorno became increasingly afraid that instead of instigating an emancipatory rupture, the students would merely destabilize the infant democracy of the Federal

Republic and plunge Germany back into fascist barbarity—which, in Adorno's estimation, lurked right below the democratic surface, as we have seen.

The confrontation between the professor and his students culminated when the latter occupied the IfS and Adorno called in the police to have them forcibly evicted. The final straw came when, in the early summer semester of 1969, Adorno's lecture on dialectical logic was interrupted by a group of female students who exposed their breasts and showered him with flowers, while calling him out on his lack of support for their cause. This was too much for the aging and increasingly fragile Adorno, who—despite his avowedly sexually liberal attitude—stormed out of the lecture theatre with tears in his eyes. The stress caused by the confrontation with his students took a major toll on Adorno, and he died of a heart attack while trekking in the Swiss Alps a few months later.

It is sad, and more than a little ironic, that Adorno should end his days in such a way: a man who had devoted his whole life to radically challenging the petrified social order, brought down by his own students out of frustration with his unwillingness to help them in their own challenge to that order. However, the confrontation was probably inevitable: in refusing to provide such assistance, Adorno displayed nothing but consistency with his beliefs that any challenge to the existing order must take the form either of theoretical critique of society, mimetic refusals to 'play along', or solitary individual resistance to 'all that the world has made of us, and intends to make of us'. Had he given the students what they demanded of him, he would have betrayed his conviction that any attempt to provoke large-scale practical change in the administered world—and, in particular, in the still latently fascist West Germany—would only risk making things infinitely worse, and such a betrayal was never forthcoming.

Moreover, Adorno was not alone in standing up to the increasingly radicalized student movement; his mentee, the young Jürgen Habermas, had by then joined him in Frankfurt as Professor of Social Philosophy, Horkheimer's old chair. Officially, his former assistant stood firmly behind Adorno, famously accusing the socialist student organization SDS of 'left-fascism'. However, in hindsight, it is clear that in the longer run Habermas in one sense took the students' side in their confrontation with his mentor. To be sure, Habermas was not prepared to countenance the student movement's most radical demands, and he consistently pointed to dangerous currents in their midst. However, he firmly shared their exasperation with the practical impasse of Adorno's negativist paradigm of critical theory. For Habermas, just as for the students, individual resistance to social heteronomy simply wasn't enough. Well before Adorno's death, Habermas had in fact begun laying the foundations for a way out of this theoretical cul-de-sac—a way that emphasized the communicative nature of rationality and the emancipatory potential of modern constitutional democracy. In doing so, Habermas had taken his first steps to developing the third paradigm of Frankfurt School critical theory, to which we now turn.

PART III
HABERMAS

Jürgen Habermas's intellectual oeuvre is as wide-ranging as it is ambitious. His work and influence spans the human and social sciences: theoretical and practical philosophy, sociology, political science, jurisprudence, media studies, historiography, linguistics, and the history of ideas. Furthermore, his ongoing presence as arguably *the* preeminent public intellectual of the postwar Federal Republic, and, more recently, of the European Union—with a veritable library of popular journal articles, opinion pieces, and public lectures to boot—spans an incredible seven decades. Richard Rorty, the perhaps leading American philosopher of his generation, once referred to him as 'the leading systematic philosopher of our time'. This is an apt description. Much more so than the young Horkheimer, and in profound contrast to Adorno, Habermas is indeed a systematic philosopher in the great tradition of German philosophy, and his thought clearly displays the same concern with 'architectonic' as that of Kant and Hegel.

I want to argue that Habermas's project for the revitalization of critical theory through a communicative paradigm-change can be understood as a response to four distinct but interconnected theoretical problems that he locates in the framework inherited from the first generation of the Frankfurt School. In this sense, we can see Habermas as picking up the baton of the learning process initiated with the young Horkheimer and his original paradigm of critical theory, and continued through Adorno's negativist paradigm, where Habermas's communicative paradigm represents both a return to a more practically engaged critical theory and a greater appreciation of the new social and political environment of postwar democratic-capitalist society. The four theoretical problems that Habermas locates in the work of his predecessors are the following:

(1) The problem of the *philosophical* and *normative grounding* of critical theory. In response to this problem—which is, for Habermas, arguably *the* central problem in the first generation of the Frankfurt School—Habermas develops a formal pragmatics of communicative reason and the acceptability conditions for different kinds of validity claims, including the normative claims that undergird a critical theory of society.

(2) The problem of Horkheimer and Adorno's philosophical entrapment in the 'philosophy of the subject'—the 'paradigm of reason' inherited from

German idealism, which ultimately leads Adorno into the practical impasse of his negativist paradigm of critical theory. In response, Habermas proposes a change to an *intersubjective* and *communicative* paradigm of reason.

(3) The problem of historical materialism's insufficient account of the *social reproduction* of complex modern societies. In response, Habermas develops a diachronic theory of social evolution along a distinction between work (strategic action) and interaction (communicative action), and a social theory that distinguishes between systems of strategic action and a lifeworld integrated through communicative action. Moreover, he reverses the explanatory hierarchy between the material base and cultural-normative superstructure in historical materialism, arguing that the symbolic differentiation of action oriented towards mutual understanding is a world-historical precondition for the functional differentiation of subsystems of strategic action. It is only in the capitalist epoch that the functional subsystems affecting the material preproduction of society achieve dominance over the lifeworld.

(4) The problem of the absence of an appreciation and account of *constitutional democracy* in the paradigms of Horkheimer and Adorno. In response, Habermas offers, first, a rational reconstruction of the moral point of view (discourse ethics), and, second, a reconstruction of the democratic rule of law (*der demokratische Rechtsstaat*). According to the latter, both the social integration and the normative legitimacy of a complex modern society organized as a democratic legal order depends on communicative action in the form of democratic will-formation in the public sphere. This 'reformist' account of practical emancipation replaces the 'revolutionary' account of the first generation.

Furthermore, in the case of Habermas's communicative paradigm, there is no need to construct the implications of his critical theory for world society from scratch, since Habermas has in recent years sought to extend his critical theory to the global context of application, in order to rethink the relationship between democratic rule and economic globalization. In Habermas's view, the globalization of the economic subsystem requires the constitutionalization of international law and the establishment of a multilevel global and transnational legal and political order with the regulative capacity to subject the systemic imperatives of economic globalization to democratically legitimate law.

Habermas is often described as a 'Kantian', which is warranted by his strong reliance on Kant's concept of reason and on his thought in the development of his normative dimension as well as his reflections on a cosmopolitan legal condition. However, it would be a grave disservice to a proper understanding of Habermas's thought if one were to reduce it to just this Kantian element, which is arguably, and unfortunately, what has too often happened in the Anglo-American reception of his work. In my view, Habermas should be interpreted as following the young Horkheimer not only in his stringent commitment to the methodological framework of critical theory, but also in his non-dogmatic and synthetic approach to theory construction. Accordingly, his communicative paradigm of critical theory is in fact much more ecumenical and eclectic than is often appreciated by political theorists. Indeed, in contrast to the received Anglo-American understanding of Habermas as a rationalist moral philosopher committed to a highly idealized ideal of deliberative democracy—an understanding that seems to be based above all on widespread ignorance of the social-theoretical dimension of his work—the following chapter will present a very different picture indeed.

In brief, this picture is of a comprehensive critical theory of society, in which Habermas's incursions into moral philosophy serve the express purpose of clarifying the normative foundations of a critical theory that seeks to illuminate the possibilities for emancipatory self-determination in modern capitalist-democratic society, and where his commitment to deliberative democracy reflects the conviction that collective self-determination can only be realized through the democratic legitimation of legal-institutional power and democratic rule over the capitalist economy. To my mind, this is a vastly more attractive picture of Habermas's work than that with which we are sometimes confronted, but it is a picture that we can bring to the fore only by viewing his work through the prism of the idea of a critical theory of society.

In Chapter 5, I will begin, in Section 5.2, by sketching the mature response that Habermas offers to problems (1) and (2) concerning the philosophical grounding of the normative dimension and the 'paradigm of reason' of his critical theory. In Section 5.3, I expound the historical dimension of his communicative paradigm, the theory of social evolution, before turning to an exposition of his two-concept theory of society as system and lifeworld in Section 5.4, which represents his response to problem (3). In Section 5.5, I account for Habermas's discourse ethics and theory of law and democracy—which constitutes his response to problem (4).

In Chapter 6, I will critically expound and discuss Habermas's argument for a multilevel global constitutional framework as a democratic response to the disruptive forces of economic globalization. I will argue that Habermas's reflections on the global context of application are overly focused on global legal institutions, which is both in tension with one of the central claims of his discourse theory of law and democracy, and, more seriously, insufficiently attentive to the *social* conditions of autonomy, of which he largely loses sight. Moreover, I will discuss the recent criticism directed at Habermas's work by Amy Allen from a postcolonial point of view, as well as Bruno Latour's criticism of the relationship between nature and society in Habermas's theoretical framework. Finally, the chapter ends with a few reflections on the reformist character of Habermas's communicative paradigm and his relationship to Marx.

5
Jürgen Habermas and the Communicative Paradigm of Critical Theory

5.1 'The Leading Systematic Philosopher of Our Time'

Jürgen Habermas was born in Düsseldorf in 1929 and reached adolescence just as Hitler's fortunes in war were beginning to turn.[1] The Nüremberg Trials—in which the extent of Nazi Germany's moral collapse began to dawn on the world—represented a profoundly formative moment for the young Habermas, who had been old enough to participate in the desperate last defence of Germany against the Allied Powers, albeit never reaching the front. He wrote his dissertation on Husserl, but his first love in philosophy was—as with so many other philosophy students of his generation—the fundamental ontology of Martin Heidegger. However, he was infuriated and deeply disappointed with the Freiburg philosopher—who had joined the NSDAP, spoken of the 'greatness and inner truth' of National Socialism, and was appointed rector of the University of Freiburg shortly after Hitler came to power—for his postwar unwillingness to reflect on the misguided and criminal nature of his Nazi commitments.[2]

After publicly disavowing Heidegger, Habermas found work at the recently resettled IfS in Frankfurt, where he became a cherished research assistant and favourite mentee of Adorno's. However, Habermas's increasingly Marxian and radical-democratic leanings led to conflicts with the ageing Horkheimer, whose intellectual journey away from his early materialism had by the early 1950s led to his embrace of *de facto* conservative political views, deeply anxious about the public standing of the IfS in the vehemently anti-communist Adenauer-West Germany. As a consequence—and in spite of Adorno's enthusiastic support for and active participation in his work—Habermas's initial and highly productive association with the IfS ended when Horkheimer refused to pass his *Habilitationsschrift*, owing to what he perceived as its dangerous Marxian radicalism, and he, somewhat perversely, derided Habermas for being too 'dialectical'.[3]

---

[1] The following biographical remarks rely on Stephan Müller-Doohm, *Jürgen Habermas: Eine Biographie* (Berlin: Suhrkamp Verlag, 2014).

[2] Jürgen Habermas, 'Martin Heidegger: Zur Veröffentlichung von Vorlesungen aus dem Jahre 1935', in *Philosophisch-politische Profile* (Frankfurt: Suhrkamp Verlag, 1981).

[3] Müller-Dohm, *Jürgen Habermas: Eine Biographie*, p. 119.

Fortunately, Habermas found a more hospitable censor in the Marburg legal scholar Wolfgang Abendroth, and his work was later published in 1962 to great acclaim as 'Structural Transformation of the Public Sphere' (*Strukturwandel der Öffentlichkeit*)—a path-breaking and highly influential account of the rise and fall of the nineteenth century bourgeois public sphere. The controversy between Habermas and Horkheimer provides illustrative testimony to how far the latter had travelled from his original paradigm of critical theory. Indeed, the contents of the *Habilitationsschrift*—which Horkheimer so forcefully disavowed—actually represents a remarkably loyal instantiation of the project of *immanent critique* of the reality of *bourgeois* society with reference to its own ideals, much as this project was conceived by Horkheimer and his associates at the IfS in the 1930s.[4] Moreover, it also contained the seeds of Habermas's lifelong philosophical project: namely, the interdisciplinary development of a comprehensive critical theory of society, which identifies structural domination and pathologies in the basic structure of postwar democratic-capitalist society from the normative point of view of Kantian autonomy and the idea of public reason.

Horkheimer's *erimitierung* in 1959 paved the way for Habermas's return to Frankfurt, and in 1964 Habermas succeeded Horkheimer as Professor for Social Philosophy, with Adorno's strong encouragement and support. Habermas continued to engage in fruitful cooperation with his former mentor and gradually rose to prominence as the leading figure in a new generation of young philosophers and social scientists profoundly influenced by the older generation of the Frankfurt School. However, in contrast to the old guard, this new generation was from the very beginning much more attuned to the immanent possibilities for critical theory and practice offered by the infant constitutional democracy, which was slowly rising like a phoenix from the ashes of the German Nazi state.[5] In this important regard, Abendroth's influence on Habermas was to prove of more lasting significance than merely that of an academic midwife.

In the early 1950s, Abendroth—who was at that time the only openly Marxist professor at a West-German university (Adorno did not assume his chair until 1953)—had participated in a debate with the conservative legal theorist Ernst Forsthoff over the interpretation of a prominent article in the new German *Grundgesetz* (Basic Law). This article describes the young *Bundesrepublik* as a '*Sozialstaat*' (literally 'social state', akin to the English term 'welfare state'). While Forsthoff found this concept to be superficial and of no legal content, Abendroth argued that it implied nothing less than a promise to every German citizen of the material and social conditions for making full effective use of their civil and political liberties; indeed, that the constitution should be understood as making

---

[4] See Habermas's reflections on the book in Jürgen Habermas, 'Concluding Remarks', in *Habermas and the Public Sphere*, ed. by Craig Calhoun (Cambridge MA: MIT Press 1993).
[5] Other central figures in this 'second generation' of the Frankfurt School include Albrecht Wellmer, Claus Offe, Ludwig von Friedeburg, Alfred Schmidt, Ralf Dahrendorf, and Oskar Negt.

effective social rights a necessary condition for the democratic legitimacy of the Federal Republic.[6]

For the young Habermas, who was searching for the theoretical means to overcome the practical impasse of Adorno's negativism, this progressive legal argument was to make a lasting impression. Indeed, in Habermas's fully developed communicative paradigm of critical theory, the key to human emancipation lies precisely in the democratic connection between law and reason: or rather, in the emancipatory potential of democratic law. In the following section, we shall first look at Habermas's evolving attempt to develop a new philosophical grounding of a critical theory of society—from his early idea of cognitive human interests to the mature, formal-pragmatic account of the universal rational infrastructure of speech.

5.2 Foundations of a Critical Theory of Society

5.2.1 The Theory of Knowledge as Social Theory

In Habermas's inaugural lecture as Professor of Social Philosophy at the Goethe University Frankfurt in 1965, he sounded a return to Horkheimer's original programme of critical theory and sketched the contours of his initial idea for redeeming its emancipatory aspirations. His strategy for doing so was to take up the theme, familiar from both the young Horkheimer and Adorno, of the origins of knowledge in lived experience—or, in Habermas's novel twist on this idea, of different domains of knowledge as expressive of certain 'cognitive human interests'. This enables Habermas to recast the Kantian critique of reason as a critique of the *historical development of the sciences* (in the broad sense of the German word '*Wissenschaft*') and their different epistemic object domains in the history of the human species.

In its original form, Kant's critique of reason answers the question 'what can I know?' through a transcendental clarification of the subjective conditions of possibility for knowledge. This Kantian programme was both meant to establish the *limits* of knowledge—which Kant put to destructive use against speculative metaphysics in the 'Transcendental Dialectic' of the *Critique of Pure Reason*—as well as the ultimate *validity* of cognition and knowledge, which he sought to establish by demonstrating the a priori character of the transcendental conditions of knowledge as such. In Habermas's early work, both of these objectives are retained and transformed in the idea of 'the theory of knowledge as social theory':

---

[6] Matthew G. Specter, *Habermas: An Intellectual Biography* (Cambridge: Cambridge University Press, 2010), p. 43.

Orientation toward technical control, toward mutual understanding in the conduct of life, and toward emancipation from seemingly 'natural' constraint establish the specific view-points from which we can apprehend reality as such in any way whatsoever ... The achievements of the transcendental subject [thus] have their basis in the natural history of the human species.[7]

This sweeping philosophical programme was subsequently substantiated in the book 'Knowledge and Human Interests' (*Erkenntnis und Interesse*), published in 1968, whose animating aspiration is nothing less than to revalidate Horkheimer's original idea of critical theory as a theory of society oriented towards human emancipation. This aspiration is pursued through a historical analysis of the collapse of the grand epistemological ambitions of German idealism and the subsequent rise of the 'scientistic' philosophy of science, which equates knowledge with observed reality and the outcome of the natural-scientific method. However, in doing so, scientism repudiates as not belonging to proper domains of knowledge both the hermeneutic method of the human sciences as well as the concept of 'reflection'—a central category of German idealism—which, Habermas claims, is also central to the idea of critical theory.

Evidently, this critique of scientism echoes both Horkheimer's critique of traditional theory in *Traditionelle und kritische Theorie* and Adorno's *Positivismusstreit* with Popper, in which Habermas was himself a very active participant. In contrast to Horkheimer, however, Habermas locates one of the roots of the collapse of 'the theory of knowledge' precisely in Marx's materialist privileging of 'instrumental action'—i.e., labour and production relations—along with the concomitant demotion of culture and ideology to the epiphenomenal superstructure. According to Habermas, this awkwardly downgrades the kind of reflective knowledge that issues from Marx's *own* critical theory, and which is supposed to serve as the impetus for emancipation, as belonging to the domain of the epiphenomenal superstructure. Marx was thereby led to misunderstand the epistemic status of his own critical theory of society according to the model of the natural sciences.[8] Paradoxically, Marx's naturalistic inclinations thus anticipated the scientistic reduction of knowledge to the natural-scientific epistemic domain at the cost of the kind of reflective knowledge, which was precisely the kind of claim to validity effectively raised by his own theory.

In order to rehabilitate the concept of reflection, Habermas argues that modern science has developed along three paths: *the empirical-analytic sciences, the historical-hermeneutic sciences,* and *the critically oriented sciences*. The empirical analytical sciences include the natural sciences and the social sciences when

---

[7] Jürgen Habermas, 'Appendix', in *Knowledge and Human Interests*, transl. by Jeremy J. Shapiro (Cambridge: Polity Press, 1987), p. 311–312.
[8] Habermas, *Knowledge and Human Interests*, p. 46, 63.

concerned with establishing 'nomological' knowledge (i.e. inductive inference of general 'laws' from observation of social reality); the historical-hermeneutic sciences include the human sciences concerned with the interpretation of meaning; and the critically oriented sciences include the social sciences (critical theory) and the human sciences (philosophy and psychoanalysis) when concerned with 'reflection'. According to Habermas, each of these three scientific branches of knowledge express and incorporate a fundamental *cognitive interest* that human beings have in this domain of knowledge: the empirical-analytic sciences incorporate a *technical interest* in understanding and controlling the natural environment; the historical-hermeneutic sciences incorporate a *practical interest* in self- and mutual understanding; and the critical sciences incorporate an *emancipatory interest* in freedom from domination and ideological illusion.

These cognitive interests are understood as *knowledge-constitutive* in the sense that Habermas argues they are conditions of possibility for knowledge in its three different epistemic branches, and as rooted in the objective structure of human life through the corresponding social domains of labour, language, and domination (*Herrschaft*). Habermas thus effectively recasts the structure of the argument of Kant's *Critique of Pure Reason*, by clarifying the necessary conditions of possibility for knowledge (the three cognitive interests) and turning these against reason's 'groundless pretensions'.[9] To be sure, the latter is not done through a destructive critique of bloated metaphysical claims to knowledge—as in Kant's case—but rather against a definition of knowledge that is *overly narrow*: namely, the scientific reduction of knowledge to the natural-scientific epistemic domain. Habermas's study thus attempts to salvage the *reconstructive dimension* of transcendental critique that Kant pursued in the *Critique of Pure Reason*, although in the form of a reflective social theory rather than the circumscribed metaphysics of transcendental idealism.

However, Habermas quickly came to recognize that this exceptionally ambitious argument is also troubled by a number of problems. First Habermas's provides little systematic clarification of the central category of reflection and its supposed connection with critique and critical theory. As Thomas McCarthy has argued, a consequence of this lack of clarity is a conflation of two forms of reflection: namely, reflection in the Kantian sense of the critique of reason, which aims at clarifying the conditions of possibility for knowledge, and reflection in the Marxian sense of critique, which aims at a practical transformation of society as a whole.[10] Habermas often seems to assume that the theory of knowledge as social theory he develops is equivalent to a critical theory of society that dispels ideological illusion and enables practical emancipation from domination, which is simply not the

---

[9] Kant, *The Critique of Pure Reason*, p. 101.
[10] Thomas McCarthy, *The Critical Theory of Jürgen Habermas* (London: Hutchinson & Co., 1978), p. 94.

case. Even if we grant that Habermas has successfully demonstrated the existence of three cognitive interests as conditions of possibility for three different branches of knowledge, this undertaking is categorically different from the meaning of critique in Marx's sense, which seeks to dissipate an ideological self-understanding of workers as commodities in order that they may see the class domination to which they are subject and emancipate themselves in practice.

Secondly, in contrast to the technical and the practical interest, Habermas actually fails to ground the emancipatory interest and the category of reflection in 'the natural history of the human species'. The different logics of inquiry characterizing the natural and cultural sciences derive from two *primordial modes* in which human beings relate to the world in their development as a species (technical control and mutual understanding). According to Habermas, two cognitive interests can be 'read off' these primordial modes of relating to the world, because the *meaning* of valid scientific claims in these two different branches of knowledge ultimately depends on the ability of such claims to further, respectively, a technical interest in the control of nature and a practical interest in mutual understanding. This suggests that scientific inquiry in the natural and cultural sciences is possible only because their respective logics of inquiry correspond to the two pre-scientifically constituted object domains. Because of the fundamental importance of these two modes of relating-to-the-world for the survival and development of the human species, they can be identified as expressing two cognitive interests, and these interests can thus be seen as fundamental conditions of possibility for scientific knowledge.

However, this attempt to ground the technical and practical cognitive interests in the *primordiality* of technical mastery of nature and mutual understanding leaves the emancipatory interest hanging in mid-air, since the cognitive interest in freedom from domination and ideological illusion would not, intuitively, seem to enjoy the same primordial status. Indeed, soon after publishing *Erkenntnis und Interesse*, Habermas would acknowledge that the emancipatory interest in freedom from domination and ideology has a 'derivative status', since power, domination, and ideology are phenomena that only arise within a communicative context of meaning once both primordial interests have found some degree of practical expression.[11] But although this clarifies that the emancipatory interest is not grounded in the same way as the two primordial interests, it does not tell us anything about what that alternative grounding would be. As we shall see in the next section, the attempt to establish an alternative grounding for a critical theory of society would ultimately lead Habermas to embrace the *linguistic turn* in analytic philosophy and abandon the language of cognitive interests.

---

[11] Habermas, *Knowledge and Human Interests*, p. 371.

5.2.2 A Formal Pragmatics of Communicative Reason

The problems that Habermas encountered in the course of his early attempt to redeem the emancipatory aspirations of critical theory through the theory of knowledge as social theory compelled him to undertake a significant change in his philosophical frame of reference, facilitated by his reception of the analytic philosophy of language. However, I should pre-empt a possible misunderstanding at this point. What we might call Habermas's *communicative turn*—which simultaneously represents the birth of what I call his communicative paradigm proper—does not, as might be supposed, represent a radical break with his earlier programme. Rather, shortly after the publication of *Erkenntnis and Interesse*, Habermas discovers the tools for recasting his programme for the redemption of critical theory within the framework of the pragmatic philosophy of language associated with Ludwig Wittgenstein, J.L. Austin, and John Searle, and the theory of linguistic competence developed by Noam Chomsky.

With this shift of philosophical framework, he does not give up the aspiration to redeem the emancipatory interest—although the theoretical language of cognitive interests is abandoned—but rather pursues that redemption through a formal pragmatics of the rational structure of ordinary language communication in terms of a *theory of communicative competence*. This account serves as the philosophical foundation of the normative dimension in Habermas's communicative paradigm of critical theory, and the systematic basis for his theory of social evolution, theory of communicative action, and discourse theory of morality, law, and democracy, to which we will return in Sections 5.3, 5.4, and 5.5.

Let us begin the exposition of this novel philosophical foundation for critical theory by seeing how this communicative turn enables Habermas to solve the obstacles encountered in the argument of *Erkenntnis und Interesse*. In response to the charge that he conflates critique in the Kantian sense with critique in the Marxian sense, Habermas draws an important distinction between *reconstruction* and *critique* (or *self-critique*).[12] Of these two, critique is the more familiar term: it is a form of reflection that seeks to 'make unconscious elements conscious in a way that has practical consequences'.[13] A critical theory of society is a form of critique in this sense, since it aspires to dispel the ideological illusions of a concrete addressee (dominated social groups) through a process of enlightenment, with the intention of enabling their self-emancipation in practice. However, Habermas now clarifies *reconstruction* as the proper heir to the method of transcendental philosophy and the key to recasting Kant's critique of reason in post-metaphysical terms for a philosophical grounding of a critical theory of society.

---

[12] Habermas, 'Appendix', in *Knowledge and Human Interests*, p. 377.
[13] Habermas, 'Appendix', in *Knowledge and Human Interests*, p. 378.

Although the term reconstruction (*Nachkonstruktion*) also has a broader meaning in Habermas' work, what he calls 'rational reconstruction' in the strict sense is consistently understood as a method for systematically *explicating* the 'pretheoretical knowledge' and 'rule consciousness' that guides the interaction of competent actors engaged in some activity.[14] According to Habermas, this method is characteristic of the reconstructive sciences—which he now distinguishes from both the empirical-analytical and the historical-hermeneutical sciences—such as logic, linguistics, and the philosophy of language. Habermas clarifies the reconstructive method with reference to Gilbert Ryle's distinction between *knowing-how* and *knowing-that*: reconstruction explicates the knowledge of the generative rules that structure a given activity, such as the logical rules that structure the formulation of formally valid propositions, thus turning the knowing-how of a competent actor *into* a knowing-that (i.e., the knowing-that of scientific knowledge).

When Habermas speaks of *rule consciousness*, he refers, for example, to the general awareness of the grammatical rules with which an agent can generate grammatically correct sentences. However, for most people, the knowledge of grammatical rules is mostly intuitive or superficial, even though they master these generative rules in practice. The linguist is concerned with reconstructing and explicating these generative rules, in the same way, in John Searle's words, as 'someone who has learned to play chess without ever having the rules formulated and who wants such a formulation'.[15] Moreover, Habermas maintains that such reconstructions are *rational* in the sense that the pretheoretical knowing-how of rule systems is understood as a complex of rational principles that provide competent agents with reasons for thought and action.

Beginning in the early 1970s, Habermas set out an ambitious reconstructive research programme in the philosophy of language that he calls *formal pragmatics*. This programme in turn serves as the philosophical foundation for his social and political theory, by allowing Habermas to identify the contours of a socially embodied and historically emergent reason in everyday communicative interaction. Briefly stated, formal pragmatics aims to 'identify and reconstruct universal conditions of possible mutual understanding (*Verständigung*)'.[16] It explicates the intuitive knowing-how and rule consciousness that a competent speaker possesses and which provides the basis of her ability to engage in successful communication with others in her own language, and Habermas maintains that this knowing-how and rule consciousness is invariant across all natural languages. For this reason, his

---

[14] Jürgen Habermas, 'Reconstruction and Interpretation in the Social Sciences', in *Moral Consciousness and Communicative Action*, transl. by Christian Lenhardt and Shierry Weber Nicholson (Cambridge: Polity Press, 1990), p 31; Jürgen Habermas, 'What is Universal Pragmatics?', in *On The Pragmatics of Communication*, ed. by Maeve Cooke (Cambridge MA: MIT Press, 1998).

[15] John Searle, *Speech Acts: An Essay in the Philosophy of Language* (Cambridge: Cambridge University Press, 1969), p. 55.

[16] Habermas, 'What is Universal Pragmatics?', p. 21.

formal-pragmatic programme was initially termed 'universal pragmatics' to distinguish Habermas's focus on reconstructing 'species competencies' from the more conventionalistic approaches inspired by the later Wittgenstein.[17]

Formal (or universal) pragmatics thus follows Noam Chomsky in drawing 'a fundamental distinction between *competence* (the speaker-hearer's knowledge of his language) and *performance* (the actual use of language in concrete situations)'.[18] However, going beyond Chomsky, formal pragmatics does not study an 'ideal speaker-hearer's intrinsic competence' in order to disclose a universal 'generative grammar' operative in the formation of well-formed sentences, but rather the communicative competences that a speaker-hearer must possess in order to reach a *mutual understanding* with another about something in the world. Crucially, an account of these competences must countenance what Habermas—here in an early formulation from his Gauss lectures in 1970—calls 'the double structure of ordinary language communication':

> a speech act is composed of a performative clause and a dependent clause with propositional content. The main clause is used in an utterance in order to establish an intersubjective relation between speakers and hearers. The dependent clause is used in an utterance in order to communicate about objects (or states of affairs) ... Communication about objects (or states of affairs) takes place only on the condition of simultaneous metacommunication about the meaning of the dependent clause. A situation where it is possible to reach a mutual understanding requires that at least two speaker-hearers simultaneously establish communication at *both* levels: at the level of intersubjectivity, where the subjects talk with one another, and at the level of the objects (or states of affairs) *about* which they communicate.[19]

To make sense of this claim, and, indeed, to fully appreciate the scope and level of ambition of the formal-pragmatic programme, we need to clarify both the 'level of intersubjectivity' and the 'level of objects (or states of affairs) about which they communicate'. Let us begin with the second level: Habermas's formal-pragmatic theory of meaning.

It might be helpful to briefly situate formal pragmatics within the broader field of the philosophy of language. Analytic philosophy rose to prominence in early

---

[17] In a footnote to the 1979 translation of the article 'What is Universal Pragmatics', Habermas notes: 'Hitherto the term "pragmatics" has referred to the analysis of particular contexts of language use and not to the reconstruction of universal features of using language (or of employing sentences in utterances). To mark this contrast, I introduced a distinction between "empirical" and "universal" pragmatics. I am no longer happy with this terminology; the term "formal pragmatics"—as an extension of "formal semantics"—would serve better'. Habermas, 'What is Universal Pragmatics?', p. 92.
[18] Noam Chomsky, *Aspects of the Theory of Syntax* (Cambridge MA: The MIT Press, 1965), p. 4.
[19] Jürgen Habermas, *On The Pragmatics of Social Interaction: Preliminary Studies in the Theory of Communicative Action*, transl. by Barbara Fultner (Cambridge MA: MIT Press, 2002), p. 74.

twentieth century Anglophone philosophy driven by the work of Gottlob Frege, Bertrand Russell, and the early Wittgenstein. The heart of this 'philosophical revolution'[20] was to introduce the theory of meaning (semantics) in place of the theory of knowledge (epistemology), which had served as 'first philosophy' since Descartes—i.e., as the 'foundation of all of philosophy'.[21] Following Frege, 'formal semantics' generally holds that understanding the meaning of a sentence depends on grasping what Donald Davidson would later call its 'truth conditions'—i.e., what would have to be the case for the sentence to be true.[22] For example, understanding the meaning of the sentence 'Elvis has left the building' depends on grasping that the sentence is true only if the person carrying the proper name 'Elvis' is, as a matter of fact, no longer in the building. Formal semantics thus connects meaning with truth—or, rather, it connects the meaning of sentences with grasping what must be the case for a sentence to be true.

Broadly speaking, Habermas criticizes formal semantics in the Fregean tradition on three separate counts. First, formal semantics commits a *semantic abstraction* by ignoring how language is used in practice and reducing the question of meaning to the meaning of sentences. Habermas maintains that *both* language use and sentence meaning have implications for meaning. Second, it commits a *cognitive abstraction* by effectively limiting meaning to declarative sentences, such as 'Elvis has left the building'.[23] As Habermas insists, actual linguistic communication is a much richer and more diverse phenomenon than declarative or 'assertoric' sentences. Finally, formal semantics commits a third abstraction by making meaning dependent on an objective conception of truth. On this final issue, Habermas is in agreement with Michael Dummett, who argues that the definition of meaning in terms of grasping objective truth conditions founders on the problem of perfectly intelligible sentences whose truth conditions cannot be decided—such as quantification over an infinite or unsurveyable domain. According to Dummett, this problem implies that we cannot conceive of meaning as grasping these (sometimes unknowable) truth conditions. Instead, Dummett argues, 'an understanding of a statement consists in a capacity to recognize *whatever is counted as verifying it*, i.e., as conclusively establishing it as true'.[24]

---

[20] Richard Rorty, 'Introduction: Metaphilosophical Difficulties in Linguistic Philosophy', in *The Linguistic Turn: Essays in Philosophical Method*, ed. by Richard Rorty (Chicago: Chicago University Press, 1967).

[21] Michael Dummett, *Frege: Philosophy of Language* (New York: Harper & Row, 1973), Ch. 19.

[22] Donald Davidson, 'Truth and Meaning', in *Inquiries into Truth and Interpretation* (Oxford: Oxford University Press, 2001).

[23] The term 'cognitive abstraction' is potentially misleading, since Habermas does not mean to claim that non-declarative sentences (such as moral sentences) do not have cognitive content. However, the point here, I take it, is that formal semantics reduces meaning to declarative sentences with an uncontroversial cognitive content, i.e., that some claim can either be true or false and can be adjudicated with reference to reasons for and against.

[24] Michael Dummett, 'What Is a Theory of Meaning? (II)', in *The Seas of Language* (Oxford: Oxford University Press, 1996), p. 71 [emphasis added].

According to Habermas, Dummett's *epistemic turn* rightly overcomes the third abstraction by construing meaning in terms of the knowledge that a speaker and hearer has of the *criteria* according to which the truth of a sentence can be established, rather than directly grasping its truth conditions. However, to overcome the first two abstractions, Dummett's epistemic revision does not suffice; rather, the framework of formal semantics must be conclusively abandoned in favour of a *pragmatic* approach to meaning. In his 'Philosophical Investigations', Wittgenstein famously laid the foundations of such an approach, arguing that 'the meaning of a word is its use in the language'.[25] However, in his own philosophical practice, the later Wittgenstein also encouraged a conventionalistic focus on local contexts of communication and circumscribed language games, effectively severing the connection between meaning and truth, understanding and validity, which was established in formal semantics. In Habermas's view, however, crucial steps towards correcting this misguided conventionalism are taken in the work of J.L. Austin.

Austin captures the pragmatic dimension of meaning in the notion of performative speech, which can be analysed in terms of its *locutionary* (or propositional) content, *illocutionary* force, and *perlocutionary* effect.[26] In Austin's terminology, formal semantics only studies 'locution': the formal meaning or propositional content of sentences. By contrast, the distinction between illocutionary force and perlocutionary effect takes us beyond mere sentence meaning and into the question of what a speaker *does* by uttering a sentence—in short, referring to *speech* rather than language. The predicate 'illocutionary' refers to speech, which is *simultaneously* the performance of an act of a certain kind, such as the utterance 'I now pronounce you man and wife'. Illocutionary force thus aims at securing what Austin calls an 'uptake'.[27] The predicate 'perlocutionary', on the other hand, refers to speech where the intention is to produce a certain effect upon the hearer that is not itself constituted by that utterance—such as attempts to threaten or manipulate. Pragmatics is thus distinguished from semantics by extending the study of meaning beyond sentences to *utterances*, or what John Searle calls 'speech acts'.[28]

---

[25] Ludwig Wittgenstein, *Philosophical Investigations*, rev. 4th ed., trans. by G.E.M. Anscombe, P.M.S. Hacker, and Joachim Schulte (Chichester: Wiley-Blackwell, 2009), p. 25.

[26] These distinctions are not exactly Austin's, who initially distinguishes between locutionary and illocutionary acts, but rather Habermas's revised reconstruction of Austin's terminology, which corresponds closer (but not exactly) to Austin's later use. As Habermas says: 'this demarcation of locutionary and illocutionary acts could not be maintained when it became apparent that all speech acts—the constatives included—contain a locutionary component (in the form of a sentence with propositional content) and an illocutionary component (in the form of a performative sentence). What Austin had initially introduced as the locutionary act was now replaced by (a) the propositional component contained in every explicit speech act, and (b) a special class of illocutionary acts—constative speech acts—that imply the validity claim of truth'. Habermas, 'What is Universal Pragmatics', p. 73.

[27] J.L. Austin, *How To Do Things With Words* (Oxford: Oxford University Press, 1962).

[28] Habermas wavers on the question whether semantics and pragmatics are complementary or mutually exclusionary, but in his later work he argues that formal semantics is a legitimate if restricted

Moreover, according to Habermas, Austin's 'concept of an illocutionary act opens up the *entire* spectrum of speech to linguistic analysis'.[29] Accordingly, Austin's pragmatism also harbours the potential to definitively overcome the second (cognitive) abstraction, by allowing us to analyse the many different ways in which language is actually *used* in communicative practice. Habermas's research programme of formal pragmatics thus represents a synthesis of certain distinctive elements from Fregean formal semantics (the connection between meaning and validity), Dummett's epistemic revision of formal semantics (the definition of meaning in terms of grasping 'acceptability conditions' rather than truth conditions), and Austin's pragmatics (the performativity, illocutionary force [and perlocutionary effect] of speech). However, Habermas also makes original—that is, non-synthetic—contributions to the pragmatic philosophy of language. Most importantly, Habermas develops an account of the *modus operandi* of illocutionary force, which construes the intersubjective 'uptake' in communicative interaction as given by the rational contestability of the *claims to validity* exchanged by speakers and hearers, enabling him to disclose a universal rational infrastructure of communication that cuts across all natural languages.

To properly grasp this far-reaching undertaking, we have to briefly sketch Habermas's account of the rational infrastructure of speech. Habermas's analysis focuses on one particular form of speech act, namely speech acts that are primarily characterized by their illocutionary (as opposed to perlocutionary) force. As we have seen, all such speech acts have, according to Habermas, a double structure in that they possess both propositional content and illocutionary force, and speech acts can be distinguished as belonging to a 'cognitive' or an 'interactive' use of language depending on which side of the 'double structure of speech' they emphasize. If the propositional content is explicated in a 'constative' speech act, then the speech act represents a cognitive use of language, and if it is assumed as part of what Habermas calls a 'regulative' speech, then they belong to the interactive use of language.

Habermas maintains that these are irreducible different *modes of communication* concerned with different *domains of meaning*: the cognitive use of language (constative speech acts) is concerned with the *truth* of claims about events or objects, whereas the interactive use of language (regulative speech acts) is concerned with the *rightness* or *appropriateness* of norms. Furthermore, in addition to these two basic modes of communication, Habermas adds what he calls the 'expressive use of language', which is concerned with the 'truthfulness with which a speaker expresses her intentions'.[30] Accordingly, in illocutionary speech acts,

---

approach to meaning. John Searle argues that the two approaches are complementary and both necessary for a comprehensive philosophy of language. See Searle, *Speech Acts: An Essay in the Philosophy of Language*, pp. 18–19.

[29] Habermas, 'Communicative Rationality and the Theories of Meaning and Action', in *On The Pragmatics of Communication*.

[30] Habermas, 'What is Universal Pragmatics?', p. 80.

we can distinguish three different modes of communication: the cognitive, the interactive, and the expressive use of language, which correspond to the respective domains of meaning of truth, rightness, and truthfulness.[31]

Moreover, Habermas also argues that in each of these three modes of communication, we assume three categorially different relations towards the world that carve out three different object domains of reality: in the cognitive use of language, we relate ourselves to an *objective world*; in the interactive use of language, we relate ourselves to a *social world* (or 'society'); and in the expressive use of language, we relate ourselves to a *subjective world*.[32] These should not be understood as three different worlds in an ontological sense, but rather as three different 'aspects' of the same world whose existence we pragmatically presuppose in these three different modes of communication. Accordingly, in making claims about states of affairs in the objective word, we are concerned with the truth of the propositional content of constative speech acts; in making claims about the social world, we are concerned with the rightness or appropriateness of regulative speech; and in making claims about our personal experiences in the subjective world, we are concerned with the truthfulness, sincerity, or authenticity of expressive speech acts.

With this formal-pragmatic theory of meaning in view, we can now flesh out Habermas's account of the 'level of intersubjectivity' in the double structure of ordinary language communication: the nature of the illocutionary uptake that 'binds' or 'bonds' speakers and hearers in communicative interaction. As suggested above, the concept that Habermas introduces to establish this bridge is the notion of a *validity claim* (*Geltungsanspruch*). According to Habermas, 'anyone acting communicatively must, in performing any speech act, raise universal validity claims and suppose that they can be vindicated'. More specifically,

> The speaker must choose an intelligible (*verständlich*) expression so that speaker and hearer can comprehend one another. The speaker must have the intention of communicating a true (*wahr*) proposition (or a propositional content, the existential presuppositions of which are satisfied) so that the hearer can *share the knowledge* of the speaker. The speaker must want to express her intentions truthfully (*wahrhaftig*) so that the hearer can find the utterance of the speaker credible (can trust her). Finally, the speaker must choose an utterance that is right (*richtig*) with respect to prevailing norms and values so that the hearer can accept the utterance, and both speaker and hearer can, in the utterance, thereby agree *with* one another with respect to a recognized normative background.[33]

---

[31] See also, Jürgen Habermas, *The Theory of Communicative Action: Vol I: Reason and the Rationalization of Society*, transl. by Thomas McCarthy (Cambridge: Polity Press, 1986), Ch. 3.
[32] Habermas, *The Theory of Communicative Action: Vol I*, p. 84.
[33] Habermas, 'What is Universal Pragmatics?', p. 22–23.

The last three validity claims correspond to each of the three uses of language sketched above, whereas the first claim to intelligibility is 'the only universal claim that is to be fulfilled immanently to language' as such.[34]

Now, what exactly does Habermas mean by calling these supposedly universal claims 'validity claims'? According to Habermas, if I claim that it is raining, I am not merely reporting an irreproachable observation about the weather. Rather, in claiming that it is raining, I am ultimately expressing the belief that I have *justifiable reasons* for making that claim—reasons that I would be able to defend if called upon to do so. This means that if you utter a disagreement with my observation, I would be compelled to support and redeem my claim with reasons for my belief, such as 'drops are falling from the sky' or 'my hair is getting wet'. Of course, if I am engaged in a regulative use of speech, by criticizing your conduct with reference to a shared norm, then it won't do to cite such 'facts' as drops of rain falling from the sky. Rather, then I must appeal to *different kinds* of reasons, namely those normative reasons that have weight in the domain of meaning characteristic of the social world, such as 'you promised me that you would clean the apartment before my parents arrived'. The central idea is that, in making a claim to validity in any of the three uses of language, I *performatively commit to justify that claim with appropriate reasons* if called upon to do so.

Indeed, on Habermas's view, it is precisely this concept of a validity claim that represents the *internal connection between language and rationality*. More specifically, his thesis is that 'the speaker can illocutionarily influence the hearer, and vice versa, because speech-act-typical obligations are connected with cognitively testable validity claims—that is, because the reciprocal binding and bonding relationship has a rational basis'.[35] This rational basis can always be relied upon to question any kind of validity claim, whether to the truth of an assertion, the rightness of a recommendation, or the sincerity of the speaker's intentions. For Habermas, 'being rational' is thus essentially a matter of being able to master the acceptability conditions of a given validity claim; it is a question of knowing what *kind of reasons* could establish the illocutionary success of a given speech act in communicative interaction, and what kind of reasons one can invoke in criticizing the speech act of another. Habermas calls this formal-pragmatic conception of rationality, understood 'in terms of the justifiability and criticizability of expressions' and as inherent in the structure of communicative interaction: *communicative reason*.[36]

---

[34] Habermas, 'What is Universal Pragmatics?', p. 49.
[35] Habermas, 'What is Universal Pragmatics?', p. 85 [emphasis removed].
[36] Habermas, *On the Pragmatics of Communication*, p. 307. In fact, Habermas considers communicative reason merely one of three constitutive 'roots of rationality', namely that of the communicative structure of validity claims. The other two roots are the propositional or representational structure of knowledge (epistemic rationality, the subject of truth semantics), and the teleological structure of action (intentional rationality, the subject of rational choice theory). However, he argues that all three roots are integrated by the justificatory structure of discursive rationality, which he understands as a

5.2.3 'A Social Life in Uncoerced Communication'

This reconstructive account of communicative reason provides Habermas's mature response to the first problem that he detected in the first generation of the Frankfurt School, namely the problem of the *philosophical grounding* of the normative dimension in critical theory. In an essay on Adorno's negativist philosophy written on the occasion of his death in 1969, Habermas already raises the question, 'how critical thinking itself might be justified'.[37] As we saw in Chapter 1, the young Horkheimer developed a conception of immanent critique that brings the *bourgeois* ideals of justice and freedom to bear on the miserable state of actual *bourgeois* society through a critical theory of society. However, immanent critique evidently presupposes that the society in question *actually makes* the required claims to justice and freedom; that it pretends to be something it is not. But if, as Habermas once expressed it, 'bourgeois consciousness has become cynical ... [and] the bourgeois ideals have gone into retirement'—as was manifestly the case in Nazi Germany, but, as we shall see, Habermas also believes is a systematic tendency in post-war capitalist democracies—'[then] there are no norms and values to which an immanent critique might appeal'.[38]

Moreover, Habermas also maintains that the attempt to ground critical theory in a return to the Marxian injection of utopian ideals into the teleological structure of a materialist philosophy of history, which still undergirded the revolutionary optimism of Horkheimer's original paradigm of critical theory, is equally closed off for three reasons—anticipated by Horkheimer and Adorno but brought to their logical concision by Habermas. The first reason is the changed practical situation resulting from the social and political disintegration of the proletariat, which, as we have seen, was one of the problems that convinced Horkheimer to give up his early materialist programme. Following Adorno, the second reason is the productive forces' 'loss of innocence' through utilization for purposes of industrial genocide and weapons of mass destruction. The third reason, also present *in nuce* in Horkheimer's early thought, is that critical theory, according to Habermas, cannot disregard the disciplinary specialization and fallibilism that characterizes modern science. Rather,

> a critical theory of society ... must one the one hand, under the two-fold pressure of theoretical generalisation and specialisation, attempt to dismantle

---

specific form of communicative rationality concerning the reflexive criticism of epistemic, intentional, or communicative claims: 'Communicative rationality does not constitute the *overarching* structure of rationality but rather one of three core structures that are, however, interwoven with one another by way of the discursive rationality that emerges out of communicative rationality'. Habermas, *On the Pragmatics of Communication*, p. 309

[37] Jürgen Habarmas, 'Urgeschichte der Subjektivität und verwilderte Selbstbehauptung', in *Philosophisch-politische Profile. Erweiterte Ausgabe* (Frankfurt: Suhrkamp Verlag, 1987), p. 175.

[38] Jürgen Habermas, *Communication and the Evolution of Society*, transl. by Thomas McCarthy (Boston, MA: Beacon Press, 1979), p. 97.

philosophical questions into scientifically workable problems; on the other hand, it must ... accept the fundamentally hypothetical nature of its theses.[39]

Accordingly, Habermas concludes: a critical theory of society 'is possible today only if we can reconstruct general presuppositions of communication and procedures for justifying norms and value'.[40] However, Habermas also argues that the substantial content of such a formal-pragmatic reconstruction tallies with the emancipatory aspirations of the first generation of the Frankfurt School—ambitions that *point beyond* the procedure of immanent critique. He maintains that the 'reconciled state', to which Adorno always implicitly but no less consistently appealed,

> has the structure of a social life in uncoerced communication. And we anticipate such a state, every time we mean to say something true. Indeed, the idea of truth, which was already implicit in the first sentence spoken, can only be formed with appeal to the model of an idealised agreement, obtained in communication free from domination. The truth of statements is therefore bound up with the intention of a true form of life. Critique must make appeal to nothing more than such a form life, implicit in everyday speech, but also to nothing less.[41]

Habermas's argument against Horkheimer and Adorno thus amounts to the claim that, for both empirical and historical reasons, as well as reasons that have to do with the epistemic refinement of modern science, a critical theory of society—which aspires to be empirically accurate, normatively justifiable, and defensible according to state-of-the-art scientific standards—must be able to ground its critical intentions in a philosophical foundation that renders its emancipatory dimension less question-begging from a scientific point of view. In Habermas's view, formal-pragmatics is able to provide this foundation.

In order bring the critical potential of this foundation fully into view, we must first introduce a distinction that is of fundamental importance to the whole architectonic of Habermas's communicative paradigm: namely, the distinction between *communicative action* and *discourse*. The difference between communicative action and discourse is their different functions in communication.

---

[39] Jürgen Habermas, 'Replik auf Einwände', in *Vorstudien und Ergänzungen zur Theorie des Kommunikativen Handelns* (Frankfurt: Suhrkamp Verlag, 1984), p. 481.
[40] Habermas, *Communication and the Evolution of Society*, p. 97.
[41] Habermas, 'Urgeschichte der Subjektivität und verwilderte Selbstbehauptung', p. 176. As this passage suggests, in his early work Habermas understood the ideal speech situation (discussed below) in more substantive terms, 'as necessary conditions of an emancipated form of life [... and as recasting] in linguistic terms what we have traditionally sought to capture in the ideas of truth, freedom, and justice'. [Habermas, *On the Pragmatics of Social Interaction*, p. 99]. It should be noted, however, that Habermas fairly quickly gives up the idea that a 'true form of life' is directly given by the ideal speech situation, maintaining instead that the idealizing formal-pragmatic presuppositions that undergird the ideal speech situation can always be turned critically against social reality.

Communicative action is defined by Habermas as *action oriented towards mutual understanding*. The defining aspect of communicative action is that orientation towards mutual understanding serves the purpose of *coordinating action* between two or more interaction partners: 'Reaching an understanding functions as a mechanism for coordinating actions only through the participants in interaction coming to an agreement concerning the claimed *validity* of their utterances.'[42] In communicative action, validity claims are taken for granted in the sense that they remain unproblematized. Of course, this can only go on for so long as the hearer of a claim does not actually raise an objection that problematizes the claim in question, but as soon as this happens, the only alternative to cutting off interaction altogether is to transcend communicative action and enter into the reflective conditions of discourse (I expound Habermas's theory of communicative action in greater detail in Section 5.4).

The crucial aspect that distinguishes discourse from communicative action is that the *pressure to act*—the orientation towards *coordinating action* through reaching a mutual understanding—recedes into the background, and the focus of interaction partners is directed towards the criticism and justification of problematized claims to validity about something in the objective world, in their shared social world, or in the subjective world of the speakers. What is distinctive about discourse is thus that speaker and hearer are *only* oriented towards reaching an understanding by invoking reasons for and against claims, while they are, to the extent their situation allows, momentarily suspended from the hustle and bustle of action coordination. Moreover, Habermas's claim is that discourses obey a logic *entirely of their own*. In his 1972 essay 'Theories of Truth' (*Wahrheitstheorien*), Habermas attempts, in his famous formulation, to 'clarify the peculiar unforced force of the better argument through the formal properties of discourse.'[43] The finer details of his discourse 'theory of argumentation' need not concern us here, but the central point of this early essay is that the formal properties of discourses can be captured by what Habermas calls an *ideal speech situation* and that this ideal speech situation can serve as a critical standard for a critical theory of society.

The ideal speech situation is characterized by four *formal-pragmatic presuppositions*, which require:

(a) that nobody who could make a relevant contribution may be excluded;
(b) that all participants are afforded an equal opportunity to make contributions;
(c) that the participants must mean what they say: only truthful utterances are admissible; and (d) that communication must be freed from external and internal

---

[42] Habermas, *The Theory of Communicative Action. Vol. I*, p. 99.
[43] Habermas, 'Wahrheitstheorien', in *Vorstudien und Ergänzungen zur Theorie des Kommunikativen Handelns*, p. 161. Habermas has never allowed this essay to appear in English, since he soon regretted and retracted the so-called 'consensus theory of truth'.

compulsion so that the 'yes'/'no' stances that participants adopt on criticizable validity claims are motivated solely by the rational force of the better reason.[44]

These four formal-pragmatic presuppositions of discourse imply that an ideal speech situation would be free from any kind of domination or systematically distorted communication. Crucially: 'Therefore, every consensus argumentatively reached under the conditions of an ideal speech situation can be regarded as a criterion for the redemption of any given thematised validity claim'.[45]

According to Habermas, these formal-pragmatic presuppositions are immanent in any rational discourse. To be sure, this does not mean that they are *always realized*—indeed, as we are all aware from personal experience, this is never actually the case. However, Habermas claims that these formal-pragmatic presuppositions have the peculiar function of being an 'operatively effective fiction':

> It belongs to the presuppositions of argumentation that, in the course of raising speech acts, we counterfactually act as if the ideal speech situation wasn't merely fictive, but real—and this is precisely what we call a presupposition. The normative foundation of understanding reached through speech is therefore both: anticipated, but as an anticipated grounding also effective.[46]

In other words, the formal-pragmatic presuppositions of discourse are at once *factual* and *counterfactual*: they are factual in the sense that 'they are actually effective in structuring processes of mutual understanding and in organizing contexts of interaction'[47] and counterfactual in the sense that they operate through idealization, *as if* the discourse weren't subject to the inevitable limiting conditions of the context at hand. The ideal speech situation is thus immanent in any actual and always imperfect discursive context, but it also simultaneously transcends any context in which it is pragmatically anticipated, and this tension is precisely what enables *critique*:

> A set of unavoidable idealisations forms the counterfactual basis of an actual practice of reaching understanding, a practice that can critically turn against its own results and thus *transcend* itself. Thus the tension between idea and reality breaks into the very facticity of linguistically structured forms of life.[48]

---

[44] This later and more intuitive formulation of the four presuppositions of discourse is from Jürgen Habermas, 'A Genealogical Analysis of the Cognitive Content of Morality', in *The Inclusion of the Other: Studies in Political Theory*, ed. and transl. by Ciaran Cronin and Pablo de Greiff (Cambridge: Polity Press, 1998).
[45] Habermas, 'Wahrheitstheorien', p. 179.
[46] Jürgen Habermas, 'Wahrheitstheorien', p. 181.
[47] Jürgen Habermas, 'Communicative Action and the Detranscendentalized Use of Reason' in *Between Naturalism and Religion*, transl. by Ciaran Cronin (Cambridge: Polity Press, 2008), p. 27.
[48] Jürgen Habermas, *Between Facts and Norms. Contributions to a Discourse Theory of Law and Democracy*, trans. by William Rehg (Cambridge: Polity Press, 1996), p. 4.

The ideal speech situation represents a kind of thought experiment, in which the idealizing formal-pragmatic presuppositions of rational discourse are brought together in a 'methodological fiction'[49] that can serve as a critical standard for evaluating agreements reached in actual discourses. Since real discourses can never actually realize the implicit ideal on which they are counterfactually predicated, the ideal speech situation can *always* be brought to bear on the conditions of discourse in actual social and political life. However, Habermas makes it clear that the 'quasi-transcendental necessity'[50] of the formal-pragmatic presuppositions cannot make a claim to the strong *a priori grounding* of Kant's critique of reason:

> Formal pragmatics holds that the rational structure of action oriented toward mutual understanding is reflected in the presuppositions that actors *must* make if they are to engage in this practice at all. The necessity of this 'must' has a Wittgensteinian rather than a Kantian character. That is, it does not have the transcendental meaning of universal, necessary, and noumenal (*intelligiblen*) conditions of possible experience, but has the grammatical meaning of an 'unavoidability' stemming from the conceptual connections of a system of learned—but for us inescapable—rule-governed behaviour.[51]

Now, Habermas's idea of an ideal speech situation has also been subject to forceful objections, leading him to undertake a number of significant revisions of his original account. Most importantly, as an epistemic account of truth defined in terms of ideal consensus, the ideal speech situation has been met with the objection that it conflates *truth* with *justification*.[52] In reply to this objection, Habermas has in later work responded by repudiating the 'consensus theory of truth' associated with the ideal speech situation and replacing it with a pragmatist version of epistemological realism.[53]

Moreover, *the very idea* of an ideal speech situation has been criticized as paradoxical and conceptually incoherent: if participants in discourse always *strive for a consensus* reached under perfectly ideal communicative conditions, they are in

---

[49] Habermas, *Between Facts and Norms*, p. 323.
[50] Jürgen Habermas, *Moral Consciousness and Communicative Action*, transl. by Christian Lenhardt and Shierry Weber Nicholson (Cambridge: Polity Press, 1990), p. 203.
[51] Habermas, 'Communicative Action and the Detranscendentalized "Use of Reason"', p. 27.
[52] McCarthy, *The Critical Theory of Jürgen Habermas*, p. 303.
[53] On this view, he returns to the traditional definition of the concept of truth as correspondence with an objective world. But in contrast to traditional epistemological realism, which assumes direct epistemic access to a world of brute facts, Habermas's 'Kantian pragmatism' conceives of truth as always linguistically mediated—as a concept that primarily refers to the unconditional validity that participants in discourse *assume* on behalf of their constative validity claims about a presupposed objective world. However, Habermas also retains a non-linguistic or empirical aspect in his later conception of truth, by accepting the realist proviso of the possibility for a discrepancy between truth and our best justifications. With the American pragmatists, Habermas thus accounts for the possibility of *learning* with reference to the inconsistencies between our always fallible knowledge of the world and the practical problems encountered in our coping with the world. Jürgen Habermas, *Truth and Justification*, trans. by Barbara Fultner (Cambridge, MA: The MIT Press, 2003).

a significant sense striving for conditions under which communication would *no longer be necessary*. That is to say, the idea of a situation in which all possible hindrances to communication have been removed is dangerously close to the idea of a situation in which a universal and perfectly rational consensus *already* exists. In this case, the presupposed ideal of communication would, paradoxically, be a condition in which communication is no longer necessary.[54] In response to this objection, Habermas has transformed his conception of the ideal speech situation, as an ideal pertaining to the *outcome* of discourse, towards a more consistently *proceduralistic* view of the idealizing presuppositions of discourse, as guiding the *process* of rational argumentation.[55]

Summing up, we can observe that, just as in his earlier work, Habermas's mature programme of formal pragmatics follows Kant in seeking to rehabilitate the reconstructive dimension of the critique of reason, by providing a reconstruction of the rational infrastructure of ordinary language communication and the formal-pragmatic presuppositions of discourse. But in contrast to Kant, communicative reason is 'detranscendentalized'—that is, it understands reason as socially embodied in historically emergent structures of communication, rather than as a 'pure' faculty of the mind whose properties can be investigated a priori. Although this dependence on historically emergent linguistic practices might seem to reduce its scope to more local linguistic contexts—a charge often levelled at Habermas from 'postmodern' quarters[56]—Habermas is adamant that communicative reason retains a universal thrust by tapping into 'species competences' that *all* speaker-hearers irrespective of their natural language must be able to master in order to reach a mutual understanding with someone about something in the world. Accordingly, insofar as Habermas's formal-pragmatic programme stands to reason, the emancipatory aspirations of critical theory can be philosophically redeemed and founded in communicative reason, enabling a reconstruction of the ideal speech situation, and—as we shall see in Section 5.5—the idea of discourse ethics and the discourse principle of democracy that, Habermas claims, represents the very 'self-understanding' of modern democratic legal orders.

Before concluding this section on the philosophical foundations of Habermas's communicative paradigm, it must be observed that, in the course of developing his communicative revitalization of critical theory, Habermas came to realize

---

[54] Albrecht Wellmer, *Ethik und Dialog. Elemente des moralischen Urteils bei Kant und in der Diskursethik* (Frankfurt: Suhrkamp Verlag, 1986).

[55] That is to say, rather than anticipating an ideal consensus toward which participants strive, Habermas now understands the unconditional validity that speakers in rational discourse assume for their claims to objective truth, subjective truthfulness, and normative rightness, and the presupposed conditions of acceptability within each of these discursive domains, as guiding the *conduct* of intersubjective communication. Maeve Cooke, 'Introduction', in Jürgen Habermas, *On the Pragmatics of Communication*.

[56] See for example Richard Rorty's 'Response to Jürgen Habermas', in *Rorty and his Critics*, ed. by Robert Brandom (Oxford: Blackwell Publishing, 2000), pp. 56-64.

that the philosophical framework he had inherited from the first generation of the Frankfurt School had undergone a crucial structural transformation. That is to say, whereas Adorno still understood his philosophical project in terms of an immanent critique of German idealism, Habermas's turn to the philosophy of language as the philosophical foundation for his communicative paradigm involves a *fundamentally different* way of construing the thinking and acting subject:

> Already Hegel had brought Kant's transcendental subject from the foundationalism of transcendental status into the historical movement of objective *Geist*; and Marx had transferred the ethical life of the objective *Geist* into the material reproduction of society. But neither one nor the other had broken free of the conceptual form of subject philosophy: the world-historical learning process plays out in macro-subjects like peoples or social classes. Also the idea of a history of the species, although it was no longer conceived merely in the form of socially organised work, but also at the same time as a communicatively mediated process of self-constitution, remained captive to the model of the philosophy of reflection.[57]

As the last sentence of this passage suggests, Habermas has later come to recognize that *Erkenntnis und Interesse* still followed Horkheimer and Adorno in conceiving of human history as the self-constitutive process of the human species as a kind of macro-subject. However, following the turn to his formal-pragmatic programme, it becomes clear that this tacit construal of human kind as a macro-subject engaged in a simultaneous process of self-constitution and self-learning is no longer appropriate or adequate. Rather, Habermas's communicative turn enables him to break with the 'philosophy of the subject' and cast historical learning processes as predicated on linguistically mediated *intersubjective relationships*.

Moreover, and just as fundamentally, Habermas's break with the philosophy of the subject also implies a structurally different conceptualization of *reason itself*. Instead of construing reason as a cognitive faculty of the thinking and acting subject, communicative reason also represents what we might call an *intersubjective paradigm of reason*. This paradigm shift to an intersubjective construal of reason represents Habermas's response to the second problem that he located in the first generation of critical theory. It implies a change of primary focus from what the individual or macro-subject *knows* and *does* to what individual subjects *can agree on*. Instead of the individual or macro-subject relating to itself and others from the first-person perspective as *objects* to be subsumed under concepts or manipulated in purposive action, Habermas sees subjects as relating to each other from a

---

[57] Jürgen Habermas, 'Einleitung', in *Sprachtheoretische Grundlegung der Soziologie. Philosophische Texte, Band 1* (Frankfurt: Suhrkamp Verlag, 2009), pp. 10–11.

first-person *and* second-person perspective, *as fellow subjects*, who depend upon one another for reaching mutual understanding. In Habermas's words,

> the objectifying attitude in which the knowing subject regards itself as it would entities in the external world is no longer *privileged*. Fundamental to the paradigm of mutual understanding is, rather, the performative attitude of participants in interaction, who coordinate their plans for action by coming to an understanding about something in the world.[58]

In a series of lectures given in Paris and Frankfurt in 1983–1984 and published as 'The Philosophical of Modernity' (*Der philosophische Diskurs der Moderne*), which were cast in grandiose terms as a defence of modernity against its postmodern critics, Habermas includes a lecture on Horkheimer and Adorno's *Dialektik der Aufklärung*, in which this paradigm shift to an intersubjective reason is brought to bear on 'their blackest book'. The lecture comes off as a peculiar mixture of defence and repudiation: on the one hand, Habermas wants to protect his old mentors from the embrace of what he sees as postmodern counter-enlightenment, but at the same time, he seeks to illustrate how Horkheimer and Adorno were led into a philosophical cul-de-sac precisely through their entrapment in the philosophy of the subject.

According to Habermas, the central thesis of Horkheimer and Adorno's negative universal history—i.e., that the historical unfolding of instrumental reason progressively undermines the subject's capacity for critical thinking, and thereby enlightenment proper—reveals the inherent limits of *Ideologiekritik* in a world where *bourgeois* ideals have lost their social currency. In the two authors' disclosure of the dialectic of enlightenment,

> what is unexplained throughout is their certain lack of concern in dealing with the (to put it in the form of a slogan) achievements of Occidental rationality. How can these two men of the Enlightenment (which they both remain) be so unappreciative of the rational content of cultural modernity that all they perceive everywhere is a binding of reason and domination, power and validity?[59]

As we saw in Chapter 3, Adorno's central but theoretically underdeveloped concept of *mimesis* may indeed harbour Adorno's intuitive insight into the cul-de-sac of the 'philosophy of the subject' as a paradigm of reason and an ultimately futile attempt to push beyond this paradigm towards a notion of undistorted intersubjectivity, a reconciled or non-dominating attitude to the other. Habermas's

---

[58] Jürgen Habermas, *The Philosophical Discourse of Modernity. Twelve Lectures*, trans. by Frederick Lawrence (Cambridge: Polity Press, 1990), p. 296.

[59] Habermas, *The Philosophical Discourse of Modernity*, p. 121.

response to the second problem identified in the first generation of the Frankfurt School holds that Adorno need have looked no further than to *language* to identify the deep normative resources of an always present but at the same time always denied communicative reconciliation with his fellow language speakers—if not with nature—on which he drew with such masterful precision and great moral sensitivity.

There is another side to this change in the paradigm of reason undergirding critical theory. Notwithstanding the fact that, in the course of his highly polemical argument, Habermas exhibits a regrettable tendency to lump Adorno together with Foucault and Derrida as figures of the counter-enlightenment—uncharitably forgetting his own point that Adorno's negativist paradigm of critical theory was precisely characterized by a *fundamental ambivalence* towards the enlightenment, and that he never once strayed from his commitment to mobilize the enlightenment promise of autonomy *against the perversion of enlightenment*[60]—Habermas nevertheless puts his finger on a soft spot. For in the final analysis, Horkheimer and Adorno *did* conceive of emancipation as a great *either-or*, rather than as a gradual learning process.

Following Marx, the reconciled state that they had in mind was always imagined in the form of a historically emergent utopian end-state, whether as a reasonable society of self-conscious subjects who rule themselves and their economic life democratically, or in the form of the messianic 'light of redemption' shone by the totally reconciled state beyond the dialectic of enlightenment. Despite his firm rejection of the affirmative moment in Hegel's dialectic, even Adorno was nonetheless unwilling to eschew the ideal of a utopian end-state—as expressed, for example, in the opening sentence of *Negative Dialektik*: 'Philosophy, which once seemed passé, clings to life because the moment of its realisation was missed'.[61] Only this unacknowledged assumption can truly explain why the regression of human civilization experienced in the first half of the twentieth century seemed to them a final entrapment in a radically evil society, from which there was no practical escape, and why they were both unable to theoretically countenance the fundamental discontinuities between the social context of totalitarian fascism and postwar democratic capitalism. And even though Habermas's early programme for the theory of knowledge as social theory, as well as his initial construal of the ideal speech situation as anticipating a true form of life, still remain captive to this Marxian figure of total, once-and-for-all redemption, his formal pragmatics does eventually pave the way for a more consistently processual and gradualist construal of emancipation that enables him to develop an account of the immanent possibilities for emancipation in capitalist democracies. In order to expound this account

---

[60] E.g., Habermas, *The Philosophical Discourse of Modernity*, p. 336. Note also that Habermas seems to have subsequently changed his mind about at least describing Foucault as a counter-enlightenment figure, as reported in personal conversation.

[61] Adorno, *Negative Dialektik*, p. 13.

in its full depth and scope, we must now turn to the historical and sociological dimensions of Habermas's communicative paradigm of critical theory.

5.3 The Theory of Social Evolution

After the previous section's reconstruction of Habermas's early and later programmes for philosophically grounding his communicative paradigm of critical theory, in this section I want to expound Habermas's theory of social evolution—i.e., the diachronic or historical dimension of his communicative paradigm of critical theory. In one sense, this dimension plays a less systematic role for Habermas than it did for the young Horkheimer and even Adorno, since he is less dependent on a philosophy of history to provide the emancipatory standard for his critical theory. On the other hand, it is also clear that Habermas's formal-pragmatic account of the rational infrastructure of ordinary language communication must be able to account for this socially embedded rationality from a historical point of view; since communicative reason is not conceived of as a *metaphysical* faculty, but rather as embedded in the objective social structures of human life, Habermas must support his formal pragmatics with an account of how these 'normative structures' have emerged in the course of human history. However, in comparison with the first two paradigms of critical theory—and, indeed, with his own earlier programme in *Erkenntnis und Interesse*—Habermas's later theory of social evolution is not burdened with the same foundational tasks; rather, the theory of social evolution that he develops is presented explicitly as a fallibilistic *theory* of history, rather than as a *philosophy* of history.

5.3.1 A Reconstruction of Historical Materialism

Habermas's theory of social revolution is cast as a reconstruction of historical materialism, and, from a more general point of view, it might be understood as his attempt to grasp the systematic importance of language for the species history of human kind. In his 1976 book 'Towards a Reconstruction of Historical Materialism' (*Zur Rekonstruktion des historischen Materialismus*), Habermas attempts to rethink the Marxian thesis that historical development follows the rule that different production relations come and go as they further or fetter the development of the production forces. This is—as we saw in Chapter 1—a functionalist thesis, insofar as forms of consciousness, superstructures, production relations, and productive forces are ordered in an explanatory hierarchy, where forms of consciousness, superstructures, and production relations are ultimately explained in terms of their functional capacity to further or fetter the development of the production forces. While Habermas's theory of social evolution does not break with the functionalist structure of historical materialism, he points—echoing the young Horkheimer—to a fundamental problem in the theory's ability to explain social change: namely, its lack of specification of the mechanism through which the members of a society *learn* to utilize the surplus productivity that spells doom for an old mode of production and institutionalize this surplus in a new and superior mode.[62]

This leads Habermas to introduce a basic and, for his communicative paradigm, crucially important distinction in extension of his longstanding distinction between work and interaction—familiar from *Erkenntnis und Interesse*[63]—namely the distinction between *instrumental action* and *communicative action*.[64] As we have seen, Marx's focus was on the first of these two classes of action—the human instrumentalization of nature for human ends—and he generally understood progress in technical knowledge as the 'engine' of human history. Indeed, for Marx, it is ultimately *technological innovation* that drives human mastery of nature forward from one epoch to the next through the dialectical contradiction between production forces and production relations and social struggles to overcome modes of production that have exhausted their productive potential.

Habermas is in agreement with Marx that the development of *technical knowledge* stored in the productive forces is essential for grasping social evolution, but he maintains that this is only *one* part of the story: to understand the leap from one epoch of history to the other, we must also include the development of *moral-practical* knowledge that enables a society to replace an outdated mode of production with a new one and institutionalize unutilized technical knowledge in more efficient relations of production. The development of technical knowledge and moral-practical knowledge represent two irreducible dimensions of human social evolution, obeying different, independent logics of their own. That is to say, Habermas argues that we can only grasp social evolution by understanding it as a dialectic between the technical knowledge produced in increasingly complex systems of instrumental action and the moral-practical knowledge produced in communicative action.

However, such a reconstruction of historical materialism simultaneously implies a move to a higher level of abstraction. Marx's focus on different 'epochs' of production relations—e.g. the ancient (slavery-based), the feudal, the capitalist, and the socialist and ultimately communist modes of production—is

---

[62] Habermas, *Zur Rekonstruktion des historischen Materialismus*, p. 160. Although Habermas does not seem to realize it, there is, as suggested, a clear echo here of the young Horkheimer's complaint that historical materialism's inability to account for how transformations in the production forces affect individuals (which Horkheimer understood in psychoanalytic terms) severely compromised its scientific credentials.

[63] See also, Jürgen Habermas, 'Technology and Science as Ideology', in *Toward a Rational Society: Student Protest, Science, and Politics* (Cambridge: Polity Press, 2014).

[64] Note that instrumental action is distinct from strategic action in being 'non-social', as concerned with bringing about some state of affairs, whereas strategic action is 'social' in being concerned with influencing the decisions of a rational agent.

thus replaced by Habermas with a focus on different 'principles of organisation'. These principles of organization describe 'innovations that become possible through developmental-logically reconstructible stages of learning, and which institutionalize new levels of societal learning'.[65] The idea here is that a principle of organization refers to the fundamental and constitutive social rules for rational action according to which a society is organized. Social evolution follows a pattern or series of stages that can be diachronically reconstructed, in which hitherto-dominant principles of organization are replaced by new ones. The introduction of a new organizational principle introduces a new form of 'social integration' (a concept that will be expounded in the next section), which enables society to utilize and institutionalize the productive surplus in technical knowledge contained in the production forces. Examples of such principles of organization are the 'primary roles of age and sex' in 'primitive societies', institutionalized as a 'kinship system', or the 'relationship between labour and capital' in 'liberal-capitalist' societies.[66] Principles of organization thus define the basic structure of social relations in a society and the 'basic terms of social cooperation'—to use an expression of John Rawls's.

Moreover, in order to fully exorcise the spectre of technological determinism from his reconstructed historical materialism, Habermas draws a distinction between 'developmental logic' and 'developmental dynamics'. The idea here is that social evolution follows a universal pattern of stages of different principles of organization, which can be reconstructed as a cumulative learning process in both the domains of technical knowledge and moral-practical knowledge. However, this developmental logic does not *determine* the actual historical paths of societies, which play out in historically contingent developmental dynamics. The actual developmental dynamics of a society do not imply that society necessarily *must* develop along the lines of the developmental logic, or that society cannot regress and fall back onto an antecedent stage of development; rather, Habermas's claim is hypothetical: *if* societies develop to a higher stage of social evolution, *then* they must follow the developmental logic. A developmental logic thus describes the *range* of possibilities within which a developmental dynamic can operate at a certain stage, and the range within the principle of organization available at a higher stage, but it does not predetermine the exact place of a society within this range, nor does it predict that progress will necessarily occur:

> The systematically reconstructible patterns of development of normative structures ... depict a *developmental logic* inherent in cultural traditions and institutional change. This logic says nothing about the *mechanisms* of development; it says something only about the range of variations within which cultural

---

[65] Habermas, *Communication and the Evolution of Society*, p. 153.
[66] Jürgen Habermas, *Legitimation Crisis*, transl. by Thomas McCarthy (Cambridge: Polity Press, 1988), pp. 19–20.

values, moral representations, norms, and the like—at a given level of social organization—can be changed and can find different historical expression. In its developmental *dynamics,* the change of normative structures remains dependent on evolutionary challenges posed by unresolved, economically conditioned, system problems and on learning processes that are a response to them. In other words, culture remains a superstructural phenomenon, even if it does seem to play a more prominent role in the transition to new developmental levels than many Marxists have heretofore supposed.[67]

As the last sentence in this passage suggests, Habermas maintains the basic claim of historical materialism, namely that it is development in technical knowledge in the domain of instrumental action which serves as the impetus for epochal transformations. But such transformations depend on the availability of sufficiently developed moral-practical knowledge, in order for the technical knowledge to find institutional expression.

Moreover, Habermas also maintains the claim that disequilibria between production forces and production relations—understood here as an institutional arrangement within a specific principle of organization—manifests itself in the form of systemic problems, i.e., crises. Habermas's theory of social evolution thus maintains the essentially *dialectical* structure of historical materialism. For example, the transition from the principle of organization of feudal societies to that of liberal-capitalist societies through a *bourgeois* revolution re-establishes an equilibrium between technical and moral-practical knowledge in the sense that a society organized according to the relationship between labour and capital is able to overcome crises within the older mode of production, by utilizing the unused productive potential for an explosive degree of capital accumulation. But it does so only at the cost of enabling an *intensification* of the conflict between the degree of social inequality permitted by the new principle of organization and the egalitarian consciousness developed in the moral-practical domain. This gives rise to *legitimation crises,* which, in the case of liberal-capitalist societies, can only ultimately be resolved by transitioning to a new principle of organization, or tamed by restricting these inequalities within the range of institutional arrangements allowed by the ruling principle.[68]

5.3.2 The Rationalization of the Lifeworld

In his 1981 'Theory of Communicative Action' (*Theorie des kommunikativen Handelns*), Habermas adds several layers to his theory of social evolution. The central

---

[67] Habermas, *Communication and the Evolution of Society*, p. 98.
[68] Habermas, *Communication and the Evolution of Society*, pp. 163–164; Habermas, *Legitimation Crisis*.

diachronic thesis of that study, couched in the conceptual vocabulary that Habermas develops in the course of the book, is that social evolution takes the form of a *rationalization of the lifeworld*, and that this process of rationalization causes the lifeworld to break up and fragment into different communicative structures and functional subsystems of action:

> I understand social evolution as a second-order process of differentiation: system and lifeworld are differentiated in the sense that the complexity of one and the rationality of the other grow. But it is not only qua system and qua lifeworld they are differentiated; they get differentiated from one another at the same time.[69]

I will postpone exposition of the concepts of system and lifeworld to the next section and here merely indicate the slightly revised theory of social evolution to which they give rise. In the briefest of terms, we can understand the rationalization of the lifeworld as a development in the structure of communicative action originating in what Habermas calls *the linguistification of the sacred*. This latter thesis holds that the semantic content of pre-linguistic rites is 'transferred' into everyday language by way of mythical narratives and worldviews.[70] As this process continues forth through the millennia, meaning becomes increasingly independent of the ritual context, and 'the authority of the holy is gradually replaced by the authority of an achieved consensus.'[71]

In the earliest human communities, the lifeworld does not yet contain the pragmatic distinctions between different validity spheres or relations to the world expounded in Subsection 5.2.2. Rather, human experience and meaning is constituted within a monolithic and structurally homogenous lifeworld, in which every action, social event, or natural occurrence is understood in terms of some overarching symbolic significance, such as the manifestations of spirits or the will of gods.[72] However, as a result of the functional requirements associated with survival of the tribe (such as increasingly specialized crafts and the incest taboo), a primitive division of labour arises along with an authoritative kinship system and a *segmented differentiation* of society into different social groups. This increased segmentation of society eventually requires a stabilizing authority, a centralized form of political power, which—over centuries—evolves into a state-like entity. However, with the birth of the state, the authority embedded in the kinship system is replaced with the authority of a centralized political sovereign, who commands the resources of the law. Moreover, with the advent of the medium of law, primitive

---

[69] Jürgen Habermas, *The Theory of Communicative Action. Vol. II: The Critique of Functionalist Reason*, transl. by Thomas McCarthy (Cambridge: Polity Press, 1987), p. 153.
[70] Jürgen Habermas, *Nachmetaphysisches Denken II: Aufsätze und Repliken* (Berlin: Suhrkamp Verlag, 2012), p. 15.
[71] Habermas, *The Theory of Communicative Action: Vol. II*, p. 77.
[72] Habermas, *The Theory of Communicative Action: Vol. II*, p. 43.

forms of exchange are legally institutionalized by means of private law and administrative power institutionalized by means of public law, which gives rise to a division of labour and an ever-increasing *functional differentiation*. At the threshold of modernity, this process of functional differentiation gives rise to functional subsystems such as the economy and the bureaucracy, which become responsible for the material reproduction of society and take on an increasingly autonomous character independently of the lifeworld.[73]

Moreover, this world-historical process of social evolution is undergirded by the development of distinctions between different spheres of validity and relations to the world in the structure of communicative action, and developments in legal and moral norms and consciousness, from the preconventional (archaic), over the conventional (traditional), to the postconventional (modern) level.[74] According to Habermas, social evolution thus represents the long and painstaking *learning process* in which the lifeworld is progressively rationalized in terms of the differentiation of human communication, cognition, and different domains of action. The rationalization of the lifeworld is a world-historical precondition for the differentiation and independence of the functional subsystems—or stated in the older terms: the development of moral-practical knowledge is a necessary condition for the possibility of utilizing and institutionalizing surplus productive potential in technical knowledge.

In segmentally differentiated feudal societies, the infant functional subsystem of the state takes pride of place in material reproduction, and it is only with the advent of modern society and the infinitely more productive capitalist mode of production that the economic subsystem is able to break free and assume the role of historical engine in social evolution. In the following section, I turn to a more systematic exposition of the sociological dimension of Habermas's communicative paradigm, including the concepts of system and lifeworld and the two different social-scientific points of view from which we can understand society as simultaneously a lifeworld and a social system of functional subsystems, before, in the end of that section, I briefly return to the theory of social evolution for a few final points of clarification.

5.4 The Theory of Communicative Action

5.4.1 System and Lifeworld

Habermas's *Theorie des kommunikativen Handelns* is a monumental study of social theory and history, which has already achieved the status of a modern

---

[73] Habermas, *The Theory of Communicative Action: Vol. II*, p. 153.
[74] Habermas, *The Theory of Communicative Action: Vol. II*, p. 174.

classic. Along with its companion volume on legal and political theory, 'Between Facts and Norms' (*Faktizität und Geltung*) from 1992, it represents Habermas's *magnum opus* and the mature expression of his communicative paradigm of critical theory. In the former, two-volume 1200-page study, written while Habermas was codirector of the (hopelessly named) 'Marx Planck Institute for Research into the Conditions of Life in the Scientific-Technical World' from 1971 to 1981 in Starnberg, Habermas pulls together the different strings of his work into a comprehensive social-theoretical attempt to resurrect Horkheimer's original aspirations for a critical theory of society.

In the course of developing his two-concept theory of society as system and lifeworld, Habermas engages in critical, in-depth reconstruction of sociological classics such as Max Weber's theory of modernity as social rationalization, Emile Durkheim's theory of the division of labour, George Herbert Mead's social psychology, Talcott Parsons's action and systems theory, Marx's theory of labour as a real abstraction, and Lukács's, Horkheimer's, and Adorno's concern with reification. The sociological position that emerges is a remarkable synthesis of these different strands, bringing together the hermeneutic concept of the lifeworld with the functionalist concept of the social system in a general theory of modern society that aspires to account for the systematic sources of social and individual pathologies. It is a work of breathtaking scope and ambition, of which, in what follows, I can only skirt the surface.

The structure of this two-concept theory of society is given by Habermas's long-standing distinction between work and interaction, or instrumental/strategic action and communicative action. This distinction is developed into a two-pronged methodological perspective, which approaches society as an object of study simultaneously from the *internal perspective* of the participating members of social groups, and from the *external perspective* of the social-scientific observer. The internal perspective allows Habermas to hermeneutically reconstruct the communicative structures of the lifeworld with reference to the pre-theoretical knowledge of participants in social action, whereas the external perspective allows him to develop a functionalist-explanatory account of society as a system of strategic actions. The central concept of the internal perspective is the notion of society as a *lifeworld*, whereas the central concept of the external perspective is the notion of society as a *system*. Let us first look at the lifeworld before moving on to the concept of the system and the relationship between the two.

The concept of the lifeworld, which Habermas appropriates from Edmund Husserl's and Alfred's Schutz's phenomenological work, is introduced to describe the 'the horizon within which communicative actions are "always already" moving'.[75] Habermas sketches the communicative structure of the lifeworld with appeal to the three world-relations (discussed in Subsection 5.2.2) with reference to which

---

[75] Habermas, *The Theory of Communicative Action: Vol. II*, p. 119.

speakers can raise claims to validity: the subjective world ('as the totality of experiences to which a speaker has privileged access and which he can express before a public'), the objective world ('as the totality of entities about which true statements are possible'), and the social world ('as the totality of legitimately regulated interpersonal relations').[76] Constituted through language and culture, the lifeworld thus represents an intuitive background knowledge and shared pool of meaning on which communicative participants can rely in action oriented towards mutual understanding: 'The lifeworld is the intuitively present, in this sense familiar and transparent, and at the same time vast and incalculable web of presuppositions that have to be satisfied if an actual utterance is to be at all meaningful, that is, valid *or* invalid'.[77]

This abstract 'communication-theoretical' account of the lifeworld is complemented by what Habermas calls the *everyday concept of the sociocultural lifeworld*, which 'refers to the totality of sociocultural facts' as a 'cognitive reference system', which can be analysed in terms of the different functions that language fulfils for the 'reproduction or self-maintenance of communicatively structured lifeworlds'.[78] There are three such core functions, corresponding to three processes of reproduction in three structural lifeworld components:

> Under the functional aspect of *mutual understanding,* communicative action serves to transmit and renew cultural knowledge; under the aspect of *coordinating action,* it serves social integration and the establishment of solidarity; finally, under the aspect of *socialization,* communicative action serves the formation of personal identities. The symbolic structures of the lifeworld are reproduced by way of the continuation of valid knowledge, stabilization of group solidarity, and socialization of responsible actors. The process of reproduction connects up new situations with the existing conditions of the lifeworld; it does this in the *semantic* dimension of meanings or contents (of the cultural tradition), as well as in the dimensions of *social space* (of socially integrated groups), and *historical time* (of successive generations). Corresponding to these processes of *cultural reproduction, social integration,* and *socialization* are the structural components of the lifeworld: culture, society, person.[79]

The latter three concepts thus take on a technical meaning in Habermas's social theory: the concept of 'culture' refers to 'the stock of knowledge from which participants in communication supply themselves with interpretations as they come to an understanding about something in the world'; the concept of 'society' refers to 'the legitimate [in the sociological sense] orders through which participants

---

[76] Habermas, *The Theory of Communicative Action: Vol. II,* p. 120.
[77] Habermas, *The Theory of Communicative Action: Vol. II,* p. 131.
[78] Habermas, *The Theory of Communicative Action: Vol. II,* pp. 136–137.
[79] Habermas, *The Theory of Communicative Action: Vol. II,* pp. 137–138.

regulate their memberships in social groups and thereby secure solidarity'; while the concept of 'personality' refers to 'the competences that make a subject capable of speaking and acting, that put him in a position to take part in processes of reaching understanding and thereby to assert his own identity'.[80]

In his subsequent work, Habermas has emphasized the *rational constitution* of the lifeworld as a 'space of symbolically embodied reasons'. This flourish implies that in 'everyday communication, reasons are in the first instance a lubricant of undisturbed cooperation. Reasons enable as well as repair the linking up of the action orientations of one participant with those of another, that is, the social intermeshing of actions'.[81] However, it is important to distinguish two levels of normativity here: the weaker normativity inherent in language, 'which makes the human spirit sensitive to reasons', that Habermas reconstructs in terms of communicative reason, and the stronger normativity of social solidarity and social integration, which, according to Habermas, ultimately derives from the linguistification of the sacred.[82]

However, the concept of the lifeworld only captures those structures of society that are *symbolically reproduced* through communicative action. Habermas maintains that a theory of society couched exhaustively in terms of the lifeworld would amount to a form of 'hermeneutic idealism', which commits itself to three related 'fictions'. First, if society is construed solely in terms of the intentional interactions of responsible agents in communicative action, it results in the idealization of society as consisting 'only of relations entered into by subjects acting autonomously' and a 'picture of a process of sociation that takes place with the will and consciousness of adult members'. Second, it 'also suggests that culture is independent from external constraints', and third, it suggests that processes of reaching mutual understanding are completely transparent and that 'communicative actors cannot reckon with a systematic distortion of their communication'.[83] However, none of these fictions are an appropriate reflection of the social reality of modern society:

> In fact, however, [the] goal-directed actions [of members of a sociocultural lifeworld] are coordinated not only through processes of reaching understanding, but also through functional interconnections that are not intended by them and are usually not even perceived within the horizon of everyday practice. In capitalist societies, the market is the most important example of a norm-free regulation of cooperative contexts.[84]

---

[80] Habermas, *The Theory of Communicative Action: Vol. II*, p. 138.
[81] Habermas, *Nachmetaphysisches Denken II*, p. 56.
[82] Habermas, *Nachmetaphysisches Denken II*, p. 69.
[83] Habermas, *The Theory of Communicative Action: Vol. II*, pp. 149–150.
[84] Habermas, *The Theory of Communicative Action: Vol. II*, p. 150.

Habermas's refusal to countenance the hermeneutic idealism of a conception of society understood only as a lifeworld is thus derivative of his aspirations to redeem the original aspirations of critical theory. As we saw in Chapters 1 and 3, despite the many ruptures and developments leading from Horkheimer's interdisciplinary materialism to Adorno's negativism, the first generation of the Frankfurt School consistently identified the central evil of modern capitalist society precisely in terms of its objectification of subjects and imposition of social heteronomy on individual lives. And the reason that Habermas objects to a monistic theory of society as *nothing but* a lifeworld is in part that he wants to be able to capture the concern of the first generation of the Frankfurt School with *reification*.

Although Habermas believes that Horkheimer and Adorno were led astray by their commitment to the philosophy of the subject—a mistake that can only be undone by shifting to an intersubjective paradigm of reason—this change of paradigm is undertaken precisely in order to provide a plausible philosophical grounding of a critical theory of society, pursued by way of formal pragmatics of communicative reason. The concept of the lifeworld enables Habermas to connect his formal-pragmatic reconstruction of communicative reason with the sociological concepts of culture, society, and personality. But for a critical theory of society that ultimately seeks to develop a framework for *reconceptualizing* such concerns as the problem of reification, this can only be half the story: in order to discern the other half—the structural source of reification *of* the lifeworld—he introduces the perspective of the social-scientific observer of *functional subsystems* that maintain the *material reproduction* of society. Habermas explains the need for this second perspective as follows:

> It is only possible to analyze these connections ['between stages of system differentiation and forms of social integration'] by distinguishing mechanisms of coordinating action that harmonize the *action orientations* of participants from mechanisms that stabilize nonintended interconnections of actions by way of functionally intermeshing *action consequences.* In one case, the integration of an action system is established by a normatively secured or communicatively achieved consensus, in the other case, by a nonnormative regulation of individual decisions that extends beyond the actors' consciousnesses. This distinction between a *social integration* of society, which takes effect in action orientations, and a *systemic integration,* which reaches through and beyond action orientations, calls for a corresponding differentiation in the concept of society itself. No matter whether one starts with Mead from basic concepts of social interaction or with Durkheim from basic concepts of collective representation, in either case society is conceived from the perspective of acting subjects as the *lifeworld of a social group.* In contrast, from the observer's perspective of someone not involved, society can be conceived only as a *system of actions* such that each action has a

functional significance according to its contribution to the maintenance of the system.[85]

As suggested in this passage, functional subsystems differ from lifeworld contexts essentially in virtue of the mechanism through which actions are coordinated. Whereas action coordination in the lifeworld is achieved by way of linking the action orientations of participants through the intersubjective exchange of reasons and the reliance-on-*cum*-reestablishment of a background consensus, the systemic integration of functional subsystems proceeds by way of coordinating the *consequences* of actions and it is thus indifferent to participants' action orientations and reasons for action. As Habermas suggests in a passage quoted above, this mechanism is intuitively familiar from economic markets in particular, in which large-scale systems of action are coordinated simply through the supply and demand of goods and services, independently of whatever reasons participants have for entering into those transactions. Habermas calls such action *strategic*, since it is concerned with influencing the decisions of the opponent through rules of rational choice.[86]

Habermas clarifies his concept of the functional subsystem with reference to Parson's systems theory and, in particular, his notion of 'steering media'. The basic idea behind steering media is that the communicative coordination of actions is 'delinguistified' and reduced to a binary 'code' to which participants can orient themselves strategically. This relieves action coordination from the risk of dissensus and the potential instability associated with an orientation towards mutual understanding, and it enables stabilized systems of action to become 'uncoupled from lifeworld contexts'.[87] The preeminent steering medium of modern society is money. As a generalized and standardized value, money has the capacity to transfer precise information between the parties to an exchange: namely, x's offer of a good or a service to y. Faced with this offer, y can choose to either accept or decline, depending on their preferences or 'indifference curves', but the coordination of actions thus takes place without appealing at any point to participants' reasons for action. According to Habermas, the second-most important steering medium of modern society is that of 'power'. Homologous to money, power functions as a code by schematizing the possible responses of an agent 'in a binary fashion: he can either submit to or oppose [the other agent's] demands'.[88] Accordingly, power can

---

[85] Habermas, *The Theory of Communicative Action: Vol. II*, p. 117.
[86] Habermas, *The Theory of Communicative Action: Vol. I*, p. 285. This of course echoes Adam Smith's famous remark: 'It is not from the benevolence of the butcher, the brewer, or the baker, that we expect our dinner, but from their regard to their own interest. We address ourselves, not to their humanity, but to their self-love, and never talk to them of our own necessities, but of their advantages'. Adam Smith, *An Inquiry into the Nature and Causes of The Wealth of Nations* (Petersfield: Harriman House, 2007), pp. 9–10.
[87] Habermas, *The Theory of Communicative Action: Vol. II*, p. 263.
[88] Habermas, *The Theory of Communicative Action: Vol. II*, p. 268.

serve the same stabilizing and standardizing function as money, by coordinating actions without recourse to reasons.

In modern society, the steering media of money and power have enabled two distinct functional subsystems of strategic action to uncouple from the lifeworld: the capitalist market and the bureaucracy. According to Habermas, both of these functional subsystems have achieved an ever-increasing independence and autonomy from the lifeworld, by growing in both intensity and extent. However, no functional subsystem can completely detach from the lifeworld: in order to inspire the required confidence, the subsystem of the market needs to be institutionally anchored in the lifeworld 'through the basic institutions of civil law (property and contract)',[89] whereas the steering medium of power 'needs an *additional* basis of confidence, namely, *legitimation*'.[90] Habermas's thought here is that if power loses its perceived legitimacy with reference to shared collective goals, its basis is eventually undermined; accordingly, power must rest not only on the fear of sanction, but also on 'obligation—a duty based on the recognition of normative validity claims'.[91]

Moreover, Habermas also suggests another crucial limitation to steering media and the functional subsystems they undergird, namely that the 'only functional domains that can be differentiated out of the lifeworld by steering media are those of material reproduction'.[92] Habermas defends this claim by showing how the additional two steering media suggested by Parsons, namely 'influence' and 'prestige', are in fact unable to uncouple from the lifeworld, since these 'generalized forms of communication' remain dependent on lifeworld resources.[93] This restriction is important because it suggests that the structural components of the lifeworld—culture, society, and personality—*cannot* be systemically integrated but *necessarily* rely on communicative action and the coordination of action by means of an orientation towards mutual understanding.

Habermas describes as the 'fundamental problem of social theory ... how to connect in a satisfactory way the two conceptual strategies indicated by the notions of "system" and "lifeworld"'.[94] To fully account for Habermas's solution to this problem, we must briefly return to his theory of social evolution. In the conceptual vocabulary of *Theorie des kommunikativen Handelns*, it is the modern emergence of the functionally differentiated subsystems that accounts for the explosion in the productive power of capitalist societies since the Industrial Revolution: 'A capitalist path of modernization opens up as soon as the economic system develops its own intrinsic dynamic of growth and, with its endogenously produced problems,

---

[89] Habermas, *The Theory of Communicative Action: Vol. II*, p. 266.
[90] Habermas, *The Theory of Communicative Action: Vol. II*, p. 270.
[91] Habermas, *The Theory of Communicative Action: Vol. II*, p. 271.
[92] Habermas, *The Theory of Communicative Action: Vol. II*, p. 261.
[93] Habermas, *The Theory of Communicative Action: Vol. II*, p. 276.
[94] Habermas, *The Theory of Communicative Action: Vol. II*, p. 151.

takes the lead, that is, the evolutionary primacy, for society as a whole'.[95] However, as we have also seen, the rationalization of the lifeworld and the differentiation of structures in communicative action is a necessary condition of possibility for the formation of functional subsystems, and, specifically, for the uncoupling of the economic system from lifeworld contexts.

Together with his earlier theory of social evolution, Habermas's *Theorie des kommunikativen Handelns* thus represents his answer to the third problem that Habermas located in the first generation of the Frankfurt School: namely, historical materialism's insufficient account of the social reproduction of complex modern societies. In his response to this problem, Habermas's intention is not to repudiate historical materialism but to revise and put certain central theses of historical materialism on a more secure footing, in the form of a two-pronged theory of social evolution in terms of development of technical and moral-practical knowledge (the rationalization of the lifeworld) and a two-concept sociological theory of the basic structure of modern capitalist society as system and lifeworld.

5.4.2 The Colonization Thesis

Habermas's reconstruction of the central concerns of Western Marxism does not stop with the diachronic theory of social evolution and the synchronic account of the basic structure of modern capitalist society: he also develops an account of the distinctive form of social heteronomy to which individuals living in a modern capitalist society are subject. This account starts from the claim that, following the increased autonomy of the economic subsystem, the phenomenon that Marx sought to capture with the notion of a 'real abstraction' arises, which 'takes place when interactions are no longer coordinated via norms and values, or via processes of reaching understanding, but via the medium of exchange value'.[96] This concept is of course intimately linked with the concern that Lukács, and, following him, Horkheimer and Adorno, sought to capture with the concept of 'reification': namely, the social objectification and self-objectification of subjects. On the basis of his two-concept theory of society as system and lifeworld, Habermas is able to recast the concept of reification as the thesis that the lifeworld is *colonized* by system imperatives of strategic action: 'the rationalization of the lifeworld makes possible a heightening of systemic complexity which becomes so hypertrophied that it unleashes system imperatives that burst the capacity of the lifeworld they instrumentalize'.[97]

---

[95] Habermas, *The Theory of Communicative Action: Vol. II*, p. 384.
[96] Habermas, *The Theory of Communicative Action: Vol. II*, p. 336.
[97] Habermas, *The Theory of Communicative Action: Vol. II*, p. 155.

According to Habermas, this far-reaching *colonization thesis* replaces the traditional and early modern problem of ideology (which, in Habermas's view, is distinct from Adorno's concept of ideology as 'societally necessary illusion' encountered in Chapter 3), where the 'whole' is justified as natural or God-given. Such false justifications have been undermined by the progressive rationalization of the lifeworld, since the modern differentiation of communicative structures no longer allows for such a 'global interpretation of the whole'. Instead,

> Everyday consciousness sees itself thrown back on traditions whose claims to validity have already been suspended; where it does escape the spell of traditionalism, it is hopelessly splintered. In place of 'false consciousness' we today have a 'fragmented consciousness' that blocks enlightenment by the mechanism of reification. It is only with this that the conditions for a *colonization of the lifeworld* are met. When stripped of their ideological veils, the imperatives of autonomous subsystems make their way into the lifeworld from the outside—like colonial masters coming into a tribal society—and force a process of assimilation upon it. The diffused perspectives of the local culture cannot be sufficiently coordinated to permit the play of the metropolis and the world market to be grasped from the periphery.[98]

The colonial metaphor is not only supposed to invoke the picture of an economic subsystem that structurally *dominates* the lifeworld, but also the idea of systemic disequilibria (crises) that can only be resolved within a given principle of organization by *plundering* the resources necessary for cultural reproduction, social integration, and socialization. In modern welfare states, Habermas's thesis is thus that system imperatives colonize the lifeworld, when 'system problems arise ... from the crisis-ridden course of economic growth, [and] economic disequilibria can be balanced through the state jumping into the functional gaps of the market'.[99] This implies that

> capitalist growth triggers conflicts within the lifeworld ... as a consequence of the expansion and the increasing density of the monetary-bureaucratic complex; this happens, first of all, where socially integrated contexts of life are redefined around the roles of consumer and client and assimilated to systematically integrated domains of action.[100]

Habermas thus argues that before systemic crises result in more destabilizing legitimation crises (large scale withdrawal of support from governing institutions) or *anomie* ('group identity breaking down'), they might be 'successfully intercepted

---

[98] Habermas, *The Theory of Communicative Action: Vol. II*, p. 355.
[99] Habermas, *The Theory of Communicative Action: Vol. II*, p. 343.
[100] Habermas, *The Theory of Communicative Action: Vol. II*, p. 351.

by having recourse to lifeworld resources', resulting in 'social pathologies' such as 'phenomena of alienation and the unsettling of collective identity'.[101] The systems imperatives' encroachment on lifeworld resources threatens both the reproduction of cultural knowledge and the socialization of agents into communicatively competent personalities and thus both the objective *and* the subjective conditions of individual autonomy, or *Mündigkeit*.

As clients and as consumers, agents are objectified and self-objectify: their consciousness is reified, in Lukács's terms. This undermines not only societies' symbolic reproduction, but also the normative resources for critical reflection and resistance towards social heteronomy. In some passages of *Theorie des kommunikativen Handelns*, we find Habermas clearly calling forth the spectre of Adorno's concept of the administered world as the dystopian end-point of systems' colonization of the lifeworld:

> To the degree that the economic system subjects the life-forms of private households and the life conduct of consumers and employees to its imperatives, consumerism and possessive individualism, motives of performance, and competition gain the force to shape behavior. The communicative practice of everyday life is one-sidedly rationalized into a utilitarian life-style; this media-induced shift to purposive-rational action orientations calls forth the reaction of a hedonism freed from the pressures of rationality. As the private sphere is undermined and eroded by the economic system, so too is the public sphere by the administrative system. The bureaucratic disempowering and desiccation of spontaneous processes of opinion- and will-formation expands the scope for engineering mass loyalty and makes it easier to uncouple political decision-making from concrete, identity-forming contexts of life. Insofar as such tendencies establish themselves, we get Weber's (stylized) picture of a legal domination that redefines practical questions as technical ones and dismisses demands for substantive justice with a legalistic reference to legitimation through procedure.[102]

With his colonization thesis, Habermas thus reconstructs and refines—within his two-concept account of the basic structure of modern capitalist society as system and lifeworld—the central animating idea of both Horkheimer's original paradigm and Adorno's negativist paradigm of critical theory: namely, the claim that the basic structure of modern capitalist society has an in-built tendency to undermine the necessary social and psychological conditions for individual autonomy. However, since this concern is reconstructed in the intersubjective terms of his communication paradigm of critical theory, Habermas is able to clearly distinguish the forces that *cause* reification from those object domains

---

[101] Habermas, *The Theory of Communicative Action: Vol. II*, p. 386.
[102] Habermas, *The Theory of Communicative Action: Vol. II*, p. 325

subject to reification: that is, the functional subsystems coordinated through the steering media of money and power, vis-à-vis those structural components of the lifeworld that can only relinquish coordination through communicative action on pain of social pathology.

Accordingly, although the mature Habermas has largely given up the language of domination and emancipation so ubiquitous in earlier work such as *Erkenntnis und Interesse*, his *Theorie des kommnikativen Handelns* can nonetheless clearly be interpreted as an account of a distinctive form of *structural domination* to which individuals living in postwar capitalist democracies are subject: namely, an assault on the normative resources necessary for the socialization of autonomous persons caused by the displacement of systemic crises into the lifeworld. To be sure, we have yet to expound the full scope of the *normative* dimension of Habermas's communicative paradigm of critical theory: the discourse-theoretical account of freedom as autonomy that tacitly informs this colonization thesis and the discourse theory of modern constitutional democracy that specifies how individuals can resist and possibly overcome such structural domination in practice. These two aspects of the normative dimension of Habermas's communicative paradigm are developed in his 'discourse ethics' and 'discourse theory of law and democracy' respectively, and it is to the exposition of these that we now turn.

5.5 The Normative Content of Modernity

As we saw in Subsection 5.2.2, the philosophical grounding of the normative dimension of Habermas's communicative paradigm is provided by a formal-pragmatic reconstruction of the idealizing presuppositions of practical discourse. This elicits the ideal speech situation, which Habermas initially understands in substantive terms both as a *theory of truth* and as an *ideal of a just society*: namely, as a 'structure of a social life in uncoerced communication'. However, Habermas has subsequently revised his theory of truth and specified that the ideal speech situation should not be understood in substantive terms but only as an account of the pragmatic presuppositions of argumentation. Following this revision, it is necessary to clarify the relationship between the ideal speech situation and the normative dimension of Habermas's communicative paradigm of critical theory. In Habermas's later work, it is clear that the ideal speech situation does not *itself* constitute the normative dimension of his critical theory, but rather, in the first instance, a step in the philosophical *grounding* of this dimension. The ideal speech situation is a formalized model of the pragmatic presuppositions of discourse, and, as such, it clarifies the constitutive rules of discourse; a set of rules that, as we saw in Subsection 5.2.2, Habermas understands as an 'operatively effective fiction' in that they enable rational discourse precisely in virtue of their counterfactually idealizing character. However, the genuinely normative dimension of

Habermas's communicative paradigm only begins to become visible when we turn to the acceptability conditions that are constitutive of *the moral point of view*.

5.5.1 Discourse Ethics

Recall the pragmatic presuppositions of discourse: that (a) no one may be excluded; (b) that all enjoy equal opportunity to contribute; (c) that participants must only make truthful contributions; and (d) that communication must not be subject to any form of internal or external compulsion. Now, if 'everyone who engages in argumentation must make at least these pragmatic presuppositions', Habermas claims,

> then in virtue of (a) the public character of practical discourses and the inclusion of all concerned and (b) the equal communicative rights of all participants, only reasons which take account of the interests and evaluative orientations of all equally can have an impact on the outcome of practical discourses; and because of the absence of (c) deception and (d) compulsion, only reasons can be decisive in the acceptance of a controversial norm. Finally, this 'free' acceptance can only occur 'jointly' on the assumption that the orientation to communicative agreement is reciprocally imputed to all participants.[103]

According to Habermas, the pragmatic presuppositions of discourse thus suggest—in an abductive manner (inference from best explanation)—the following *principle of universalization* (the 'U' principle), as a 'rule of argumentation' for moral discourses:

> A [moral] norm is valid when the foreseeable consequences and side effects of its general observance for the interests and value-orientations of *each individual* could be freely accepted *jointly* by *all* concerned.[104]

The 'U' principle represents nothing less than a reconstruction of *the moral point of view*. It is thus important to recognize that the 'U' principle is not in itself an action-guiding moral norm, but rather an operative second-order rule in moral discourses that specifies the acceptability conditions of first-order moral norms. As such, the procedural moral content of the 'U' principle—which, Habermas claims, we necessarily presuppose whenever we engage in moral discourse—is grounded in the more general *discourse principle*, which specifies the following condition for the justification of all norms (including, but not limited to moral norms):

---

[103] Habermas, 'A Genealogical Analysis of the Cognitive Content of Morality', p. 44.
[104] Habermas, 'A Genealogical Analysis of the Cognitive Content of Morality', p. 42.

> Only those norms can claim validity that could meet with the agreement of all concerned in their capacity as participants in a practical discourse.[105]

These are the basic principles of Habermas's 'moral philosophy', which he—somewhat misleadingly, as we shall see—calls 'discourse ethics', and, more importantly for our purposes, the discourse principle can be seen as the *foundational principle* of the normative dimension of his communicative paradigm of critical theory. By specifying impartial justifiability as a necessary and sufficient condition for the *justification* of any norm, the discourse principle is a *procedural* rather than a substantive normative principle: it is a *second-order criterion* for the justification of norms as such.[106]

As its name suggests, Habermas offers the 'U' principle as a reconstruction of Kant's categorical imperative—which I shall expound in greater detail in Chapter 7—since it captures the practical universalization requirement that Kant specifies as a both necessary and sufficient condition for the validity of moral principles. To be sure, with its vocabulary of 'social pathology' and 'colonisation of the lifeworld', it may seem that the social theory unfolded by Habermas in *Theorie des kommunikativen Handelns* appeals to substantial first-order moral principles of the kind more at home in the Aristotelian and Hegelian tradition than the procedural Kantian tradition. There is an obvious sense in which this is right: the social pathologies associated with systems-colonization of the lifeworld refer to substantial and very 'un-Kantian' concerns relating to psychodynamic development and the reproduction of cultural knowledge. However, I would argue that Habermas's simultaneous commitment to the *normative content* of a Kantian conception of a morality of autonomy and to a Hegelian-Marxian concern with the *social reality* of such a conception reflects a fundamental double-sided concern that we have found in all three paradigms of Frankfurt School critical theory hitherto reconstructed. Indeed, in a way closely reminiscent of Horkheimer's original paradigm and Adorno's negativist paradigm, Habermas's communicative paradigm of critical theory can be interpreted as an attempt to account for the psychological, social, and political conditions for each individual to enjoy an *effective capacity* of autonomy.

In his Kantian construal of discourse ethics, Habermas follows his friend and collaborator Kart-Otto Apel, who, in his path-breaking work 'Towards a Transformation of Philosophy' (*Transformation der Philosophie*) from 1972, unfolds a 'transcendental-pragmatic' programme that draws on the philosophy of language and the American pragmatists in an ambitious attempt to recast philosophy as a whole—including an ultimate justification (*Letztbegründung*) of morality.

---

[105] Habermas, 'A Genealogical Analysis of the Cognitive Content of Morality', p. 41.
[106] As such, it is reminiscent of Thomas's Scanlon's 'Contractualism' and Rainer Forst's principle of general and reciprocal justification, to which we return in Chapter 10.

Habermas's extensive reliance on Apel's transcendental-pragmatic programme also raises the question of the 'transcendental status' of the philosophical grounding of the normative dimension in Habermas's communicative paradigm. In Apel's view, participants in discourse always necessarily accept a first-order moral principle requiring the realization of an ideal of an unrestricted communication community '*as a precondition for the possibility and validity of argumentation*' as such.[107] That is to say, Apel seeks to preserve the strong transcendental status of the categorical imperative in his transcendental-pragmatic justification of morality, by arguing that participation in argumentation commits us *in a categorically obligatory sense* to an unconditional first-order moral principle.

Although Habermas's grounding of the discourse principle in the pragmatic presuppositions of discourse is indeed profoundly inspired by Apel's work, he is not willing to endorse his friend's stronger transcendental commitments. By contrast, Habermas draws a sharp distinction between norms of argumentation and obligatory moral norms, and he denies that the latter can be derived from the former:

> The [communicatively acting] agent thereby becomes the subject of a 'must' in the sense of weak transcendental necessitation, without encountering the prescriptive 'must' of a rule of action ... Communicative reason, unlike practical reason, is not itself a source of norms of right action. It spans the full spectrum of validity claims (of assertoric truth, subjective truthfulness, and normative rightness) and hence extends beyond the sphere of moral-practical questions. Normativity in the more restricted sense of a binding practical orientation is not identical with the rationality of action oriented to reaching understanding as a whole.[108]

According to Habermas, there is no reason to regret that philosophy is no longer able to fulfil the foundationalist role of *Letztbegründer*; rather, discourse ethics happily 'takes its place among the reconstructive sciences concerned with the rational basis of knowing, speaking, and acting.'[109] Discourse ethics is therefore not really a moral theory or 'ethics' in the conventional philosophical sense at all, in that it does not attempt to offer obligatory moral norms or principles of justice, but rather seeks to clarify *the rational and discursive basis on which moral norms and principles of justice are constructed and intersubjectively justified*. Indeed, in Habermas's view, the '*moral* intuitions of everyday life are not in need of clarification by the philosopher.'[110]

---

[107] Karl-Otto Apel, *Towards a Transformation of Philosophy*, transl. by Glyn Adey and David Fisby (Milwaukee: Marquette University Press, 1998), p. 274.
[108] Jürgen Habermas, 'Remarks on Discourse Ethics', in *Justification and Application*, transl. by Ciaran Cronin (Cambridge MA: The MIT Press, 1994), p. 81.
[109] Habermas, *Moral Consciousness and Communicative Action*, p. 98.
[110] Habermas, *Moral Consciousness and Communicative Action*, p. 98.

To be sure, this also suggests—and Habermas is very forthright in recognizing this—that discourse ethics *presupposes* a discursive moral practice, from which it can reconstruct (in the formal-pragmatic sense) the moral point of view, but which discourse ethics cannot itself ground:

> This much is true: any universalistic morality is dependent upon a form of life that *meets it halfway*. There has to be a modicum of congruence between morality and the practices of socialization and education. The latter must promote the requisite internalization of superego controls and the abstractness of ego identities. In addition, there must be a modicum of fit between morality and socio-political institutions. Not just any institutions will do. Morality thrives only in an environment in which postconventional ideas about law and morality have already been institutionalized to a certain extent.[111]

Habermas recognizes that this forthright acknowledgement of the limits of moral theory and the theory of justice is not what many of us have come to expect from practical philosophy. However, this limitation might seem to reflect not only what Habermas sees as the limits of moral theory, but also the disciplinary limits of philosophy as such. As we have seen, it is a highly familiar idea in the Frankfurt School tradition that a clarification of the normative dimension of a critical theory—which, to a less systematic extent, we also find in Horkheimer's original paradigm and in Adorno's negativist paradigm—represents but one dimension of a comprehensive critical theory. Accordingly, one might argue that Habermas's modest view of moral theory and the theory of justice is actually true to Horkheimer's claim that a critical theory provides the correct methodological instantiation of morality by incorporating its normative content in an account of existing injustices in the basic structure of society, with the practical aim of enabling human emancipation. Indeed, this interpretation is confirmed by Habermas, who maintains, with explicit appeal to Horkheimer, that

> philosophy cannot absolve anyone of moral responsibility. And that includes philosophers, for like everyone else, they face moral-practical issues of great complexity, and the first thing they might profitably do is to get a clearer view of the situation they find themselves in. The historical and social sciences can be of greater help in this endeavor than philosophy. On this note I want to end with a quote from Max Horkheimer from the year 1933: 'What is needed to get beyond the utopian character of Kant's idea of a perfect constitution of humankind, is a materialist theory of society'.[112]

---

[111] Habermas, *Moral Consciousness and Communicative Action*, pp. 207–208.
[112] Habermas, *Moral Consciousness and Communicative Action*, p. 211. In Chapter 6, I will argue that Habermas's meta-ethical modesty comes with serious costs, especially when his communicative

Note that in this passage, we find explicit reference to the three methodological dimensions of a critical theory, namely the historical (given by Habermas's theory of social evolution), the sociological (given by his two-concept theory of society), and the normative (given by discourse ethics). However, the normative dimension in Habermas's communicative paradigm of critical theory is only completed by his ambitious discourse theory of democracy and the rule of law, to which we now turn.

5.5.2 A Discourse Theory of Law and Democracy

Although *Faktizität und Geltung* from 1992 can fruitfully be read as a companion volume to *Theorie des kommunikativen Handelns*, which complements Habermas's account of the historical and sociological dimension of critical theory with a more elaborate *political-theoretical* account of the normative dimension of critical theory, there is a sense in which such a reading belittles the book's ambition and achievement: independently of its place within Habermas's communicative paradigm, the study represents a monumental interdisciplinary contribution to political and legal theory and the theory of democracy in its own right. According to Habermas, *Faktizität und Geltung* represents nothing less than a reconstruction of the 'self-understanding' of a modern constitutional democracy, which charts a path between the reality and the ideal of constitutional democracy (*der demokratische Rechtsstaat*) through a combination of political sociology, jurisprudence, and democratic theory. The centrepiece of Habermas's theory is a reconstruction of the normative content of constitutional democracy in terms of 'the democratic principle' and the 'system of rights', which is supplemented by a 'two-track' sociological account of the circulation of power in 'deliberative politics'; a reconceptualization of the 'public sphere' as the ultimate discursive source of legitimacy through the formation of 'communicative power'; and a 'discourse paradigm of law' that incorporates insights from both the theory of justice and legal positivism. This section will only be able to provide a highly superficial exposition of the book's rich and complex argument.

The key to understanding Habermas's discourse theory of law and democracy is to read it as an attempt to capture a tension between 'facticity' and 'validity'— as the book's title suggests—which, Habermas claims, is *inherent in democratic law*. According to Habermas, this tension can only be methodologically grasped by maintaining both the internal perspective of the participant and the external perspective of the social-scientific observer—two perspectives that, as we have seen,

---

paradigm is applied to the global context of application. Moreover, as we shall see in Chapter 10's discussion of Rainer Forst's justification paradigm of critical theory, there is reason to think that it may be more difficult for Habermas to maintain this modest interpretation of a deontological, Kantian morality than he himself suggests.

inform his entire social theory. Indeed, by retaining this methodological dualism, Habermas is able to rely on insights from both legal positivism, which defines the law as a social system of rules and thus privileges its facticity, and normative legal theories such as Kant's, which derive the legitimate authority of law from principles of justice (or 'right') and thus privilege its validity.

From the external perspective of legal positivism, law as a legal system appears simply as a set of social facts or positive rules that represent and structure part of social reality. The primary function of law, from this perspective, is to maintain a system of action by stabilizing participants' behavioural expectations: if a rule has been produced by the relevant institutions, and it is recognized as valid by the relevant agents, then that rule is law.[113] The positivist understanding of law as a social fact thus corresponds to the objectifying attitude of the citizen engaged in strategic action, who can only be motivated to act in accordance with the law with a view to its facticity—that is, who can view law merely as a limiting condition on possible courses of action, e.g. for fear of *state-backed sanctions*.[114]

From the internal perspective of the participant—associated in the jurisprudential literature above all with Ronald Dworkin's method of 'constructive interpretation'—law appears as the institutional manifestation of a normative ideal: as an embodiment of normative principle that can and must be rationally reconstructed by the legal scholar (or judge) in order to make sense of the law.[115] From this internal point of view, the primary function of law is to regulate society according to a rationally justifiable interpretation of the principles of justice to which the legal community is committed. This interpretive perspective corresponds to the point of view of the citizen engaged in communicative action, who is motivated to act in accordance with the law with a view to its validity—that is, who can view law as an enabling condition for a just society, and choose not to break the law because of its *claim to legitimacy*.

Rather than attempting to reduce one of these points of view to the other, Habermas argues that *both* perspectives on democratic law are methodologically ineliminable, because of the inherent tension between facticity and validity *in* democratic law *itself*: between its positivity as a coercive system of social rules and its claim to legitimacy as a putatively justified legal order. According to Habermas, discourse theory is uniquely situated to account for this duality within democratic law, since it recognizes—as we have seen—the double-sided nature of the pragmatic presuppositions of discourse as having both a factual and a counterfactual

---

[113] H.L.A. Hart, *The Concept of Law* (Oxford: Oxford University Press, 1961).
[114] This coercive element is emphasized by John Austin in his seminal 1832 argument for legal positivism. John Austin, *The Province of Jurisprudence Determined*, ed. by W.E. Rumble (Cambridge: Cambridge University Press, 1995).
[115] Ronald Dworkin, *Law's Empire* (Cambridge MA: Harvard University Press, 1986).

side.[116] That is to say, because every rationally achieved agreement is always comprised of *shared reasons*, it can be understood both as a *social fact*, in so far as it actually serves to coordinate action, and as making an always-fallible *claim to validity*, which in turn renders it permanently vulnerable to the destabilizing force of the better argument:

> With reasons, the facticity-validity tension inhabiting language and its use penetrates society. Insofar as it is supported by shared beliefs, the integration of society is susceptible to the destabilizing effect of invalidating reasons (and is all the more susceptible to the invalidation of an entire category of reasons). The ideal tension breaking into social reality stems from the fact that the acceptance of validity claims, which generates and perpetuates social facts, rests on the context-dependent acceptability of reasons that are constantly exposed to the risk of being invalidated by better reasons and context-altering learning processes.[117]

As we have seen, Habermas construes the backbone of modern society in terms of social integration through communicative action—action that is coordinated ultimately through the *exchange of reasons*. To be sure, action coordination achieved by nothing more than participants' insight into the justifiability of given reasons is of course highly precarious, owing not least to the individual agents' epistemic and motivational limitations. However, positive law is able to functionally mitigate this precariousness, by complementing and supporting rationally motivated action in three ways: by relieving the individual agent of having to decide on a case-by-case basis if actions are justified; by enforcing general compliance; and by providing the organizational means to solve complex collective action problems.[118]

Accordingly, *Faktizität und Geltung* should also be read as providing part of the answer to the third problem that Habermas's detects in Horkheimer and Adorno's respective paradigms of critical theory, concerning the social reproduction of complex modern societies. Habermas's basic claim is that it is only by relying on the functional support of positive law that social integration, through communicative action, can become the medium for the social reproduction of complex modern societies. Law can support everyday forms of communicative action precisely because it shares the latter's inbuilt structural tension between facticity and validity, and, as we will see, its coordinative and organizational advantages allow law to transpose the results of communicative action *beyond* the lifeworld, thus *reconnecting* the functional subsystems of strategic actions back into the domains of action oriented towards mutual understanding.

---

[116] To be sure, Hart also draws a similar distinction between the 'internal' and the 'external' perspective on law, but his conventionalist account denies the connection between the facticity of law and morality, which Habermas's discourse theory seeks to account for.
[117] Habermas, *Between Facts and Norms*, pp. 35–36.
[118] Habermas, *Between Facts and Norms*, p. 114.

Now, as we have seen, Habermas's account of the duality of law is meant to represent a reconstruction of the 'self-understanding' of 'modern legal orders'.[119] This idea should be understood in intersubjective terms, as concerned with the 'legal rules the members (or different parts of the membership) follow, how they go about using, interpreting and changing them, for what reasons they accept or reject a legal order or parts of it as binding'.[120] Yet Habermas's reconstruction does not limit itself to explicating the self-understanding of participants, but attempts to provide a rationally reconstructible interpretation of those historically embedded 'paradigms' of background knowledge, beliefs, values, and norms that inform and make intelligible the explicit self-understanding and practices of a historically determinate legal order. Habermas's reconstruction thus begins at an *even more* abstract, conceptual level by asking, what 'rights citizens must accord one another if they want to legitimately regulate their common life by means of positive law'?[121] The true systematic intention of Habermas's discourse theory of law and democracy only emerges when we see that his answer to this question is given by 'the interpenetration of the discourse principle and the legal form'.[122]

This central but difficult idea refers to the incorporation of the normative content of the discourse principle—according to which a norm is justified only if it can command the assent in a practical discourse of all those affected by it—into the legal system, understood in legal-positivist terms as a system of social rules. Habermas maintains (with Weber) that any modern legal order is motivationally dependent on the belief of the legal subjects that that order is in fact sufficiently justified—i.e., that its claim to legitimacy can be redeemed in rational discourse. Furthermore, he maintains that the discourse principle, when thus embodied in positive law, also represents the necessary and sufficient condition for the *normative* justification of that claim to legitimacy in the form of what he calls 'the democratic principle':

> Only those statutes may claim legitimacy that can meet with the assent of all citizens in a discursive process of legislation that in turn has been legally constituted.[123]

This argument enables Habermas to advance the original claim that basic rights and democratic self-determination are *not*—in contrast to what is often assumed—competing normative demands on a modern legal order, but rather *cooriginal (gleichursprünglich)*. The crucial idea here is that in the incorporation of the discourse principle into the legal form, the pragmatic presuppositions of

---

[119] Habermas, *Between Facts and Norms*, p. 82.
[120] Bernhard Peters, 'On Reconstructive Legal and Political Theory', Philosophy & Social Criticism (20/101), 1994: pp. 101–134, p. 107.
[121] Habermas, *Between Facts and Norms*, p. 82.
[122] Habermas, *Between Facts and Norms*, p. 121.
[123] Habermas, *Between Facts and Norms*, p. 110

discourse are legally institutionalized as *a system of rights*, including five basic classes of rights.

These five classes include rights to equal negative liberties, membership status, equal legal protection, equal opportunities for discursive-democratic participation, and rights to the social, technological, and ecological provision of living standards for the effective enjoyment—or, in Rawls's sense, the 'fair value'—of these basic rights.[124] By conceptually *enabling* the simultaneous exercise of *private autonomy* (equal liberties) and *political autonomy* (participatory rights) as well as establishing the *rule of law* within a constitutionally defined political context, the interpenetration of the discourse principle and the legal form can thus be understood as giving rise to *both* basic human rights and democratic self-determination. Human rights and democratic self-determination, as well as the concomitant normative ideas of private and political autonomy, are in turn seen as *conceptually interdependent*: just as democratic self-determination presupposes basic rights as a condition of possibility, basic rights require discursive-democratic contextualization in order to determine their lifeworld-specific meaning, relative priority, and appropriate contexts of applicability.[125] Habermas thus argues that his *cooriginality thesis* resolves the tension between the traditional *liberal* privileging of rights as restricting the will of the people (in the tradition from Locke) and the traditional *republican* privileging of the *volonté générale* (in the tradition from Rousseau): since basic rights are seen as *enabling conditions* for democratic self-determination, they cannot coherently be conceptualized as limiting its exercise, and neither can democratic self-determination infringe on basic rights, since that would undermine its own condition of possibility (i.e. it would cease to be democratic self-determination).

This complex and sophisticated reconstruction of the internal conceptual connection between democracy and the rule of law (understood as a system of rights) provides the basis for a sociologically informed conception of democratic legitimacy. This deliberative-democratic line of argument defines legitimacy in terms of the translation of one form of power into another: of *communicative power*, which is constituted in processes of collective opinion- and will-formation in the political public sphere, into *administrative power*, as wielded by the government and the public administration. However, these two concepts of power do not merely represent two different specifications of one and the same phenomenon: in contrast to the Weberian conception of power, as the instrumental ability of an agent to impose his or her will on others, communicative power is understood in Arendtian terms, as the *constitutive* formation of an intersubjective consensus in communicative action.[126] Communicative power thus refers to the constitution

---

[124] Habermas, *Between Facts and Norms*, p. 122. Note also the echo of Abendroth here.
[125] Habermas, *Between Facts and Norms*, pp. 122–131.
[126] Jürgen Habermas, 'Hanna Arendts Begriff der Macht', in *Philosophisch-politische Profile. Erweiterte Ausgabe* (Frankfurt: Suhrkamp Verlag, 1987). I will have more to say about power—and this difference in particular—in Chapter 7.

of a collective will, which is in turn understood as the intersubjective basis for all forms of instrumental political power. Such power is formed in *the public sphere*, in which communication must flow as freely and uninhibited from asymmetrical relations of social power as possible in order to avoid manipulation and distortion of processes of opinion- and will-formation.

However, only through the binding decisions of a democratically elected parliament can communicative power be 'transformed' into the code of law and find application to the functional subsystems—directly to the subsystem of administrative power, and indirectly to the economic subsystem *through* the administrative system. For Habermas, law thus functions as a *medium of legitimation* through a 'two-track' model, which translates (1) communicative power formed in the political public sphere into (2) authoritative legislation issuing from the formal deliberations of an elected parliament, which can in turn steer, regulate, and 'anchor' the functional subsystems in the lifeworld. Law is thus able to serve a mediating role between the lifeworld and functional subsystems, since it can translate the content of democratic will-formation from the political public sphere into a language that the subsystems can 'understand', whereby it serves to reconnect the economy and the bureaucracy to the collective will of communicatively acting subjects in the lifeworld.[127]

Habermas is adamant that the democratic principle is *not subordinate* to the moral 'U' principle. Rather, he explicitly argues that, although both are 'grounded' in the discourse principle, the democratic principle and the principle of morality lie at *different levels* of rational reconstruction:

> The moral principle first results when one specifies the general discourse principle for those norms that can be justified if and only if equal consideration is given to the interests of all those who are possibly involved. The principle of democracy results from a corresponding specification for those action norms that appear in legal form. Such norms can be justified by calling on pragmatic, ethical-political, and moral reasons—here justification is not restricted to moral reasons alone.[128]

This latter point is very important to Habermas, since it implies that democratic legitimacy is a much broader notion than moral justifiability. Besides moral considerations, a conception of democratic legitimacy must be able to countenance some forms of 'procedurally regulated bargaining' as well as citizens' 'strong evaluations', i.e., their individual and collective 'ethical' commitments. What Habermas refers to as 'pragmatic reasons' are reasons where the function of practical reason is limited to calculating the optimal means to achieve a required end: what Kant's calls 'hypothetical imperatives'. Such purposive use of practical reason is distinct from ethical reasons, which refer to the self-realization of an individual

---

[127] Habermas, *Between Facts and Norms*, chs. 7 and 8.
[128] Habermas, *Between Facts and Norms*, p. 108.

or the collective aspirations of a community. Finally, in distinction to both of the preceding classes, moral reasons obey a logic entirely of their own:

> The categorical 'ought' of moral injunctions, finally, is directed to the *free will* (*freien Willen*), emphatically construed, of a person who acts in accordance with self-given laws; this will alone is autonomous in the sense that it is completely open to determination by moral insights. In the sphere of validity of the moral law, neither contingent dispositions nor life histories and personal identities set limits to the determination of the will by practical reason. Only a will that is guided by moral insight, and hence is completely rational, can be called autonomous.[129]

Democratic legitimacy requires that legal norms are impartially justified, but such a requirement does not a priori prejudge the kind of reasons that suffice for the legitimacy of a given norm: although such norms must not *violate* moral reasons, they may be sufficiently legitimated with reference to ethical or pragmatic reasons—for example, in cases of procedurally regulated bargaining:

> Bargaining processes are tailored for situations in which social power relations cannot be neutralized in the way rational discourses presuppose. The compromises achieved by such bargaining contain a negotiated agreement (*Vereinbarung*) that balances conflicting interests. Whereas a rationally motivated consensus (*Einverstandnis*) rests on reasons that convince all the parties *in the same way,* a compromise can be accepted by the different parties each for its own *different* reasons... The discourse principle, which is supposed to secure an uncoerced consensus, can thus be brought to bear only indirectly, namely, through procedures that *regulate* bargaining from the standpoint of fairness. In this way, non-neutralizable bargaining power should at least be disciplined by its equal distribution among the parties.[130]

As part of the account of the normative dimension in Habermas's communicative paradigm, *Faktizität und Geltung* picks up one some of Habermas's earliest themes—as developed in *Strukturwandel der Öffentlichkeit*—relating to the public sphere as a source of democratic legitimacy within a constitutional democracy. The book thus also represents Habermas's formidable response to the fourth and final problem that he detected in the first generation of the Frankfurt School, concerning the unsatisfactory conception and appreciation of *constitutional democracy* in the first generation of critical theory. Following the lead of his early mentor Wolfgang Abendroth, Habermas's mature identification of a practical emancipatory potential in a modern capitalist society organized as a

---

[129] Habermas, 'On the Pragmatic, the Ethical, and the Moral Employments of Practical Reason', in *Justification and Application*, pp. 9–10.
[130] Habermas, *Between Facts and Norms*, p. 166.

constitutional democracy thus emphasizes the internal connection between basic constitutional rights and democratic self-determination—or, more specifically: the emancipatory possibilities for democratic self-determination opened up by the legal institutionalization of the pragmatic presuppositions of rational discourse.

In developing this constitutional-democratic alternative to the much less institutionally specified accounts of practical emancipation that we find in the paradigms of the young Horkheimer and Adorno, however, he retains their basic normative commitment to an ideal of socially effective autonomy—or *Mündigkeit*. Indeed, what is emerging as one of the central findings of the present reconstruction of the Frankfurt School tradition—namely its distinctive fusion of a 'Kantian' normative concern with freedom as autonomy and a 'Hegelian-Marxian' concern with the psychological, social, and legal-political conditions of autonomy in the basic structure of society—is, as I have already argued, clearly also one that we can locate in Habermas's work.

In Habermas's communicative paradigm, the Kantian concept of autonomy is understood in intersubjective terms, as a discourse principle for the impartial justification of norms immanent in the rational infrastructure of language communication. Furthermore, his discourse theory of law and democracy is tailored specifically to the question of how this principle might be brought to bear on the basic structure of a complex modern society, which must be integrated in both a social and a systemic fashion, but in which citizens nonetheless expect to be able to democratically determine the social conditions of their individual lives. The beating heart of his communicative paradigm is the claim that, in the pragmatic presuppositions of discourse, we can glean the contours of—in Adorno's words—'an organisation of reality such that autonomous human beings are able to live in it'. Or, as stated in Habermas's own words from the closing passage of *Faktizität und Geltung*:

> The project of realizing the system of rights—a project specifically designed for the conditions of our society, and hence for a particular, historically emergent society ... states the necessary conditions under which legal subjects in their role of enfranchised citizens can reach an understanding with one another about what their problems are and how they are to be solved ... Certainly this understanding, like the rule of law itself, retains a dogmatic core: *the idea of autonomy according to which human beings act as free subjects only insofar as they obey just those laws they give themselves in accordance with insights they have acquired intersubjectively.* This is 'dogmatic' only in a harmless sense. It expresses a tension between facticity and validity, a tension that is 'given' with the fact of the symbolic infrastructure of sociocultural forms of life, which is to say that *for us*, who have developed our identity in such a form of life, it cannot be circumvented.[131]

---

[131] Jürgen Habermas, *Between Facts and Norms*, pp. 445–446 [emphasis added].

6
Habermas's Communicative Paradigm and the Idea of Critical Theory of World Society

6.1 A Kantian Cosmopolitanism

After Chapter 5's reconstruction of Habermas's communicative paradigm, it is the task of this chapter to ascertain the implications of this paradigm for a critical theory of world society. However, as I noted in the introduction to Part III, this does not require the kind of independent theoretical construction that I have undertaken in Chapters 2 and 4, since Habermas has in recent years offered just such an application of his communicative paradigm to the global context. In doing so, he has developed a proposal for a multilevel framework of functionally differentiated legal and political institutions, integrating the world organization of the UN, regional polities on the model of the European Union, and existing democratic nation-states.

However, this proposal does not represent mere normative stipulation; rather, it is rooted in a historically and sociologically informed analysis of economic globalization that sees the global extension of the economic subsystem as submitting territorially circumscribed nation-states to global system imperatives that undermine the steering capacity of existing legal-political institutions and colonize fragmented lifeworlds. In short, as long as economic globalization is not followed by a concomitant *legal-political* globalization, Habermas argues that the virulent forces of the globalized economic subsystem will *gradually undermine* the necessary institutional, cultural, and psychological conditions for democratic self-determination.

6.1.1 The Postnational Constellation and a Multilevel Global Constitutional Framework

The starting point for Habermas's reflections on world society is a 'diagnosis of the times' that he calls *the postnational constellation*. With this term, Habermas not only intends to capture the increasingly questionable viability of the culturally homogenous 'nation' in a globally integrated world society, but also, just as importantly, the problematic relationship between globalized markets and territorially demarcated nation-states:

> The phenomena of the territorial state, the nation, and a popular economy constituted within national borders formed a historical constellation in which the democratic process assumed a more or less convincing institutional form. And the idea that one part of a democratic society is capable of a reflexive intervention into society as a whole has, until now, only been realized in the context of nation-states. Today, developments summarized under the term 'globalization' have put this entire constellation into question.[1]

For Habermas, the immense historical significance of the nation-state as a political entity lies in three achievements: in its development of a territorially demarcated administrative system financed through taxation; in the idea of the nation as a political community and locus of civic solidarity; and, of course, in the historical transformation of a system of hierarchical political authority into a constitutional democracy that has taken place within its borders.

For the last 200 years or so, the nation-state has been *the site* for the democratization of the power of an administrative system, which has gradually branched out of the lifeworld, while the lifeworld has, to a large extent, itself been indexed to the linguistic and cultural community of the nation. However, alongside the formation of the democratic nation-state, an ever more complex and autonomous economic subsystem has developed as the increasingly predominant action system, responsible for the material reproduction of society. In the postwar context of Western Europe, the combination of strong states, national economies devastated by World War II, and extensive international regulation of economic life through the Bretton Woods system allowed for a democratic 'taming' of the economic subsystem through the regulative power of the administrative system. In the process of postwar reconstruction, this enabled the development of the democratic constitutional state into a democratic welfare state (or *Sozialstaat*) with a flourishing middle-class, enjoying a historically unprecedented degree of socioeconomic equality and a fairly robust democratic legitimation of political power.[2]

However, no sooner had this unique historical constellation of strong nation-states, a subdued economic subsystem, and robust democratic self-determination come into being than it started falling apart. The chief instigator of this collapse was the resurgent economic subsystem, which gradually escaped the administrative straightjacket of the nation-state through a combination of politically orchestrated deregulation, technological innovations, and geopolitical

---

[1] Jürgen Habermas, *The Postnational Constellation: Political Essays*, ed. and transl. by Max Pensky (Cambridge: Polity Press, 2001), p. 60.
[2] Habermas, *The Postnational Constellation*, p. 62. See also Habermas, *Between Facts and Norms*, Ch. 9.

transformations—such as the collapse of the Soviet Union and the opening of China towards Western capitalism. The emergence of the postnational constellation has a number of highly disruptive consequences.

First, increased 'capital mobility makes the state's access to profits and monetary wealth more difficult, and heightened local competition reduces the state's capacity to collect taxes'.[3] Second, the globalization of the economic subsystem translates into fundamental *steering problems* for the territorially demarcated nation-state, since its administrative system becomes increasingly incapable of mitigating the human costs of unperturbed global market forces:

> where a vicious circle of unemployment, overburdened social security systems, and shrinking tax base exhausts the financial capacities of the state, growth-stimulating measures become both far more important and far less possible ... 'Keynesianism in one country' is no longer possible.[4]

Third, the resurgence of the economic subsystem directly impairs the ability of democratic parliaments to translate democratic will-formation into administratively efficacious law:

> Increasingly globalized markets have clearly worked to the disadvantage of the state's autonomy and its capacity for economic interventions. At the same time, multinational corporations have emerged as powerful competitors to nation-states. This shift of power is better grasped with the concepts of a theory of different steering media than with a theory of power: money replaces power. The regulatory power of collectively binding decisions operates according to a different logic than the regulatory mechanism of the market. Power can be democratized; money cannot. Thus the possibilities for a democratic self-steering of society slip away as the regulation of social spheres is transferred from one medium to another.[5]

Accordingly, as 'markets drive out politics, the nation-state increasingly loses its capacities to raise taxes and stimulate growth, and with them the ability to secure the essential foundations of its own legitimacy'.[6] In fact, and fourthly, the very concept of state sovereignty and the notion that a determinate *demos* can reflexively manage its own affairs through state institutions is called into question by increased international interdependence: 'there is less and less congruence between the group of participants in a collective decision and the total of all those affected by their decision'.[7] Moreover, and fifthly, the transfer of regulative

---

[3] Habermas, *The Postnational Constellation*, p. 69.
[4] Habermas, *The Postnational Constellation*, pp. 78–79.
[5] Habermas, *The Postnational Constellation*, p. 78.
[6] Habermas, *The Postnational Constellation*, p. 79,
[7] Habermas, *The Postnational Constellation*, p. 70.

competence from the nation-state to intergovernmental organizations such as the IMF, the World Bank, and the WTO necessary for meeting transnational steering problems has opened up serious 'legitimation gaps' between administrative power and channels of democratic will-formation. Finally, and sixthly, in modern multicultural societies, the notion of an ethno-culturally homogenous nation has become untenable, and, as a consequence, the task of furnishing civic solidarity has increasingly shifted to the democratic process—a basis for civil solidarity that Habermas has famously called 'constitutional patriotism'.[8] But since the ability of the democratic process to furnish solidarity depends on its ability to accommodate democratic will-formation in the political public sphere, the globalized economic subsystem's assault on the political institutions of the nation-state also represents an indirect but powerful threat to civic solidarity.

As is obvious, these six currents converge in a fairly disheartening estimation of the prospects for democratic self-determination within the territorially demarcated nation-state in an age of economic globalization:

> The (not exactly encouraging) diagnosis has led politicians to scrap social programs, and has driven voters to apathy or protest. The broad renunciation of the power of politics to shape social relations, and the readiness to abandon normative points of view in favour of adaptations to supposedly unavoidable systemic imperatives, now dominate the political arenas of the Western world.[9]

Although Habermas penned these lines in the late 1990s, his diagnosis of a postnational constellation has lost none of its plausibility or urgency: not only does economic globalization wreak a frontal assault on the steering capacities of existing political institutions; it also submits political decision-making within the faltering nation-state to a structural dynamic of interstate competition and a concomitant 'race to the bottom' of constraints on the profits of private investment, such as living wages, progressive taxation, and decent social policy.[10] As a consequence, substantive political disagreement is increasingly replaced by technical debates in which the parameters have been set by the functional requirements of a globalized economic subsystem.[11] Accordingly, Habermas also sees in the advent of neoliberal globalization—where the predicate 'neoliberal' is understood in terms of the increased marketization of state and social relations—a formidable confirmation of the *colonization thesis*, where system imperatives rob politics of its normative

---

[8] Jürgen Habermas, *The New Conservatism: Cultural Criticism and the Historian's Debate*, transl. by Shierry Weber Nicholsen (Cambridge: Polity Press, 1989).
[9] Habermas, *The Postnational Constellation*, p. 79.
[10] Peter Dietsch, *Catching Capital: The Ethics of Tax Competition* (Oxford: Oxford University Press, 2015).
[11] Claus Offe, *Europe Entrapped* (Cambridge: Polity Press, 2016).

dimension by undercutting the cultural and psychological resources for citizens' very ability to, in an emphatic sense, *think and act politically*.[12]

For Habermas, the fundamental problem posed by economic globalization can be understood in the sense that it represents a severe challenge to the legal form in which the discourse principle has hitherto been institutionalized, namely the legal-political institutions of the nation-state. But this way of formulating the problem also indirectly points to its solution: *the discourse principle must be given a new legal-institutional form that is adequate to the conditions of the postnational constellation.* Habermas's proposed solution to this problem relies on two sources: one empirical-historical, and the other normative. The first is given by a reconstruction of the historically evolved framework of legal-political institutions that has developed in different stages all the way back to the ancient empires (such as China or Persia); the Treaty of Westphalia in 1648 (which marks the official birth of the European state); European colonization and imposition of peripheral state structures on their subject peoples around the world, as well as subsequent anticolonial revolutions; and the trans- and supranational political institutions that developed in the wake of World War II—most importantly, the EU and the UN. Habermas interprets this history of legal-political institutional formation and differentiation as a world-historical *learning process*, from which we can anticipate a certain developmental direction for our present practical purposes. Specifically, along with a growing number of international legal scholars, he interprets this history as tending towards the *constitutionalization of international law*.[13]

The most important normative source for this account is—above all—Kant's political writings. One of Kant's most basic insights is that a *legal (or civil) condition* is a fundamental enabling condition of freedom, peace, and justice, and even at the international level of states, he did not shy away from pushing this insight to its logical conclusion:

> In accordance with reason there is only one way that states in relation with one another can leave the lawless condition, which involves nothing but war; it is that, like individual human beings, they give up their savage (lawless) freedom, accommodate themselves to public coercive laws, and so form an (always growing) *state of nations* (*civitas gentium*) that would finally encompass all the nations of the earth.[14]

However, since Kant feared that a world republic would degenerate 'into a universal monarchy, since as the range of government expands laws progressively

---

[12] Habermas has confirmed this last observation in personal conversation.

[13] See, for example, Bardo Fassbender, 'The United Nations Charter as Constitution of the International Community', *Columbia Journal of Transnational Law*, (36/3), 1998: 529–619.

[14] Immanuel Kant, 'Toward Perpetual Peace', in *Practical Philosophy*, ed. and transl. by Mary J. Gregor (Cambridge: Cambridge University Press, 1996), p. 328.

lose their vigor, and a soulless despotism, after it has destroyed the seed of the good, finally deteriorating into anarchy',[15] he settled for the compromise solution of a 'pacific league of nations'.[16] Notwithstanding this seeming loss of nerve, Kant consistently maintained that all human beings have a 'cosmopolitan right' to 'conditions of universal *hospitality*': a *'right to visit'* that 'belongs to all human beings by virtue of the right of possession in common of the earth's surface on which, as a sphere, they cannot disperse infinitely but must finally put up with being near one another'.[17] Without getting further into the details of Kant's evolving vision for a cosmopolitan legal condition, it is the basic dilemma sketched by Kant between a *sovereign world republic* and a *voluntary league of nations* that forms the starting point for Habermas's normative proposal for a multilevel global constitutional framework more adequate to the functional-systemic challenges of globalization.

According to Habermas, the root of Kant's dilemma between a sovereign world state and a voluntary league of sovereign nation-states is that he perceived sovereignty as 'indivisible'. However, as existing federal polities such as the US show, a model of 'divided sovereignty' developed alongside the mode of unitary and centralized sovereignty that Kant observed in the French Revolution, and, in such models of divided sovereignty, 'the democratic will of the people already branches out at its very source into parallel channels of legitimation through elections to local, state, and federal parliaments'.[18] Such a model of divided and functionally differentiated sovereignty can serve as the basis for a multilevel constitutional framework of supranational, transnational, and national legal-political institutions. Moreover, departing from the premises of *Faktizität und Geltung*, Habermas appeals to the less demanding account of the rule of law that one finds in the liberal tradition (as compared with the republican tradition), which 'limits the power of the state without constituting it', and he argues that such a 'liberal type of constitution ... also provides a conceptual model for a constitutionalization of international law in the form a politically constituted world society without a world government'.[19] As we shall see below, this amounts to a serious weakening of the central conceptual claim of his legal and democratic theory: namely, that basic human rights and popular sovereignty are *cooriginal*.

With these preliminaries in place, we can now sketch Habermas's proposal for a multilevel global constitutional framework. This framework is developed at three different levels of functionally differentiated policy-making, in which three different kinds of collective actors predominate. First, the *supranational* level is characterized by a single collective actor, the *world organization* of the

---

[15] Kant, 'Toward Perpetual Peace', p. 336.
[16] Kant, 'Toward Perpetual Peace', pp. 328–329.
[17] Kant, 'Toward Perpetual Peace', p. 329.
[18] Habermas, 'A Political Constitution for the Pluralist World Society?', in *Between Naturalism and Religion*, p. 315.
[19] Habermas, 'A Political Constitution for the Pluralist World Society?', p. 316.

United Nations. Although more powerful and autonomous than the UN at present, Habermas's vision for a world organization is no world state, but a global polity with a carefully circumscribed mandate for 'securing peace and human rights on a global scale'.[20] The world organization would come into being through the constitutionalization of a suitably reformed UN Charter and the Universal Declaration of Human Rights, establishing the universal jurisdiction of the International Court of Justice and the International Criminal Court. The global constitution would recognize all human beings as citizens and legal subjects of a cosmopolitan legal order, above and beyond states.

As Kant intended, the constitutionalization of the UN Charter would thus abolish war in the traditional sense and transform the meaning of conflict in the global arena: 'Once war has been overcome, the key issue becomes that of obligating a global *police force* to act on behalf of the basic rights of cosmopolitan citizens who need protection against their own criminal governments or other violent gangs operating within states'.[21] The world organization would include a General Assembly of directly elected representatives of 'cosmopolitan citizens' while retaining the existing state representatives; accordingly, the global constitution would establish the representation of *both* cosmopolitan citizens and states in the global parliament. The Assembly would be 'the institutional locus of an inclusive formation of opinion and will concerning the principles of transnational justice'—by which Habermas refers to 'the interpretation and elaboration of the Charter' and the determination of the concrete meaning of human rights through the reconciliation of 'competing justice perspectives'.[22] As states would retain their monopoly on force, they would have to furnish the world organization with sufficient military resources to uphold peace and conduct interventions on carefully circumscribed grounds—including, of course, humanitarian grounds—which determine both when the security council is 'authorized *and obligated*' to use force.[23]

Second, the *transnational* level is characterized by what Habermas calls *regional* or *continental regimes*, modelled on transnational polities such as the European Union. Since some of the most important collective action problems we face today are global in scope—most importantly, in addition to those mentioned above, climate change and global poverty—the plethora of smaller nation-states must coalesce into larger regional powers 'with a sufficiently representative mandate to negotiate for whole continents and to wield the necessary powers of implementation for whole territories'.[24] This (far from trivial) requirement of Habermas's

---

[20] Habermas, 'A Political Constitution for the Pluralist World Society?', p. 322.
[21] Habermas, 'A Political Constitution for the Pluralist World Society?', p. 339.
[22] Jürgen Habermas, 'The Constitutionalization of International Law and the Legitimation Problems of a Constitution for a World Society', in *Europe: The Faltering Project*, transl. by Ciaran Cronin (Cambridge: Cambridge University Press, 2009), pp. 120–121 [emphasis omitted].
[23] Jürgen Habermas, 'Does the Constitutionalization of International Law Still Have a Chance?', in *The Divided West*, ed. and transl. by Ciaran Cronin (Cambridge: Polity Press, 2006), p. 173.
[24] Habermas, 'A Political Constitution for the Pluralist World Society?', p. 324.

multilevel global constitutional framework is thus motivated purely by functional considerations, since polities with a continental regulative scope and mandate are necessary for addressing the steering problems caused by the globalized economic subsystem and reintroduce the more democratically congenial steering medium of power:

> At the intermediate, transnational level, the major powers would address the difficult problem of a global domestic politics which are no longer restricted to mere coordination but extend to actively promoting a rebalanced world order. They would have to cope with global economic and ecological problems within the framework of permanent conferences and negotiating forums.[25]

These continental polities should not necessarily be understood as states—although some states, such as China, Russia, and the US are already near-continental in scope—but rather as regional organizations such as the EU and the (much less cohesive) African Union. In his most recent work, Habermas has developed a constitutional proposal for a democratization of the European Union, which leaves a considerable extent of nation-state sovereignty intact through a system of 'double sovereignty': the European Commission would become an actual government anchored in the parliamentary majority in the European Parliament, but the Commission would answer both to the Parliament and the European Council of member states—the latter as a second parliamentary chamber.[26]

As in the cosmopolitan case, the continental constitutions would not usurp the sovereignty of the states, but form composite polities in which individuals and states stand in a *'heterarchical relationship',*[27] where citizens enjoy dual citizenship of the transnational polity and of their nation-state, but in which continental law holds primacy over national law. Although the *global domestic politics* that would arise in permanent negotiation forums between the continental polities would retain parts of the power-politics and coalition-building of present-day international affairs, it would be far from international politics as we know it, since the extreme option of recourse to war would be off the table and the continental polities would be constrained by the normative parameters laid down by the General Assembly of the world organization: 'From a normative point of view, the power-driven process of compromise formation can also be understood as an application of the principles of transnational justice negotiated at the supranational level'.[28]

---

[25] Habermas, 'Does the Constitutionalization of International Law Still Have a Chance?', p. 136 [emphasis omitted].
[26] Jürgen Habermas, *The Crisis of the European Union: A Response*, trans. Ciaran Cronin (Cambridge: Polity Press, 2012), pp. 28–53.
[27] Jürgen Habermas, 'Democracy in Europe: Why the Development of the European Union into a Transnational Democracy is Necessary and How it is Possible', *ARENA Working Paper* (13/2014), December 2014, p. 11.
[28] Habermas, 'The Constitutionalization of International Law', p. 126.

Third, the *national* level would comprise *nation-states* much as we know them—although having relinquished sovereignty over the maintenance of peace and human rights to the world organization, and regulation of global economic and ecological systems to the continental polities, they would evidently not enjoy anything like absolute 'Hobbesian' sovereignty. To be sure, insofar as Habermas's diagnosis of the postnational constellation is correct, such an absolute notion of state sovereignty is already untenable in the world of today. Indeed, his multi-level global constitutional framework is motivated precisely by a hope to *win back sovereignty for the political domain* that it has largely relinquished to global markets, and which nation-states cannot hope to achieve on their own. In rethinking democracy for the postnational constellation, however, Habermas is in no rush to leave the nation-state behind; he rather emphasizes its crucial importance within his multilevel framework:

> As democratic states characterized by the rule of law, the nation states are not only actors on the long historical path towards civilizing the violence at the core of political power; as vital embodiments of 'existent justice' (Hegel), they also represent lasting achievements. Therefore, the citizens of the Union have a justified interest in their respective nation states continuing to perform their proven role as guarantors of law and freedom also in their role as member states. The nation states are more than just embodiments of national cultures worthy of preservation; they vouch for a level of justice and freedom which citizens rightly want to see preserved.[29]

To sum up, Habermas proposes a multilevel global constitutional framework in which a world organization is charged with upholding peace and human rights, continental polities are charged with regulating global economic and ecological systems, and the nation-state charged with maintaining its traditional role as a guarantor of justice and freedom for its citizens and its monopoly on force. If Habermas's proposal were realized in practice, all human beings would thus simultaneously be legal subjects of a cosmopolitan constitution, a continental constitution, and a state constitution, and citizens of a world organization, continental polity, and a nation-state.

6.1.2 The Limits of Law

The starting question for Habermas's proposal, as outlined above, is 'whether the normative core of the vanishing world of democratic nation-states can be

---

[29] Habermas, *The Crisis of the European Union*, p. 41.

recovered within the postnational constellation'[30]—or, in other words, whether the discourse principle can be institutionalized at higher legal-political levels that can establish the effective global rule of the democratic principle. Clearly, it is therefore essential for Habermas that his multilevel global constitutional framework admits of sufficient democratic legitimation. In Habermas's view, democratic legitimacy has both a normative and a functional component. From a normative point of view, as we have seen, the democratic principle represents the legally institutionalized form of Habermas's discourse-theoretical reconstruction of the Kantian conception of freedom as autonomy: namely, the discourse principle. Habermas can thus be interpreted as claiming that democratic legitimation of the multilevel global constitutional framework is necessary for *re-establishing the conditions for autonomy in our globalized world*. From a functional point of view, since the task of furnishing civil solidary has increasingly been displaced from the national culture to the democratic process, insufficiently legitimate legal-political institutions will also be motivationally unsustainable. In a complex world society, sufficient legitimation is therefore also *functionally necessary* for securing civil solidarity and upholding a just social and political order.

However, as above, Habermas faces a serious conceptual obstacle at this point, which derives from one of the central claims of his discourse theory of law and democracy. Recall the perhaps central argument of *Faktizität und Geltung* that basic human rights and popular sovereignty are cooriginal and, conceptually speaking, mutually dependent: just as popular sovereignty depends on the institutionalization of the enabling conditions of discourse in the form of a system of rights, the rule of law depends on a political legislature and political public sphere through which the system of rights can be given a substantive content within a specific lifeworld. As conceptualized in *Faktizität und Geltung*, the democratic constitutional state is able to meet both the normative requirement and the functional requirement in a way that accords with the cooriginality thesis: from a normative point of view, a state parliament ensures legitimacy by deliberating on and enacting law that translates the democratic will formed in the political public sphere into the legal code; and from a functional point of view, the combined regulative efficaciousness and legitimacy of the democratic process, and the perceived justice of its results, secures the required civic solidarity. However, the implication of the postnational constellation is precisely that in the existing context of the nation-state, both of these conditions are increasingly eroded, and this supplies the reason for transitioning to Habermas's multilevel global constitutional framework. But can the latter framework live up to the demanding presuppositions of the cooriginality thesis?

The short answer is, no. First, it is clear that we will never have a global lifeworld, or perhaps even a single European, African, or South-American lifeworld.

---

[30] Habermas, 'A Political Constitution for the Pluralist World Society?', p 327.

To be sure, we might imagine global and continental *public spheres* that cut across lifeworlds. But even if we might hope for such supra- and transnational public spheres, for the moment they remain closer to hope than reality. That is to say, even if it were true, as Habermas suggests, that there is in fact a burgeoning European public sphere arising within the infrastructure of national public spheres, and even occasional spouts of an infant global public sphere, these supra- and transnational public spheres would likely have to be very robust indeed. Given the vast and persistent patterns of global socioeconomic inequality, and the more subtle neocolonial forms of domination and epistemic injustices that still permeate our present world society, the supra- and transnational decision-making fora that Habermas envisions will be extremely vulnerable to cooptation by the most powerful states and the social power of transnational corporations.

Faced with the enormous asymmetries of social and political power in the present world society, the communicative power of would-be continental and global public spheres would surely have to permanently 'besiege'[31] the transnational negotiating system in which continental polities negotiate the terms of the global economy and human interaction with the ecological system, in order to avoid backroom deals that serve only the special interests of the already-powerful few. The basic problem for Habermas here is that another way to interpret the cooriginality thesis is that human rights and popular sovereignty are *both necessary conditions* for redeeming the *emancipatory potential* of democratic law. That is to say, unless highly resourceful and robust supra- and transnational public spheres develop in support of supra- and transnational political legislatures, the global institutional structure that Habermas proposes might quickly turn out to be a potent vehicle for more pernicious forms of global power that bring to mind Kant's 'soulless despotism' rather than the institutional safeguarding of democracy in a globalized world society.

Faced with this objection, Habermas has two responses at hand. We have already touched upon the first response, namely that Habermas interprets the constitutionalization of international law on the less demanding liberal model of *domesticating* power rather than the more ambitious republican model of *constituting* legitimate power. Following this line of reasoning, Habermas introduces the notion of 'legitimacy chains'. In particular, two different legitimacy chains would operate within the global constitutional framework: one would lead from cosmopolitan citizens and state governments to the UN General Assembly, while another would lead from both citizens of states and continental polities as well as the governments of states to the transnational negotiating system.[32]

In this way, some of the 'thick' legitimacy of the national level might be preserved through the transnational level all the way to the supranational level, even

---

[31] Habermas, 'Popular Sovereignty as Procedure', in *Between Facts and Norms*, pp. 486–487.
[32] Habermas, 'The Constitutionalization of International Law', p. 118.

if permanent supra- and transnational public spheres remain underdeveloped. Moreover, this argument finds support in Habermas's claim that the narrowly circumscribed mandates of the upper levels—especially of the world organization—presupposes a lesser degree of legitimacy than the lower levels of governance. In the General Assembly of the world organization, legislation would be limited to interpreting the UN Charter and the Universal Declarations of Human Rights, and it would thus, according to Habermas, be '*juridical* rather than *political*'.[33] Accordingly, although neither the trans- nor the supranational level will be able to meet the thick legitimation requirements and demands on the governments of states, where the public sphere is supported by a shared lifeworld and shared political culture, 'the chain of legitimacy could extend without interruption from national states via regional regimes such as the European Union to the world organization'.[34]

The second response available to Habermas would be to follow Seyla Benhabib and others in their emphasis on the 'jurisgenerativity of law'—in particular 'the power of those most prominent cosmopolitan norms, namely universal human rights, to empower local movements'.[35] This response effectively amounts to a revision of the cooriginality thesis, in that it suggests that constitutionalization *as such*—i.e., becoming a legal subject of a constitution predicated on human rights—can 'create a normative universe of meaning that can often escape the "provenance of formal lawmaking"'.[36] According to this revision, the legal recognition of basic human rights precedes and 'generates' popular sovereignty; the establishment of a global constitutional framework could thus be supposed to generate public spheres and its own chains of legitimacy. That Habermas might have something like this in mind is suggested by the following remark:

> The constitutional norms and legal constructs introduced by political elites in supranational arenas exercise anticipatory effects in the sense of a *self-fulfilling prophecy*. This kind of lawmaking anticipates the change in consciousness that it provokes among the addressees only in the course of its gradual implementation. The accompanying political discourses provide the medium in which the spirit of legal regulations, whose letter is initially recognized only in a declamatory manner, can be gradually internalized.[37]

Unfortunately, neither of these two responses seems sufficient to counter the worries expressed above. To my mind, both founder on a systematic problem with

---

[33] Habermas, 'The Constitutionalization of International Law', p. 124.
[34] Habermas, *The Crisis of the European Union*, p. 66.
[35] Seyla Benhabib, 'Claiming Rights across Borders: International Human Rights and Democratic Sovereignty', *American Political Science Review*, (103/4), Nov. 2009: 691–704, p. 692.
[36] Benhabib, 'Claiming Rights across Borders', p. 696.
[37] Habermas, *Between Naturalism and Religion*, p. 321.

Habermas's application of his communicative paradigm to world society, which I already introduced in the discussion in Chapter 3 on the disappearance of the perspective of political economy from the work of later generations of Frankfurt School critical theory: his circumscribed focus on the *legal-political* conditions for autonomy in the global context. Indeed, his lack of concern with the broader *social* and *economic* conditions of autonomy disregards precisely those obstacles that would be most likely to obstruct and prevent chains of legitimacy from reaching from the nation-state all the way to the world organization, as well as to undercut the possibility for the jurisgenerativity of cosmopolitan law: namely, those vast socioeconomic inequalities and asymmetries of power that persist between the affluent parts (mainly the West and parts of Asia) and the poorer regions (such as Africa, the South-Asian Subcontinent, and South America) of the present global order—which is still very much structured along past colonial and imperial lines[38]—and between social classes and other social groups across geographical regions.

These global inequalities and asymmetries are 'social' or 'economic' rather than legal-political in nature, but they would obviously have an immense impact on the possibility for legally empowered subjects to make emancipatory use of their cosmopolitan legal status. If certain social classes, states, or even continents continue to be as systematically deprived of even the most basic resources as they are today, their populations are as unlikely to be able to make their voices heard in transnational and global public spheres and decision-making fora as they are today—whether because they are overtly excluded by more powerful agents, or because they lack the material or educational resources to give public voice to their grievances.[39]

Of course, in an important sense, Habermas is right to focus on legal-political institutions, precisely because they represent those institutions by means of which the individuals belonging to a political community can 'reflexively' influence and organize the basic structure of their society. That is to say, it is only through legal-political institutions that a democratic community is able to 'govern itself', which is also true of those social spheres that Habermas largely leaves out of consideration in his proposal for a multilevel global constitutional framework. However, the fact that it is only *politically* and *legally* that we govern ourselves as a community does not justify excluding from theoretical consideration those *social* and *economic* inequalities and asymmetries in an account of how subjects might aspire to practical emancipation under conditions of globalization, especially when those social

---

[38] See James Tully's discussion of 'Neo-Kantian imperialism' in his *Public Philosophy in a New Key: Volume II: Imperialism and Civic Freedom* (Cambridge: Cambridge University Press, 2008). I take up this question in a more systematic manner in Chapter 9.

[39] I will return to a discussion of the sense in which Habermas's communicative paradigm may be blind to injustices that prevent subjects from discursively articulating their experience of socially compelled suffering in the first place in Chapter 7.

and economic conditions so dramatically impact on the ability of the 'wretched of the Earth' to engage in legal-political action.

In Habermas's application of his communicative paradigm to world society, the question of how to deal with global socioeconomic inequalities and power asymmetries is simply entrusted to the transnational negotiation of global domestic politics between continental regimes, guided by principles of transnational justice embedded in international law. However, having thus delegated the problem to political practice, Habermas assumes that theory has nothing more to add. But a critical theory of world society cannot countenance such a crippling self-imposed limitation: it must not blind its theoretical gaze to those global social and economic conditions that would systematically frustrate political autonomy even within a full-fledged cosmopolitan constitution.

6.1.3 The Limit of Proceduralism

It seems to me that the root of this circumscribed focus on legal-political institutions—or, as I have also expressed it, on the legal-political conditions for autonomy—is Habermas's thoroughgoing *proceduralism*. This discourse-theoretical proceduralism is much less pronounced in his earlier work, and even in *Theorie des kommunikativen Handels*, the colonization thesis is a clear example of a concern with the social conditions of autonomy more broadly conceived. But the narrower focus on legal-political autonomy comes to the fore in *Faktizität und Geltung*, and, in particular, in his later work on globalization. This uncompromising proceduralism implies that Habermas eschews any reliance on first-order principles of justice in his critique of world society, but limits his normative point of view to the legal institutionalization of the second-order principles that guide the discursive redemption of first-order normative claims. The upshot is that Habermas does not actually provide a critical theory of global *justice*, in the sense envisioned by the young Horkheimer, but rather, as I have suggested, a procedural account of the legal-political institutions necessary for the discourse principle to receive a new legal expression more appropriate for the conditions of globalization.

To be sure, as I have argued, we can interpret Habermas's guiding normative concern as continuous with the concerns that we located in the young Horkheimer's original paradigm and in Adorno's negativist paradigm: namely, as a concern with the *social reality of autonomy*. But Habermas explicitly denies that we can and should understand such a normative concern as a first-order moral concern of an *immediately practical reason*, insisting instead that communicative reason is not a source of first-order moral claims. However, in abstaining from a substantive first-order critique of injustice, or in delegating these judgements to political practice, Habermas also deprives himself of immediate theoretical access to those social relations and structures in the global basic structure that are the proper subject of first-order discourses of justice—and in doing so, he offers at best a *partial* and foreshortened perspective on the social reality of autonomy.

Indeed, it seems to me that his unwillingness to theorize the social conditions of political autonomy in the global context is partly driven by his commitment to eschewing first-order principles of justice. However, instead of leaving such substantive concerns of social injustice to practice and hoping for better times, in which legal subjects might have the social and psychological wherewithal to make effective use of their cosmopolitan legal status, a critical theory of world society should also be able to theorize such social impairments to individual autonomy. In order to do so, however, we must go beyond Habermas's thoroughgoing proceduralism and, like the young Horkheimer, embrace the concept of justice, as I will argue in the Conclusion.

6.1.4 The Limits of Western Modernity

In *The End of Progress*, Amy Allen mounts a sweeping objection to the basic assumptions that undergird Habermas's communicative paradigm of critical theory: namely, that Habermas's emphasis on socio-cultural learning and the rationalization of the lifeworld commits him to an irredeemably Eurocentric 'view of history according to which European modernity represents a moral-political advance over premodern forms of life', which sees European modernity as developmentally superior to temporally coexisting cultures classified as traditional or premodern.[40] This in turn violates Habermas's own injunction that the children of European modernity must encounter non-European participants in the emergent 'global public sphere' with openness 'to being enlightened by others about our own blind spots'.

Allen's argument proceeds in three steps. First, she argues that Habermas's theory of social revolution renders him vulnerable 'to the frequently levelled charge of Eurocentrism', as it posits lifeworld structures that are specific to European modernity as both universally valid and as the culmination to a world-historical developmental process, thus effectively assigning to non-Western cultures the pernicious status of being developmentally inferior. This argument follows Gurminder K. Bhambra's incisive claim that 'the dominant ideas of modernity' involve a 'temporal and spatial disjuncture', a 'temporal rupture that distinguishes a traditional, agrarian past from the modern, industrial present; and a fundamental difference that distinguishes Europe from the rest of the world'.[41]

Second, Allen argues that the theory of social evolution is no mere add-on to his critical theory but does important 'metanormative work', serving a 'crucial

---

[40] Allen, *The End of Progress*, p. 72.
[41] Gurminder K. Bhambra, *Rethinking Modernity: Postcolonialism and the Sociological Imagination* (New York: Palgrave MacMillan, 2007), p. 1.

role in Habermas's attempts to validate his own critical standards'. This implies that Habermas cannot simply abandon the theory of social evolution, since this theory is necessary for 'grounding the normativity of Habermasian critical theory'.[42] Third, and finally, she therefore argues that the problem of Eurocentrism emerges in a 'seemingly intractable form in Habermas's work', since he 'positions the European or Euro-American participant [in the global public sphere] as developmentally superior to members of traditional or "nonmodern" cultures'.[43] In other words: from a post- or decolonial point of view, Habermas's communicative paradigm is effectively beyond redemption.

This objection should hardly come as a surprise to Habermas. In a 1985 interview with Perry Anderson and Peter Dews, we find Habermas practically conceding the point in response to a question concerning the Frankfurt School tradition's neglect of 'capitalism as a global system':

> *[Anderson/Dews:] The Frankfurt School Tradition as a whole has concentrated its analyses upon the most advanced capitalist societies, at the comparative expense of any considerations of capitalism as a global system. In your view, do conceptions of socialism developed in the course of anti-imperialist and anti-capitalist struggles in the Third World have any bearing on the tasks of a democratic socialism in the advanced capitalist world? Conversely, does your own analysis of advanced capitalism have any lessons for socialist forces in the Third World?*
>
> [Habermas:] I am tempted to say 'no' in both cases. I am aware of the fact that this is a eurocentrically limited view. I would rather pass the question.[44]

But whereas the charge of Eurocentrism seemed to catch Habermas off-guard in the 1980s, in recent years, Habermas's work on the global application of his communicative paradigm has spurred sustained reflection on questions of how to conceive of a global modernity, the relationship between faith and secular reason, and the status of post-metaphysical thinking, culminating in the momentous 1700-page study *Auch eine Geschicte der Philosophie*, published in 2019 shortly after his 90th birthday.[45]

Let's be clear about the stakes here. The question before us is not whether Habermas, especially in his earlier work, was prone to using language and employing ideas that reflect the prejudices of his historical, cultural, and intellectual context— this is surely, and trivially, the case. The question is also not whether Habermas has incorporated more systematic elements into his communicative paradigm, which lend credence to Allen's charge—a worry which, for example, indeed seems to arise

---

[42] Allen, *The End of Progress*, p. 39.
[43] Allen, *The End of Progress*, p. 39, 73.
[44] Jürgen Habermas, 'A Philosophico-Political Profile', written interview with Perry Anderson and Peter Dews, *New Left Review* (1/151), May-June 1985: pp. 75–105.
[45] Alas, published too late for me to do justice to this last *magnum opus* in what follows.

in the cross-cultural application of Jean Piaget's and Lawrence Kohlberg's theories of cognitive and moral development, to which Habermas appeals for support of his discourse ethics.[46] The question must be whether Habermas' communicative paradigm is, as Allen charges, irredeemably and *intractably intertwined with Eurocentric assumptions*, because those assumptions serve to ground the normativity of his communicative paradigm of critical theory. And the answer to this question seems to turn on whether her charge, that the basic categories of the theory of social revolution are irredeemably Eurocentric, is sound.

In my view, there are reasons to resist this inference. In her critique of Habermas, Allen recognizes his efforts to mitigate the potentially Eurocentric implications of 'modernisation theory' by appealing to the concept of 'multiple modernities', which holds that the globalized, modernizing infrastructure of functional subsystems historically emanating from the West is 'compatible with a high degree of cultural hybridity', and that modernity should therefore be understood as a common global infrastructure adaptable to many different cultural contexts, rather than simply the transposition of a single Western or European modernity across the world. However, following Bhambra, Allen rejects this argument, as the concept of multiple modernities in her view 'does nothing to address the fundamental problems with the conceptualization of modernity itself' and thus leaves intact the 'progressive view of history' that renders Habermas vulnerable to decolonial critique in the first place. In Bhambra's words: 'to the extent that these multiple modernities continue to be understood as derived from the creative appropriation, by those that followed, of the institutional frameworks of modernity that are seen to originate in Europe, the problem of Eurocentrism remains integral' to this view.[47]

But this objection misses its mark—not only because it may seem to confuse questions of genesis and validity. More importantly, as Allen actually recognizes earlier in her discussion, Habermas insists that 'no purely premodern societies remain in our globalized world'.[48] That is to say, while Habermas clearly accepts Bhambra's claim that modernity involves a 'temporal disjuncture'—which is indeed a long-running theme in his work[49]—he explicitly *rejects* the claim that modernity also involves a 'spatial disjuncture' between Europe and the rest of the world, at least in the present day context of globalized modernity and its common but, in diverging ways, culturally-embedded global infrastructure.

Indeed, in *Auch eine Geschichte der Philosophie*, Habermas insists that we must instead conceive of globalized modernity as 'something like the arena, in which

---

[46] See Thomas McCarthy, 'Reason and Rationalization: Habermas's "Overcoming" of Hermeneutics', in *Ideals and Illusions: On Reconstruction and Deconstruction in Contemporary Critical Theory* (Cambridge MA: The MIT Press, 1991), and Jürgen Habermas, 'Moral Consciousness and Communicative Action', in *Moral Consciousness and Communicative Action*.
[47] Bhambra, *Rethinking Modernity*, p. 65.
[48] Allen, *The End of Progress*, p. 68.
[49] See, most notably, Habermas, *The Philosophical Discourse of Modernity*.

different civilizations encounter one another within more or less culturally specific mouldings of this common infrastructure'.[50] With this proposal, Habermas rejects the 'culturalist' image of world civilizations as incommensurable and mutually enclosed entities in favour of a more complex picture, where 'the great civilisations' are characterized by 'family resemblances', 'which imply similar cognitive developmental paths'.[51] Accordingly, the view that contrasts 'European modernity' with temporally coexisting 'traditional' or 'premodern' forms of life in non-Western cultures, and which therefore necessarily regards the latter as developmentally inferior, is one that Allen *imputes* to Habermas, rather than a view that she identifies within his work. In other words, it is *her* assumption, rather than his.

Of course, this does not mean that Habermas is necessarily *right* in claiming that we today live in a globalized modernity with similar cognitive developmental paths across cultures, in which we must all come to terms with what it does and should mean to be modern in a global intercultural discourse with one another. But it does mean that, strictly speaking, Allen's charge that Habermas's theory of social evolution is irredeemably Eurocentric does not stick—at least not on the grounds that she has offered. What Allen's critique of Habermas's communicative paradigm does manifestly demonstrate, in my view, is that any critical theory that interprets social rationalization in terms of socio-cultural and moral learning processes must be ever mindful that such a view risks *lending itself* to pernicious developmentalist interpretations, which would introduce a spatial disjuncture between 'civilized' Europe and the ostensibly 'primitive' Third World. Accordingly, a critical theory of world society that understands itself as anchored in moral learning processes must have built into itself a reflexive check against such abuses and misuses of its categorical framework to prop up neocolonial forms of domination between Europe or the West and 'the Global South'. I will return to Allen's decolonial critique of Axel Honneth's recognition paradigm of critical theory in Chapter 8, before offering a more systematic discussion of her proposed rehabilitation of Adorno's negativism as a basis for rethinking the normative grounds of a critical theory of world society in Chapter 9.

6.1.5 The Limits of Intersubjectivity

Habermas has been forcefully criticized by ecological thinkers for drawing an overly robust conceptual distinction between communicative reason and instrumental reason, or society and nature, which 'falls behind' the first generation of the Frankfurt School in construing nature solely as an object of instrumental mastery

---

[50] Jürgen Habermas, *Auch eine Geschichte der Philosophie. Band I: Die okzidentale Konstellation von Glauben und Wissen* (Berlin: Suhrkamp, 2019), p. 119 [translated by me].
[51] Habermas, *Auch eine Geschichte der Philosophie. Band I*, 134.

and control.[52] As we saw in Chapter 5, Habermas distinguishes two modes of integration, communicative action and strategic action, where the former enables social integration with a view to action orientations and the latter systemic integration through action consequences, whereas the relation to nature is conceptualized solely in terms of instrumental action and technological mastery.

This tripartite distinction is undertaken precisely in order to escape the theoretical cul-de-sac in which Adorno's negativist paradigm ends up, where enlightenment reason is reduced to a totalizing instrumental orientation in the course of its historical realization. This move has obvious theoretical advantages, as we have seen—but the question is whether it also deprives Habermas of the conceptual resources to make sense of the ecological dialectic of enlightenment playing out before our very eyes: namely, the disruption of global ecosystems and fossil-powered industrial society's undermining of its natural existential conditions. I will argue that this is indeed the case.

In his *We Have Never Been Modern* from 1991, Bruno Latour influentially argues that modernity is characterized by a foundational distinction between society and nature, which is no longer tenable. Latour explicitly singles Habermas out for criticism, arguing that 'Habermas wants to make the two poles [between subject and object] incommensurable, at the very moment when quasi-objects are multiplying to such an extent that it appears impossible to find a single one that more or less resembles a free speaking subject or a reified natural object'.[53] According to Latour, 'quasi-objects' refer to phenomena that can neither be classified as purely subject or object, as neither existing purely within the domain of society or nature:

> So long as Nature was remote and under control, it still vaguely resembled the constitutional pole of tradition, and science could still be seen as a mere intermediary to uncover it. Nature seemed to be held in reserve, transcendent, inexhaustible, distant enough. But where are we to classify the ozone hole story, or global warming or deforestation? Where are we to put these hybrids? Are they human? Human because they are our work. Are they natural? Natural because they are not our doing. Are they local or global? Both.[54]

In my view, this objection seems to represent a forceful challenge to the whole conceptual framework of Habermas's communicative paradigm, which meets its limit in what Timothy Morton has called 'hyperobjects' such as a global warming, which are defined precisely in terms of the way that social and natural influences

---

[52] Joel Whitbook, 'The Problem of Nature in Habermas', *Telos: Critical Theory of the Contemporary* (40/41), 1979: 41–69.
[53] Bruno Latour, *We Have Never Been Modern* (Cambridge MA: Harvard University Press, 1991), p. 60.
[54] Latour, *We Have Never Been Modern*, p. 50.

interact and assemble to such disastrous effect.[55] As Adorno insisted, escaping this ecological dialectic of enlightenment requires that we learn to assume a wholly different attitude towards nature than mere instrumental control and technological mastery and reconceive of the relationship between society and nature, reason and its object. This may seem impossible from the point of view of communicative reason, at least as Habermas develops this communicative turn, since his account of the intersubjective relationship is restricted to discursive participants, to human speakers and hearers. In Chapter 8 and in the Conclusion, however, I will argue that it may be possible to reconceive the intersubjective paradigm of reason in a way that takes account not only of the social conditions but also of the *natural conditions* of human autonomy, and which reconceives the methodological holism characteristic of the Frankfurt School tradition of critical theory to include the ecological relationship between society and nature.

6.2 The Last Marxist?

In a Q-and-A-session in the early 1990s, Habermas made the following remark on the developmental trajectory of his theoretical and political outlook:

> I do think that I have been a reformist all my life, and I may have become a bit more so in recent years. Nevertheless, I mostly feel that I am the last Marxist.[56]

This extraordinary claim is profoundly revealing not only of Habermas's political self-understanding, but also of his understanding of his whole intellectual project. In standard political nomenclature, 'Marxist' and 'reformist' are almost understood as antonyms—but not so for Habermas. In the context of this book's reconstruction of the Frankfurt School tradition, the reason is not difficult to grasp: Habermas does not see the core of the Marxian programme in a revolutionary political attitude, but rather in the methodological project of a *critical theory of society*. Since he is one of the few philosophers who still adheres to the comprehensive meaning of the methodological idea of critical theory as understood in the Frankfurt School tradition, Habermas could indeed—in an intellectual landscape influenced by postmodernism and extensive disciplinary fragmentation—with some justifiability claim to be 'the last Marxist'. However, his claim that he has always been a reformist, and has become more so in recent years, points to an interesting schism within the Frankfurt School tradition, in which we can indeed see Habermas's communicative paradigm as an important turning point.

---

[55] Timothy Morton, *Hyperobjects: Philosophy and Ecology after the End of the World* (Minneapolis: University of Minnesota Press, 2013).
[56] Jürgen Habermas, 'Concluding Remarks', p. 471.

An illuminating way to clarify this schism is by taking a look back at how critical theory's practical criterion of validity is understood in the first generation of the Frankfurt School and how it is understood by Habermas. For the young Horkheimer, the practical criterion of validity is clearly still a revolutionary call to arms; the test of a critical theory's validity lies in its ability to guide transformation of society *as a whole*, and this requires the revolutionary overthrow of the capitalist mode of production. In Adorno's negativist paradigm, the implicit revolutionary spirit is—contrary to appearances—perhaps *even stronger*. According to Adorno, we are so entrapped in an administered world and a universal system of delusion that only a total rupture—a dramatic upheaval, such as a man-made or natural catastrophe—might release us from our self-imposed fetters. To be sure, Adorno does not think that revolutionary *practice* is likely to succeed in the administered world—indeed, as we saw in his conflict with the student movement, he thinks that revolutionary action is extremely dangerous in the context of late-capitalist society—but like the young Horkheimer, he nevertheless tacitly retains an understanding of true emancipation as a radical, once-and-for-all transformation of society as a whole. Indeed, it is precisely the uncompromising nature, the quasi-eschatological radicalism of the 'Messianic light' of this presupposed revolutionary ideal, which accounts for Adorno's extremely bleak outlook on the actual society of his day.

In Habermas's communicative paradigm, however, we find a clear structural discontinuity when compared with the paradigms of the young Horkheimer and Adorno: as we have seen, Habermas does not hold up a non-dominated (*herrschaftsfrei*) speech situation and a discourse principle as standards for the revolutionary transformation of society as a whole, but rather as a *processual ideal*. In accordance with this processual construal of practical emancipation, his commitment to the democratic process as a vehicle of emancipation is clearly a *reformist view*—and for some of the Frankfurt School's more radical sympathizers, the question has naturally posed itself whether Habermas concedes too much ground to the unjust social reality of late capitalism?

At this point, it is important to understand Habermas's reasons for giving up (or rather, for never having nurtured) any revolutionary commitments. To be sure, he explicitly maintains that between 'capitalism and democracy there is an *indissoluble* tension; in them two opposed principles of societal integration compete for primacy'.[57] However, he also rejects the notion that 'there can be any type of revolution in societies that have such a degree of complexity'.[58] In his view, the solution to this tension is therefore *not* the wholesale overthrow of capitalism in a social revolution, but rather a *proper balancing* of the competing principles of democracy and capitalism:

---

[57] Habermas, *The Theory of Communicative Action: Vol. II*, p. 345
[58] Habermas, 'Concluding Remarks', p. 469.

> [T]he instruments that politics has available in law and administrative power have a limited effectiveness in functionally differentiated societies. Politics indeed continues to be the addressee for all unmanaged integration problems. But political steering can often take only an indirect approach, and must, as we have seen, leave intact the modes of operation internal to functional subsystems and other highly organized spheres of action. As a result, democratic movements emerging from civil society must give up holistic aspirations to a self-organizing of society, aspirations that also undergirded Marxist ideas of social revolution ... In no way does [civil society] occupy *the position* of a macrosubject supposed to bring society as a whole under control and simultaneously act for it.[59]

In other words, in Habermas's lifelong attempt to reinvigorate the original emancipatory aspirations of critical theory, he forfeits the politically radical idea of a complete revolutionary transformation of capitalism into a reasonable society in Horkheimer and Adorno's sense—of democratic self-determination, *all the way down*. For Habermas, the high degree of functional differentiation that characterizes modernity is here to stay; indeed, the Soviet attempt to completely displace the economic subsystem by the abolition of private property only resulted in a totalization of the bureaucratic subsystem, with well-known deleterious consequences:

> After fifty to sixty years of Soviet Russian development, no one can now fail to see that Max Weber was right, in other words: that the abolition of private ownership of the means of production in no sense does away with class structures as such. Personally, I no longer believe that a differentiated economic system can be transformed from within in accordance with the simple recipes of workers' self-management. The problem seems to be rather one of how capacities for self-organization can be sufficiently developed in autonomous public spheres for the goal-orientated processes of will-formation of a use-value orientated life-world to hold the systemic imperatives of economic system and state apparatus in check, and to bring *both* media-controlled subsystems into dependence on life-world imperatives. I cannot imagine that this would be possible without a gradual abolition of the capitalist labour market, and without a radical-democratic implantation of political parties in their public spheres.[60]

What Habermas seems to be saying here is that the differences between an actually existing democratic-capitalist society and a truly self-determining society of autonomous individuals—which remains the ultimately normative aim of Habermas's communicative paradigm of critical theory—has the limited and

---

[59] Habermas, *Between Facts and Norms*, p. 372.
[60] Jürgen Habermas, 'Politico-Philosophical Profile', *New Left Review* (1/151), May–June 1985: pp. 75–105, p. 103.

reformist character of differences in *degree* rather than the utopian and revolutionary character of differences in *kind*. Against this continuum of a *more or less* reasonable society, one can interpret the development of Habermas's communicative paradigm of critical theory as the theoretical identification of ways to unleash the emancipatory potential in ordinary language communication upon the functionally differentiated subsystems, through democratically legitimated law.

Of course, it remains unclear just how far Habermas thinks that such a 'reigning in' of the subsystems can go—although his casual and perhaps surprising remark that it requires 'a gradual abolition of the capitalist labour market' suggests that he thinks it can go quite far indeed. In general, however, the proper relationship between democratic self-determination and the capitalist economy seems to remain an unclarified issue in Habermas's communicative paradigm, which is of course also derivative of Habermas's convictions that the capitalist economy represents a irrevocably differentiated functional subsystem, which cannot be fully re-embedded in the lifeworld, and that philosophy can only specify conditions for the justification of norms of justice, whereas the determination of the exact nature of a just society is a matter of communicative practice. However, as we shall see in the next chapter of this reconstruction of the Frankfurt School tradition as four paradigms of critical theory, both of these convictions have been forcefully challenged by Axel Honneth's recognition paradigm of critical theory, to which we now turn.

PART IV
HONNETH

As we have seen, the theoretical history of the Frankfurt School tradition is profoundly influenced by the dramatic events that took place on the European continent during the first half of the twentieth century. The young Horkheimer's original paradigm can largely be interpreted as a process of coming to terms with the simultaneous disintegration of proletarian class-consciousness and the rise of German fascism. This attempt to comprehend a society descending into catastrophe culminates in Adorno's negativist paradigm and the contention that fascism is an endogenous political corollary to state capitalism, which is itself the culmination of a world-historical dialectic of enlightenment. To be sure, Habermas's historical experience has primarily been marked by the founding and consolidation of the German Federal Republic. But as someone who was old enough to be conscripted into military service during Hitler's desperate last stand against the Allies—which he avoided only by coincidence—Habermas's work is clearly informed by an acute awareness that neither the legal-democratic achievements of the Federal Republic nor his own attempt to capture the emancipatory potential of these achievements in thought can be so easily disentangled from the human catastrophes out of which they emerged.[1]

In comparison with his three predecessors, the historical experience of Axel Honneth's generation has been considerably less horrifying. Of course, postwar Europe was profoundly marked by the division of Europe along the icy battlefronts of the Cold War and the coercive entrapment of East Germany behind the Iron Curtain. But at the same time, the citizens of the Federal Republic—first in its West German, and later in its reunited form—have demonstrated a robust democratic learning curve and proved remarkably resilient in their commitment to solve even severe social and political conflicts through peaceful democratic means, a feat never accomplished by the chronically troubled Weimar Republic.[2] Just as importantly, postwar Germany rode on the back of a *Wirtschaftswunder* fuelled by the

---

[1] Jürgen Habermas, *Eine Art Schadensabwicklung. Kleine politische Schriften VI* (Frankfurt: Suhrkamp Verlag, 1987).
[2] In particular, the student revolts of the late 1960s, and the controversial American offer to deploy hundreds of intermediate-range nuclear missiles in West Germany—and the social-democratic chancellor Helmut Schmidt's decision in 1979 to accept the deployment—seems to have been a powerful

Marshall Plan and rapid catch-up growth in a physically devastated economy rich on technological knowledge, and a growing middle-class quickly became accustomed to an unprecedented standard of living. As we shall see, the undeniable moral achievements of the democratic welfare state, which flourished across the continent in postwar Western Europe, have left a profound mark on Honneth's recognition paradigm of critical theory, which relies to an even greater extent than Habermas's communicative paradigm on the socially embodied morality of modern democratic-capitalist society.

Much like Habermas, I want to argue that Honneth's recognition paradigm can be interpreted as reacting to three related problems that he locates in the Frankfurt School tradition of critical theory, and, in particular, in Habermas's communicative paradigm.

(1) Despite the Frankfurt School's central concern with the basic structure of society, Honneth argues that Horkheimer and Adorno lose sight of the distinctive object domain of the 'social'. Consequently, they fail to appreciate the extent to which social actors are actively engaged in the normative reproduction of society. In response to this problem, Honneth embraces Habermas's transition to an intersubjective paradigm of reason and his concept of the lifeworld.

(2) However, despite its advantages, Honneth argues that Habermas's communicative paradigm is insufficiently sensitive to the crucial role of power struggles in the intersubjective constitution of society. According to Honneth, the distinction between system and lifeworld implies a dualistic fiction of the former as a norm-free sphere and the latter as a power-free sphere of action coordination, which misses the practical intertwinement of reason and power in moral learning processes. Habermas's two-concept theory of society is therefore unable, on the one hand, to plausibly account for the historical development of the social institutions of modern society, and, on the other, to connect with the experiences of injustice of individual subjects. In response to this problem, Honneth renounces systems theory and develops a 'monistic' social theory, which understands struggles for recognition as power-mediated moral learning processes within the lifeworld.

(3) According to Honneth, the discourse principle cannot be a sufficient explication of the moral point of view, since that principle is substantively dependent on an already operative normative background of ethical life (*Sittlichkeit*), which exhibits a greater normative complexity than

---

formative moment in the consolidation of German democracy. The incident provoked huge controversy, widespread practices of civil disobedience, and the biggest public demonstrations in the history of the Federal Republic.

the discourse principle's procedural standard of impartial justifiability allows. In response to this problem, Honneth renounces Habermas's proceduralism in favour of a more substantive normative dimension. This critique implies a categorially different account of normativity that eschews recourse to a second-order constructivist moral principle, but which envisions the task of moral justification as the reconstruction of first-order socially embodied normativity, which can subsequently be turned against existing society by way of immanent critique. In his mature work, Honneth develops this conception into a reconstructive account of democratic ethical life, which is understood in terms of the necessary contribution that existing institutions of social freedom make to the realization of individual autonomy.

Following (3), Honneth's mature work is explicitly conceived in the methodological terms of a *theory of justice as social analysis*. Accordingly, in the Frankfurt School tradition of critical theory, it is only with Honneth's recognition paradigm that we find a systematic development of a theory of justice within the framework of a critical theory of society.

Following the insights gained in the discussion of Horkheimer's original paradigm in Chapter 1, I interpret this project in accordance with the claim that a critical theory of society can *itself* be understood as a theory of justice, although of a very different kind than that which predominates in the contemporary philosophical literature. In contrast to the predominant focus on distributive justice, Honneth's theory of justice as social analysis is centrally concerned with the concept of *communicative freedom*, which describes intersubjective relationships in which individual subjects mutually empower one another and reciprocally enable each other's individual autonomy. This enables Honneth to develop a theory of justice with a much broader institutional focus than Habermas's circumscribed focus on legal-political institutions allows, submitting all the major institutions of modern society to critical social analysis with reference to their respective contributions to the realization of individual autonomy. Accordingly, Honneth's recognition paradigm also offers a theoretical resolution of the problem encountered towards the end of Chapter 6 in the discussion of Habermas's global application of his communicative paradigm—that is, it offers a conceptualization of the *social* conditions of autonomy in terms of a critical theory of *justice*.

However, when one reads through Honneth's oeuvre in search for reflections on world society, one is quickly struck by the fact that, although Honneth has developed his recognition paradigm during a historical period profoundly marked by the disruptive forces of globalization, one looks in vain for sustained engagements with the global context of application, and only in the most recent work do we find a systematic if methodologically circumscribed engagement with globalization. Accordingly, just as in Chapter 1 and Chapter 2, we must construct the implications for a critical theory of world society of Honneth's recognition paradigm—a task that I undertake in Chapter 8. However, in attempting such a construction, we quickly find that Honneth's hesitation to engage with the global context stems from systematic methodological presuppositions in his recognition paradigm of critical theory. More specifically, I will argue that Honneth's commitment to the method of normative reconstruction and reconstructive critique of already (if imperfectly) realized institutions of social freedom undercuts the possibility of a critical theory of world society, since the global context of application is distinguished precisely by the absence of those social institutions.

From the point of view of a critical theory of world society, I thus want to suggest that Honneth's recognition paradigm offers inherently ambivalent insights. On the one hand, I will argue that Honneth's idea of a theory of justice as social analysis, concerned with communicative relations as social conditions of individual autonomy, can be interpreted as an exemplary clarification of the way in which a critical theory can itself be understood as a theory of justice. On the other hand, I will argue that the restrictive implications for world society chiefly derive from the reconstructive Hegelian methodology that he employs in fleshing out this idea. Accordingly, we might say that although Honneth offers the theoretical means for developing a critical theory of *justice*, his methodological commitments preclude the development of a critical theory of *global* justice.

7
Axel Honneth and the Recognition Paradigm of Critical Theory

7.1 Introduction

Born in Essen in 1949, Honneth studied philosophy and sociology in Bonn and Bochum before writing his doctoral dissertation at the Free University in West Berlin. He subsequently spent several periods as a scientific assistant for Habermas, first under the latter's directorship at the Max-Planck Institute in Starnberg, and later at the Goethe University in Frankfurt, where Honneth received his *Habilitation* in 1990 and was appointed to the Chair of Social Philosophy—formerly held by both Horkheimer and Habermas—six years later. In 2001, Honneth also assumed the directorship at the IfS, which had by then become marginalized in the years following Adorno's death and Habermas's disassociation from the Institute.

After his conflict with Horkheimer in the late 1950s, Habermas was never again formally affiliated with the IfS, which subsequently lost much of its status as the institutional base of the Frankfurt School. However, one of Honneth's achievements has been to revive the IfS as a centre for interdisciplinary social inquiry, firmly grounded in the recognition paradigm of critical theory that Honneth has been developing since the 1980s. Moreover, one of the remarkable aspects of Honneth's intellectual development has been his willingness to augment even fundamental tenets of his critical theory in response to theoretical criticism and empirical insight—most significantly, concerning the foundational concept of recognition. Indeed, Honneth's willingness to undertake such revisions seems to me a testament to his exemplary commitment to Horkheimer's original idea of a dialectical relationship between philosophy and empirical social inquiry.

A note on the structure of the chapter: The four dimensions of critical theory are more tightly interwoven in Honneth's recognition paradigm than they are in Habermas's communicative paradigm, or even in the paradigms of Horkheimer and Adorno. Furthermore, it seems to me fruitful to make a distinction between Honneth's earlier and more mature work. Both his earlier and more mature work is informed by historical, sociological, and normative considerations, developed at different levels of abstraction: while Honneth's earlier work is concerned with developing a more abstract account of the 'moral grammar of social conflicts' in terms of three patterns of mutual recognition and their associated subjective relations-to-self, his later work is concerned with laying bare the existing social institutions in which these patterns are (or can be) realized in modern Western society. Accordingly, the present chapter does not follow the structure of the three previous chapters.

Given the extent to which the three methodological dimensions are fused in Honneth's Hegelian approach, the chapter instead presents these dimensions in a less differentiated and more holistic way, first within Honneth's earlier work, and, secondly, in his more mature work. The chapter is thus structured as follows. In Section 7.2, I account for the guiding themes of Honneth's earliest work: namely, the concept of power, and the attempt to recover the object domain of the 'social' for a critical theory of society. In Section 7.3, I account for Honneth's early theory of the struggle for recognition as the moral grammar of social conflicts. In Section 7.4, I offer an account of his more mature work: his reconstruction and critique of the 'reality of freedom' in the democratic ethical life of modern Western society.

7.2 Early Themes: Power, and the Recovery of the Social

In the early 1980s, whilst Habermas was engaged in a polemical dispute with Michel Foucault and the French poststructuralists over the possibility of distinguishing reason from power—two concepts that Habermas is anxious to keep unequivocally distinct—the young Axel Honneth drew a very different lesson from his careful study of Foucault's work: critical theory must be brought *closer to power*. At first sight, this claim might seem paradoxical. As we have seen in the last six chapters, the concept of domination (*Herrschaft* or *Beherrschung*) is absolutely central to the idea of a critical theory of society. Indeed, notwithstanding the considerable theoretical heterogeneity that this book's reconstruction of the Frankfurt School tradition has uncovered, it is nonetheless clear that one of its principal and continuous concerns is the aspiration to expose, criticize, and practically overcome illegitimate forms of power, understood as relations and structures of domination. However, in Honneth's earliest work, he suggests that the nature of this concern with domination remains fundamentally ambiguous, leading to serious problems and limitations in all three preceding paradigms of critical theory.

7.2.1 The Critique of Power

In his doctoral dissertation, published as 'The Critique of Power' (*Kritik der Macht*) in 1988, Honneth identifies the primary cause of the Frankfurt School's difficulty with the concepts of power and domination in the first generation's systematic underappreciation of what Honneth calls the object domain of 'the social'. With this charge, Honneth has a quite specific conception of sociality in mind: namely, 'the cognitive and moral synthetic accomplishments of which social groups are capable through the cooperative interpretive efforts of their members'.[3] According to Honneth, this distinctively social domain of intersubjective normativity disappears in the functionalist account of the relationship between political economy and psychology in Horkheimer's original paradigm of critical theory, and it is 'definitively repressed' in Adorno's negativist paradigm, which depicts 'the oppressed individual as a passive victim of the techniques of domination'.[4]

It is only with Habermas's communicative paradigm that critical theory begins to take seriously the degree to which individuals actively participate in the normative reproduction of their social world. With the conceptual complex of communicative action, lifeworld, and social integration, as well as the internal methodological perspective of the participant in social interaction, Habermas carves out a social sphere of communicative reproduction for social-scientific inquiry that the two preceding paradigms of critical theory marginalize and ignore:

> In this way [Habermas] is, from the beginning, on the watch for a reductionism that interprets society as a norm-free relation of instrumental or strategic action. Everyday linguistic understanding about action-guiding norms is recognized as the supporting dimension of societies. For the first time in the history of Marxism, communicative understanding [*Verständigung*] is treated systematically as the paradigm of the social.[5]

While Habermas thus remedies the 'sociological deficit' of the Frankfurt School's first generation, and thereby brings into view the object domain of the social, his social theory nevertheless—according to Honneth—suffers from a peculiarly one-sided construal of this domain. In *Kritik der Macht*, Honneth suggests that this one-sidedness ultimately derives from Habermas's attempt to conceptualize reification in terms of the distinction between system and lifeworld.

Recall that Habermas introduces this distinction in order to conceptualize both the functional integration of society as a social system and the social integration of society as a lifeworld, and to explain social pathologies in terms of the effects of the former upon the latter. The concept of the lifeworld thus enables Habermas to theoretically comprehend those social domains—culture, society, personality—which can only be reproduced through systemic integration on pains of social pathology. Moreover, in *Theorie des kommunikativen Handelns*, Habermas construes power solely as the steering medium of the bureaucratic subsystem,

---

[3] Axel Honneth, The Critique of Power: *Reflective Stages in a Critical Social Theory*, transl. by Kenneth Baynes (Cambridge, MA: The MIT Press, 1991), p. 100.
[4] Honneth, *The Critique of Power*, p. 95.
[5] Honneth, *The Critique of Power*, p. 243.

and he locates a central form of colonization in the 'juridification' of lifeworld structures—that is, in the integration of lifeworld contexts through strategic action and the bureaucratic steering medium of power. In doing so, however, Habermas not only construes communicative action but also the lifeworld writ large as *conceptually purified* of the steering medium of power. In Honneth's view, this has the counterintuitive consequence that 'the social lifeworld already assumes at the conceptual level the character of a *power-free* sphere of communication'.[6]

The reverse problem of this one-sided construal of the social, as a lifeworld integrated through power-free communicative action, is that Habermas understands the functional subsystems of the market and the bureaucracy as operating independently of participants' active normative engagement, since they are construed as coordinating action purely with a view to action consequences in abstraction from participants' intentions. The market and the bureaucracy are thereby understood as *norm-free* spheres of media-steered systemic integration, within which actors can only navigate with recourse to strategic action. Honneth maintains that these complementary 'fictions' of a power-free sphere of normative reproduction and a norm-free sphere of material reproduction represent a counterintuitive dualism, which ultimate undermines the empirical plausibility and critical purchase of Habermas's social theory:

> Whereas purposive-rational domains of action seem to be separated out from all processes of the integration of the lifeworld, the social lifeworld is represented as freed from all forms of the exercise of power. 'Power', as a means for the coordination of social action, is considered only at the level of systems integration, so all presystemic processes of the [normative] constitution and reproduction of domination must fall out of view. On the other hand, the socially integrative achievements of the lifeworld are observed only in those spheres of social action that aid the symbolic reproduction of a society, so all processes of moral consensus formation internal to an organization [such as the market or the bureaucracy] must fall out of view. The first fiction contradicts ... the importance of pre-state, situationally bound forms of the exercise of everyday domination in the reproduction of a society. The second fiction contradicts ... the importance of processes of social integration internal to an organization for the functioning of social organizations.[7]

To be sure, *Kritik der Macht* was published before Habermas's wrote *Faktizität und Geltung*, in which—as we have seen—he complements his systemic account of power as a steering medium with a lifeworld account of social and communicative power. But in Honneth's view, the underlying problem is that Habermas's

---

[6] Honneth, *The Critique of Power*, p. 300 [emphasis added].
[7] Honneth, *The Critique of Power*, p. 301.

account of the lifeworld, as integrated only through action orienteered towards mutual understanding, is bound to construe power as conceptually independent of individual normative agency, and *vice versa*. As a result, Habermas is unable to theoretically comprehend how both individuals and social groups can be *normatively engaged* in relationships of power and domination. Moreover, Honneth plausibly maintains that advances in moral-practical knowledge do not merely issue from a rationalization of the lifeworld in power-free discourse and communicative action, but rather from conflicts and power struggles between social groups and their reflection on experienced injustice. Accordingly, Habermas's theory of social evolution, no less than his social theory, seems to be predicated on a miscomprehension of the relationship between power and reason. By contrast, Honneth maintains, 'the dynamic that arises in the historical development of social order can be fully explained only by extending the sphere of communicative action to include the negative dimension of struggle'.[8]

This problem also points to a serious gap between the philosophical grounding of Habermas's communicative paradigm and the motivation of actual social agents for embarking on emancipatory struggles against injustice. Recall that formal pragmatics provides a rational reconstruction of the knowing-how that speakers must possess and the idealizing presuppositions they must undertake in order to successfully redeem validity claims and reach a mutual understanding. From a diachronic perspective, Habermas argues that the historical development of these linguistic and epistemic structures has taken the form of progressive rationalization of the lifeworld: a process in which the lifeworld is linguistically and symbolically differentiated and the inherent rational potential of language is unleashed. However, since this world-historical rationalization of linguistic structures largely takes place 'behind the backs' of individuals, they do not *experience* this process as constitutive of their moral consciousness, which is rather—as the young Horkheimer also emphasized—born out of the experience of being subject to unjust forms of power and domination. In Honneth's words:

> The emancipatory process in which Habermas socially anchors the normative perspective of his critical theory in no way appears as an emancipatory process in the moral experiences of the subjects involved. *They experience an impairment of what we can call their moral experiences, i.e., their 'moral point of view,' not as a restriction of intuitively mastered rules of language, but as a violation of identity claims acquired in socialization.* The communicative rationalization of the life-world may unfold historically, but it does not appear as a moral state of affairs in the experiences of human subjects. For this reason, a correlate cannot be found within social reality for the pre-theoretical resource referred to in Habermas's normative perspective; his conception is not aimed in the same way

---

[8] Honneth, *The Critique of Power*, p. xxviii.

as Horkheimer's (which was of course also under the influence of a destructive illusion) at giving expression to an existing experience of social injustice.[9]

According to Honneth, this foundational problem is of particular moment in modern class societies, in which marginalized groups forced to shoulder injustice might not—for a number of reasons, having to do with their structural disempowerment—be in possession of the discursive and rhetorical means to publicly express their legitimate grievances in the form of coherent and principled rational arguments, of which others will be able to recognize the 'peculiar unforced force'.

For Habermas, who, following Lawrence Kohlberg, relies on the idea of a 'postconventional moral consciousness' oriented towards universal moral principles as the highest and paradigmatically modern stage of moral development,[10] and whose discourse theory of democratic legitimacy is predicated on citizens' ability to publicly voice their experiences of injustice and contribute to the formation of a democratic will, such a structurally conditioned inability to express one's concerns in a publicly acceptable language represents a potentially very serious problem.[11] In *Faktizität und Geltung*, Habermas often seems to presuppose that citizens will in fact be able to make coherent and intelligible public claims based on their social experience, and this assumption risks blinding his communicative paradigm to precisely those substrata of injustice that are so pervasive and insidious so as to never attain public articulation. In the context of an unjust class society, all that dominated groups have to go on might be their unarticulated 'consciousness of injustice', and, for Honneth, it is imperative that a critical theory be able to gain hermeneutic access to such moral experiences, formed at a subterranean level below 'official' discourses of public contestation.[12]

Against the background of these objections to Habermas's communicative paradigm, Honneth locates the potential for a solution in two sources: in the work of Michel Foucault, and in an early but largely unexplored thesis of Habermas's. Firstly, in *Kritik der Macht*, Honneth develops an original—but, it seems to me, ultimately unsuccessful—interpretation of the 'theory of society' implicit in Foucault's later work as a continuation in spirit of the Frankfurt School tradition of critical theory. Honneth's interest is sparked by Foucault's innovative conception of power, according to which 'power should be thought of not as a fixable property, as the enduring characteristic of an individual subject of a social group, but rather

---

[9] Axel Honneth, 'The Social Dynamics of Disrespect: On the Location of Critical Theory Today' in *Disrespect. The Normative Foundations of Critical Theory* (Cambridge: Polity Press, 2007), p. 70 [emphasis added].
[10] Habermas, *Moral Consciousness and Communicative Action*, pp. 116–195.
[11] For similar concerns, see also Pierre Bourdieu, *Language and Symbolic Power*, ed. by John B. Thompson (Cambridge MA: Harvard University Press, 1991).
[12] For this important argument, see the early essay 'Moral Consciousness and Class Domination: Some Problems in the Analysis of Hidden Morality', published in Axel Honneth, *Disrespect*.

as the in principle fragile and open-ended product of strategic conflicts between subjects'.[13] This suggests that power is acquired and maintained 'not in the form of a one-sided appropriation and exercise of rights of decree or instruments of compulsion but rather in the shape of a continuous struggle of social actors among themselves'.[14]

I have already discussed some of the similarities and differences between Adorno and Foucault in Chapter 4. However, as I argued in that context, the attempt to 'adopt' Foucault into the Frankfurt School tradition seems to falter on the French philosopher's avowed methodological nominalism and staunch repudiation of any attempt to comprehend reason in a universal and emancipatory sense, rather than in terms of discrete rationalities as techniques of power. But Honneth smells a different rat; he locates two inconsistent programmes in Foucault's work, both of which ultimately render his theory of struggle as the 'paradigm of the social' unfit for a critical theory of society. One the one hand, Foucault's underdeveloped theoretical reflections on social struggle are foreshortened to *strategic conflicts*, which exclude an immanent moral dimension and the kind of engagement of normative agency that Honneth takes to be constitutive of the social. On the other hand, in his historical genealogies, Foucault tacitly abandons his conception of power struggles in favour of a 'systems-theoretical' conception of power that 'portrays subjects behavioristically, as formless, conditionable creatures'[15] in a way reminiscent of Adorno's 'definitive repression' of the social.

Honneth identifies a more promising conception of power struggles that includes a constitutive moral dimension in Habermas's early article 'Labor and Interaction: Remarks on Hegel's Jena *Philosophy of Mind*', published in the collection 'Theory and Practice' (*Theorie und Praxis*) from 1963. Indeed, Honneth's engagement with Habermas's interpretation of Hegel's early Jena writings seems to have had a profoundly formative impact on his recognition paradigm as a whole. According to Habermas's interpretation, these early writings contain the seeds of an account of the formation of *Geist*—a micro-level account later abandoned by Hegel in favour of a more holistic view—as the result of 'struggles for recognition' between individual subjects: a dialectic of intersubjective conflict through which individual consciousness and moral relationships are formed.[16] Honneth's interest in the concept of recognition is thus stirred by its conceptual fusion of power and moral normativity. Indeed, in Honneth's early work, following *Kritik der Macht*, he sets himself the task of unfolding the full theoretical potential of the struggle for recognition that Hegel and later Habermas took up and subsequently abandoned.

---

[13] Honneth, *The Critique of Power*, pp. 154–155.
[14] Honneth, *The Critique of Power*, p. 155.
[15] Honneth, *The Critique of Power*, p. 199.
[16] Jürgen Habermas, 'Labor and Interaction: Remarks on Hegel's Jena *Philosophy of Mind*', in *Theory and Practice*, transl. by John Viertel (Cambridge: Polity Press, 1988).

This idea enables Honneth to reject the norm-free fiction of systems theory and to develop a monistic social theory that conceives of power as struggles for recognition *within the lifeworld*, where moral consciousness and individual identity are forged in the heat of social conflict.

7.2.2 Three Conceptions of Power

Before proceeding to an account of this theory, it seems to me that we can clarify the basic concerns behind Honneth's early programme by explicating a tripartite distinction between three different kinds of power that we have until now only implicitly observed. In the Frankfurt School tradition as a whole, I want to argue, we find *three conceptually distinct conceptions of power*, and—following Honneth—the four paradigms of critical theory can be distinguished according to the degree and kind of emphasis (or lack of emphasis) that they place on these conceptions.

First, we find what we can call an *agential* conception of power. The agential conception of power is the predominant conception of power in the tradition of Western political thought coming down from Hobbes and Weber,[17] and it refers to a capacity of agents, whether individual or corporate. I call this conception of power agential because of its intimate connection with *agency*: the capacity for intentional action specific to individual and corporate agents. Secondly, we also find what we can call a *structural* conception of power. Compared with agential power, the structural conception of power operates on a completely different conceptual register: structural power is not a capacity that presupposes intentional agency—although it does presuppose what we might call 'mediated' agency—but it refers to the empowering and disempowering effects upon the individual of the *structure of social relations* in which social agents find themselves. The structural conception of power suggests that agents are subject to power even in the absence of direct and unmediated agential power; when their social circumstances empower and disempower them in certain systemic ways.

Thirdly, we find a conception of power that is only thematized as such within the Frankfurt School tradition in Honneth's earliest work: namely, what we can call a *relational* conception of power.[18] The relational conception does not conceive of power as a capacity of agents or as structural effects—or, indeed, in terms of the conceptual opposition of power and freedom—but rather as a phenomenon that arises in relations of conflict and cooperation *between* agents, and which constitutes (or empowers) them *as* social agents in the first place. It is the relational conception of power that animates Honneth's aspiration to recover the object

---

[17] Martin Saar, 'Power and Critique', *Journal of Power* (3/1), 2010: 7–20.
[18] Danielle Petherbridge, *The Critical Theory of Axel Honneth* (Plymouth: Lexington Books, 2013).

domain of the social in Frankfurt School critical theory, and which he locates in both Foucault's work and Habermas's early interpretation of Hegel.

In distinguishing these three conceptions of power, I merely intend to sketch the contours of three broad conceptual classes of power, each of which can be spelled out in substantially different ways. In general, however, a claim about agential power will be a claim about the *capacity* of an agent to do and make other agents do certain things; a claim about structural power will be a claim about the *systematic effects* that social structures can have upon agents and their self-relation and practical situation; whereas a claim about relational power will be a more basic claim about the determinate field of possible *social relations* and *forms of subjective self-relations* that arise in social interaction.[19] In different but familiar terminology, we might say that the agential conception is a *subjective* conception of power, the structural conception is an *objective* conception of power, and the relational conception is an *intersubjective* conception of power. With this in mind, we can identify the problems with which Honneth is concerned in the preceding three paradigms of critical theory in terms of the tradition's attempt to grapple with this tripartite distinction between agential, structural, and relational power.

In Horkheimer's original paradigm of critical theory, power is understood in orthodox Marxian terms as *bourgeois* class domination of the proletariat. This clearly suggests an agential conception power, as a capacity of classes conceived as collective agents. However, Horkheimer is also concerned with conceptualizing both the kind of structural power suggested by Lukács's account of reification, and the kind that agents are subjected to by the economically irrational structure of capitalist society. The early interdisciplinary-materialist programme of social inquiry is therefore primarily concerned with accounting for the absence of revolutionary consciousness among the proletariat, which can be understood as an account of a form of structural power that *undermines* the conditions for the agential power of the proletariat, both as individual agents and as a class. However, what Horkheimer thereby really wants to explain can be interpreted in terms of the relational conception of power that, to be sure, remains wholly undeveloped in his work: namely, the tendency within monopoly capitalism towards a *suspension of class struggle*.

Indeed, Honneth reconstructs a conception of class struggle that he sees as implicit in parts of Horkheimer's early work (but which he later abandoned), which conceptualizes the social domain in terms of relational power:

> In their everyday action, members of a social group have harmonized their class-conditioned interests and their specific needs within relatively stable value orientations and interpretive patterns that enable them, without losing their

---

[19] Martin Saar, *Die Immanenz der Macht: Politische Theorie nach Spinoza* (Berlin: Suhrkamp Verlag, 2013).

psychic identity, to participate actively in the institutionalized structures of a social order ... The disruption of culturally secured everyday action forces the group member to correct and expand the traditional horizon of orientation in the face of unmasked reality. [The critical attitude] is thus also the reflexive continuation of an everyday communication shaken in its self-understanding. On this basis, social struggle can be conceived as the cooperative organization of this everyday critique: It would be the attempt by social groups, forced by the conditions of the class-specific division of labor and excessive burdens, to realize within the normative structures of social life the norms of action acquired in the repeated experience of suffered injustice.[20]

However, notwithstanding these gestures at a conceptualization of the social in terms of a relational conception of power, Horkheimer's attempt to explain the suspension of the class struggle ultimately reduces the social domain in an economic-psychological account of relatively unmediated structural effects on the individual psyche—and, in doing so, he also forgoes the possibility of comprehending this suspension with reference to a moral logic inherent in power struggles as such.

This explanatory deficiency points to a larger inconsistency in Horkheimer's original paradigm, between his reductive social theory and the fact that his paradigm is nonetheless—in a sense—*grounded* in the relational conception of the class struggle that Honneth reconstructs. Indeed, Horkheimer's original idea of a critical theory *presupposes* and is explicitly conceived as an epistemic input to the proletariat's struggle for self-emancipation, in that a critical theory illuminates the relations and structures of domination to which the downtrodden workers are subject, such that proletarians can recognize their shackles and cast them aside. Within his Marxian-Freudian framework, the young Horkheimer aspires to a kind of second-order enlightenment that seeks to inform proletarians of the structural forces that undermine the requisite class-consciousness for the proletariat to overcome monopoly capitalism and realize a reasonable society (as opposed to a first-order kind of enlightenment that seeks to inform proletarians of their interest in overthrowing capitalist relations of production).

However, Horkheimer is able to claim that materialism 'understands itself as the theoretical side of the struggle to rid the world of existing misery'[21] only because he tacitly presupposes an account of the social in terms of the relational power of the class struggle, in which proletarians both *learn from* their suffering and struggles and *reflectively apply* the resulting insights in emancipatory practice, with critical theory serving as a vehicle of social and moral learning. Following Marx and Lukács, the young Horkheimer's original paradigm can thus be interpreted as

[20] Honneth, *The Critique of Power*, pp. 28–29.
[21] Horkheimer, 'Materialismus und Moral', p. 131.

concerned with the triadic conceptual structure of the proletariat seeking the *agential power* to emancipate itself from the *structural power* of capitalist production relations (and the agential power of *bourgeois* class domination that they enable) by reflecting on its *relational power* struggle with the *bourgeoisie*. Given the centrality of this triadic conceptual structure to Horkheimer's original paradigm, it is easy to appreciate the disruptive effects of the empirically observed structural disempowerment and fragmentation of the proletariat, which leads Horkheimer to, first, reorient his critical theory towards the more elusive addressee of anyone exhibiting a critical attitude, and, ultimately, to seek refuge in the negativism of *Dialektik der Aufklärung*.

In Adorno's negativist paradigm, the class struggle and the domain of the social recedes fully into the background and the structural power of reification comes to the fore; Adorno thus consistently construes power in abstract and anonymous structural terms, at the cost of any discernible agential or relational conception of power. Structural domination is conceptualized as the systemic administration of individual subjects, and their ideological manipulation through a system of delusion, which penetrates so deeply into late-capitalist subjectivity that it effectively undermines the individual capacity for critical thinking, spontaneity, and even freedom of the will. In doing so, it completely undercuts the social and psychological conditions for the agential power of practical emancipation. Accordingly, Adorno simply abstains from specifying an agent of emancipation and construes his practical dimension in terms of an individualistic ethics of resistance towards all-pervasive forces of social heteronomy.

Of course, this abandonment of hope for practical emancipation is precisely what makes Adorno's negativist paradigm so unpalatable *as* a paradigm of critical theory: since he disavows any notion of relational power and reduces agential power to a defensive individual posture of resistance, because he believes that agents in the administered world are so overwhelmingly in thrall to objectifying structural power, he is also effectively compelled to disavow the specification of an agent of emancipation and a practical route by which emancipation may be reached. The disconcerting practical implications of this effective reduction of the triadic conceptual structure of power to structural power is amply illustrated by his conflict with the student movement of the late 1960s, and it was precisely this practical impasse that motivated the young Habermas to seek to resurrect the emancipatory aspirations of Horkheimer's original paradigm of critical theory.

In Habermas's communicative paradigm of critical theory, his two-concept theory of society enables him to conceptualize the economy and the bureaucracy as *systems* of agential power and recast the *structural* power of reification in terms of system imperatives' colonization of the lifeworld and the displacement of action oriented towards mutual understanding by strategic action. In *Faktizität und Geltung*, Habermas further introduces the concepts of social power and communicative power, developed within the participant perspective of the lifeworld, which may be interpreted, respectively, in terms of an agential and a relational conception of power.[22] Habermas's two-perspective methodology thus enables him to develop a complex view of power, with a systemic or structural conception of power developed from the external perspective of the observer of society as a system of social systems, and an agential and a relational conception of power developed from the internal perspective of the participant in society as a lifeworld. The bridge between these three conceptions of power is democratic law, in which functional subsystems are steered and anchored in the lifeworld through a legal code informed by processes of collective will-formation within the political public sphere.

However, Habermas's introduction of an agential and a relational conception of power in *Faktizität und Geltung* does not repudiate Honneth's objection that these conceptions play little if any systematic role in his theory of social evolution and two-concept theory of society, in which the object domain of the social is not interpreted in terms of relational power, but rather in terms of power-free discourse and communicative action. In other words, the agential and relational conceptions of power play only a limited role in the historical and sociological dimension of Habermas's communicative paradigm. This *power-deficit* might seem to be an implication of the way that Habermas cashes out his turn to an intersubjective paradigm of reason—which irrevocably undercuts the possibility of construing social class as unitary subjects—as well as his acknowledgement of the irrevocable fragmentation of the proletariat, since these revisions combine to undermine the assumptions that undergird the class struggle.

The starting point for Honneth's recognition paradigm of critical theory is a refusal to accept that this power-deficit is a price that a critical theory, which is firmly rooted in the intersubjective paradigm of reason and which acknowledges the fragmentation of the proletariat, must pay. In his earliest work, the continuous theme that stands out is precisely the attempt to carve out a relational conception of power which rises to the systematic emancipatory importance that power struggles held for the young Horkheimer, but without falling back into Marxian orthodoxy: to discover 'in the structural conflicts of a social system the signs of a historical movement in which the moral learning processes of the species consistently achieves expression.'[23] In other words, we can understand Honneth's

---

[22] With reference to Hannah Arendt, Habermas remarks of communicative power that 'legislation depends on the generation of another type of power, namely, on the *communicative power* that, as Hannah Arendt says, no one is really able to 'possess': 'Power springs up between men when they act together, and it vanishes the moment they disperse'. According to this model, both law and communicative power have their cooriginal source in the 'opinion upon which many publicly were in agreement'.' Habermas, *Between Facts and Norms*, p. 147.

[23] Honneth, 'Moral Consciousness and Class Domination: Some Problems in the Analysis of Hidden Morality', p. 81.

recognition paradigm as an attempt to develop a conception of the triadic conceptual structure of agential, structural, and relational power that is immune to the problems faced by the preceding three paradigms of critical theory. As suggested, the centrepiece of this account is an account of the social domain in terms of a relational conception of power as the struggle for recognition, where the normative structures and forms of subjectivity in the lifeworld are seen as deriving from—and thus constituted by—intersubjective relations of conflict and cooperation. It is to an exposition of this account that we now turn.

7.3 The Struggle for Recognition

7.3.1 The Original Programme

In 1992, Honneth published his *Habilitationsschrift*, written under the supervision of Habermas in Frankfurt, as 'The Struggle for Recognition: The Moral Grammar of Social Conflicts' (*Kampf um Anerkennung*). In this widely influential book, Honneth follows the unexplored implications of Habermas's thesis that Hegel's Jena writings contain a number of philosophical and conceptual breakthroughs that did not come to full fruition in the idealist system of his mature works. Even in the early stages of his philosophical career, Hegel found himself deeply unsatisfied with the atomistic individualism that had dominated political theory since the days of Machiavelli and Hobbes. Inspired by Aristotle's communitarian conception of the human being as a *zoon politikon*, Hegel instead conceived of society as resting on an intersubjective basis—in terms of relations *between* mutually dependent individuals, rather than an aggregate of solitary individuals in a struggle for self-preservation.

According to Hegel, it is possible to understand human society only if we abandon the atomistic conception of struggle as a purely strategic conflict between self-interested individuals and instead construe struggle as the driving force in the formation and moral development of social orders. In Honneth's view, Hegel was thus the first in the history of social philosophy to propose a truly *holistic* and yet undeniably modern conception of society—according to which society is something categorially different from an aggregate sum of self-interested individuals—but in which the idea of the individual struggle for self-preservation still finds its place. The organizing idea of this conception is that

> a struggle among subjects for the mutual recognition of their identity [generates] inner-societal pressure toward the practical, political establishment of institutions that would guarantee freedom. It is individuals' claim to the intersubjective recognition of their identity that is built into social life from the very beginning as a moral tension, transcends the level of social progress institutionalized thus far,

and so gradually leads—via the negative path of recurring stages of conflict—to a state of communicatively lived freedom.[24]

In the view of the young Hegel, the idea of mutual recognition is key to accounting not only for the historical *development* but also the relative *stability* of a given social order, by shifting theoretical attention 'to the intersubjective social relations that always already guarantee a minimal normative consensus in advance'.[25] Furthermore, from early on, Hegel believed that a stable and justified social and political order is one that properly and appropriately represents and regulates intersubjective recognition in the three distinct normative spheres of the family, civil society (the economic market), and the state. As we shall see in Section 7.4, Hegel's mature political philosophy construes the three normative spheres of the family, civil society, and the state as constitutive of the whole of a society's 'ethical life' (*Sittlichkeit*) and as the full realization of objective *Geist* in the institutional framework of society.

Now, Honneth accepts the tripartite structure of Hegel's view, but he rejects its speculative underpinnings and seeks instead to place the insights of Hegel's Jena writings on a 'materialist' foundation. Accordingly, *Kampf um Anerkennung* primarily represents an attempt to replace the idealist metaphysics undergirding this structure with a post-metaphysical and empirically falsifiable basis developed from recent social theory and developmental psychology. Honneth's first revision of Hegel's argument is to broaden the concepts of his tripartite structure. Seeking to avoid not only Hegel's embrace of the patriarchal *bourgeois* family, but also his metaphysical hypostatization of the capitalist market and proto-authoritarian conception of the state as a constitutional monarchy, Honneth instead generalizes Hegel's categories according to their embodied normative content.

This engenders a tripartite distinction between primary relationships (love, care, friendship), legal relations (rights), and communities of value (solidarity). Honneth maintains that each of these 'patterns of recognition' represents a necessary condition for developing what he calls 'a positive practical relation-to-self': they represent 'those forms of practical affirmation by which [the subject] gains a normative understanding of itself as a certain kind of person',[26] and 'ways of relating positively to oneself'[27] that are experienced by the subject as forms of self-realization.[28] This 'connection between the experience of recognition and one's

---

[24] Axel Honneth, *The Struggle for Recognition: The Moral Grammar of Social Conflicts*, transl. by Joel Anderson (Cambridge: Polity Press, 1995), p. 5.
[25] Honneth, *The Struggle for Recognition*, p. 42.
[26] Honneth, *The Struggle for Recognition*, p. 76.
[27] Honneth, *The Struggle for Recognition*, p. 143.
[28] Honneth's definition of 'practical self-relation' is close to Christine Korsgaard's definition of what she calls 'practical identity': 'The conception of one's identity in question here is not a theoretical one, a view about what as a matter of inescapable scientific fact you are. It is better understood as a description under which you value yourself, a description under which you find your life to be worth living and

relation-to-self stems from the intersubjective structure of personal identity',[29] and each pattern represents a distinct and necessary (but by itself insufficient) condition for developing a positive practical self-relation. More specifically, the three practical relations-to-self that one achieves in the three patterns of recognition are: the *basic self-confidence* derived from the experience of love, the *self-respect* derived from the experience of legal recognition as a rights-bearing subject, and the *self-esteem* derived from the experience of societal solidarity.

Honneth's post-metaphysical justification of these three practical relations-to-self, which aims to establish both that the three patterns of recognition represent the fundamental normative infrastructure of the modern social world and necessary conditions for individual self-realization, relies on a number of sources. From George Herbert Mead's social psychology, Honneth appropriates the idea of a naturalistic justification of Hegel's tripartite distinction between different patterns of recognition, as well as the generic normative content of this structure. From the object relations psychology of Donald W. Winnicott and Jessica Benjamin, Honneth appropriates the thesis that the development of infant subjectivity follows the model of a struggle for recognition between mother (understood as 'care-giver') and child.[30]

From the work of T.H. Marshall, Honneth derives the historical thesis that the development of the different classes of basic rights—civil rights, political rights, and social rights—have arisen through struggles for legal recognition, in which the pre-modern idea of honour has increasingly given way to the idea of equal citizenship, which has in turn been continuously expanded both in terms of its scope and normative content. Indeed, as a result of the latter process, in 'being legally recognized, one is now respected with regard not only to the abstract capacity to orient oneself vis-à-vis moral norms, but also to the concrete human feature that one deserves the social standard of living necessary for this'.[31] Finally, from Rudolp von Ihering and Stephen Darwall, Honneth appropriates the distinction between *respect* and *esteem*, where the former is predicated on recognizing a concrete other simply as a person (an absolute parameter)—as a moral agent able to act autonomously on reasonable insight and with the moral responsibility and universal constraints on action that this entails—while the latter is predicated on recognizing the other as a person with *particular* qualities that one values according to shared commitments and values (a relative parameter).

---

your actions to be worth undertaking'. Christine Korsgaard, *The Sources of Normativity* (Cambridge: Cambridge University Press, 1996), p. 101.

[29] Honneth, *The Struggle for Recognition*, p. 173.

[30] This struggle is understood as a dialectical process of initial 'absolute dependency' or undifferentiated intersubjectivity, subsequent 'relative dependency' in which the child gradually learns to differentiate between the mother and itself, and ultimately differentiated intersubjectivity, where both mother and child learn how to 'be oneself in another' and thus experience love between themselves as independent but mutually caring subjects. Honneth, *The Struggle for Recognition*, pp. 95–107.

[31] Honneth, *The Struggle for Recognition*, p. 117.

Building on this theoretical foundation, Honneth argues, first, that the struggle for recognition between mother and child is a necessary condition for developing a basic degree of self-confidence, enabling one to form primary relationships of love and friendship and to become properly responsive to inner needs and impulses. Second, he argues that the experience of legal recognition is a necessary condition for developing the self-respect that enables one to regard oneself—and others—as moral subjects capable of autonomous action:

> Just as, in the case of love, children acquire, via the continuous experience of 'maternal' care, the basic self-confidence to assert their needs in an unforced manner, adult subjects acquire, via the experience of legal recognition, the possibility of seeing their actions as the universally respected expressions of their own autonomy ... Whereas [the former] generates, in every human being, the psychological foundation for trusting one's own sense of one's needs and urges, [the latter] gives rise to the form of consciousness in which one is able to respect oneself because one deserves the respect of everyone else.[32]

Indeed, in legal recognition one experiences both the institutional recognition of membership in a concrete political community *and* the moral recognition of one's individual autonomy, enabling one to participate—both in the legal-institutional and in the moral sense—in processes of discursive will-formation.[33] Thirdly and finally, although the first two forms of recognition are both necessary for developing a positive practical relation-to-self, they are—according to Honneth—insufficient without the third form of recognition, namely the form experienced when one is esteemed by the other members of one's community of value as a biographically differentiated individual with particular qualities. This third form of recognition, which should be understood not in terms of a 'positive learning process ("expansion")', but as a 'negative process of overcoming the constraints of narrow horizons of interpretation',[34] is thus a necessary condition for developing basic self-esteem 'accompanied by a felt confidence that one's achievements or abilities will be recognized as "valuable" by other members of society'. Since 'solidarity' is defined as 'an interactive relationship in which subjects mutually sympathize with their various different ways of life because, among themselves, they esteem each other symmetrically', Honneth argues that to 'the extent to which every member of a society is in a position to esteem himself or herself, one can speak of a state of societal solidarity'.[35]

Now, while the form of recognition found in love serves a crucial but more limited purpose in the sense of enabling one to participate in the latter two forms

---

[32] Honneth, *The Struggle for Recognition*, pp. 118–119.
[33] Honneth, *The Struggle for Recognition*, p. 120.
[34] Axel Honneth and Nancy Fraser, *Redistribution or Recognition: A Political-Philosophical Exchange* (New York: Verso Books, 2003), p. 264.
[35] Honneth, *The Struggle for Recognition*, p. 128–129.

of recognition, the forms of recognition inherent in rights and solidarity enable Honneth to understand the 'moral grammar of social conflicts' as *struggles for recognition*, either to be recognized as a moral subject with equal rights (as exemplified by the suffragette-movement, or the civil rights movement and the contemporary Black Lives Matter movement in the United States), or to be recognized as a valuable person or social group relative to society's evaluative framework (as exemplified, in part, by contemporary struggles for social inclusion in multicultural societies). In other words, Honneth's post-metaphysical account of the struggle for recognition enables him to understand the historical development and relative stability of social orders as driven by the intersubjective interplay between power and normative agency—by struggles over which groups get to define the limits and content of legal rights and moral autonomy, or who has interpretive primacy over shared values, and as sustained by subsequent general acceptance of the outcomes. In Honneth's hands, the moral achievements inherent in the development of modern law and societal solidarity is thus seen as the outcome of a *moral learning process*, in which social agents increasingly learn, through struggles for recognition, to *include* others within the scope of the socially effective legal and moral community and as individuals with particular qualities relative to societal values.

Of course, Honneth recognizes that if this tripartite structure of patterns of recognition is to serve as the basis for a critical theory, it requires not only an account of how the three forms of recognition are necessary conditions for the development of positive practical relations-to-oneself, but also of why the withholding, denial, obstruction, or distortion of recognition in *any* of these three patterns should be considered a wrong above and beyond the injury experienced by the 'misrecognized' person in question. In Honneth's early work, he thus advances an account of the three patterns of recognition as collectively constitutive of the *moral point of view*, and of these diverse, systematic forms of misrecognition as constituting *injustices*. More specifically, Honneth develops a negative moral phenomenology of the *three forms of disrespect* (*Misachtung*) that a subject is liable to experience if he or she is denied recognition according to any of the three patterns.

In the pattern of primary relationships, the most basic form of disrespect takes the form of violations of physical integrity, or physical abuse, which impairs one's basic self-confidence not only through the experience of pain, but also, and perhaps more importantly, through the experience of being fully at the mercy of another.[36] In the pattern of legal relations, the second form of disrespect refers to the impairment of one's basic self-respect derivative of being excluded from the legal community of equals and denied certain basic rights, as well as, crucially, the impairment to self-respect suffered when one is treated as a being without

---

[36] Honneth, *The Struggle for Recognition*, p. 132.

basic moral autonomy and responsibility.[37] Finally, in the context of one's community of value, the third form of disrespect represents an 'evaluative degradation of certain patterns of self-realization', which implies for the disrespected groups and individuals that 'they cannot relate to their mode of life as something of positive significance within their community'. Because such evaluative disrespect denies public recognition and approval of their way of life as 'estimable', 'the experience of this public devaluation typically brings with it a loss of personal self-esteem'.[38]

Moreover, bringing to mind Peter Strawson's reflections on 'reactive attitudes', Honneth argues that denial of recognition in any of the three patterns of recognition is associated with certain negative emotional reactions such as shame, rage, hurt, or indignation. According to Honneth, these affective reactions can serve as a cognitive bridge between the experience of the *denial* of recognition and the practical struggle *for* recognition, by disclosing the 'moral knowledge' that one has been subject to an injustice, which can in turn serve as a motivational impetus for action.[39] With this account of the moral grammar of struggles for recognition, Honneth thus develops a conception of the moral point of view that has a clear 'foothold in social reality': namely, in the *affective reactions* of subjects who experience injustice.

Honneth's account of the moral point of view in *Kampf um Anerkennung* thereby highlights a major difference between his recognition paradigm and Habermas's communicative paradigm, namely Honneth's critique of the 'empty formalism' of Habermas's discourse principle. Indeed, in contrast to Habermas's deontological specification of the moral point of view, Honneth presents a much more structurally complex account of morality, comprising rights and duties associated with the positive practical relations-to-self that one derives from being recognized in *all three* patterns of recognition, suggesting three moral principles concerning 'the reciprocity of love, the universalism of rights and the egalitarianism of solidarity'.[40] Because the rights and duties associated with these principles are derivative of the subject's possibility for developing a positive practical relation-to-self, Honneth's conception of morality is, in the traditional terms of moral theory, *teleological* rather than deontological; his moral conception as a whole is thus predicated on what he calls a 'formal conception of the ethical life': a moral ideal of society that we ought to realize because it affords every subject equal recognition across all three patterns, which includes but simultaneously goes beyond the idea of a categorically valid moral duty that no one ought to transgress.

More specifically, this formal conception of the ethical or good life suggests an ideal of society in which all its members are equally recognized through love and friendship in their primary relationships, in their moral and legal relationships

---

[37] Honneth, *The Struggle for Recognition*, pp. 133–134.
[38] Honneth, *The Struggle for Recognition*, p. 134.
[39] Honneth, *The Struggle for Recognition*, p. 138.
[40] Honneth, 'Between Aristotle and Kant: Recognition and Moral Obligation', in *Disrespect*, Ch. 6.

as autonomous agents and rights-bearers, and where all have equal opportunity through an overarching framework of mutual solidarity to be recognized in their individual way of life, as particular individuals with qualities that contribute to the realization of society's shared values. In other words, such a formal conception of ethical life must 'contain everything that is intersubjectively presupposed today in order for subjects to know that the conditions for their self-realization are safeguarded'.[41] To be sure, Honneth recognizes that 'in the case of a moral conflict, the claims of all subjects to equal respect for their moral autonomy enjoy absolute priority'.[42] He thus conceives of his recognition theory of morality as located 'between Aristotle and Kant', countenancing both the categorical ought of moral autonomy and the necessary social and psychological conditions for self-realization. Importantly, this tripartite, teleological account of morality is not meant to specify a *substantive* conception of the good life—something that Honneth recognizes as impossible under post-metaphysical conditions. It is rather meant to track those 'structural elements of ethical life, which, from the general point of view of the communicative enabling of self-realization, can be normatively extracted from the plurality of *all particular forms of life*'.[43]

Moreover, Honneth explicitly understands the struggle for recognition as 'a critical framework for interpreting the processes by which societies develop'.[44] The formal conception of ethical life is, correspondingly, conceived as a 'hypothetical end-state' to a process of historical development projected on the basis of the moral developmental logic of the three patterns of recognition. Of course, this projected end-state is not intended as a theoretical *prediction*, but rather as a *normative standard* for a critical theory of society. However, while the formal conception of the good life offered in *Kampf um Anerkennung* develops a fairly abstract account of patterns of recognition necessary for developing a positive practical relation-to-self, which is supposed to enable a deciphering of the moral grammar of social conflicts, it does not tell us much by way of the concrete *social institutions* that have actually been brought about by struggles for recognition; for an account of the latter, we must turn to the re-actualization of Hegel's *Rechtsphilosophie* developed in Honneth's more mature work.

Before doing so, however, I want to provide a sketch of the work pursued by Honneth in the period between his earlier and later work, since this period offers important clues for understanding the overall coherence of his recognition paradigm. In the almost twenty years between *Kampf um Anerkennung* (1992) and his mature *magnum opus, Das Recht der Freiheit* (2011), Honneth pursues (at least) two research programmes: a systematic attempt to pave the way for a post-metaphysical reconstruction of Hegel's *Rechtsphilosophie* ultimately realized

---

[41] Honneth, *The Struggle for Recognition*, p. 172.
[42] Honneth, 'Between Aristotle and Kant: Recognition and Moral Obligation', p. 141.
[43] Honneth, *The Struggle for Recognition*, p. 172 [my emphasis].
[44] Honneth, *The Struggle for Recognition*, p. 170.

in *Das Recht der Freiheit*, and a more heterogeneous research programme concerned with defending, revising, and developing his early account of the struggle for recognition while exploring its implications for a variety of thematic contexts. I begin by charting the second of these two strands in the following subsection, before moving on the first in Section 7.4.

7.3.2 Innovations and Revisions

In Honneth's reflections on recognition after the publication of *Kampf um Anerkennung*, two things are of particular note: firstly, his ingenuity in using the concept to open up and develop new and surprising lines of inquiry, and, secondly, his remarkable willingness to countenance criticism of the original statement of his ideas. Of particular moment is Honneth's debate with Nancy Fraser in their coauthored 'Redistribution or Recognition? A Political-Philosophical Exchange' from 2003. In Honneth's exchange with Fraser, the question on which their discussion turns is whether it is necessary to categorically distinguish struggles for recognition from struggles for redistribution, or whether, as Honneth contends, the latter can fruitfully be understood in terms of the former. I will not go into the details of their far-reaching discussion, but merely note what seems to me one of its more illuminating points for our concerns: the extent to which it is necessary to distinguish and allow for the two perspectives of social and systemic integration (as in Habermas's communicative paradigm), or whether the former alone is sufficient.

In his response to Fraser's—in my view, fairly uncharitable—reconstruction of his view,[45] Honneth clarifies his conception of the relationship between social and systemic integration. Interestingly, Honneth acknowledges that his monistic lifeworld approach 'is not sufficient to explain the dynamics of developmental processes in contemporary capitalism', but that it is 'only meant to make clear the *normative constraints* embedded in such processes because subjects face them with certain expectations of recognition'.[46] Although Honneth affords a 'certain primacy to social integration as against system integration', since 'the development of the capitalist market can only occur in the form of a process of symbolically mediated negotiation directed toward the interpretation of underlying normative principles', he also concedes that capitalist markets, which are ''embedded' in the normatively structured social order', may constitute 'an institution in which a complex network of individual actions is coordinated seemingly automatically by the

---

[45] She interprets Honneth's theory as reducing the sociological dimension to moral psychology, capitalism to 'cultural schemas of evaluation', and morality to an ethics of identity, whereby she completely misses the foundational concern with power and moral normativity. Honneth and Fraser, *Redistribution or Recognition*, pp. 198–236.

[46] Honneth and Fraser, *Redistribution or Recognition*, p. 250 [emphasis added].

interplay of utility considerations'.[47] I will return to this question concerning the relationship between social and systemic integration, which has lost none of its urgency in an age of economic globalization, in Sections 7.4 and 7.5 below.

Since the publication of *Kampf um Anerkennung*, Honneth has made at least three important revisions to his theory of the struggle for recognition. The first important revision is to draw a stronger and more explicit connection between *recognition* and *reason*. Already in a 'Postscript' to *Kampf um Anerkennung* published in 2003, Honneth had taken steps towards clarifying the concept of recognition, which suffers from a significant ambiguity: assuming that recognition is a kind of intentional affirmative act or attitude towards another subject, it is unclear whether an act of recognition should be understood as an *attribution* of a hitherto-absent property to another subject, or whether recognition is a *receptive* attitude towards an already-present property in the subject. In Honneth's view, the attributive interpretation of recognition is ruled out by its ineliminable openness as to *what* is attributed, since if recognition is understood merely in terms of such attribution, we are left with no internal criteria for distinguishing right from wrong attributions; we would have no *moral reasons* to discriminate between different kinds of attributions. However, although the receptive model is superior on this account, it raises another problem: if the concept of recognition is to be understood as perception of recognition-internal moral reasons to recognize already-present properties in another subject, then that may seem to lead down a path towards a form of value realism that is at odds with the post-metaphysical assumptions of the Frankfurt School tradition.

Honneth's way out of this cul-de-sac is by way of appeal to John McDowell's Aristotelian account of the concept of 'second nature'. McDowell's account is cast as an objection to the disenchanted 'empiricistic naturalism' encouraged by modern natural science and familiar from Habermas's attack on 'scientism' in *Erkenntnis und Interesse*: the kind of naturalism that restricts objective knowledge to the domain of 'facts of nature', as observed by the natural-scientific method. The problem with such a disenchanted naturalism is, in McDowell's view, that it excludes the 'space of reasons' from the domain of nature and thus renders it—from a naturalistic point of view—inherently suspect. McDowell thus agrees with Habermas that empiricistic naturalism unduly restricts the scope of knowledge, but his strategy for developing an alternative is to go back to Aristotle's idea of *phronesis*, or practical wisdom. The central thought in this modified Aristotelian account is that a subject's practical wisdom is cultivated through an educative process that enables the subject to be habitually receptive to the space of reasons—and, among them, ethical (or moral) reasons:

> We cannot credit appreciation of [the rational demands of ethics] to human nature as it figures in a naturalism of disenchanted nature, because disenchanted

[47] Honneth and Fraser, *Redistribution or Recognition*, pp. 250–256.

nature does not embrace the space of reasons. But human beings are intelligibly initiated into this stretch of the space of reasons by ethical upbringing, which instils the appropriate shape into their lives. The resulting habits of thought and action are second nature.[48]

Accordingly, the concept of second nature is introduced to account for the object domain to which 'practically wise' subjects are receptive, namely the space of reasons, which is understood as 'natural' relative to *the human form of life*.[49] Since the space of reasons has been socialized into our habits, desires, and even perception of the world, it has become part of our very nature as human beings. While our 'first nature' still refers to our physical and bodily existence, we would not be human beings if we did not know our way around a socially embodied space of reasons, which ensures that the nature *we humans* face is already conceptually structured; accordingly, practical wisdom is simply receptivity to our 'rationally' structured second nature.

McDowell's Aristotelian conception of second nature allows Honneth to argue that 'the human lifeworld can be understood as the result of the emergence of a "second nature", in which we habitually orient ourselves in a changing "space of reasons"'[50], and that recognition implies a receptive attitude towards the properties of other subjects relative to the space of reasons thus embedded as a second nature in our social practices. This establishes a much stronger and more explicit connection between recognition and reasonable insight than what seemed to be the case in *Kampf um Anerkennung*, which, Honneth claims, is necessary for preserving its intrinsic moral dimension: 'only if our recognition of other persons is motivated by reasons, which we can also try to articulate as necessary, can we understand it as a matter of acting on the basis of insight and thus, in a broad sense, expand the domain of the moral.'[51] However, if we understand the space of reasons in terms of a historically developed lifeworld in which subjects habitually learn to orient themselves, the dilemma between value relativism and realism simply returns in another form, since such a lifeworld would seem to either provide reasons only for the individuals socialized into its space of reasons, implying a form of moral relativism, or it would seem to imply the equally implausible and ontologically awkward picture of the lifeworld developing towards a ready-made index of moral reasons that pre-exist their socially embodied form.

Honneth ultimately overcomes this dilemma only with the second revision of his theory of recognition that he undertakes, which is to commit his theory of

---

[48] John McDowell, *Mind and World* (Cambridge MA: Harvard University Press, 1994), p. 84.
[49] John McDowell, 'Two Sorts of Naturalism', in *Mind, Value, and Reality* (Cambridge MA: Harvard University Press, 1998), pp. 196–197.
[50] Axel Honneth, 'Grounding Recognition: A Rejoinder to Critical Questions', *Inquiry: An Interdisciplinary Journal of Philosophy* (45/4), 2002: 499–519, p. 500.
[51] Honneth, 'Grounding Recognition, p. 507.

recognition to the 'moderate realism' of a fairly robust notion of moral progress in history. In Honneth's discussion of McDowell's work, he argues that the latter fails to provide an account of how subjects, who face novel moral challenges or disagree in their interpretations of the moral significance of the situation at hand, are to resolve such disputes. This failure stems, in Honneth's view, from McDowell's sceptical view of a picture of morality as deduction from first principles, but Honneth argues that a principle-based morality need not be understood as contradictory to McDowell's more habitualized account if the two are construed as *complementary*. Indeed, *pace* McDowell, Honneth maintains that knowledge of 'principles of construction' is simply part and parcel of the second nature of our lifeworlds:

> We are not only initiated into the moral modes of perception and the corresponding reaction patters, but, in the same process, we also learn to understand these grid-like connections between attitudinal dispositions as limited embodiments of principles, which ought to legitimately regulate our relationships of interaction through consideration of justified claims.[52]

Honneth's account of this moral principle of construction, on which morally dissenting individuals within a shared lifeworld must ultimately fall back to resolve their disputes, appeals to Mead's idea of mutual perspective-taking and gradual internalization of the 'generalised other'. Indeed, it is in this search for a shared standpoint through 'reciprocally compelled generalisation' that we find the seeds of an account of moral progress: namely, the two criteria of 'inclusivity' and 'individualisation'.[53]

The basic idea here is to measure progress in history according to the extent to which norms of recognition *include* affected subjects and the intensity to which they display openness and are able to *integrate* their particular points of view. The moral criteria of extensive generalization and intensive differentiation thus enable Honneth to interpret the development of the three patterns of recognition as a rational *learning process* of moral progress in history, since our highly conflictual and violent history has nonetheless brought about increased inclusivity and individualization in the three recognition patterns of love, legal respect, and social esteem. Moreover, taking a page from Kant, Honneth attempts to resist the potentially troubling meta-ethical implications of such transhistorical criteria of progress by insisting that a commitment to moral progress is irreducible from a

---

[52] Axel Honneth, 'Zwischen Hermeneutik und Hegelianismus: John McDowell und die Herausforderung des moralischen Realismus', *Unsichtbarkeit: Stationen einer Theorie der Intersubjektivität* (Frankfurt: Suhrkamp Verlag, 2003), p. 134 [translated by me].
[53] Honneth, 'Zwischen Hermeneutik und Hegelianismus', p. 135. See also, Honneth, 'Redistribution as Recognition: A Response to Nancy Fraser', in *Redistribution or Recognition: A Political-Philosophical Exchange*.

practical point of view: 'All those who actively side with the moral achievements of the Enlightenment are thus forced to see the history preceding them as a conflict-ridden learning process, which, as heirs of this process, they have to continue in their own time'.[54]

Finally, all of this points to Honneth's third revision of his early theory of recognition, namely his decision to draw a much tighter connection between *recognition* and freedom as *autonomy*. More specifically, Honneth now argues 'that social recognition represents the necessary condition for subjects being able to identify with their valuable qualities and, accordingly, develop genuine autonomy'.[55] The basic idea is to see mutual recognition as a necessary social and psychological condition not only for developing a positive practical relation-to-self but for human beings to unfold their potential for individual autonomy: recognition is a moral demand, because only on account of being recognized through love, legal respect, and social esteem for their particular qualities can modern subjects come to realize their autonomous selves.

Compared with the more complex account of morality that we find in Honneth's early work, this revised view integrates the three principles of morality as moral requirements of one overarching norm of individual autonomy. In his own words: 'I do indeed assume that we should understand autonomy or self-realization as the overarching *telos* of our human form of life, in terms of which our internal critique can orient itself'.[56] With this account of mutual recognition as a moral requirement of freedom as autonomy, owing to its being a necessary social and psychological condition for its *realization*, Honneth not only falls in line with the preceding paradigms of the Frankfurt School tradition—which, as we have seen, all express a foundational concern with illuminating social and psychological impairments to individual autonomy, or *Mündigkeit*—but he also erects the final pillar for the bridge to Hegel's mature political philosophy, as developed in his *Rechtsphilosophie*. It is to Honneth's ambitious re-actualization of that controversial classic that we now turn.

7.4 The Reality of Freedom as Democratic Ethical Life

7.4.1 The Turn to Hegel's Mature Political Philosophy

As noted in the preceding section, Honneth pursued another and more focused research agenda alongside the more heterogeneous body of work defending and

---

[54] Axel Honneth, 'The Irreducibility of Progress: Kant's Account of the Relationship between Morality and History', in *Pathologies of Reason: On the Legacy of Critical Theory*, transl. by James Ingram et al. (New York: Columbia University Press, 2009), p. 18.
[55] Honneth, 'Grounding Recognition: A Rejoinder to Critical Questions', p. 515.
[56] Honneth, 'Grounding Recognition, p. 516.

revising his early theory of the struggle for recognition expounded in the above subsection: namely, his ambitious attempt to 'reactualize' Hegel's mature political philosophy: the 'Elements of the Philosophy of Right' (*Grundlinien der Philosophie des Rechts*) from 1820/1821. When he wrote *Kampf um Anerkennung*, Honneth seems to have accepted Habermas's contention that only Hegel's early Jena writings could provide a suitable basis for a post-metaphysical conception of recognition, since Hegel's later work was consumed by his 'ontological' conception of *Geist* and his aspiration to develop an all-encompassing idealist philosophical system.[57]

However, in his book 'The Pathologies of Individual Freedom' (*Leiden an Unbestimmtheit*) from 2001, Honneth develops a reading of the 'basic intention' and 'structure' of the *Rechtsphilosophie*, which is supposed to overcome the 'ontological concept of spirit' as well as the undemocratic, 'substantialist concept of the state', which—in Honneth's view—beset Hegel's original project.[58] The preparatory work undertaken in *Leiden an Unbestimmtheit* thus paves the way for his later and significantly more ambitious work, *Das Recht der Freiheit*, which represents a comprehensive attempt to recast Hegel's mature political philosophy in a form that is at once more appropriate for, and critical of, modern capitalist-democratic society. I will begin, in this subsection, by identifying what Honneth thinks can and must be salvaged from Hegel's mature political philosophy, before moving on to reconstruct the more ambitious project undertaken in *Das Recht der Freiheit* in the Subsection 7.4.3 that follows.

Honneth's sustained engagement with Hegel's *Rechtsphilosophie* can be interpreted as guided by two overarching concerns: on the one hand, by a concern to demonstrate the relevance and fruitfulness of Hegel's mature political philosophy *as a theory of justice* (a task undertaken in *Leiden an Unbestimmtheit*) and, on the other, by a concern to demonstrate its relevance and fruitfulness for a *critical theory of society* (a task undertaken in *Das Recht der Freiheit*). Indeed, what is truly remarkable about Honneth's mature work is precisely the extent to which these two notions are *fused*: for the first time in our reconstruction of the Frankfurt School tradition, we thus find the explicit comprehensive development of a theory of justice within the framework of critical theory. In *Leiden an Unbestimmtheit*, Honneth's express purpose is thus

> to demonstrate the current relevance of *The Philosophy of Right* by proving that it can be understood as a draft of a normative theory of those spheres of reciprocal recognition that must be preserved intact because they constitute the moral identities of modern societies.[59]

---

[57] Honneth, *The Struggle for Recognition*, pp. 5–6.
[58] Axel Honneth, *The Pathologies of Individual Freedom; Hegel's Social Theory*, transl. by Ladislaus Löb (Princeton: Princeton University Press, 2010), p. 5.
[59] Honneth, *The Pathologies of Individual Freedom*, p. 5.

He takes the two core ideas of that work, which are relevant for a theory of justice and which can still be defended under post-metaphysical conditions, to be: firstly, the concept of 'objective spirit', which refers to the thesis that 'social reality has a rational structure and any breach of that structure by using false or inadequate concepts to try to understand it will necessarily have negative effects on social life as soon as those concepts come to be applied in practice'; and, secondly, the concept of 'ethical life', which refers to the thesis that the social reality of modern society reveals 'spheres of action in which inclinations and moral norms, interests, and values are already fused in the form of institutionalized interactions'.[60] Together, these two ideas point to 'all those social conditions that can be proved to be necessary for the realization of the "free will" of every subject'—which, for Hegel, is the general meaning of the term 'right' (*Recht*), and which it is the purpose of his *Rechtsphilosophie* to reconstruct and bring to consciousness.[61]

Moreover, Honneth is also concerned to show that the *Rechtsphilosophie* does not necessarily have the conservative implications that some—notably the young Marx, and Adorno—have argued. Indeed, as suggested, a central aspiration of Honneth's work is to bring out the concerns shared by Hegel's mature political philosophy and the Frankfurt School tradition, and the fruitfulness of the *Rechtsphilosophie* as both a methodological and social-theoretical basis for developing a critical theory of contemporary society. In particular, Hegel's concern with the social conditions for the realization of the will allows us to see a perhaps somewhat overlooked sense in which the Frankfurt School tradition can indeed be understood as decidedly 'Left-Hegelian'. As we have seen, all four paradigms of critical theory clearly follow Hegel in his theoretical emphasis on the social and psychological conditions of individual freedom; for Horkheimer and Adorno no less than for Habermas and Honneth, individual autonomy is in the first instance a question of social relations that furnish subjects with the internal and external conditions for a non-dominated coexistence.

Following Michael Theunissen, the concept that Honneth introduces to describe this concern is 'communicative freedom' (*kommunikative Freiheit*).[62] Of course, we have also encountered this concept in Habermas's communicative paradigm, but Honneth uses the concept in a different sense: whereas Habermas invokes communicative freedom with inspiration from Hannah Arendt to refer specifically to the cooperative power of citizens who reach a discursive agreement in the political public sphere, Honneth employs the concept in reference to Hegel's famous definition of freedom as 'being with oneself in the other'.[63] In Theunissen's words: 'Communicative freedom means that the subject does not experience the

---

[60] Honneth, *The Pathologies of Individual Freedom*, p. 6.
[61] Honneth, *The Pathologies of Individual Freedom*, p. 9.
[62] Michael Theunissen, *Sein und Schein. Die kritische Funktion der Hegelschen Logik* (Frankfurt: Surhkamp Verlag, 1978).
[63] Hegel, *Grundlinien der Philosophie des Rechts*, §7 Zusatz, p. 57.

other subject as a limiting condition, but as a condition of possibility for his own self-realisation', implying that 'communicative freedom is possible at all only as the freedom of all'.[64] In order to clarify the meaning of this communicative conception of freedom and appreciating its importance for the Frankfurt School, we must backtrack a bit and view that conception in light of Hegel's critique of Kant's idea of freedom as autonomy—or, more precisely, we must understand the sense in which communicative freedom can be seen as a *radicalization* of Kant's idea of freedom as autonomy.

7.4.2 Communicative Freedom: An Excursus on Kant and Hegel

For Kant, of course, an autonomous human being is a self-legislating being, as the ancient-Greek etymological root of the word, *autos* (self) and *nomos* (law), implies. This might be taken to mean that we are autonomous whenever we resolve to act according to what particular edicts suit our fancy—but this voluntarism is far from Kant's view. Rather, Kant thinks that we are only autonomous—and, thus, truly *free*—when we act according to a principle that we could *will* to be a universal law for all rational beings. In *Kritik der reinen Vernunft*, Kant argues that the possibility of knowledge depends on both the concepts of our understanding (which enable us to think) and the intuitions that issue from our sense apparatus (which enable us to represent objects in cognition): we can acquire knowledge of (or cognize) empirical reality only when an object is represented in the form of a sense impression and when this 'intuition' is subsumed under a concept.[65]

However, Kant also maintains that our sense apparatus inevitably leaves its mark on the intuitions that reach our understanding. Specifically, it forms our sense impressions in the dimensions of time and space, which, according to Kant, are inescapable epistemological filters of our faculty of sense. Because our knowledge of the world is therefore always cast by our sense apparatus in the dimensions of time and space, we can never have representations of the empirical world that isn't moulded by our senses. Accordingly, Kant argues, we only have access to objects as *phenomena*, and whatever lies beyond our subjective filters, objects as *noumena*, is beyond the scope of our epistemic capacities. In his famous expression: we can have no knowledge of the object or thing as such (*an sich*), but only as it appears to us (*für uns*). This is Kant's doctrine of transcendental idealism.

Moreover, Kant also argues that cognition is necessarily structured according to the categories (or pure concepts) inherent in the faculty of understanding—and,

---

[64] Theunissen, *Sein und Schein*, p. 46 [translated by me].
[65] The only kind of 'metaphysical' speculation that rises to the rank of knowledge is the a priori kind that specifies the necessary and sufficient conditions for knowing anything at all—in other words, the transcendental conditions that Kant elaborates in the first part of *Kritik der reinen Vernunft*.

among these, the category of causation. He thus claims that the world of *phenomena* is a world of thoroughgoing natural causation. However, given that we only have epistemic access to objects in the world of phenomena, and given that we only have access to ourselves as empirical beings, *we* must also be subject to thoroughgoing causation through our natural desires and drives, our 'inclinations'. And here lies the central problem of Kant's critical philosophy: if we are indeed causally determined all the way down, not only does any defensible notion of free will and agency seem to be impossible, but so does morality, since moral action presupposes freedom of the will.

But this is, of course, only one half of Kant's story. Indeed, in the 'Groundwork for the Metaphysics of Morals' (*Grundlegung zur Metaphysik der Sitten*), he maintains that the denial of free will is impossible from the *practical point of view*—the point of view in which we find ourselves when we deliberate on what actions to pursue. The reason we might be led to the determinist conclusion owes to a mistaken reduction of human life to the theoretical standpoint—the point of view in which we are concerned with knowledge and explanation. However, we cannot act under the assumption that the outcome of our deliberations is already causally determined; in considering possible courses of action, I inevitably assume that the choice between them is ultimately *up to me*.

According to Kant, to be confronted with these two equally ineliminable points of view is simply what it is to be a rational agent, who employs reason both for explanatory and for justificatory purposes. All rational agents are endowed with the ability for both a theoretical *and* a practical use of reason. From the point of view of practical reason, we always act under what Kant calls 'the idea of freedom' as a necessary presupposition for all practical cognition and action. To be sure, this does not explain anything—in particular, it doesn't mean that we can *know* that we are free, since that judgement belongs to the theoretical domain—but it does mean that we must, for practical purposes, *assume* that we are free.[66]

Now, in assuming that we are free, we assume that we are exempt from the closed system of natural causation; we assume that we—with our will and practical reason (which, for Kant, comes down to the same faculty)—can initiate and produce causal effects in the world without that initiation itself being caused. But this means, in the terms of Kant's transcendental idealism, that we have to assume that we are *also* part of the world of *noumena*; that our practical reason somehow issues from beyond the world of *phenomena* and natural causation. The phenomenal part of our selves is indeed naturally caused—the part that contains our feelings, desires, sexual drives, and so on. However, this also means that if I choose to act on the whim of feeling, desire, or sexual drive, then the grounds of my action lie firmly

---

[66] Immanuel Kant, *Grundlegung zur Metaphysik der Sitten* (Hamburg: Felix Meiner Verlag, 1999), Abschnitt III. Kant later abandoned this account, attempting instead to derive freedom of the will from the moral law as a 'fact of reason', which I discuss further in Chapter 10. Immanuel Kant, *Kritik der praktischen Vernunft* (Hamburg: Felix Meiner Verlag, 2003), §7.

within the phenomenal world, and I thus in a sense choose to be compelled by natural forces, in spite of my necessary presupposition that I do so freely. The only way to escape natural causation and to act as an uncaused cause in the world—to be free, in the transcendental sense—is thus to empty my will of all phenomenal grounds for action and seek a ground that is *not* naturally caused. If I am to act freely in this transcendental sense, I must act from an *unconditioned ground*.

Because Kant thinks that practical reasoning involves acting from principles, this is equivalent to acting from a principle that does not issue from the phenomenal world of causation. But, Kant argues, if I empty my will of all such phenomenal grounds, then there is really nothing left but the *structure* of acting from a principle. Since Kant also thinks that, as a rational being, I must take any reason for action to be in principle valid for all rational beings, he can express this claim by saying that I must act from a *universal law*. Moreover, since what is at stake here is that I must be able to *will* to act from a law—i.e., that I have to think of myself as an uncaused cause acting from the structure of a principle valid for all rational beings—I must be able to let my will be determined by the structure of a principle that I can at the same time will to be able to move all rational beings to the same action: a principle that I can will to be universally valid, to bind everyone. Kant thus reaches the conclusion that insofar as I am to act freely in the transcendental sense—insofar as I am to act as an unconditioned ground, or uncaused cause—I must *act only according to a principle that I could at the same time will should also become a universal law*.[67]

This, of course, is the *categorical imperative*. The categorical imperative requires that I act only on universalizable principles; principles that I could will all rational beings to adopt as the determining grounds of action. This should be understood in the following sense. In willing an end, Kant thinks that I also at the same will the means to that end.[68] If I cannot realize the end—e.g., if the means are beyond my reach—then I can only wish for the end, but I cannot will it, in the sense that I cannot will to travel to the moons orbiting Saturn, but only wish for it. The categorical imperative requires that I be willing to act from a principle in a way that is compatible with all rational beings acting from this principle. This has the implication, Kant believes, that I cannot consistently will to enrich myself by issuing a promise that I have no intention of keeping, since if all rational beings were to act in such a way, my strategy would be self-defeating: if promises were never kept, rational beings would (with good reason) cease to believe in promises, and enriching oneself by issuing false promises would no longer be a means to that end.[69] My

---

[67] Kant, *Grundlegung*, p. 45 [421].
[68] Indeed, Kant thinks that this is analytically true: that it is contained in the very thought of an action.
[69] Christine Korsgaard, *Creating the Kingdom of Ends* (Cambridge: Cambridge University Press, 1996), Ch. 3.

willing the end and my willing the particular means to that end (here: lying for self-enrichment) would not be universalizable.

It is precisely in acting from such universalizable principles that rational beings are self-legislating, or *autonomous*. As autonomous beings, we act only according to laws that we ourselves legislate—or, in other words, we act only according to principles that are valid for all rational beings. Autonomy, for Kant, therefore implies that we are only rationally moved by those principles that we could will all rational beings to act from. Of course, this is also Kant's definition of the moral point of view. The categorical imperative is an unconditional rule for practical cognition that allows us to act freely, as uncaused causes, and in acting freely, we at the same time act morally. In a word, the categorical imperative is *the moral law*, and only *moral action is free* (in the transcendental sense). The categorical imperative forbids me to do certain things; to act in a way that I cannot universalize. The fact that I am free to act on arbitrary whims issues from the fact that I am both equipped with what Kant calls *Willkür*, or executive freedom of choice, and *Wille*, the legislative ability to act from a conception of the law. In choosing to act immorally, I am not caused to do so, but I am also not free in the transcendental sense, since such freedom implies for Kant that my will is determined by universalizable grounds. This complex account of freedom thus allows Kant to identify morality and freedom with 'self-legislation', and, on that basis, distinguish between *autonomy* and *heteronomy*: between morally required (and transcendentally free) action in accordance with the moral law, and contingent (and transcendentally unfree) action from inclination—which, in the worst case, is an action in violation of the moral law.[70]

Now, Hegel confronts Kant's account of freedom as autonomy with a number of forceful objections, which locate the problems that beset Kant's account in the fundamental dualisms that run through the whole architectonic of his critical philosophy. There are roughly two different interpretations of the nature of this critique in the literature on Hegel's philosophy, which differ on how radically they take Hegel to depart from Kant's conception of freedom as autonomy. What we might call the *Romantic Interpretation* holds that 'Hegel rejects this entire conception of autonomy'[71] as the basis for freedom and that he instead claims that I am free only when my desires and choices '*harmonize* with the practical system constituting my self-identity as an agent'.[72] By contrast, what we might call the *Enlightenment Interpretation* holds that, rather than rejecting it, Hegel maintains that Kant does not *go far enough* in conceiving of freedom as autonomy. I will assume that the Enlightenment Interpretation is correct, both because I believe

---

[70] For a sympathetic discussion, see Henry E. Allison, *Kant's Theory of Freedom* (Cambridge: Cambridge University Press, 1990).
[71] Allen Wood, *Hegel's Ethical Thought* (Cambridge: Cambridge University Press, 1990), p. 44.
[72] Wood, *Hegel's Ethical Thought*, p. 49 [emphasis added].

it is, but also, and more importantly in this context, because it is the interpretation of Hegel espoused by Honneth and the rest of the Frankfurt School.[73] On the Enlightenment Interpretation, Hegel's central objection to Kant is that, in spite of the latter's path-breaking insight in having identified freedom with autonomy, his metaphysical dualism between *noumena* and *phenomena* forces him to cede far too much ground to the heteronomy of natural causation.

To appreciate this objection, we must draw a distinction between the determining *ground* (*Bestimmungsgrund*) of an action, which must be a reason (or maxim) of some kind issuing from principles (whether universalizable or from inclination), and the *end* of an action, which is the intended purpose or consequence of the action.[74] The idea here is that I can pursue an end for different reasons (i.e., I can help the little old lady cross the street because it is right or because I happen to have great affection for little old ladies), just as I can pursue different ends for the same reason. In *Grundlegung*, Kant's well-known thought experiments ask us to consider the decisions whether to commit suicide, whether to borrow money one cannot repay, and whether to cultivate one's talents.[75] On Kant's account, it is solely the ground of an action that determines whether that action is autonomous or heteronomous. That is, what is decisive in evaluating the moral quality of an action is that I pursue a given end from duty or respect for the moral law.

However, even an autonomous will, which is determined by universalizable principles rather than mere inclination, is of course still dependent on the causally determined world of phenomena for *pursuing anything at all*. That is to say, although my grounds of actions may be perfectly autonomous, and thus noumenal, whatever I make the end of my action will always be subject to casual determination, even other human beings, because phenomenal. Whatever I do, I find myself poised against an empirical reality of thoroughgoing natural causation, both in terms of the material objects of the will and the actions of others. In a word, even when the moral law plays the part of 'rudder' on the ship of the self, the latter still sails on an ocean of natural compulsion, in which the idea of freedom is admitted no place by Kant.

For Hegel, however, Kant's account of freedom as autonomy is not only problematic because it construes the ends of actions as dependent on a phenomenal world bereft of freedom; he also rejects Kant's characterization of the relationship between the rational self and bodily nature as a perpetual struggle for reason to gain the upper hand over and against the causally determined inclinations as reflecting a fundamental misunderstanding of moral action as necessarily

---

[73] For other proponents of the Enlightenment Interpretation, see Alan Patten, *Hegel's Idea of Freedom* (Oxford: Oxford University Press, 1999)and the brilliant exposition in Robert B. Pippin, *Hegel's Practical Philosophy: Rational Agency as Ethical Life* (Cambridge: Cambridge University Press, 2008).
[74] Allison, *Kant's Theory of Freedom*, p. 189.
[75] Kant, *Grundlegung*, p. 46 [p. 421].

reflective rather than habitual.[76] In other words, Hegel rejects both Kant's claim that the *ends* of the will's determination is beyond the pale of autonomy, as well as his claim that inclination as the *grounds* of the will is necessarily heteronomous. Evidently, since these two-fold restrictions on freedom as autonomy ultimately derive from Kant's distinction between *phenomena* and *noumena*, Hegel overcomes these two problems only by abandoning Kant's dualistic metaphysical framework. Indeed, according to Hegel, the only way to broaden the grounds of autonomous action and to bring the ends of action within the scope of autonomy is to recast freedom as autonomy within a *historical* and *social-theoretical* framework.[77]

However, in order to truly appreciate the radical implications of this historical and social-theoretical turn, we must first achieve a better grasp of the nature of Hegel's communicative conception of freedom—defined above as 'being with oneself in the other'—which he expounds in the 'Introduction' to his *Rechtsphilosophie*.[78] In the course of this exposition, Hegel makes two particularly noteworthy arguments. First, he claims that we can construe the inclinations of a subject as within the scope of autonomy by explicating the social circumstances that have conditioned them (§19). In Honneth's words:

> Hegel wanted to draw the idea of individual self-determination so deeply into the structure of human motivation that every subject, and correspondingly every social community, as it were, 'naturally' and 'spontaneously' sets itself the task of developing and cultivating within itself inclinations and impulses that were consistent with, and in fact an integral part of, true human freedom.[79]

Second, Hegel claims that we can understand those social circumstances as *themselves* expressive of free will. To this purpose, he draws a distinction between 'subjective will' and 'objective will', where the former is understood as 'the will's self-conscious aspect, its individuality', and the latter as 'the will immersed in its object or condition', its 'external existence' (§§25–26). Hegel's basic idea here is that we can understand both subjective and objective will as autonomous if we can somehow comprehend the social and political institutions of society and their corresponding forms of subjective relations-to-self as expressive of reason, by being constitutive conditions for the very possibility of free agency.[80]

---

[76] In his earliest and most 'romantic' work, Hegel understood this conflict within the self precisely in terms of the tyranny of the 'general' over the 'particular', which would later be so central to Adorno. See G.W.F. Hegel, *Frühe Schriften: Werke 1* (Frankfurt: Suhrkamp Verlag, 1986), p. 323.

[77] In *Hegel's Practical Philosophy*, Robert B. Pippin emphasizes these historical and social-theoretical aspects of Hegel's thought over the ontological conception of *Geist*.

[78] In the following paragraphs, references in the text are to G.W.F. Hegel, *Grundlinien der Philosophie des Rechts*, with quotes from the English translation, G.W.F. Hegel, Elements of the Philosophy of Right, ed. by Allen W. Wood, transl. by H.B. Nisbet (Cambridge: Cambridge University Press, 1991).

[79] Honneth, *Pathologies of Individual Freedom*, p. 13.

[80] See, again, Pippin, *Hegel's Practical Philosophy*.

As we have seen, his concept for a social order that fulfils these conditions is 'ethical life': in a fully unfolded ethical life, the social and political institutions that condition the content of subjects' choices and the actions of others embody an objective will, while the subject's desires and inclinations are socialized in such a way that the subject will habitually and unreflectively act autonomously, making it unnecessary—and, Hegel believes, potentially perverse—to incessantly apply the categorical imperative in individual moral reflection. By thus viewing inclinations as the habitual outcome of socialization through social and political institutions, and by viewing those social and political institutions as embodying an objective will and reason (objective *Geist*), Hegel breaks through both of Kant's restrictions on autonomy. Indeed, we can only speak of true autonomy in a situation of congruence between subjective and objective will, since only in such a situation 'is the will completely with itself (*bei sich*), because it has reference to nothing but itself, so that every relationship of *dependence* on something *other* than itself is thereby eliminated' (§23).

This brings us full circle to Hegel's communicative conception of freedom as 'being with oneself in the other'. We can now see how, as noted in the discussion above, communicative freedom refers to the social and physical conditions of freedom—or, more specifically, to social relationships that are constitutive of an autonomous will.[81] The central point is this: subjects that are 'with themselves in their other' act and are socialized *only within social and political institutions that are reciprocally conducive to their autonomy*. In his *Rechtsphilosophie*, Hegel develops his vision of a society that he believes satisfies this condition. In accordance with Hegel's affirmative dialectic, he embraces both the modern conception of freedom as negative liberty as well as Kant's reflective construal of freedom as autonomy as necessary but in themselves insufficient dimensions of freedom, which he finds, respectively, in 'abstract right' to external objects and things, and in the reflective 'morality' governing actions, while maintaining that both of these limited conceptions of freedom presuppose and depend upon society's ethical life as 'their support and foundation' (§141).

As was noted in Section 7.2, Hegel believed that such an ethical life was fundamentally (if imperfectly) realized in the social and political institutions of his day: namely, in the patriarchal *bourgeois* family, in the civil society (or market economy) at the dawn of the Industrial Revolution, and in the state organized as a constitutional monarchy. Although Hegel can no doubt be seen as a reformist or perhaps even a progressive in his own historical context, his political endorsement of a social and political order conspicuously similar to his native Prussia has led many—including his most famous student, the young Marx, and Adorno, as we have seen—to reject Hegel's political philosophy as conservative and parochial.

---

[81] Compare this with Adorno's claim, as discussed in Chapter 3, that the forces of social heteronomy in the administered world undermines freedom of the will.

Notwithstanding such concerns with Hegel's estimation of the extent to which the social institutions of his day expressed and realized a free and ethical life, the point I want to make here is a different one.

An important but perhaps less obvious part of what warrants the characterization of the Frankfurt School as 'Left-Hegelian' is their shared and unwavering commitment to Hegel's communicative construal of Kant's conception of freedom as autonomy, and the claim that a just society is one in which social relations are ordered such that subjects have the social and psychological wherewithal for individual and collective self-determination.[82] That is to say, Horkheimer, Adorno, Habermas, and Honneth all agree that the institutionalized relationships of a society must provide subjects with sufficient inner and outer opportunities to lead an autonomous life, as expressed in Adorno's demand for 'an organisation of reality such that autonomous human beings are able to live in it'. Moreover, they all assume that such an organization is possible only when subjects participate in social relationships in which subjects do not encounter each other as limiting conditions on their freedom but in which they *mutually* enable one another's autonomy.

Autonomy is thus understood partly as a function of social relationships, and, ultimately, of the structural totality of social relationships, rather than uncaused self-legislation *in foro interno*. We might express this commitment to communicative freedom by saying that, for the Frankfurt School, social relationships must be reciprocally *autonomy-enabling* rather than *autonomy-impairing* (whether reciprocally or asymmetrically). Moreover, the communicative conception of freedom as autonomy is also, I want to argue, the conceptual basis for the conception of domination (*Herrschaft/Beherrschung*) that we find throughout the Frankfurt School tradition of critical theory. Where social relations are such that subjects mutually enable one another's autonomy, we can thus speak of individual subjects as free or *non-dominated*, and where relations *impair* the autonomy of subjects, whether because some individuals are able to impose heteronomy on others, or because the structure of social relations deprives everyone (or large groups) of the social and psychological conditions for autonomy, we can speak of individual subjects being *dominated* (*beherrscht*).

Accordingly, we can say that Hegel's communicative construal of freedom as autonomy represents the shared overarching commitment in the normative dimension of the different paradigms of Frankfurt School critical theory, albeit cashed out in different ways. On this interpretation, it is this normative ideal of a society of enabling autonomy-enabling social relationships, which Horkheimer ultimately has in mind with his idea of a reasonable society, which we find intimations of in Adorno's idea of a society fit for *mündigen Menschen*, which Habermas

---

[82] I owe the suggestion that the Frankfurt School is committed to a communicative conception of freedom to personal conversation with Honneth.

captures in his discursive reconstruction of autonomy in terms of the principles of discourse and democracy, and which Honneth pursues in terms of the formal conception of ethical life in his early work. Conversely, it is precisely a critique of social relations that structurally impair individual autonomy, which we find at work in Horkheimer's critique of monopoly capitalism, in Adorno's critique of socially imposed heteronomy in late-capitalism, in Habermas's critique of systems colonization of the lifeworld, and—as we shall see in what follows—in Honneth's reconstructive critique of misdevelopments in the 'reality of freedom' of modern capitalist democracies.

7.4.3 Das Recht der Freiheit

Honneth unfolds his mature programme for a theory of justice as social analysis in *Das Recht der Freiheit* from 2011. The outline and structure of the book follows Hegel's *Rechtsphilosophie*, with its attempt to demonstrate the legitimate but limited place of 'legal freedom' (*abstrakte Recht*) and reflective or 'moral freedom' (*Moralität*) within the more comprehensive conception of ethical life (*Sittlichkeit*), or, the reality of freedom (*die Wirklichkeit der Freiheit*) in the institutional spheres of 'social freedom'. At the root of this demonstration lies the idea of communicative freedom, understood in terms of relationships of mutual recognition, the purpose of which—as we have seen—Honneth now explicitly understands as the realization of individual autonomy:

> A subject is only 'free' if it encounters another subject, within the framework of institutional practices, to whom it is joined in a relationship of mutual recognition; only then can it regard the aims of the other as the condition for the realization of its own aims. 'To be with oneself in the other' thus necessarily entails a relation to social institutions, for only established and routine practices can guarantee that subjects will recognize each other as the other of their self.[83]

Honneth recognizes that other conceptions of freedom and indeed other values than freedom are found in the collective normative imagination of modern society, but he maintains that all of these values and alternative conceptions of freedom have ultimately 'been placed under the spell' of freedom as autonomy:

> Of all the ethical values prevailing and competing for dominance in modern society, only one has been capable of leaving a truly lasting impression on our institutional order: freedom, i.e. the autonomy of the individual ... Today, at the

---

[83] Axel Honneth, *Freedom's Right: The Social Foundations of Democratic Ethical Life*, transl. by Joseph Ganahl (New York: Columbia University Press, 2014), p. 44–45.

beginning of the twenty-first century, it is nearly impossible to articulate one of these other values of modernity without immediately grasping them as facets of the constitutive idea of individual autonomy.[84]

Departing somewhat from his earlier work, Honneth now follows Hegel more closely in maintaining that the three central institutional spheres of social freedom are those of personal relationships, the market economy, and democratic will-formation (in the original German: *Öffentlichkeit*), the latter of which replaces Hegel's substantialist conception of the state. Moreover, to uncover the normative infrastructure of these three spheres of social freedom, Honneth develops the methodological procedure of 'normative reconstruction' that he sees at work not only in Hegel's political philosophy, but also in the work of such sociologists as Parsons and Durkheim.

The central idea of normative reconstruction is to 'determine the order of social spheres according to the respective function they fulfil when it comes to stabilizing and realizing the modern hierarchy of values'.[85] The method thus aims to uncover those spheres of social life that contribute, each in their own way, to the realization of individual autonomy, which are not only understood as having achieved a modicum of reality in the institutional framework of society, but also as *necessary* for social reproduction. Normative reconstruction thus relies on the arguably very strong premise that 'the normative point of reference employed by a theory of justice should draw on those values or ideals that, as normative claims, also constitute the conditions of reproduction of a given society'.[86] This suggests, firstly, that the spheres of value into which normative reconstruction taps must be functionally necessary for the social reproduction of society, and, secondly, that a theory of justice must be conceived such that the normative conception of a just society that it develops can be seen as a representation of these socially necessary spheres of communicative freedom:

> This procedure implements the normative aims *of a theory of justice through social analysis*, taking immanently justified values as a criterion for processing and sorting out the empirical material. Given institutions and practices will be analysed in terms of their normative achievements and recounted in order of their significance for the social embodiment and realization of socially legitimated values. In the context of this procedure, 'reconstruction' thus means that out of the entirety of social routines and institutions, we will only pick out those that are indispensable for social reproduction. And because the aims of social reproduction are essentially determined by accepted values, 'normative' reconstruction means categorizing and ordering these routines and institutions according to the

---

[84] Honneth, *Freedom's Right*, p. 15.
[85] Honneth, *Freedom's Right*, p. 6.
[86] Honneth, *Freedom's Right*, p. 4.

impact of their individual contribution to the stabilization and implementation of these values.[87]

Now, Honneth is well aware that such a methodological procedure is immediately vulnerable to the objection that it risks producing little more than a stylized account of the status quo and, in the worst case, complacent apologetics for existing injustice. Accordingly, much more so than Hegel, Honneth is at pains to develop this procedure such that it allows for *critical* evaluation of society, and he thus complements normative reconstruction with what he calls the method of *reconstructive critique*.

The purpose of reconstructive critique is to enable evaluation of the institutions of society with reference to normative standards that are *immanent* in existing spheres of social freedom, such that 'the same standards according to which these institutions and practices are picked out of the chaos of social reality are used to criticize insufficient, still imperfect embodiments of universally accepted values'.[88] In a broader sense, the idea of *immanent* critique—understood as social criticism with reference to normative standards that are already institutionalized in the political institutions or social practices subject to criticism[89]—is of course in some way or another endorsed and practiced in all the four paradigms of critical theory. This commitment is closely connected with the left-Hegelian premise that a critical theory is supposed to contribute to bringing an unfinished process of societal rationalization to completion, by bringing socially embedded normative ideals of society to bear on social reality and inspire the need for its practical transformation out of reasonable insight.[90] To be sure, this shared commitment to immanent critique is cashed out in very different ways in the respective paradigms, ranging from Horkheimer's critique of monopoly capitalism with reference to *bourgeois* moral concepts, over Adorno's negative dialectics (which can be understood as a general philosophical method of immanent critique), to Habermas's rational reconstruction of the formal pragmatics of linguistic communication and the self-understanding of the democratic constitutional state.

On the one hand, Honneth's conception of reconstructive critique is quite distinct from the conceptions of immanent critique found in Horkheimer's and Adorno's work: although he shares the young Horkheimer's (and Adorno's) project of scrutinizing social reality with reference to 'its own' moral values, as with Habermas, Honneth does not believe that a 'reasonable society' requires the revolutionary overthrow of capitalism. On the other hand, the similarities and

---

[87] Honneth, *Freedom's Right*, p. 6 [emphasis added].
[88] Honneth, *Freedom's Right*, p. 9.
[89] See Titus Stahl, *Immanente Kritik*, p. 34.
[90] Axel Honneth, 'Reconstructive Social Criticism with a Genealogical Proviso: On the Idea of 'Critique' in the Frankfurt School', in *Pathologies of Reason. On the Legacy of Critical Theory*, transl. by James Ingram (New York: Columbia University Press, 2009), p. 50.

differences with Habermas's position are also instructive: Honneth not only shares Habermas's political reformism, but also, on a broader level, the commitment to the intersubjective paradigm of reason, and to grounding the normative dimension of critical theory through a 'reconstructive' method.[91] However, the crucial difference between their respective methodological procedures can be brought out by seeing that whereas Habermas's rational reconstruction takes aim at the *second-order* norms that govern the discursive redemption of first-order validity claims (including moral claims), Honneth's normative reconstruction takes aim at the *first-order* moral norms institutionalized in communicative spheres of mutual recognition. The normative dimensions of their respective paradigms reflect this difference: whereas Habermas's discourse principle represents a second-order principle of moral constructivism (in the form of the 'U' principle], Honneth painstakingly reconstructs those first-order socially embodied moral values that Horkheimer largely took for granted in his critique of *bourgeois* society. As we shall see in the end of this section, this difference in their modes of criticism reflects a basic disagreement in moral theory between Habermas and Honneth, where, roughly speaking, Habermas sides with Kant, and Honneth with Hegel.

Before expounding Honneth's normative reconstruction of personal relationships, the market economy, and democratic will-formation as spheres of social freedom, let us take a look at his argument that legal freedom and reflective moral freedom represent two necessary but by themselves insufficient 'models of freedom'. Honneth develops an ambitious argument that the conceptions of legal freedom and moral freedom are both conceptually inadequate and unable to unilaterally secure their own claims in social reality. According to Honneth, legal (or negative) freedom and moral (or reflective) freedom are indeed necessary conditions of possibility for a democratic ethical life, since in recognizing each other as legal and moral subjects, the citizens of modern capitalist democracies invest each other with both the necessary protection of their private lives as well as the individual status and ability to reflectively question existing social affairs. In struggles for legal freedom throughout history, subjects have demanded an individual space free from all voluntary obligations; a legally secured 'sphere of individual privacy':

> As diverse as the social reasons and political-moral conflicts might have been, the expansion and reformulation of liberties has essentially followed the idea that we all deserve a sphere of negative freedom that allows us to retreat from the communicative space of mutual obligations and take up a reflective and critical stance.[92]

---

[91] Mattias Iser, *Empörung und Fortschritt: Grundlagen einer kritischen Theorie der Gesellschaft* (Frankfurt: Campus Verlag, 2008).
[92] Honneth, *Freedom's Right*, p. 76.

THE REALITY OF FREEDOM AS DEMOCRATIC ETHICAL LIFE 265

Following this legally secured space of privacy, Honneth interprets moral freedom as an intersubjectively (or culturally) secured reflective capacity to question and criticize social relations in which one partakes:

> In the first instance, Kant's idea of moral autonomy does not instruct us on how we should in fact structure our lives and our actions, rather it conveys the ever-present possibility of questioning the legitimacy of existing social relations ... Hence in this negative form, Kant's notion of moral autonomy consists in the freedom to reject unreasonable social demands or circumstances that do not stand the test of social universalizability.[93]

Accordingly, Honneth views both legal and moral freedom as essentially *negative* and *reactive* models of freedom, which allow us retreat from or reflectively question existing social relations.

However, because this is the case, legal freedom and moral freedom are also insufficient conditions for a democratic ethical life, because they *presuppose* an already-existing order of norms, practices and institutions; they rest on an intersubjective foundation that they do not conceptually acknowledge.[94] This also implies, Honneth argues, that they cannot *guarantee* the reality of freedom, but must rely on a social reality that is sufficiently accommodating for their applicability in practice, and such accommodation can only be understood as external conditions for their own possibility.[95] However, in contrast to the 'regulative' models of moral of freedom, social freedom represents a 'constitutive' model of freedom; it *establishes* certain intersubjective norms, practice, and institutions that the participants realize through mutual recognition and social cooperation.[96] Only if social freedom is sufficiently realized in communicative relations of mutual recognition can legal and moral freedom be realized on that basis, and only if all three conceptions of freedom are realized such that they institutionally complement and support rather than compete with one another can we speak of the reality of freedom and of a truly democratic ethical life. This also means, Honneth argues, that if either legal or moral freedom are absolutized or mistaken for 'the whole' of freedom, the reality of freedom will suffer as a result, since subjects will then orient themselves according to merely negative and reactive models of freedom and lose sight of the positive intersubjectivity of social freedom, without which the former are bereft of all points of orientation.

Indeed, Honneth wants to show how a one-sided absolutization of the model and institutional complex of both legal and moral freedom results in distinctive

---

[93] Honneth, *Freedom's Right*, p. 98.
[94] This argument is of course a version of Hegel's critique of Kant's truncated conception of autonomy, discussed in the previous subsection on the idea of communicative freedom.
[95] As Habermas freely admits, as we have seen.
[96] Honneth, *Freedom's Right*, p. 125.

social pathologies. A social pathology, on Honneth's definition, 'indicates any social development that significantly impairs the ability to take part rationally in important forms of social cooperation'.[97] Social pathologies represent 'second-order ... deficits of rationality', where a subject has 'lost the ability, due to social causes, to practice adequately the normative grammar of an intuitively familiar system of action'.[98] In this definition of social pathology as a social-structural impairment of communicative freedom, we see clearly how Honneth intends to mobilize the conceptual resources of Hegel's *Rechtsphilosophie* for restating the concerns of the Frankfurt School tradition.

Without delving too deeply into Honneth's account of the pathologies of legal and moral freedom—which he primarily supports through interpretative analysis of history, novels, movies, and works of art—we can mention two illustrative and particularly interesting cases that appear in the course of his discussion: the tendency to reduce one's relation-to-self to the legal personality that comes to the fore in the increase in legal resolutions of conflicts in personal relationships, such as a juridification of marital divorce (which Honneth sees paradigmatically expressed in the film *Kramer vs. Kramer*); and the tendency for a perversion of moral freedom into the detached moral legislation of political extremism or even terrorism, which puts an absolute premium on individual judgement and thus allows a wholesale and even violent rejection of the existing social and political order where the original universalist restrictions have been sufficiently suppressed (Honneth sees this tendency at work in the case of Ulrike Meinhoff of the *Rote Armee Fraktion* terrorist group that haunted West Germany in the 1970s). In both cases—as well as in Honneth's version of the more traditional Hegelian charge of 'moral rigorism' against the Kantian moral self-legislator—what comes to pass is a kind of loss of orientation within the normative infrastructure of social freedom in society. Moreover, the crucial point is that it is to some extent these models and institutional complexes of freedom, which are *to blame* for these pathologies:

> The pathologies of legal and moral freedom represent social embodiments of misinterpretations for which the rules of action themselves are at least partly responsible; after all, the normative practices in both of these spheres are incomplete on their own and require supplementation by lifeworld relations, without, however, this being made apparent in the performance of these practices. Such pathologies could thus be said to derive from an 'invitation' on the part of the underlying system of action to perceive the mere 'possibility' of freedom as the entire 'reality' of freedom.[99]

---

[97] Honneth, *Freedom's Right*, p. 86.
[98] Honneth, *Freedom's Right*, p. 86.
[99] Honneth, *Freedom's Right*, p. 128.

This leads us, finally, to Honneth's ambitious normative reconstruction of the three spheres of social freedom in modern society: the institutions of personal relations, the economic market, and democratic will-formation. Clearly, this tripartite distinction between spheres of social freedom loosely follows Honneth's tripartite distinction between three patterns of recognition found in his early work, but they are developed at two different levels of abstraction: whereas *Kampf um Anerkennung* is ultimately concerned with disclosing the moral grammar of social conflicts with reference to the ontogenetic development of a positive practical relation-to-self, the normative reconstructions of *Das Recht der Freiheit* are concerned with laying bare the normative infrastructure embodied in the concrete institutions of social freedom of modern Western society, as these institutions functionally contribute to the compound social reality of individual autonomy. In what follows, it will not be possible to do justice to the sweeping historical narratives of dialectical struggle, progress, and regress that Honneth sketches in the course of his normative reconstructions, so I will mostly limit myself to accounting for their systematic results.

In the first sphere of personal relations, Honneth locates three distinct but complementary institutions of social freedom: namely, friendships, intimate relations of love, and the family. Firstly, the modern form of friendship is an institution of social freedom—indeed, Honneth suggests, it is 'the most elementary foundation of democratic ethical life'—because the mutual role-obligations that parties to a friendship undertake allow subjects to experience their own wills as desired for their own sake by an 'other', whom they can place their trust and confide in: 'It is this experience of self-articulation, both desired and fulfilled, that makes friendship a homestead of social freedom'.[100] Secondly, in the institution of intimate relationships of love, we expect to be loved for not just our present but also our future particular qualities, and we further accept mutual role-obligations that secure and affirm our sexual needs and need for physical intimacy: 'In the intimacy of love, being with ourselves in the other therefore means recovering the natural neediness of our own self in physical interaction, without fear of being humiliated or hurt'.[101] Finally, in the institution of the family, the dyadic structure of intimate relationships is transformed into a triadic structure, between parents and the child(ren), in which Honneth finds not only a realized social freedom in mutual 'care and sympathy' between family members, but also a shared room for the virtual 'playful bracketing and suspension of age differences', as well as the very real reversal of relationships of care when parents reach old age. Indeed, he contends that the family may even provide a form of 'secular consolation': 'a measure of relief from the oppressive solitude and fear of death'. Finally, the

---

[100] Honneth, *Freedom's Right*, p. 140.
[101] Honneth, *Freedom's Right*, p. 151.

modern democratic family has also become a nursery for learning the 'attitudes and dispositions' necessary for shared cooperation in a democratic society.[102]

In all of Honneth's normative reconstructions of spheres of social freedom, he conducts historical analyses not only in order to lay bare the normative content of each institution of social freedom, but also to disclose systematic 'misdevelopments' by way of reconstructive critique. Such misdevelopments are different from the social pathologies that he detects in the institutional complexes of legal and moral freedom, since misdevelopments are 'anomalies whose sources must be sought elsewhere, not in the constitutive rules of the respective system of action.'[103] Clearly, the notion of misdevelopments depends on the idea of a correct of *normal* development of a relational action system, and this standard of normality is given by the moral norms constitutive of each institution of social freedom: where institutions systematically 'fail to meet the demand of social freedom underlying the respective sphere of action', they exhibit such social misdevelopments. Moreover, these misdevelopments are of course influenced by government policy and other kinds of agential power, but it is clear that Honneth most often has subtler and less intentional transformations in the institutions of social freedom in mind— that is, various *structural transformations* that undermine the social conditions of individual autonomy embodied in communicative relations of intersubjective recognition.

In the sphere of personal relations, Honneth does indeed locate a number of potential misdevelopments—especially concerning market-induced commodification of friendships and intimate relations, and insufficient legal support for the democratized family—but the overall picture that emerges is that the institutions of social freedom found in the action systems of personal relations are, alone among the three spheres of social freedom, in fairly good shape: not only has the institution of friendship proven remarkably resilient in the face of attempts to convert the mutual articulation and affirmation of each other's will for its own sake into strategic forms of 'networking', but as a consequence of the explosive learning process of moral individualization and inclusivity that took place in the affluent postwar European democracies, intimate relationships, and the institution of the family have become increasingly inclusive, heterogeneous, and democratized. With the progress in recognition of non-heterosexual couples and greater equality not only between mothers and fathers, but also between parents and children, the sphere of social freedom that is personal relations tends—in Honneth's view—to actually deliver on its promise of social freedom.

Things could not be more different with the second sphere of social freedom: the market economy. In the institutions of the 'sphere of consumption' and the 'capitalist labour market', Honneth finds in recent misdevelopments a glaring

---

[102] Honneth, *Freedom's Right*, pp. 164–176
[103] Honneth, *Freedom's Right*, pp. 128–129.

contradiction between the promise of social freedom on which they rest and the dire reality of what they actually deliver. Of course, in viewing the institutional sphere of the market economy as resting on a promise of social freedom, Honneth departs quite radically not only from Marx, but also, following him, from Horkheimer, Adorno, and Habermas: where Horkheimer speaks in categorical terms of fact that 'there exists no reasonable relationship between the free competition amongst individuals ... and society as a whole' as 'the great defect of the *bourgeois* economic model',[104] Habermas views the market economy as a functional subsystem that relies only on strategic interaction between economic agents, and which therefore offers no internal normative criteria for immanent critique. By contrast, Honneth follows Hegel and Durkheim in their more positive estimation of the moral foundations of economic interaction, which goes beyond viewing markets merely as strategic action systems predicated on negative freedom of contract to interpreting them as institutions of social freedom in their own right:

> According to Hegel and Durkheim, the market can only fulfil its function of harmoniously integrating individual economic activities in an unforced manner and by means of contractual relations if it is embedded in feelings of solidarity that precede all contracts and obligate economic actors to treat each other fairly and justly.[105]

More specifically, Honneth interprets this view of the market in terms of a 'normative functionalism', which holds that 'the market economy relies on an "ethical" framework of pre-contractual norms because it is only under this normative condition that it can garner the consent of all economic actors'.[106] Accordingly, Honneth maintains that there is an 'intrinsic connection' between the conditions of economic interaction and the generally accepted norms of the lifeworld, which implies that 'markets must be able to reflect the rules prevailing outside the market to a certain degree in order to be able to fulfil their function of coordinating economic action'. If markets do not reflect these normative expectations, 'then we can expect not only a disruption of the market mechanism itself, but also a subtle or publicly articulated withdrawal of legitimacy on the part of the population'.[107] The norm of social freedom that Honneth identifies as the moral foundation of market institutions is that

> the purely individual self-interest constitutive of market behaviour must be able to fulfil the normative condition that all participants can understand it

---

[104] Horkheimer, 'Materialismus und Moral', p. 116.
[105] Honneth, *Freedom's Right*, p. 181.
[106] Honneth, *Freedom's Right*, p. 183.
[107] Honneth, *Freedom's Right*, p. 191.

as a suitable means for the complementary realization of their own respective purposes. Negative or contractual freedom, whose institutionalization is what enables the dynamism of the capitalist economy, is limited by a threshold beyond which actors can no longer regard this freedom as a form of their social freedom.[108]

Accordingly, the legitimacy of the increases in economic efficiency enabled by markets thus depends upon their ability to fulfil the higher-order moral promise of participants' mutual recognition of the freedom of one as a condition for the freedom of the other.[109] That is to say, on Honneth's view, it is only when participants can actually see competition as complimentarily realizing their individual aims that the institutions of the market constitute a sphere of social freedom. As a consequence of this view of markets as a sphere of social freedom, Honneth maintains, *pace* Marx:

> Neither the problem of exploitation nor that of enforced contracts should be grasped as structural deficits that can only be removed by abolishing the capitalist market economy, but as challenges posed by the market's own normative promise, which can thus only be solved within the market system itself.[110]

This also implies that purely economic transactions enabled by negative freedom must be complemented by what Honneth calls 'discursive procedures for coordinating interests' and 'bastions of equality of opportunity' that can legally secure the mutual solidarity and complimentary satisfaction of individual ends on which both the functional requirements and moral legitimacy of markets ultimately depend. Indeed, Honneth takes the presence and degree of influence of such discursive mechanisms for interest articulation and coordination as labour unions and consumer cooperatives to be the principal criterion of moral progress or misdevelopment in the institutions of the market.

As I noted above, Honneth locates two institutions of social freedom in the market economy: the 'sphere of consumption', and the 'labour market'. In the first case, 'the market for consumer goods can be understood as an institutionalized relation of mutual recognition, provided that the relationship between sellers and consumers contributes to the complementary realization of each party's legitimate interests'.[111] Historically, demands for such recognition have been expressed by collective actors such as 'social movements that demand "fair" prices in the face of massive supply shortages, ethically motivated movements that demand restrictions on luxury consumption, political forces that call for government protection

---

[108] Honneth, *Freedom's Right*, pp. 191–192.
[109] Honneth, *Freedom's Right*, p. 192.
[110] Honneth, *Freedom's Right*, p. 196.
[111] Honneth, *Freedom's Right*, p. 208.

of consumers, and finally, numerous consumer cooperatives'.[112] Honneth details the dialectical history of progress and regress, in which the democratic labour movement and the student movement represent high points. However, he ultimately reaches the disconcerting conclusion that 'the market-mediated sphere of consumption has not become an element of democratic ethical life over the last several decades'.[113]

To the contrary, globalization and cultural shifts have in recent years conjoined to facilitate a comprehensive 'privatization' of consumption, where the monumental asymmetries between the immense commercial power of multinational corporations and the lone consumer have left the latter in a situation of isolated vulnerability that seem to confirm Horkheimer and Adorno's most dire conclusions about the culture industry's manufacturing of needs. Multinational conglomerates are free to pursue their economic advantage with few legal restrictions or opposition in civil society, and consumers are bereft of any possibility of exercising informed collective influence on both the *kinds* of goods marketed, the supporting marketing infrastructure, and the extent to which the level and form of consumption contributes to potentially catastrophic climate change. Indeed, the sphere of consumption is today almost clinically cleansed of the consumer cooperatives, social movements, and other discursive mechanisms of the past. This leads Honneth to the conclusion that, when regarded as a prospective sphere of social freedom, the market for consumer goods is characterized by such all-pervasive misdevelopments that its inherent promise of institutionalized reciprocal realization of the legitimate interests of both sellers and consumers is comprehensively contradicted by its present-day reality.

In the case of the labour market, things are no less alarming. According to Honneth, the moral content of social freedom in the labour market can be gauged not only, as before, in the works of Hegel and Durkheim, but also in the demands written on the banners of the early labour movement, which sought 'a radical socialization of the freedom of contract presupposed by the capitalist labour market by defining income, social protections and an adequate recognition of their labour skills as core elements of this freedom'.[114] That is to say, the labour market can be understood as an institution of social freedom only if such demands as a decent income, unemployment insurance, and public affirmation of a worker's productive contribution are established as necessary conditions for the legitimacy of labour contracts. Conversely,

> the capitalist labour market is regarded as unjustified or illegitimate as soon as it no longer guarantees participants a living wage, does not adequately honour

---

[112] Honneth, *Freedom's Right*, p. 208.
[113] Honneth, *Freedom's Right*, p. 220.
[114] Honneth, *Freedom's Right*, pp. 228–229.

work in terms of wage levels and social reputation, or no longer offers a sense of being cooperatively involved in the social division of labour.[115]

Tracing the dialectical back and forth between progress and regress, Honneth uncovers a moral developmental path, which may initially have suggested a future in which 'legal, educational and workplace conditions were to be institutionalized, thus ultimately enabling all wage labourers to see themselves involved in the social division of labour under conditions of true equality of opportunity'.[116] Indeed, Honneth's point is that these demands for a proper wage, for social recognition of the labourer's productive contribution, and for a modicum of influence in the 'sphere of production' should be seen as moral demands that are *intrinsic* to the labour market. Since they are articulated in the labour market's own terms, as basic conditions for its moral legitimacy as a social institution, those demands should be seen as constitutive of the capitalist labour market as a sphere of social freedom, which requires reciprocity of power and equality of opportunity amongst workers and between workers and capital owners.

However, in spite of all his efforts to bolster the claim that the labour market should indeed be interpreted as an institution of social freedom, Honneth paradoxically ends up concluding that this promise of social freedom is today so thoroughgoingly contradicted by recent developments that the labour market effectively tends towards becoming an institution of mere negative freedom and egotistical conduct. Again, the misdevelopments are traced out in terms of the absence of discursive mechanisms that can help participants to coordinate interests and adopt the perspective of others. Honneth again locates the causes of their absence in the confluence of globalization and monumental cultural shifts—from an understanding of the labour market as a sphere of collective action, responsibility, and solidarity to an almost complete 'privatization' of the responsibility for the individual's own fate.[117] As a consequence of this misdeveloped individualization, workers are increasingly stripped of any bulwark of protection that might mitigate the disruptive effects of economic globalization and the 'gradual autonomization of the imperatives of the financial and capital markets'.[118] Indeed, it 'is perhaps in this last impression, in this feeling of being solely responsible for one's own occupational destiny, that the key lies to explaining the oppressive silence with which all the growing insecurity and flexibility in the sphere of social labour are currently accepted'.[119]

This leads to the following, sobering conclusion: 'The market is no longer viewed as a social institution for which we all share responsibility as members of a

---

[115] Honneth, *Freedom's Right*, p. 246.
[116] Honneth, *Freedom's Right*, p. 249.
[117] One might not only point to consistently falling rates of union membership but also to the rise of the new platform or 'gig' economy as clear indications of these trends.
[118] Honneth, *Freedom's Right*, p. 245.
[119] Honneth, *Freedom's Right*, p. 248.

cooperating community, but as an arena of competition in which the aim is to maximize the utility for which we are all individually responsible'.[120] In other words, in its contemporary reality, the crucially important institution of the capitalist labour market is no longer an institution of social freedom, in which individuals are able to see each other's freedom as conditions of their own. Rather, while the labour movement's past achievements in legal protection, living wages, and social recognition are gradually being eroded under the pressures of globalization and financialization, the labour market has *in fact* been reduced to the internally depoliticized system of purely strategic action orientations that Habermas's more cynical view of its normative foundations suggests.

On a side note, one enabling condition for these misdevelopments that Honneth fails to consider is that, despite some efforts, above all in Scandinavia, the labour movement across the West has completely failed to *democratize* ownership of the means of production. As research in political economy in recent years has shown, economic inequality is today very much driven by increased concentration of wealth, which—along with economic globalization, which has itself been a main driver of both wealth and income inequality—has contributed to exacerbating the power asymmetries between organized labour and capital that Honneth rightly bemoans.[121] According to a number of prominent scholars of economic inequality, these asymmetries can only be effectively curtailed by *deconcentrating* ownership through alternatives to private ownership, such as public ownership, workers' ownership funds, 'community wealth building' and other forms of democratic ownership.[122] It may not be completely off the mark to speculate that Honneth's blindness to the role that questions of *ownership* play as a crucial enabling condition for the structural misdevelopments in the economic life of Western societies that he identifies can be traced back to his systematic concern with repudiating Marx's more cynical view of the capitalist market—questions that, as I argued in Chapter 1, a critical theory of world society must be able to address.

Finally, in the third sphere of social freedom that Honneth reconstructs—the sphere of 'democratic will-formation'—we are already broadly familiar with the moral content of the mutually dependent institutions of the 'public sphere' and the 'democratic rule of law' (*demokratischer Rechtsstaat*) that Honneth uncovers, since his normative reconstruction of this sphere closely follows Habermas's reconstruction of the self-understanding of the democratic constitutional state. First, in the institution of the public sphere, Honneth defends Habermas's account of the public

---

[120] Honneth, *Freedom's Right*, p. 251.
[121] Piketty, *Capital in the Twenty-First Century*.
[122] Anthony B. Atkinson, *Inequality: What Can Be Done* (Cambridge MA: Harvard University Press, 2015); Branko Milanovic, *Capitalism Alone: The Future of the System that Rules the World* (Cambridge MA: Harvard University Press, 2019); Joe Guinan and Martin O'Neill, *The Case for Community Wealth Building* (London: Wiley, 2019).

sphere first sketched in *Strukturwandel der Öffentlichkeit* against Hannah Arendt's more institutionally decoupled account of 'public spaces':

> With the gradual synthesis of the universal right to vote with the right to assemble and form political associations, the communicative conditions arose, more incidentally than intentionally, under which citizens in free association could reach an understanding about which practical and political principles should be enforced by the representative bodies involved in parliamentary legislation.[123]

To be sure, even as these conditions were gradually transformed into a principle of legitimacy for political rule, the legal inclusion of women and the propertyless was significantly slower to take hold, and powerful informal cultural mechanisms of exclusion were operative far into the postwar period. Moreover, in addition to the first and foundational condition of constitutional rights, Honneth emphasizes that the norm of social freedom in the democratic public sphere rests on a set of more informal but fairly demanding and often-underappreciated conditions of possibility. Second, the public sphere also rests on 'material conditions' such as the availability of 'leisure time' and the unpaid willingness of citizens to engage in the more pedestrian logistical tasks of arranging and advertising town hall meetings and public debate, as well as, third, an all-important medial infrastructure. Indeed, in the generalized political context of the nation-state, to which the idea of the democratic public sphere became intimately attached from early on, the existence of mass media that are able to fulfil their original *raison d'être* of informing citizens about existing state of affairs emerges as an all-important condition of possibility for the social freedom of the democratic public sphere:

> As soon as the media fulfil their task of providing the general knowledge required for dealing with social problems, the members of society will be capable, under conditions of equal rights to freedom and participation, to commonly explore appropriate solutions and work cooperatively toward the experimental consummation of their community.[124]

Fourth, a democratic public sphere also presupposes the existence of a 'class-transcending, universal communicative space that enables different groups and classes affected by political decisions to enter into an exchange of opinions.'[125] Fifth, it crucially relies on the uncoerced motivation of citizens to engage in public will-formation, and, when this motivation is absent, it risks being undermined by widespread political 'apathy' or 'depoliticization', with negative and potentially disruptive consequences for the legitimation of political power. Both the universal

---

[123] Honneth, *Freedom's Right*, p. 260.
[124] Honneth, *Freedom's Right*, p. 274.
[125] Honneth, *Freedom's Right*, p. 290.

communicative space and motivational support has long been provided by a national political culture, which has engendered the necessary norms of solidarity and sufficient sense of shared commonality across political and class differences. Finally, a no less important sixth condition is that 'members of society who supplement each other in their communicative exchange of views must feel that the products of their will-formation are effective enough to be practised in social reality'[126]—which points to the second institution of democratic will-formation: namely, the democratic constitutional state.

In Honneth's normative reconstruction of the democratic constitutional state as an institution of social freedom, it is Habermas's democratic principle that serves as the guiding moral criterion. In this view,

> the modern state is conceived on the basis of the conditions of social freedom for members of society who recognize each other's capacity for judgement; it represents the 'reflexive organ' or the network of political authorities that help communicating individuals implement their 'experimentally' or 'deliberatively' derived ideas of the morally and practically appropriate solution to social problems in reality.[127]

In the course of its conflictual twentieth century developmental process towards the postwar welfare state—which was, in many European countries, completely interrupted during the time of Europe's fascist dictatorships—the democratic constitutional state won an ever-greater degree of regulative competence and ability to intervene in the spheres of personal relations and the economic market, with massive increases in the reach of its authority that were not always followed by corresponding increases in its legitimacy. However, throughout this development, the democratic constitutional state always stood in a conflictual relationship of tension not only with the capitalist economic structure, but also with the growing and passing strength of nationalist sentiments. These tensions are also Honneth's key to disclosing the misdevelopments that the democratic constitutional state and the intrinsically connected democratic public sphere have undergone in recent years, when interpreted as institutions of social freedom.

In the institution of the public sphere, Honneth sees two recent misdevelopments. First, he laments the failure of the mass media to serve their morally required function of facilitating information about actual states of affairs. Indeed, as a result of increasingly being sucked into the vortex of commercial supply and demand, the mass media has degenerated into a sensationalist industry, in which the profound epistemic problem arises that existing states of affairs are no longer merely reported but virtual realities are increasingly *created*:

---

[126] Honneth, *Freedom's Right*, p. 304.
[127] Honneth, *Freedom's Right*, pp. 305–306.

These virtualizing tendencies of traditional media pose a significant difficulty for our normative reconstruction; according to the criteria inherent in the democratic public sphere itself, these tendencies must be regarded as a misdevelopment because they no longer sufficiently inform the public, but rather produce reality self-referentially. Even stronger than in other social spheres, the communication processes in the public sphere have been so dramatized by media reporting that it is quite difficult to separate reality from fiction and get a sober look at real social developments.[128]

This tendency for the mass media to abandon the function of serving to enlighten and inform the citizenry in favour of mere entertainment and a virtualization of reality is only reinforced by the second misdevelopment. This is the increasing fragmentation of the public sphere brought about by globalization-driven tendencies towards the formation of transnational publics, reserved for a cosmopolitan elite while excluding and effectively disenfranchising the 'new "services proletariat", migrants and welfare recipients'.[129] Honneth considers the myriad forums and platforms of social media on the Internet as a digital infrastructure with the potential to reinvigorate the public sphere across class and political divides, but because of the internal segmentation and fragmentation of online public discussion, he fears that

> the digitally enabled expansion and unbounding of the political communicative space could have the paradoxical effect of destroying or at least weakening the very political culture in mature democracies that had previously motivated moral efforts to include all citizens in the space of collective self-legislation.[130]

Although the jury is still out when it comes to the overall effects of the Internet on the public sphere—my own inclination would lean towards a somewhat more ambivalent estimation—Honneth suggests that it could potentially support the uncoupling of new transnational public spheres reserved for a privileged elite and effectively inaccessible for those who need new channels of public articulation the most.

In the institution of the democratic constitutional state, Honneth locates misdevelopments that will again be familiar from Chapter 5 on Habermas's communicative paradigm. Specifically, Honneth follows Habermas in observing 'an increasing decoupling of the political system from democratic will-formation', which is reflected in the suspicion among large parts of the population that 'state authorities' are no longer 'committed to the principle of neutrality demanded by

---

[128] Honneth, *Freedom's Right*, p. 297.
[129] Honneth, *Freedom's Right*, p. 303.
[130] Honneth, *Freedom's Right*, p. 303.

the democratic constitution'. However, whereas such suspicions were in an earlier age aroused by more obvious corporatist practices or the political rulers' open preferential treatment of capital interests,

> today the bias of the state in favour of capitalist profit interests seems to be entirely hidden from public view, because the corresponding governmental measures are either not addressed in parliament at all or are justified with reference to objective constraints [*Sachzwänge*].[131]

The 'more freedom that business has gained over the last quarter century to pursue its profit interests, the more the state has been put at the mercy of the former's increased capacity for obstruction'; however, what is perhaps most disconcerting about these developments is that 'the mere suspicion, substantiated by occasional journalistic research, that individual state decisions add up to a systematic privileging of business interests is enough for citizens to retreat from public arenas of political will-formation'.[132] In Honneth's view, this reaction of withdrawal is not simply caused by a lack of interest in political affairs, but rather due to 'the sober realization that the social freedom of democratic self-legislation has not been extended to the corresponding organs of the constitutional state'.[133]

The sum of this critical social analysis of the reality of freedom in modern Western society is hardly uplifting. To be sure, Honneth paints a highly differentiated picture, which is sensitive both to the forms of moral progress that have received institutionalized expression, particularly in the sphere of personal relations, as well as the substantial and disheartening misdevelopments that presently characterize the institutions of the capitalist market and democratic will-formation. However, because European national cultures are 'drying up' as sources of solidarity and social recognition under the sustained pressure from economic globalization, and we thus seem bereft of the only existing pool of normative resources that would enable and motivate a 'public, multi-voiced opposition' against the might of globalized markets, Honneth—just like Habermas—sees the only way out of the cul-de-sac that the democratic constitutional state presently finds itself in as being the possibility of an inclusive European political culture and transnational constitutional-democratic framework. However, before I proceed, in Chapter 8, to a more systematic discussion of Honneth's reflections on the injustices of neoliberal globalization, as well as the possibilities for countering them, I want to add a few further remarks to the conception of moral normativity and moral-theoretical method realized in Honneth's mature work.

---

[131] Honneth, *Freedom's Right*, p. 326.
[132] Honneth, *Freedom's Right*, p. 326 [translation amended—or rather, translation appears incomplete].
[133] Honneth, *Freedom's Right*, p. 326.

7.4.4 A Hegelian Account of Moral Normativity

The starting point for Honneth's account of moral normativity and his moral-theoretical method is the claim that once a theory of justice sets its eyes on relations of communicative freedom rather than individual rights claims to resources or well-being, it has a systematic impact on what *kind* of theory of justice it is:

> Our conception of justice is thereby stripped of its character as a theory of distribute justice and takes on the form of a normative theory of communication; in the place of principles for distributive fairness, we instead have principles oriented towards state guarantees of the social presuppositions of mutual recognition.[134]

This seems to me an extremely important insight, which is as true of all the paradigms of critical theory as it is of systematic interest for the overall project pursued in this book: given the Frankfurt School commitment to communicative freedom, we should not expect what I have called a critical theory of justice to bear any close resemblance to mainstream distributive conceptions of justice in contemporary political theory, since a critical theory of justice is concerned—from a normative point of view—with the establishment of intersubjective relationships that enable subjects' individual autonomy through mutual recognition and reciprocal empowerment. Moreover, for the same reason, a critical theory of justice is not concerned with distributive patterns for their own sake, but rather with illuminating and evaluating existing relationships and identifying ways of overcoming relations and structures that impair the autonomy of individual subjects—including, of course, the structure of the distribution of wealth and resources.

In Honneth's reflections on this question, he draws a very close connection—and, I will argue, closer than necessary—between a concern with intersubjective relations of communicative freedom on the one hand, and the theoretical structure of Hegel's *Rechtsphilosophie*, as well as Hegel's *moral-theoretical method* and account of *moral normativity* on the other. Perhaps the most straightforward way to clarify the latter two aspects is to contrast them with the Kantian account of moral theory and normativity that we find in Habermas's communicative paradigm. In Habermas's discourse ethics, we find a *constructivist* account of moral normativity, where Habermas sees the universalization principle as the procedure implicitly at work when we construct the cognitive content of moral norms in communicative interaction. To be sure, we should not understand Habermas as claiming that morally acting individuals must incessantly apply the universalization principle, such as in Kant's 'monological' account of the categorical imperative;

---

[134] Axel Honneth, 'Gerechtigkeit und kommunikative Freiheit. Überlegungen im Anschluss an Hegel', *Eurozine* 15/1-2007: p. 7 [my translation].

rather, Habermas sketches a 'dialogical' form of moral constructivism, in which moral norms are intersubjectively constructed through a rule for moral argumentation that derives from the very nature of moral validity claims. Moreover, as we saw in Chapter 5, Habermas does not believe that moral theory can *justify* substantive moral norms or intuitions, but it must limit itself to a reconstructive account of the moral point of view. Accordingly, Habermas explicitly refuses to provide a theory of justice, but offers, in some sense, a more normatively modest account of how the discursive conditions for the justification of moral, ethical, and pragmatic norms can be sufficiently realized in the system of rights of a democratic constitutional state.

Honneth's Hegelian account of moral theory and normativity is in an important sense considerably more demanding than Habermas's Kantian account: rather than understanding moral theory in terms of a procedure for the construction of moral norms, Honneth follows Hegel in construing moral theory as concerned with those habitually learned norms that have been embedded into spheres of action, and thus as expressed in what Hegel's calls the 'objective will'. This moves the focus of moral theory from the procedure at work in moral construction towards those spheres of social freedom that actually contribute to enabling and realizing individual autonomy in modern society. Indeed, according to Honneth, the distinctive Hegelian claim is precisely that even a Kantian account of a constructivist moral procedure *cannot do without* an already-realized and logically antecedent framework of moral norms, i.e. that 'the general validity of certain moral norms must already be presupposed in order for the procedure of individual or communicative self-determination to be intelligible in the first place'.[135] Of course, these norms can only be described as moral to the extent that the communicative relations in which they are embedded *actually* enable the autonomy of individuals:

> Thus for Hegel, the standard model of the social efficacy of morality is the collective appropriation of ethical norms, whose validity is owed to the fact that the members of a group mutually grant each other the authority to evaluate their respective applications of those norms.[136]

It is precisely because of this 'social embedding' of morality that—as we saw at the end of Section 7.3—Honneth no less than Hegel needs a criterion of moral progress in history to safeguard this conception of moral normativity as ethical life from the suspicion of conventionalism.

Honneth's account of moral theory and normativity is also stronger than Habermas's in a further sense, since he is convinced that the demonstration that certain

---

[135] Axel Honneth, 'The Normativity of Ethical Life', transl. by Felix Koch, *Philosophy and Social Criticism* (40/8), 2014: pp. 817–826, p. 817.
[136] Honneth, 'The Normativity of Ethical Life', pp. 821–822.

spheres of social freedom are necessary conditions for individual autonomy also *justifies* these spheres, and that such a demonstration is *sufficient* for justifying them. That is to say, Honneth construes the analysis offered in *Das Recht der Freitheit* not as a second-order procedural account that leaves the content of moral norms unspecified, but as a first-order *substantive theory of justice* that sketches the basic institutional requirements of societal morality. Moreover, what is particularly striking about this theory is that Honneth follows Hegel in not justifying his theory of a just basic structure with reference to an independent principle of moral construction, but construes such constructivist principles as a necessary but inherently limited aspect of morality, with the emphasis on the spheres of social freedom that establish the reality of freedom and morality. As we shall see in the next chapter, this Hegelian conception of moral theory and normativity presents us with a significant dilemma, if we seek to employ this reconstructive methodology as a basis for a critical theory of world society—a dilemma, which suggests that Honneth may have wedded his recognition paradigm *too closely* to existing spheres of social freedom.

I want to close this section by addressing a criticism levelled at *Leiden an Unbestimmtheit* and other parts of Honneth's earlier work by Robert Pippin, which is also of more general relevance for the systematic intentions of this book. According to Pippin, Honneth's earlier work in fact remains *insufficiently Hegelian*, so to speak, in construing the spheres of communicative freedom necessary for individual autonomy as derivative of rights claims—although, somewhat curiously, not of the rights of individuals but rather of *social spheres*. According to Pippin, Honneth thereby construes the social conditions for the free will's existence as 'entitlement claims', which, Pippin claims, is simply incoherent:

> A common ethical life cannot be understood as the object of a rights or general entitlement claim if that life amounts to a necessary pre-condition of the determinate meaning and binding force of such a rights claim ... (The somewhat paradoxical situation here is captured by a nice image used by Martin Hollis: how could Eve have possibly known whether it was right or wrong to eat of the fruit of the tree of the knowledge of good and evil, before she did? [there is no point at which Eve could have said: 'Adam, let's invent language'.]) ... It does not, I think, help much to argue, as Honneth does, that these 'social forms of existence' can themselves be said to have rights ... The notion of a right, no matter the bearer, is tied necessarily to the capacity to place others under an obligation, and if such social forms are said to have a right to existence, then by parity of reasoning we will have to ask again, under what social pre-pre-conditions could such claim to entitlement have binding actual force?[137]

---

[137] Pippin, *Hegel's Practical Philosophy*, p. 257 [the text in square brackets is imported from a footnote].

It seems to me that Pippin misunderstands what Honneth means by claiming that 'social spheres' are 'bearers of rights', although Honneth's language certainly invites the misinterpretation.[138] The point of that claim is not to construe the social conditions of individual autonomy—and, perforce, of the capacity to make entitlement claims—as entitlement claims enjoyed *by those spheres* (which would indeed be nonsensical), but rather to construe rights as having the 'double meaning of a "necessary condition" and a "justifiable claim"'.[139] Indeed, it is of course precisely the fact that these spheres are necessary conditions for the autonomy of *individual* subjects that makes their 'claim' to existence justifiable.[140] Individual autonomy therefore also has the parallel double meaning of what we might call a *socially enabled capacity* and a *normative status*, where it is the normative status of autonomy that *justifies* the conditions necessary for its social and psychological efficacy.

Moreover, contrary to what Pippin suggests, there is nothing incoherent about the idea that the normative status of individual autonomy justifies its own necessary social conditions. Indeed, as is obvious from his analogy with pre-linguistic Eve, Pippin's claim that individuals cannot have a moral right to the social conditions that establish 'the determinate meaning and binding force' of rights in the first place falsely relies on the extreme picture in which somebody who does not possess even the concept of a right is supposed to enjoy a right to the conditions for doing so. But such an extreme and arguably problematic situation is not relevant to the question at hand: we are not talking about the abstract question, whether it makes sense for x to have a right to y, which he does not yet have access to, and where having access to y is a necessary condition for x to even begin to understand what having a right means; rather, we are talking about the kind of historical developmental processes that Honneth sketches in *Kampf um Anerkennung* and *Das Recht der Freiheit*—that is, long conflictual processes of struggle for emancipation from domination, which should be understood as a relative continuum rather than as an absolute either-or.

From this historical point of view, as soon as the conditions for individuals and social groups to articulate their grievances in terms of rights claims had been *sufficiently* realized—as was the case, for example, with the early labour movement's invocation of rights to a shorter working day—such that they were able to appreciate the contradiction between the normative ideals and harsh reality of modern *bourgeois* society, these individuals and groups began to struggle for the *full* realization of the conditions for individual and collective self-determination. Therefore, Pippin's analogy with pre-linguistic Eve doesn't hold up; what we are talking about is not equivalent to the suggestion 'let's invent rights' before any

---

[138] Honneth, *The Pathologies of Individual Freedom*, p. 17.
[139] Honneth, *The Pathologies of Individual Freedom*, p. 15.
[140] Honneth, *The Pathologies of Individual Freedom*, p. 18.

degree of social freedom is even realized, but is rather a graduated demand for the *full realization* of a normative promise that is sufficiently embedded in social institutions for individual subjects to take that promise as a point of normative orientation. Within *our modern normative horizon*, there is nothing incoherent about the claim that individuals have a right to the full realization of the social and psychological conditions necessary for their individual autonomy.

8
Honneth's Recognition Paradigm and the Idea of a Critical Theory of World Society

8.1 Beyond Social Freedom?

In this chapter, I construct the implications of Honneth's recognition paradigm for a critical theory of world society. Before doing so, it is worth noting that before *Das Recht der Freiheit*, one would be hard pressed to find much sustained discussion or even a mention of globalization in Honneth's work—which strongly suggests that he has not been much concerned with the global implications of his thought, or of the implications of questions relating to the global context, before writing that book. In what follows, I will briefly expound the implications for world society of his earlier theory of the struggle for recognition, before moving on to the more mature work.

8.1.1 A Western-European 'Culture of Freedom'

In the 'Postscript' to *Kamp um Anerkennung*, Honneth clarifies what we might call the *ontological status* of recognition:

> I now distinguish much more sharply than in my original approach between 'anthropological' starting conditions and historical contingency: although the human form of life as a whole is marked by the fact that individuals can gain social membership and thus a positive relation-to-self only via mutual recognition, its form and content change during the differentiation of normatively regulated spheres of action.[1]

This distinction makes clear that while Honneth believes that *recognition simpliciter* is a universal or 'basic' human practice necessary for any kind of social interaction, he now also suggests that *all the three patterns* of recognition are historically contingent. For a critical theory of world society, this implies that there

---

[1] Honneth, 'Grounding Recognition', p. 501.

is no natural presumption that all societies on Earth must necessarily contain the patterns of recognition characteristic of Western modernity, i.e., the patterns of primary relationships, legal relations, and communities of value.

To be sure, the claim that these patterns are historically contingent does not necessarily imply a very wide scope of global variation. If, say, Habermas's claim that the great civilizations have generally followed similar cognitive developmental paths and that all cultures must today exist within the same modernizing global infrastructure, the picture would of course be less heterogeneous than one might be tempted to suspect. For example, as Honneth initially suggests, some form of love and care does seem like an effectively universal human need, and global pluralism has also been kept in check by such historical factors as ancient empires; colonialism and anticolonialism; world wars; successive waves of capitalist expansion, economic development, and—more recently—the forces of economic globalization; the global spread of information technology and the rise of the Internet; and the radiating force of the world's commercial cultural centres, such as Hollywood. Owing to these past and present forces of global integration, the global variance among patterns of recognition is likely to be less extensive than their ontological status as historically contingent would in theory allow.

However, the putative historical contingency of patterns of recognition also suggests that the more interesting implications of Honneth's recognition paradigm for a critical theory of world society are to be found in those institutions of social freedom in which the three different patterns of recognition receive concrete social expression. Accordingly, this turns our attention towards the theory of justice as critical social analysis that Honneth develops in *Das Recht der Freiheit*. To begin with, it is clear that globalization plays a, if not *the*, leading role in Honneth's account of misdevelopments in the spheres of social freedom—but it is at the same time conspicuously absent from the book's theoretical framework. Indeed, globalization generally seems to have the character of an external force that disrupts the institutions of social freedom from without, but which does not—as Honneth emphasizes in his contradistinction between misdevelopments and social pathologies—*itself* derive from those spheres of social freedom. Indeed, because Honneth is explicitly concerned with reconstructing the 'culture of freedom'[2] within 'Western Europe',[3] globalization inevitably has the character of a virulent and somewhat mysterious disruptive force that tears apart the moral fabric of social freedom realized in a long and painstaking history of moral progress and regress—arguably, much as it is today experienced by many citizens of Western-European welfare states.

This brings us back to the question concerning the relationship between social integration and system integration, as discussed in Section 7.3. Recall that in

---

[2] Honneth, *Freedom's Right*, p. 62.
[3] Honneth, *Freedom's Right*, p. 334.

Honneth's debate with Nancy Fraser, he emphasizes that his 'monistic' recognition paradigm, which attempts to make do without the systems concept of Habermas's communicative paradigm and instead aspires to develop a critical theory of society from the singular perspective of the lifeworld, should be understood as sketching the normative *constraints* on the possibilities for capitalist development, rather than as accounting for that development as such. Indeed, consistent with this claim, Honneth insists that, as a sphere of social freedom, 'even the globalized economy is subject to the officially confirmed claim of universal equality of opportunity'.[4] That is to say, he insists that since labour and consumption markets have gradually become truly global institutions, their internal normative criteria of the reciprocal serving of interests and equality of opportunity are today also global in scope.

However, recall that in *Das Recht der Freiheit*, Honneth also speaks of 'a gradual autonomization of the imperatives of the financial and capital markets, which not only has consequences for the labour market, but also for the neighbouring social spheres'.[5] Part of this gradual autonomization can be explained by the increasing digitalization of financial markets and the so-called 'financialization' of capitalism—where the financial sector comes to represent a virtual economy of ever-greater size and importance vis-à-vis the 'real economy'. As he himself suggests, the particularly troubling thought for Honneth here is that in spite of its promise of social freedom—which, he maintains, lies at the foundation of the social institution of the economic market—it may just be the case that large parts of the global market economy have *in effect* become a functional subsystem of purely strategic action founded on the more limited or contractual conception of *negative* freedom, as suggested by Habermas.

This last point is also suggestive of a perhaps more troubling implication of Honneth's recognition paradigm for a critical theory of world society. Honneth understands the three patterns of recognition as historically contingent and only the need for recognition as such as an anthropological fact of human nature. In order to avoid relativist implications of this assumption, Honneth introduces two criteria of moral progress in history: specifically, he argues that it is the degree of inclusivity and individualization of historically contingent patterns of recognition that is supposed to provide a transhistorical standard for distinguishing between more or less morally advanced social institutions. However, when this robust account of moral progress is combined with the substantive account of the spheres of social freedom that we find in *Das Recht der Freiheit*, it might appear as if Honneth means to establish the whole institutional structure of social freedom characteristic of modern capitalist society in Western Europe—i.e. the norms of friendship, intimate relationship, marriage, the consumption market, the labour

---

[4] Honneth, *Freedom's Right*, p. 198.
[5] Honneth, *Freedom's Right*, p. 245.

market, the public sphere, and the democratic constitutional state—as the moral culmination of world history and the pinnacle of freedom and justice. Although this would of course be an impeccably *Hegelian* implication, it is less clear that Honneth would want to follow Hegel in this unabashed global projection of all the major social institutions of European modernity as a developmental blueprint for the rest of the world to follow.

Importantly, in *Das Recht der Freitheit*, Honneth is very concerned to limit his context of application to the confines of Western Europe, which suggests that he is indeed very mindful of this potential implication. However, there seems to be a real dilemma here: either Honneth allows that freedom can be reached through a plurality of social institutions—opening the door for claims that institutions embodying, for example, more authoritarian and collectivist 'Asian values' might also represent embodiments of social freedom—which would seem to undermine his attempts to resist relativist conventionalism and cast doubt on the robustness of his two criteria of moral progress. Or, he could stand his ground and maintain that the West is indeed leading the way in a moral learning process with global implications, which would evoke some of the more unappealing aspects of the legacy of the European colonial powers—and, it seems to me, be seriously at odds with Honneth's general moral outlook.

In *The End of Progress*, Amy Allen charges that Honneth's recognition paradigm of critical theory ultimately founders on this dilemma. More specifically, Allen takes aim at Honneth's conception of human history as a conflictual learning process of 'moral rationalization'.[6] Recall that Honneth relies on this conception of moral progress—by which progress is measured according to the two moral criteria of inclusivity and individualization in norms of recognition—to protect his reconstructive theory of justice from collapsing into relativist conventionalism. However, Allen argues, because Honneth needs such a robust notion of moral progress to ground the normative dimension of his recognition paradigm, he is at the same time 'committed to a strong claim about the cognitive superiority of European modernity'; a robust form of historicism in Dipesh Chakrabarty's sense, as discussed in Chapter 2, 'whereby European modernity seems to occupy a unique and superior place in the historical development of social, political, and ethical orders'.[7]

Allen envisions two ways that Honneth might respond to this objection. He might bite the bullet and insist that European modernity is indeed developmentally superior, but that this 'doesn't licence the further claim that we are justified in forcing our form of life on them'. Alternatively, Honneth might argue that the view of moral progress as a historical learning process only applies to the 'historical

---

[6] Honneth, 'The Irreducibility of Progress: Kant's Account of the Relationship Between Morality and History', p. 15.
[7] Allen, *The End of Progress*, p. 114.

antecedents' of European societies and 'does not entail any negative judgements regarding the developmental status of the forms of ethical life found in other societies'.[8] Honneth has himself suggested this second line of argument in response to an objection that his recognition paradigm is 'unable to give voice to the moral concerns of large portions of the world's population':

> This certainly articulates a valid concern, and it seems at first glance to simply identify the price that a reconstructive theory of justice must pay for accepting as well-founded claims of justice only those that can be recast as convincing criticisms of the limited or incomplete realization of obligations which already enjoy some institutionalized legitimacy. This means that the moral grievances rightfully voiced today in many parts of the world beyond the European continent fall within the purview of such a theory of justice only to the extent that they correspond to some implications of our own institutional structure.[9]

I shall take up this implication of Honneth's reconstructive method in the next subsection, but I agree with Allen that Honneth owes a more comprehensive response to this question. As I argued in the Introduction, I would maintain that Honneth's failure to offer a more comprehensive response to this worry is indicative of the fact that he has failed to devote much if any attention to the implications of taking world society as critical theory's context of application—or, indeed, to the extent to which one is compelled to theorize the many complex interconnections between the local and the global in any society within the context of global capitalist modernity. Once we do so, it is clear that such questions are not simply marginal side issues but sit at the heart of any attempt to revitalize the project of critical theory today.

However, I also want to argue that Honneth might have recourse to a third response, which Allen fails to consider. For Allen's claim that Honneth's conception of moral progress necessarily implies a commitment to the wholesale developmental superiority of European modernity is not only unwarranted but also in conflict with the disaggregated way that Honneth employs his conception of moral progress in *Das Recht der Freitheit*. My claim here is that it is both perfectly possible and consistent to affirm, say, a specific course of moral learning within personal relationships as an institution of social freedom in European society, while at the same time denying that we can judge European modernity *in toto* as morally or developmentally superior to non-Western lifeworlds that do not, for example, permit gay marriage—a very recent instance of moral progress even within Western societies. Moreover, the claim that *I* or *we* have become responsive to certain reasons for legalizing gay marriage does not entail the further judgement

---

[8] Allen, *The End of Progress*, pp. 115–116.
[9] Axel Honneth, 'Replies', *Krisis: Journal for Contemporary Philosophy* 1, 2013: pp. 37–47, p. 46.

that anyone who holds a different view on gay marriage is cognitively inferior. That kind of judgement takes place outside the space of normative reasoning and represents an explanatory attempt to *account for* the moral disagreement (with reference to the other's ostensible cognitive inferiority). Such a shift in register within the space of reasons (from the moral to the explanatory) transforms the relationship from one of moral disagreement to the other as a *problem* to be made sense of—or to be dealt with. But such a shift already *presupposes* that I or we have stopped thinking of the other as a co-reasoner with whom I or we morally disagree, which is precisely the point at stake here.

What Allen in my view rightly identifies and objects to from a decolonial point of view is the historical intertwinement of totalizing appraisals of European modernity as cognitively and morally superior with colonial and imperial subjection of non-Western societies (and those fragmented communities that were violently forced into colonial state forms in the course of colonization). In colonial and imperialist narratives, the cognitive and moral ranking of cultures serves the nakedly ideological function of justificatorily propping up relations of domination and exploitation of those subjected to foreign rule, and as postcolonial literature and theory attests, they still to varying degrees serve that function today in less formalized relations of domination and exploitation between the former imperial centres and postcolonial states.

But that fact of historical and actual intertwinement does not commit someone, who today is committed to viewing the legalization of gay marriage as a step in a continuous and still-ongoing process of moral learning in the social institution of personal relationships within a European society, to the further judgement that lifeworlds, which do not permit gay marriage, are wholesale morally and cognitively inferior. Rather, we might just as well think that we find ourselves in *deep moral disagreement* with those, who believe that gay marriage is an abomination, whether at home or abroad. Indeed, we might reason: just as we saw in Chapter 1 that the young Horkheimer employed *bourgeois* moral ideas in critique of the ideological function of legitimating actual *bourgeois* society, we must employ the insights that we have gained in moral learning in *critique* of developmentalist narratives, including those narratives that would instrumentalize the legalization of gay marriage in Europe for pernicious claims about non-European cultures as developmentally inferior and thus serve to uphold neocolonial relations of domination and exploitation across the world, as well as continued discrimination within Western societies. But I see no reason for thinking that such a critique necessarily presupposes that we relinquish the ability to make disaggregated judgements of moral progress within specific social institutions of our own lifeworlds. Accordingly, just as I argued in Chapter 6 that Allen's decolonial critique of Habermas's communicative paradigm misses its mark but instead demonstrates that any critical theory, which anchors its emancipatory guidance in an account of socio-cultural or moral learning processes, must guard against developmentalist narratives that would abuse the theory for justifying illegitimate neocolonial forms of power, I would argue that the same holds for her attempt to decolonize Honneth's recognition paradigm.

Moreover, one might argue that it is not just Honneth who faces a dilemma—so does Allen. She distinguishes between two different perspectives on progress—a backward-looking conception of progress as a historical 'fact', and a forward-looking conception of progress as a moral-practical 'imperative'—and she is at pains to deny the former, since, she argues, a self-congratulatory appraisal of European modernity as a model of moral progress is incompatible with postcolonial insights into the intertwinement of such a view with cultural and political imperialism. Moreover, Allen also objects to Honneth's claim that gay marriage represents an instance of moral progress by insisting that the very institution of marriage is both *heteronormative*, by privileging 'a bourgeois-romantic conception of heterosexual marriage', and *homonormative*, by excluding queer relationships that do not conform to this heterosexual norm. She argues that this commits Honneth to viewing cultures that do not allow gay marriage as 'backward or inferior', and that this judgement 'evinces an imperialist sensibility'.[10]

I have argued that the latter judgement doesn't follow. But I also think that her critique of Honneth's claim that gay marriage is an instance of moral progress is unsound. For Honneth is not committed to saying that the institution of *bourgeois* marriage represents the absolute pinnacle of moral progress within the social institution of personal relationships, as opposed to a comparative claim that inclusive marriage is all things considered more just and thus a moral improvement on more exclusive rules governing marriage, even if the legalization of gay marriage still implies an unjustified exclusion of queer relationships.

However, the perhaps more serious point for Allen is that her argument also seems to deprive *her own critique* of Honneth's qualified embrace of gay marriage of moral criteria by which she could morally appraise social struggles that might eventually lead to the abandonment or loosening of the strictures of *bourgeois* marriage as in fact a case of moral progress. Indeed, it seems to me that Allen's categorical rejection of any kind of backward-looking judgements of moral progress as historical fact—although motivated by undeniable postcolonial insights into the intertwinement of the developmentalist narratives of European modernity with cultural and political imperialism—is, in fact, deeply counterintuitive. Why should we commit ourselves to a view by which we observe the forward-looking imperative to *demand* moral progress, but by which we would at the same time deprive ourselves of the backward-looking ability—if that moral demand is met in practice—to say that such achievements of emancipatory social struggles represent instances of moral progress? I will return to a more in-depth exposition and discussion of the strengths and weaknesses of Allen's view in Chapter 9.

[10] Allen, *The End of Progress*, pp. 100–101.

8.1.2 The Limits of Hegelianism

I have argued that Honneth's recognition paradigm is not quite as vulnerable to Allen's critique as she claims—even though he owes her a more comprehensive, and satisfying, response. However, I want to argue that a further and, for Honneth, more troubling problem follows from his *Hegelian methodological assumptions*. The problem that worries me here is that Honneth's methodological procedures of normative reconstruction and reconstructive critique are dependent on the existence of already (if insufficiently) realized spheres of social freedom—given that no such institutions exist at the *global* or international level. Because Honneth's recognition paradigm is so wedded to the *existing* institutional structure of social freedom in modern Western-European societies, it seems to run into serious trouble if that institutional structure is *itself part of the problem*.

This problem comes to the fore, I believe, in the final section of *Das Recht der Freiheit*, where Honneth joins Habermas in calling for a strengthening and democratization of the European Union, since the more territorially extended European political institutions have a better chance at standing up to the pressures of global markets and thus counter the causes of misdevelopments in the institutions of social freedom of European societies. Because of Honneth's broader appreciation of the social conditions for the democratic public sphere and constitutional state, he emphasizes that such a transition would require nothing short of a post-national European political culture, which would have to contain sufficient normative resources to be able to motivate the hitherto fairly unenthusiastic Europeans to give up the last vestiges of exclusionary national sovereignty in favour of continental democracy and solidarity. In justifying this proposal, Honneth points to the fact that struggles for recognition on the European continent have long since acquired a transnational dynamic—as already evident, for example, in the aftershocks of the French revolution and the wave of democratic revolutions in 1848—which suggests that Europeans can *already* look back at a long and shared history in which their destinies have been deeply interlinked.

This seems to me an extremely important insight. But given Honneth's admission that a European political culture has until now failed to emerge, his call for the establishment of such a culture also seems to me to *run up against the limits of his own methodology*. For if no truly European-wide institutions of social freedom exist that we may describe as a shared European public sphere or a functioning democratic constitutional state, where does Honneth find the internal normative criteria by which to criticize the existing state of affairs and counsel transition to European democracy? This is a much more serious problem for Honneth than for Habermas, precisely because he rejects the latter's moral constructivism and defends a reconstructive approach that presupposes existing institutions, which embody (even if imperfectly) first-order moral norms constitutive of the social reality of individual autonomy. Seemingly recognizing this problem, Honneth admits that this plea for European social and political integration rests on 'little more than the hope that on the basis of this historical consciousness, we will see the development of a European culture of shared attentiveness and broadened solidarity'.[11]

What I ultimately want to suggest is that Honneth's recognition paradigm presents not just Honneth but also critical theory as such with an exceedingly difficult dilemma: although I believe Honneth is right to emphasize critical theory's foundational concern with intersubjective relations of communicative freedom, his Hegelian reconstructive method for spelling out this concern seems to effectively undercut the possibility of a critical theory of *world society*, since it is, on the one hand, highly questionable that we find any *global* or transnational institutions of social freedom, and, on the other, the limited territorial scope of existing institutions of social freedom may *itself* be part of what we ultimately have to overcome. If this is indeed the case, it is difficult to see how a methodological programme that presupposes already (if insufficiently) realized institutions of social freedom could countenance the prospect—forcefully defended by Habermas—that *even* full-fledged European social and political integration will in itself be insufficient to counter the assault on the legal-political conditions of individual autonomy presently issuing from global capitalism.

In the metaphysically overwrought conceptual vocabulary of Horkheimer's original paradigm of critical theory, it may very well be the case that this would require that *humanity* constitutes itself as a global subject—an idea that we find in a different and more restricted form in Habermas's call for a multilevel global constitutional framework. However, as suggested in Chapter 6, I do not think this problem can be overcome by a return to Habermas's communicative paradigm, since Habermas's proceduralist trust in global legal-political institutions seems problematic even on his own conceptual presuppositions and remains theoretically blind to those vast global inequalities of resources and power that come to view only in Horkheimer's and Honneth's idea of a critical theory of justice. Indeed, as I have argued, Honneth is right to both embrace a more substantive theory of justice and to broaden the institutional focus of his recognition paradigm to a more inclusive view of the social conditions for individual autonomy. Accordingly, we will have to strike a path between the insufficient appreciation of the social conditions of autonomy that we find in Habermas's proceduralism and Honneth's methodological entrapment in existing institutions of social freedom. In Chapter 10, I will argue that the combined procedural and substantive moral constructivism of Rainer Forst's emerging justification paradigm of critical theory holds a potential for striking this path.

---

[11] Honneth, *Freedom's Right*, p. 335. See also Axel Honneth, 'Eine Geschite der moralische Selbstkorrekturen: Auf den Spuren europäischer Solidarität', in *Die Armut unserer Freiheit* (Berlin: Suhrkamp Verlag, 2020).

8.1.3 Natural Conditions of Autonomy

In the preceding chapters, we have seen how the successive paradigms of critical theory have struggled with conceptualizing the relationship between society and nature. In Horkheimer's original paradigm, nature is seen—in line with a Promethean reading of Marx—purely as an object of instrumental mastery and control. In Adorno's negativist paradigm, the relationship between society and nature is explicitly theorized as the *site* of the dialectic of enlightenment, where the emancipatory project is perverted and reverts into its opposite by the reduction of enlightenment reason into the instrumental attitude towards outer and inner nature, culminating in the permanent catastrophe of world war, the Holocaust, and the enduring threat of nuclear annihilation. We have also seen how Adorno struggled to break the bounds of the subjective paradigm of reason, identifying in the concept of *mimesis* an ultimately unsatisfactory promise of a non-instrumental attitude towards nature, which, however, threatens to explode the basic presuppositions of his negativist paradigm. Finally, Habermas is able to escape the theoretical cul-de-sac of Adorno's negativism only by introducing a tripartite distinction between communicative, strategic, and instrumental action, which reverts to Horkheimer's original paradigm in its inability to conceive of the human relationship to nature in any form other than technological mastery and control. Following Latour, I have argued that this leaves Habermas unable to conceptualize global warming as a phenomenon that is defined precisely in terms of the way that it straddles the neat conceptual boundaries of society and nature, subject and object.

Is any kind of reconciliation between reason and nature possible within the framework of Frankfurt School critical theory, if not exactly in Bennett's and Latour's sense, as discussed in Chapters 4 and 6? Although Honneth's work offers few if any reflections on this question, I nonetheless believe that it holds the conceptual resources that enable to us to answer with a qualified 'yes'. The key lies not in an ontological rethinking of nature, as the new materialists would have it, but in a *normative reconceptualization* of the communicative conception of freedom as autonomy that animates the whole Frankfurt School tradition. As we saw in Chapter 7, this conception of freedom follows Hegel's radicalization of Kant's account of the autonomous will in maintaining that Kant's two-world metaphysics conceptualizes freedom in a way that unduly restricts the scope of autonomy to internal motives for action in opposition to natural inclination—and, indeed, in a way that makes freedom from natural causation the hallmark of freedom. By contrast, Hegel holds, the social and psychological processes that condition my drives and impulses must be conceived in such a way that they can be understood as justified only insofar as they serve as a condition of possibility for individual autonomy. That is to say, they must be conceived as communicative relations of mutual recognition and empowerment, in which I am able to 'find myself in the other'.

From the point of view of this communicative conception of freedom, reconciliation with nature is possible only once we conceive of the ecosystems—indeed, of the planetary Earth system as a whole—that we inhabit as similarly conditions of possibility for individual autonomy. This does not involve 'finding ourselves in nature' in the form of non-human agency (or 'actants') or vibrant matter, as in Latour's and Bennett's work. Rather, it involves a recognition that, just as autonomous agency emerges out of and expresses inner nature, so too do the external natural conditions of human existence remain necessary enabling conditions for societal forms of life in which we can hope to realize an 'objective will' in the basic structure of society. If we destroy those natural conditions—the ecosystemic balances that sustain life on Earth—we at the same time destroy the perhaps most fundamental condition of possibility for a society fit for autonomous beings.

This may seem like a paradoxical thought. In the communicative conception of freedom, it is precisely the presumption that the social conditions of autonomy are not only given but also potentially subject to collective codetermination, which is the basis for including them as 'objective will': as social conditions of human agency. We can speak of a 'reasonable society' only when the basic structure of society is responsive to democratic will-formation and, in this sense, a social enabling condition of human autonomy. This does not seem to be the case with the natural world, which is distinguished—within the modern worldview—precisely by being non-human, or 'outside' of society. But following the discussion of Latour's work in Chapter 6, this objection misses the extent to which the boundary between society and nature is both conceptually and practically blurred precisely in the case of 'hyperobjects' such as anthropogenic climate change and global warming, which issue from the complex 'mediation' between industrial society, the atmosphere, and natural ecosystems. Just as society is infused with 'Nature', so too is the natural environment in the Anthropocene infused with the manifold consequences of human history, from the micro to the planetary level.

Such a 'remembrance' that human autonomy rests not only on purely social conditions but also on natural conditions—within a less conceptually robust distinction between these two 'poles', in Latour's phrase—clearly echoes Adorno's claim that reason includes a somatic element; that we are not only part of nature, but that true human emancipation is possible only once we recognize that the enlightenment aspiration to wrest power over human life from nature and subject nature to total human control is doomed to fail—if not by rendering us unable to assume an non-objectivating attitude towards ourselves as much as to others, then ultimately by destroying our natural habitat and making our planetary home all-but 'unliveable'. Only by fashioning ways of life that allow human beings and the other animals to coexist within an enduring, ecologically sustainable relationship between social and natural environments can we be free.

PART V
ALLEN AND FORST

In this final Part V, I engage two emerging paradigms of critical theory: the emerging contextualist paradigm developed by Amy Allen and the emerging justification paradigm conceived by Rainer Forst. Allen's and Forst's respective paradigms are particularly salient for the systematic purposes of this book, because they are explicitly and self-consciously developed, on the one hand, as critical theories in the Frankfurt School tradition, and, on the other, with a clear view to the implications for a critical theory of world society. I describe them as *emerging* paradigms of critical theory, because they do not (yet) offer a comprehensive account of all three methodological dimensions of critical theory. Indeed, in their different ways, Allen and Forst have tended to focus on the *normative dimension* of critical theory, with important and far-reaching methodological implications, but they have—in varying degrees—offered less comprehensive and systematic independent accounts of the historical and sociological dimensions of critical theory.

Amy Allen's work represents an ambitious synthesis of poststructuralist currents with the Frankfurt School tradition of critical theory. Allen wrote her dissertation on a feminist theory of power at Northwestern University under Nancy Fraser and Thomas McCarthy—two pivotal figures in the North American 'branch' of critical theory—and today, she is the Professor of Philosophy and Women's, Gender, and Sexuality Studies at Pennsylvania State University.[1] In her book *The Politics of Our Selves* from 2008, Allen develops a sophisticated contextualist account of the normative foundations of critical theory—bringing together the work of Foucault and Judith Butler with that of Habermas and Seyla Benhabib—with a particular view to the relationship between subject formation (or subjection), autonomy, and gender. In *The End of Progress* from 2016, with which I have been in sustained discussion throughout this book, this synthesis is developed in a distinctively postcolonial direction, with the explicit intention of *decolonizing* Frankfurt School critical theory. However, in the latter book, Allen's work also

---

[1] Amy Allen, *The Power of Feminist Theory: Domination, Resistance, Solidarity* (New York: Routledge, 2018).

takes a stronger *negativist* turn, aligning it more closely with Adorno's paradigm than with Habermas's.

In doing so, I will argue in Chapter 9, Allen points to crucial tasks and unearths important resources for a critical theory of world society. More specifically, I will argue that Allen's concern with subjection illuminates the objectionable neglect within the Frankfurt School tradition of critical theory of how racial and gender norms inculcate forms of domination in the very formation of the subject. Moreover, I will argue that a critical theory of world society must be able to integrate Allen's approach of self-problematizing critique as a reflexive check on its biases, blind spots, and potential ideological misuse. However, I will also argue that Allen's metanormative contextualism simultaneously ends up in some of the same theoretical cul-de-sacs and practical impasses as Adorno, and that therefore, her approach cannot stand alone.

In the work of Rainer Forst, the Frankfurt School tradition of critical theory has entered into a sustained and fruitful conversation with the Anglophone philosophical literature on justice. Indeed, Forst's justification paradigm of critical theory has been developed not only explicitly and self-consciously, as a paradigm of critical theory in the Frankfurt School tradition, but also through a careful engagement with contemporary analytical moral and political theory, and, in particular, with contemporary theories of justice. Forst wrote his dissertation under Habermas and subsequently worked as a scientific assistant for Honneth in Berlin and Frankfurt, interrupted by research visits in New York and at Harvard University—the latter under the auspices of John Rawls. In 2004, Forst assumed the chair of political theory and the history of ideas (later philosophy) at the Goethe University in Frankfurt. Importantly, Forst's theoretical framework has from the beginning been developed with an eye to its global application, and this intention is reflected down to its most basic concepts and claims.

In Chapter 10, I will argue that Forst's Kantian constructivism offers a theoretical path between the two dead-ends that we encountered in the discussion of Habermas's and Honneth's respective paradigms. In Chapter 6, I argued that Habermas places too narrow an emphasis on the legal-political conditions of autonomy and is insufficiently attentive to the broader social and psychological conditions of autonomy. I argued that this problem ultimately stems from Habermas's proceduralism and his concomitant unwillingness to offer a critical theory of *justice*. In Chapter 8, I argued that although Honneth's work exhibits a broader concern with the social and psychological conditions of autonomy through his idea of a theory of justice as social analysis, his recognition paradigm remains methodologically entrapped in existing institutions of social freedom. In other words, although Honneth offers a sophisticated insanitation of the young Horkheimer's idea of a critical theory of justice, his Hegelian reconstructive method precludes the possibility of a critical theory of *global* justice.

I will argue that Kantian constructivism as defended by Forst enables us to chart a course between these two dead-ends. Indeed, this approach integrates precisely the aspects of Habermas's paradigm that allow for application to the global context and the aspects of Honneth's paradigm that allow for the development of a critical theory of justice. Like Habermas, Forst grounds his justification paradigm in the validity claims made in the idealizing presuppositions of discourse—but unlike Habermas, Forst argues that we find in the reconstruction of criteria for justifying validity claims an immediately practical reason, from which we can derive substantive first-order claims about justice and injustice. Moreover, Forst shares Honneth's commitment to a communicative conception of freedom as autonomy but disavows Honneth's exclusive commitment to a Hegelian methodology of normative reconstruction and reconstructive critique, and he is therefore methodologically unconstrained by existing institutions of social freedom.

To be sure, Forst has also been criticized by Allen and others for being insufficiently attentive to the myriad ways in which power conditions the subject. Moreover, as postcolonial theorists have shown, sediments of the colonial and imperial origins of present-day world society are still operative in many of the concepts, ideas, and narratives that we rely on to navigate this order—such as in the stagist view of history and the concomitant belief that non-Western societies belong to a pre-modern developmental stage, as discussed throughout this book. Forst's main response to postcolonial critics such as Allen is to insist—in my view, rightly—that they must themselves presuppose the universal norms that they criticize.[2] However, this response does not absolve a critical theory of world society from continuously applying a check on the many ways that aspects of Western modernity's colonial and imperial heritage may have unwittingly found their way into its concepts, ideals, and assumptions, and the ways that such a theory may itself be liable to ideological misuse.

What I thus want to argue in the following two chapters and in the Conclusion is that a critical theory of world society is compelled *by the nature of its object* to integrate *both* Forst's Kantian constructivism *and* Allen's self-problematizing critique. On the one hand, such a theory must critically analyse the injustices of the global order and, on this basis, theorize what a more just world society would look like: it must identify relations of domination and dependence enabled and maintained by the globally integrated capitalist economy and current international political order, and it must consider, even if only in a suitably deflated sense of Horkheimer's term, what it might mean today for humanity to 'constitute itself as a conscious subject', in order to establish a more just global order and avert a planetary climate disaster. On the other hand, such a theory must at the

---

[2] See, e.g., Rainer Forst, *Normativity and Power: Analyzing Social Orders of Justification*, transl. by Ciaran Cronin (Oxford: Oxford University Press, 2017), p. 5.

same time interrogate the dark side and blind spots of Western modernity and its own potential entanglements with this heritage. My claim is that neither of these methodological perspectives can be dispensed with, and, therefore, a critical theory of world society must incorporate both.

9
Amy Allen's Contextualist Paradigm of Critical Theory

9.1 A New Synthesis with Poststructuralism

Like Honneth's early work, Amy Allen's thought expresses an aspiration to bring the question of *power* more sharply into focus for Frankfurt School critical theory, and like the first generation of the Frankfurt School, she is keenly attentive to the ways that power is sedimented into the subject's psychic constitution—its most basic needs and desires. Indeed, she sees the defining concern of critical theory in the relationship between power and autonomy, specifically as this relationship operates in processes of subject formation. And, like the young Honneth, she finds inspiration for illuminating this relationship in the work of Michel Foucault— both, as we shall see, as it relates to questions of gender and postcolonial concerns. In this sense, Allen's work goes to the heart of what I have argued are central, animating concerns of the Frankfurt School tradition of critical theory as a whole: namely, a concern with the dialectic between power and freedom, and the social and psychological conditions of individual autonomy. As we shall see, her work consistently highlights injustices and forms of domination to which the Frankfurt School tradition has generally turned a blind eye. In this chapter, I first offer a critical exposition of Allen's reflections on subjection and gender as well as her 'principled contextualism' (Section 9.2), before discussing her ambitious attempt to undertake a decolonization of critical theory (Section 9.3).

9.2 Power, Autonomy, and Allen's 'Contextualization of Habermas'

As I argued in the Introduction, the Frankfurt School's waning influence in recent years may in part be due to the remarkable silence of its most prominent standard-bearers on questions of gender and race, which have today become inescapable both within the academy and in broader political life. From this point of view, the perhaps most significant achievement of Allen's 2008 book *The Politics of Our Selves* is precisely to allow an appreciation, from within the tradition itself, of the extent to which Frankfurt School critical theory has been much too complacent about the ways that norms of gender and race structurally subordinate and impose social heteronomy on individuals beginning in the child's infancy, and the extent to which this insight requires a rethinking of the place of power in the formation of the autonomous subject. In making this argument, she develops a powerful critique of Habermas's conceptualization of the relationship between power and autonomy that dovetails with the critique of the lifeworld as a power-free sphere developed in Honneth's early work.

More specifically, Allen argues that Habermas's emphasis on power as a systemic phenomenon screens out the profound ways that power is involved in the most basic lifeworld processes of subject formation—or *subjection*, in Foucault's terms. To be sure, she locates an initially more promising account of subject formation in Habermas's essay 'Individuation through Socialization: On George Herbert Mead's Theory of Subjectivity', published in his collection *Postmetaphysical Thinking: Philosophical Essays* from 1992. In this essay, Habermas offers an account of how, in 'the process of socialization', the subject acquires 'a degree of individuation', which is at the same time an '*autonomization* of the self'. In Mead's work, Habermas argues,

> individuation is pictured not as the self-realization of an independently acting subject carried out in isolation and freedom but as a *linguistically mediated process of socialization* and the simultaneous constitution of a life-history that is conscious of itself. The identity of socialized individuals forms itself simultaneously in the medium of coming to an understanding with others in language and in the medium of coming to a life-historical and intrasubjective understanding with oneself. Individuality forms itself in relations of intersubjective acknowledgement and of intersubjectively mediated self-understanding.[3]

But as Allen points out, Habermas is 'utterly sanguine' about the role that power plays in this intersubjective process of subject-formation and the development of the autonomous subject's ability to take up 'the moral point of view'. He acknowledges that power relations are important to the formation of the subject in the asymmetrical relationship between child and parents—as paradigmatically exemplified by Freud's theory of the child's overcoming of the Oedipus complex discussed in Chapter 1. But he 'glosses over this aspect' by portraying the asymmetrical power relation between child and parent as a kind of 'contract between free and equal parties',[4] suggesting that 'the child views authority ... relations as relations of exchange' and thus in some sense as legitimate.[5]

But according to Allen, this normative claim concerning the legitimacy of parental authority cannot be the child's, who will only develop the ability to take

---

[3] Jürgen Habermas, *Postmetaphysical Thinking: Philosophical Essays*, transl. by William Mark Hohengarten (Cambridge: Polity Press, 1992) [emphasis added].
[4] Amy Allen, *The Politics of Our Selves: Power, Autonomy, and Gender in Contemporary Critical Theory* (New York: Columbia University Press, 2008), p. 116.
[5] Habermas, *Moral Consciousness and Communicative Action*, p. 153.

up the moral point of view and thus consciously enter into relations of power that it has deemed legitimate through subsequent psychic internationalization of the asymmetrical power relation in question. With appeal to Judith Butler's work on subjection, Allen instead argues that Habermas's complacency towards parental authority has troubling systematic implications, since the child is so fully at the mercy of her parent that they have no choice but to internalize even deeply subordinating norms, identities, and affective attachments:

> Because the child cannot discriminate between subordinating and nonsubordinating attachments, and because she will form an attachment to painful and subordinating modes of identity rather than not attach, her psychic attachment to subordination may well precede the development of her capacity for autonomy… For example, consider the fact that in societies that are structured by sex/gender systems, the very vehicles of recognition through which the infant's capacities for autonomy are nourished and developed—language and the familial relations into which infants are first socialized—are shot through with relations of dominance and subordination based on gender. Thus, power threatens to pervade not only the content of oppressive gender norms but also the very critical capacities that enable the gendered individual to reflect autonomously on such norms.[6]

As Allen argues, subordinating gender norms are instilled from the very moment the child begins to acquire language, structuring their identity formation around socially established gender roles and gendered self-relations that may exercise a deeply pernicious influence throughout their life. Moreover, Allen argues that such gendered relations-to-self are often so deeply rooted in the subject's psychic constitution that they resist critical self-scrutiny, in part because they form part of the child's earliest and most basic affective attachments, and in part because they are fused into the very condition of possibility for autonomous reflection—language itself.

From this compelling argument—which echoes themes in Horkheimer's and Fromm's account of the psychological predispositions nurtured by monopoly capitalism, and in Adorno's view of the administered world's weakening of the ego and displacement of the subject's capacity for critical reflection—Allen wants to draw wide-ranging meta-ethical and normative implications. She argues that the degree to which power is co-constitutive in subject formation processes 'threatens to problematize the distinction between power and validity that Habermas takes to be so central to critical theory, for if the validity of certain norms is so woven into the fabric of our form of life, our language, and our sense of who we are, that we literally cannot imagine ourselves independent of them, then these norms

---

[6] Allen, *The Politics of Our Selves*, p. 119.

will remain stubbornly resistant to attempts discursively to assess their legitimacy'.[7] That is to say, because subordinating gender norms are instilled with the earliest affective attachments and the child's acquisition of language, she may be unable to submit those norms to scrutiny and critique, because questioning them would threaten the foundational pillars of her self-relation. Moreover, Allen claims, such permanently off-limits subordinating norms make a mockery of the idea of the autonomous subject, threatening to undermine her ability to distinguish valid norms from those that have been instilled through power.

In response to this objection, and the weakening of the distinction between power and validity that she takes to be its implication, Allen develops a 'contextualized' reading of Habermas's work that moderates the claim to 'immanent transcendence' of validity claims so central to his communicative paradigm. Allen's first move in this contextualization of Habermas's communicative paradigm is to *historicize* and *provincialize* the claim to immanent transcendence, arguing that 'the very faith in context-transcending validity is itself rooted in and restricted to a specific sociocultural, historical context: the context of late *Western modernity*. On this view, it is constitutive of our modern Western form of life that we posit this idealization, and, in that sense, idealizations such as this one are necessary *for us*, but only contingently so'.[8] Secondly, Allen proposes what she calls a 'principled form of contextualism', which rejects 'the false opposition between radical contextualism and the commitment to reason's actual capacity to transcend its situatedness' by emphasizing 'our need *both* to posit context-transcending ideals *and* to continually unmask their status as illusions rooted in interest and power-laden contexts'.[9]

I agree with Allen's charge that Habermas greatly underestimates the extent to which power is operative in the most basic processes of subject formation—which was, as we saw in Chapters 1, 3 and 8, a central concern of the first generation of the Frankfurt School, especially concerning how the emancipatory dialectic between power and autonomy broke down on the eve of fascism, and also in Honneth's critique of Habermas's dualistic fiction of the lifeworld as a power-free sphere of action coordination and personality development. Moreover, I also believe she points to a more general complacency throughout the Frankfurt School tradition as a whole in relation to subordinating norms of gender and race, and as I argued above and in the Introduction, the silence of its standard-bearers on these pivotal struggles of our times may be part of the explanation for the waning influence of Frankfurt School critical theory today. Allen's work offers an indispensable contribution to remedying these theoretical blind spots.

---

[7] Allen, *The Politics of Our Selves*, p. 120.
[8] Allen, *The Politics of Our Selves*, p. 143 [emphases added].
[9] Allen, *The Politics of Our Selves*, p. 148.

But I also want to argue that, in her attempt to draw metanormative implications about context-transcending validity, she overplays her hand. Allen repeatedly stresses, with only subtle bewilderment, how imperative it is for Habermas to maintain a sharp distinction between power and validity—portraying it almost as a kind of personal eccentricity on his part. But in my view, she gravely misjudges the systematic costs of weakening the distinction. Indeed, I want to argue that Allen's 'principled contextualism' actually illustrates precisely why it is so crucial to maintain a clear distinction between power and validity, even while recognizing the extent to which power is co-constitutive in subject formation processes, and that certain sexist, racist, and other norms are so deep-seated in the subject that they will often remain stubbornly resistant to any attempts to discursively assess their legitimacy.[10]

For in drawing the implication that the distinction between power and validity breaks down, Allen effectively *collapses* the idea of context-transcending validity into a kind of historically and culturally specific predisposition limited to 'late Western modernity', which must always be held in check by an unmasking critique that reveals these ideals to be mere self-delusion by exposing their genesis in relationships of power. Having thus reduced the 'need for transcendence' to a kind of cultural obsessive compulsive disorder of the modern Westerner, Allen is of course faced with all the familiar objections—so often levelled at Foucault's work—that her principled contextualism is at a loss as to how to account for *its own normative validity* as critique.[11] For we might then wonder whether the normative criteria that guide her own critique of power from within the Western context are not merely expressive of the same contingent need to make overblown and ultimately delusional claims to a more general kind of validity? If nothing transcends power, is she not herself simply engaged in a kind of power move?

Moreover, Allen's claim that the 'need' to posit context-transcending ideals is merely a kind of delusional cultural compulsion specific to Western modernity also seems to have the straightforward implication that those ideals cannot be valid *beyond* that cultural and historical context. That is to say, even if she overcomes the first hurdle concerning the status of the normative criteria that lend her own critique its claim to validity, what is then left for critical theory but a kind of incessant intra-cultural self-critique (assuming that it is not by the same standards a stretch to make validity claims for an abstract context such as 'late Western

---

[10] In my view, Allen's argument neglects the insight—explicit in both Habermas's and Honneth's work—that autonomy is never an achieved end-state, but rather always a work in progress, and that the idea of the autonomous self as fully transparent to itself is at best an unhelpful illusion, which should not lead us to question the distinction between power and validity but rather understand this as a dialectical relationship that includes both moments within itself. In the Conclusion, I offer a more systematic account of how this dialectical relationship between power and reason can be seen as the engine of moral learning within the whole tradition of Frankfurt School critical theory.

[11] Nancy Fraser, 'Foucault on Modern Power: Empirical Insights and Normative Confusions', *PRAXIS International* (3), 1981: pp. 272–287. See also Habermas, *The Philosophical Discourse of Modernity*.

modernity', which might seem questionable), which exposes Western theories' false pretensions to universal validity?

This latter problem is of course acutely relevant for the possibility of a critical theory of world society. For how is a theory that takes the global order as its context of application supposed to get off the ground if the very possibility of a universal (or context-transcending) human norm is nothing more than a Western self-delusion that must be deconstructed and exposed? Would that not seem to render impossible any attempt to criticize global capitalist modernity with reference to norms potentially sharable with anyone beyond the Western context, and would that impossibility not seem to seriously cripple, for example, any hope of morally justified collective action to tame globalized markets or the pre-emption of runaway climate change on a global scale? I will return to a discussion of the dialectic between power and autonomy that Allen marshals against Habermas in the Conclusion. But we must first take a more general look at the systematic implications that Allen herself draws from her principled contextualism in her book *The End of Progress*, in which she submits the Frankfurt School tradition of critical theory *as such* to penetrating decolonial critique.

9.3 Decolonizing Critical Theory: The Idea of Self-Problematizing Critique

In the opening pages of *The End of Progress*, Allen observes that if critical theory 'wishes to be truly critical, then contemporary critical theory should frame its research program and its conceptual framework with an eye towards decolonial and anti-imperialist struggles and concerns'.[12] As she rightly points out, critical theorists have not appreciated 'the deep and difficult challenge that our postcolonial predicament poses to the Frankfurt School's distinctive approach to social theorizing'.[13] Elsewhere she describes as the aim of the book to speak 'across the divide' between Frankfurt School critical theorists and postcolonial theorists,

> both by showing how and why critical theory in the narrow sense of that term can and must be decolonized and by showing how a certain way of inheriting the Frankfurt School approach to critical theory, a certain way of construing and taking up its method and its aims, can be congenial to postcolonial theory, how it might even allow postcolonial theory to be criticalized.[14]

Yet, as the project of 'criticalizing postcolonial theory' takes up nothing more than the final page of her book, it is also clear that her overwhelming interest lies in the

---

[12] Allen, *The End of Progress*, p. 4.
[13] Allen, *The End of Progress*, p. 2.
[14] Allen, *The End of Progress*, p. xvi.

project of decolonizing Frankfurt School critical theory. In practice, this means submitting several of the paradigms of critical theory reconstructed in this book to decolonial arguments and lines of criticism, which have often been developed within the postcolonial literature in response to more orthodox Marxist theory and historiography. In other words, I would suggest that, rather than truly speaking across the divide between Frankfurt School critical theory and postcolonial theory, Allen effectively makes the latter the standard for one-sidedly evaluating the former.

As discussed in Chapters 6 and 8 of this book, Allen's main targets are Habermas's communicative paradigm, Honneth's recognition paradigm, and, as we shall see in the next chapter, Forst's emerging justification paradigm of critical theory. In the case of the former two paradigms, as we have seen, her main objection centres on different aspects of what she considers the 'left-Hegelian' grounding of their respective normative dimensions: Because of the centrality of the idea of socio-cultural and moral learning processes to both Habermas's and Honneth's paradigms, they are both implicated in modernist developmental narratives that have been deeply entangled with colonial and imperial domination. Specifically, Allen argues that critical theory should rid itself of any trace of the backward-looking conception of progress as 'fact' that, she claims, serves a crucial metanormative function in both Habermas's and Honneth's work, while retaining the commitment to a forward-looking conception of progress as a 'moral-political imperative'.

In Chapters 6 and 8, I argued that neither Allen's decolonial critique of Habermas's communicative paradigm nor of Honneth's recognition paradigm is fully convincing, but that she nonetheless effectively demonstrates that a critical theory committed to the left-Hegelian self-conception as a vehicle of enlightenment within socio-cultural and moral learning processes is always *liable* to be misused for the purposes of false and ideological justifications for neocolonial domination, and that a critical theory of world society must therefore integrate a reflexive check on such ideological misuse into its basic theoretical framework. However, this is not Allen's conclusion; indeed, she draws the much stronger implication that critical theory must dump its left-Hegelian baggage altogether and instead settle for a metanormative contextualism in grounding its normative dimension, as discussed in the previous section. But Allen now spells out this contextualist alternative in much greater detail, while locating in the work of Adorno and Foucault a conception of critique as 'historical problematization' that she finds to be more in accord with this metanormative contextualism.

Helpfully, Allen draws a tripartite distinction between three different 'modes of genealogical inquiry': namely, the 'subversive', the 'vindicatory', and the 'problematizing' mode. The 'common core' of these three modes is a 'historical approach that asks how specific, contingent historical processes have led human beings to develop and embrace [a] value or concept'. The subversive mode of genealogy aims, in addition, to reject, undermine, or *repudiate* those values and concepts—as familiar from Nietzsche's genealogy of Christian morality in *Zur Genealogie der Moral*.[15] By contrast, the vindicatory mode aims to *justify* the values or concepts of in question.[16] Compared with both of these, the problematizing mode of genealogy is an inherently more ambivalent and open-ended undertaking:

> the problematization of our own point of view can and should be understood not as a rejection or abstract negation of the normative inheritance of modernity but rather as a fuller realization of its central value, namely, freedom ... By allowing us to reflexively critique the social institutions and practices, the patterns of cultural meaning and subject formation, and the normative commitments that have made us who we are, problematizing critique opens up a space of critical distance on those institutions, practices, and so forth, thereby freeing us up in relation to them, and thus also in relation to ourselves.[17]

It is this problematizing mode of critique—which seeks neither to simply repudiate nor to justify, but rather to disclose as historically contingent 'all that the world has made of us, and intends to make of us', and thus enable different ways of thinking and being—that Allen locates in Foucault's and Adorno's thought. Indeed, from the discussion in Chapter 3, it should be clear that the *Dialektik der Aufklärung* can be interpreted as expressing just this ambivalent attitude of problematizing critique.

As Allen insists, the aspiration to critically problematize 'the social institutions and practices, the patterns of cultural meaning and subject formation, and the normative commitments that have made us who we are' is especially urgent precisely with regard to the global context of application, where resources and power are still distributed, wielded, and exercised along past (and now-informal) colonial and imperial lines, and where historically entrenched racist norms and exclusionary institutions and practices are reproduced through processes of subjection.[18] Indeed, this is one of the undeniable common insights of postcolonial theorists discussed throughout this book: in their different ways, Guha, Chakrabarty, Said, Spivak, and Bhambra all wrestle with the fact that categories, norms, and narratives that emerged during Western modernity and were forcibly disseminated throughout the world through Western colonial and imperial expansion are not only often still operative in social life, but also reinforce forms of exclusion and domination that are—in Allen's words—'so woven into the fabric of our form of life, our language, and our sense of who we are' that their historical origin and social function often passes without notice.

---

[15] See also Geuss, *The Idea of a Critical Theory*, for a helpful discussion.
[16] As exemplified by Habermas's 'A Genealogical Analysis of the Cognitive Content of Morality', in *The Inclusion of the Other*.
[17] Allen, *The End of Progress*, pp. 195–197.
[18] Charles W. Mills, *The Racial Contract* (Ithaca: Cornell University Press, 1997); Achille Mbembe, *Critique of Black Reason*, transl. by Laurent Dubois (Durham: Duke University Press, 2017).

Moreover, as many have argued, the global order of Westphalian states and the regime of international law on which Habermas wants to base his multilevel global constitutional framework is far from innocent; rather, they are the historical products of centuries of European imperialism and colonization.[19] Moreover, the steeply hierarchical global political order also has a *material* side, which sometimes goes unnoticed in the 'culturalist' focus of many postcolonial critics— including, I would argue, in Allen's work.[20] Indeed, many postcolonial states are still as heavily economically marginalized and subject to massive power asymmetries vis-à-vis their former colonial masters and more recent imperial centres such as the US and China—many even more so than in the immediate aftermath of decolonization—as they are massively disfavoured by the system of rules regulating international investment and trade within global capitalist markets.

To be sure, in the decades following decolonization, there was a remarkable concerted effort by anticolonial nationalist state leaders and intellectuals to establish a 'New International Economic Order', which sought to secure state rights to national resources, give states regulative sway over multinational corporations, and regulate international trade to the benefit of the economically fragile and newly decolonized states, while politicizing international economic affairs by situating distributive and regulative conflicts within the democratic decision-making forum of the UN General Assembly.[21] According to Adom Getachew, these efforts amounted to an ambitious project of anticolonial 'worldmaking', which aimed to establish 'an internationally managed global economy that was structured by equitable interdependence rather than hierarchical dependence', where this 'radically reimagined mode of sovereign equality would supply the condition of international non-domination in which postcolonial nation-building could realize the principle of equality domestically'.[22]

However, these efforts at anticolonial worldmaking—which may also serve as an exemplary source of inspiration for a critical theory of contemporary world society, as Getachew suggests—were definitively thwarted in the early 1980s, when a neoliberal vision of financialized economic globalization found powerful and willing sponsors in resurgent neoconservative world leaders such as Reagan and Thatcher. Theirs was a vision that emphasized the rights of capital over labour and even democratic government, which entrenched the veto power of the wealthy nations in technocratic international organizations such as the IMF, the

---

[19] James Tully, *Public Philosophy in a New Key: Volume II: Imperialism and Civic Freedom*; Martti Kosskeniemi, *The Gentle Civilizer of Nations: The Rise and Fall of International Law 1870–1960* (Cambridge: Cambridge University Press, 2001).

[20] Onur Ulas Ince, *Colonial Capitalism and the Dilemmas of Liberalism* (Oxford: Oxford University Press, 2018).

[21] There are clear parallels between this vision and Habermas's proposal for a multilevel global constitutional framework that seem to go unnoticed in his recent work.

[22] Adom Getachew, *Worldmaking after Empire: The Rise and Fall of Self-Determination* (Princeton: Princeton University Press, 2019), p. 167.

World Bank, and the WTO, and which subjected postcolonial societies caught in socially and economically disastrous sovereign debt traps to crippling IMF-backed structural adjustment programs.[23]

The ability to take up a critical perspective on the historically entrenched hierarchies and vast socioeconomic inequalities of existing world society calls for a critical political economy of the global economic order (the material side of neocolonial forms of domination and dependence), just as it calls for critical histories of the present world society to denaturalize and illuminate its continuing intertwinement with the legacy of European colonialism and imperialism, ideologies of racism and sexism, and the historicist and developmentalist narratives that serve to uphold its ossified structures (the cultural side).[24] As Allen rightly insists, critical theory can only eschew this crucial task at the cost of serving to reproduce and maintain global relations of domination and subjugation.

Still—once again, I would argue, Allen goes further than necessary in a way that actually seems counterproductive to this crucial task. In *The End of Progress*, she offers a more systematic account of the 'principled contextualism' that I discussed in the previous section. The first move in this account is to 'tie justification and knowledge to specific contexts', which 'encompass not just beliefs and statements but also historically specific, social, cultural, and material conditions'. Second, she argues that 'metanormative contextualism about normative validity claims' involves both the claim that 'moral principles or normative ideals are always justified relative to a set of contextually salient values, conceptions of the good life, or normative horizons—roughly speaking, forms of life or lifeworlds'—and that 'there is no über-context, no context-free or transcendent point of view from which we can adjudicate which contexts are ultimately correct or even in a position of hierarchical superiority over others'.[25] In short: the scope of justifications is bound by existing lifeworld contexts, and there is no overarching or universal context of justification that transcends those more particular contexts.

At the same time, however, Allen insists that 'contextualism about ... justification does not entail skepticism or relativism'.[26] Rather, following Adorno (and the young Horkheimer's reflections on the concept of truth, although she does not discuss his work), she claims that metanormative contextualism is first and foremost 'a point of view that is beyond the alternatives of relativism and absolutism', and that her view 'is even compatible with regarding these principles as universal in the scope of their application, so long as we don't understand these principles, from

---

[23] Joseph E. Stiglitz, *Globalization and its Discontents* (New York: Norton, 2002); Quinn Slobodian, *Globalists: The End of Empire and the Birth of Neoliberalism* (Cambridge MA: Harvard University Press, 2018).

[24] For the latter argument, see also Thomas McCarthy, *Race, Empire, and the Idea of Human Development* (Cambridge: Cambridge University Press, 2009).

[25] Allen, *The End of Progress*, p. 215.

[26] Allen, *The End of Progress*, p. 215.

a metanormative point of view, as justified insofar as they are absolute values'.[27] However, it is not fully clear what this restricted metanormative claim amounts to.

If the scope of principles of justice is categorically indexed to the specific lifeworld context within which they are formulated, how can 'regarding these principles as universal in the scope of their application' be anything but the same kind of ruse or delusion that Allen diagnosed as a cultural predisposition specific to Western modernity in *The Politics of Our Selves*? This seems to suggest that Allen's metanormative contextualism is unable to ground her own method of problematizing critique as applicable to world society (as opposed to the Western context), since this would imply subjecting the overarching context of the global order to norms of critique that are specific to a parochial lifeworld context.

The problem here is not so much that a critical theory may risk incidentally performing such a misapplication of norms to world society that are in fact specific to a more local context; rather, the problem is that Allen's view seems to categorically deny the *very possibility* of universal norms—and thus of subjecting world society to critique with reference to moral norms that cut across specific lifeworld contexts, and which could potentially be shared by all the denizens of global capitalist modernity. This pulls the rug from any conceivable sense in which humanity might 'constitute itself as a conscious subject', as I have repeatedly argued we must, in a suitably metaphysically deflated sense of the young Horkheimer's demand. I can't see a way out of this bind: if metanormative contextualism delimits the scope of norms and principles to specific lifeworld contexts *and* categorically denies that there exist or could exist any universal contexts of justification, then the scope of norms and principles cannot, even potentially, be universal.

This worry—to wit: that Allen's account of metanormative contextualism hasn't actually overcome the problem of relativism that we encountered in the discussion of *The Politics of Our Selves*—is confirmed by the fact that her account of problematizing critique is, at its core, a form of *self-criticism*, which seeks to question, unsettle, and expose as contingent the normative and conceptual foundations of Western or European modernity. It is an inward-directed form of self-questioning, performed by the heirs of the modern West on the norms, ideals, concepts, and narratives that have made us who *we* are. This is why Allen consistently speaks of a problematization of '*our* own point of view and of *our* belief in its cognitive and moral superiority', of 'a persistent critical interrogation of the power investments and effects of *our* own normative commitments and ideals', and why she describes the aim of such self-problematization as nurturing a 'modest and humble stance toward *our* own reasoning practices' and even of a willingness 'to unlearn certain aspects of *our* own taken-for-granted point of view in order to engage in a genuinely open way with various participants in debates about global modernity'.[28]

---

[27] Allen, *The End of Progress*, pp. 216–217.
[28] Emphases added.

To be sure, this is explicitly a form of self-criticism undertaken so as to do justice to the 'Other' of European modernity, and in order to confront the enduring heritage of the monstrous injustices wrought by Europe on its former colonial subjects. But it is, as such, not actually an attempt to develop a critical theory of *world* society, as much as a self-interrogation of European or Western modernity and its global crimes.

Don't get me wrong: as I have repeatedly emphasized, I believe Allen is quite right to call for such a continuous Western self-critique *precisely* in the context of a critical theory of world society, which must be ever mindful of the myriad ways in which it risks drawing on or lending itself to narratives or justifications that ideologically prop up the enduring global heritage of European colonialism. However, as crucial as this task is, I think it is just as crucial to insist that a critical theory of world society cannot *limit itself* to such a mode of European or Western self-criticism; it must also push beyond self-problematization and seek to critically comprehend and evaluate the compound structures of a global capitalist modernity, which can no longer meaningfully be understood solely as a Western imposition. Indeed, as I shall argue in the Conclusion, the reverse side of this task is that a critical theory of world society must be conceived as an interdisciplinary, cooperative, and inherently decentred 'interpenetration' of philosophy and social research, which cannot be brought to life by a single philosopher (least of all one from a Western context) but must remain able to integrate and synthesize the work of multiple philosophical and social-scientific contributions from across the world. In other words, the task of mounting a critique of global capitalist modernity must not, as Allen tends to do, be construed solely as a Western or European project of self-critique, but must also be understood as a truly *global* undertaking, which cuts across lifeworlds and continents, just as economic, cultural, and political forms of domination today cut across borders.

Let me re-emphasize this point by addressing a slightly different concern. Allen interprets problematizing critique as an expression of a stance of 'epistemic humility' that she locates in both Adorno's work and in much postcolonial theory.[29] In his lectures on *Probleme der Moralphilosophie*, Adorno argues that the only 'cardinal virtue' he would be able to think of, if he were pressed to offer such an account, would be 'modesty'—by which he means that 'we must have a conscience, but may not insist on our own conscience'. This abstention from 'self-assertiveness' is directly motivated, on Adorno's part, by a concern to do justice to the non-identical, to the otherness of the 'Other':

> if today we can at all say that subjectively there is something like a threshold, a distinction between a right life and a wrong one, we are likely to find it soonest in asking whether a person is just hitting out blindly at other people—while claiming

[29] Allen, *The End of Progress*, p. 201.

that the group to which he belongs is the only positive one, and other groups should be negated—or whether by reflecting on our own limitations we can learn to *do justice to those who are different*, and to realize that true injustice is always to be found at the precise point where you put yourself in the right and other people in the wrong.'[30]

Yet, at the same time, Adorno insists 'it is clear that something like the good life is not conceivable unless you hold fast to both conscience and responsibility'. That is to say, his point is that 'we find ourselves really and truly in a *contradictory situation*', in that we 'need to hold fast to moral norms, to self-criticism, to the question of right and wrong, and at the same time to a sense of the fallibility of the authority that has the confidence to undertake such self-criticism'.[31] Once again, this echoes the point made by the young Horkheimer, as discussed in Chapter 1, that 'critique does not merely include the negative, sceptical moment, but equally the inner independence not to lose sight of that which is true; to remain firm in its application, even though it might one day change'.[32]

It seems to me that Allen does not really do justice to the double-sidedness of these reflections; rather, she one-sidedly elaborates the negative moment—the sceptical moment of self-doubt—while ignoring the injunction to 'hold fast to moral norms' and that which one is convinced is true. In the Conclusion, I will be concerned with sketching a framework for a critical theory of world society that integrates *both* of these elements—or as I will construe them: the reconstructive and constructive moral universalism without which, I will argue, a critical theory of world society *wouldn't even get off the ground*, and the continuous reflexive self-problematization to which the global application of a theoretical tradition grounded in such a commitment to moral universalism and born out of the European Enlightenment must at the same time submit itself. Allen's work offers vital resources for the latter task, but gravely underestimates the costs of eschewing the former.

There is another downside—in my view—to Allen's close alignment with Adorno: namely, that her theory seems to run into the same practical impasse as Adorno's negativist paradigm, as it is unable to offer the kind of *practical* guidance for emancipatory collective action, which should be understood, I have argued, as the very *raison d'être* of a critical theory of society.[33] Indeed, as we have seen, the mode of critique offered by historical self-problematization does not so much have the practical aim of emancipation as the aim of denaturalization—of bringing

---

[30] Adorno, *Probleme der Moralphilosophie*, p. 251 [emphasis added].
[31] Adorno, *Probleme der Moralphilosophie*, p. 251.
[32] Horkheimer, 'Zum Problem der Wahrheit', p. 319.
[33] Allen explicitly defends a negativist conception of emancipation and critique in Amy Allen, 'Emancipation without Utopia: Subjection, Modernity, and the Normative Claims of Feminist Critical Theory', *Hypatia* (30/ 3), 2015: pp. 513–529.

theoretical blind spots and the contingency of taken-for-granted assumptions to consciousness. Again, I think this mode of self-critique is essential as an imperative *reflexive check* on a critical theory of world society, but I believe that the core task of such a theory must be understood—in line with the young Horkheimer—as facilitating emancipation *in practice*.

In *The Politics of Our Selves*, this retreat from emancipatory collective action even seems to take the explicit form of a reversal of Horkheimer's original conception of critical theory as an attempt to reflect on and guide the struggles of emancipatory social movements into an attempt to derive lessons from social movements for *individual* resistance to heteronomy. In Allen's words:

> one might hypothesize that such social movements, via experimentation with alternative modes of self-understanding and ways of living together, also can provide alternative possibilities for attachment and sources of recognition that can help individuals to form less subordinating modes of attachment.[34]

In conjunction with her close alignment with Adorno's negativism, such reflections may seem to suggest that Allen is not really concerned with *social* transformation as such, but—much like Adorno—with *individual* resistance to heteronomy. To be sure, the aim of unearthing resources for individual resistance to subordinating forms of power is of course a perfectly legitimate and worthwhile one. But I believe we can and should expect more from a critical theory of world society. In the next chapter, I want to explore another emergent paradigm of critical theory, which is—in marked contrast to Allen's—distinguished precisely by being unabashedly grounded in a *universal* context of justice, and which holds, I will argue, the resources for grounding the emancipatory intentions of a critical theory of world society: Rainer Forst's justification paradigm of critical theory.

---

[34] Allen, *The Politics of Our Selves*, p. 183.

10
Rainer Forst's Justification Paradigm of Critical Theory

10.1 Reason, Power, and Justification

At the most fundamental level, Rainer Forst's emerging justification paradigm of critical theory can be interpreted as elaborating a central theme that we have encountered again and again throughout our reconstruction of the Frankfurt School tradition of critical theory: namely, the translation of experiences of socially compelled suffering into a *demand for reasons*—into a demand for justification, and a critique and struggle to abolish relations and practices of domination within the existing basic structure of society. In this chapter, I will first expound the normative centrepiece of his justification paradigm—the right to justification, as the ground of morality (Section 10.2)—and subsequently spell out the ambitious social and political theory that Forst has recently developed on this basis (Section 10.3). I then argue that Forst's Kantian constructivism can strike the desired path between Habermas's proceduralism and Honneth's Hegelianism, promising a normative dimension for a critical theory of world society that enables a critique of genuinely global injustices (Section 10.4). Finally, I discuss Forst's own reflections on the normative implications of his theory for a critical theory of world society (Section 10.5).

10.2 The Right to Justification

The right to justification is the normative foundation of Forst's justification paradigm. His argument for the right to justification combines elements of discourse ethics with more traditional Kantian themes, as well as insights from contemporary Anglo-American moral philosophy. The argument starts from the discourse-theoretical assumption that the criteria of justification for different validity claims can be derived from the specific nature of the validity claim in question. Forst defines 'practical reason' as 'the basic capacity to respond to practical questions in appropriate ways with justifying reasons within each of the practical contexts in which they arise and must be situated'.[1] This definition allows Forst to

---

[1] Rainer Forst, *The Right to Justification. Elements of a Constructivist Theory of Justice*, transl. by Jeffrey Flynn (New York: Columbia University Press, 2012), p. 18.

countenance the fact that there are just as many 'uses' of practical reason as there are distinct practical validity claims in a given natural language, and each of these validity claims defines its respective *context of justification*. Any practically reasonable human being thus masters what Forst calls the *principle of justification*—'the fundamental principle of practical reason'—namely that 'normative answers to practical questions are [or ought] to be justified in precisely the manner referred to by their validity claims'.[2] Accordingly, a 'comprehensive analysis of practical and normative justification' can be developed by 'recursively reconstructing' the conditions for the redemption of different validity claims in their respective contexts of justification.

Following Habermas, this discourse-theoretical approach enables Forst to define *the moral point of view* through a reconstruction of the justificatory criteria of the validity claim raised in the moral context of justification. However, Forst is careful not to reduce the principle of justification to its moral context; in particular, he distinguishes between the *ethical* context (claims concerning what is good for me, my significant others, and the communities to which I belong), the *legal* context (claims concerning what ought to be legally prohibited or permitted that we raise as 'subjects of the law'), and the context of *democratic self-determination* (claims concerning the interests of the political community that we raise as 'authors of the law').[3] According to Forst, none of these contexts must be allowed to coopt the others: although they are often much less clearly demarcated in practice, an autonomous person must be capable of mastering the grammar of justification in each of these contexts and integrate the four kinds of autonomy corresponding to each context of justification: *moral autonomy, ethical autonomy, legal autonomy*, and *political autonomy*. I will return below to the final form of autonomy that he adds to this list: namely, *social autonomy*—which covers the necessary social (and psychological) conditions for autonomy.

The argument for the right to justification is developed in the course of Forst's analysis of the validity claim raised in the moral context of justification: 'The validity claim of the moral norm—according to which each person has the duty to do or refrain from doing X—basically indicates that nobody has good reasons to violate this norm'.[4] Forst's reconstructive aim is thus to capture the criterial conditions by which moral norms and actions are justified and criticized. Since the modal specification of moral norms is the obligatory and categorical *ought*, which is not limited by ethical or political membership but addressed to 'the community of all human beings', the reasons justifying a moral norm or action must be capable of being grasped and accepted by all affected by that norm of action.

---

[2] Forst, *The Right to Justification*, p. 18.
[3] Rainer Forst, *Contexts of Justice: Political Philosophy Beyond Liberalism and Communitarianism*, transl. by John M. M. Farrell (Berkeley, CA: University of California Press, 2002), pp. 256–275. See also *The Right to Justification*, Chs. 3 and 5.
[4] Forst, *The Right to Justification*, p. 19.

The moral validity claim is thus distinguished by its claim to be *universally indefeasible*—that it faces no overriding considerations or reasons against its validity. Forst captures the universal scope of the claim to validity of moral norms in terms of the two justificatory criteria that moral norms and actions must be 'reciprocally' and 'generally' justifiable—or, as Forst prefers, that valid moral norms cannot be reciprocally and generally rejected. The criterion of reciprocity implies that no one must be able to claim any privileges over others (establishing justificatory *equality*) or project their needs and interests onto others (establishing justificatory *individuation*), and the criterion of generality implies that no one affected by the norm must be excluded (establishing justificatory *universality*). This *principle of reciprocal and general justification* is 'valid for the justification of both norms and actions', which establishes a 'criterial *threshold*' that all norms and actions, which claim validity for all human beings, must pass. This account of moral validity represents Forst's alternative not only to Habermas's universalization principle, but also to other related accounts in moral theory that attempt to conceptualize the moral point of view in terms of mutual justifiability, such as John Rawls's 'justice as fairness', Thomas Scanlon's 'contractualism', or Derek Parfit's 'Kantian contractualism'.

As we have seen, the principle of reciprocal and general justification implies that moral claims (claims to validity for all human beings) can only be those claims that cannot be reciprocally and generally rejected. The concomitant justificatory requirements on moral reasons of equality, individuation, and universality effectively implies that everyone has a justificatory *veto power* against unjustified norms and actions: everyone has a claim to consider and assess the grounds for any action or norm that affects them, to express their point of view, and to test whether any counter-reasons they might advance could pass the justificatory threshold of reciprocity and generality. It is precisely this veto power against unjustified norms and actions that Forst conceptualizes by saying that every participant in moral discourse has *a basic right to justification*. This basic right can thus be inferred from the moral validity claim itself, and, ultimately, from the principle of justification, and it corresponds to a *basic duty of justification*, which all participants in moral discourse must observe. Forst's original insight here is that insofar as I claim that a norm is morally justifiable—and thus claim that an action is justified with reference to a norm that is justifiable to all persons—then I effectively claim, from a discourse-ethical point of view, that its validity depends on the both necessary and sufficient condition that *no one* to whom it applies will be able to provide a reason that defeats it. In raising moral validity claims, I therefore simultaneously posit a basic right to justification of all human beings and assume a duty of justification vis-à-vis all affected.

To be sure, the right to justification does not imply that everyone has an arbitrary veto power against any norm in a way that suits his or her fancy. Rather, it implies that (a) they have a right to demand a justification for a norm or action that affects them; and, (b) if they do not accept this justification, they must be able to present reasons to motivate their rejection; and, (c) if the reasons they mobilize pass muster according to the criteria of reciprocity and generality, then the norm falls or the action is prohibited. Note that strictly speaking, the term 'right to justification' suggests that persons only have a right to (a), but it is clear from the justificatory criteria of reciprocity and generality that Forst means this right to extend to (b) and (c) as well.

Forst explicitly develops the right to justification as a discourse-ethical reinterpretation of Kant's morality of autonomy—of his 'categorical imperative to respect others as "ends in themselves"'.[5] Just as on Kant's view, respect is owed to the 'dignity' of human nature, which is rooted in the autonomy of our wills, so, for Forst, a duty of justification is owed to other human beings due to our basic right to justification. Just as Kant's concept of autonomy has both the descriptive meaning of a capacity for rational self-determination and the normative meaning of the inviolable moral status that attaches to autonomous beings, so, for Forst, the concept of justification integrates both this descriptive and normative dimension: as justificatory beings, we have both a capacity for justification *and* an inviolable moral status, which derives from our basic right to justification. To be sure, in contrast to Kant, Forst sides with the rest of the Frankfurt School in seeing the capacity of justification chiefly as a social and historical achievement, rather than as a metaphysical faculty of the mind. However, the right to justification has also been criticized for committing Forst to an untenable moral foundationalism and for relinquishing critical theory in favour of an 'applied-ethics' approach. We must now address this most controversial aspect of Forst's idea of the right to justification: namely, his account of the right to justification as the very *ground of morality*.

10.2.1 The Ground of Morality

Forst's truly *transcendental* moment—in the strong Kantian sense not only of reconstructing the conditions of possibility for practical reason but of *grounding* practical reason—begins with an observation, which can be posed as a dilemma for anyone, who wants to defend a form of Kantian constructivism, but who thinks that Forst's more ambitious transcendental impulses go too far (such as Habermas). Recall Habermas's objection to Apel's transcendental pragmatism, as discussed in Chapter 5, that Apel conflates the 'prescriptive "must" of a rule of action' with the '"must" in the sense of weak transcendental necessitation'.[6] In Habermas's view, the universalization principle is not a direct source of first-order moral rights and duties, but rather a rule of argumentation reconstructed from

---

[5] See Forst, *The Right to Justification*, p. 2.
[6] Habermas, *Justification and Application*, p. 81.

moral validity claims, which represents 'what it means to regard something from the moral point of view'. In other words, communicative reason can at most tell us *what it means* to raise a moral validity claim, but it cannot aspire to the prescriptive moral content of an *immediately practical* reason.

However, this is precisely where Forst smells a rat: the problem with Habermas's disavowal of practical reason is that such a disavowal actually runs afoul of the moral point of view, since the *categoricality* that Habermas thereby dispenses with is exactly *what morality means*. In Forst's words:

> the normative gap between the merely transcendental 'must' and the 'must' of justified norms must be filled. Otherwise we lose sight of the practical meaning that the principle of justification acquires in the context of morality, that is, the practical meaning that consists in the insight that in the moral context (and only there, as we must insist against Apel) one has an unconditional and categorical duty to justify modes or norms of action in a reciprocal and general manner towards those who are affected in morally relevant ways. The principle of justification must be viewed, *pace* Habermas, as normatively binding, for otherwise moral persons might indeed know *how* they should justify their actions but not *that* they are obliged to do so in a moral context.[7]

Forst's point here is that understanding the *rules* of the moral language game simply isn't enough; unless we also understand that we are unconditionally *bound* by these rules—that we are morally *obliged* to others—we will remain blind to the categorical nature of the moral point of view. Accordingly, Habermas must either countenance the categoricality of the principle of justification in moral contexts—and thus trade communicative reason for practical reason in his discourse-ethical account of moral validity claims—or he must remain unable to account for the very meaning of the moral point of view.

This seems to me a genuine dilemma for a Kantian constructivist such as Habermas, who seeks to detranscendentalize Kantian morality with appeal to communicative reason, but who also insists that philosophy can no longer aspire to *justify* first-order moral norms. Forst's solution to this dilemma is to come down fully on Kant's side, accepting the burden not only to reconstruct the conditions of possibility for practical reason in moral contexts, but also to provide a *grounding* of the moral use of practical reason. In doing so, Forst bases his case on another of Kant's central insights, namely that morality must *itself be autonomous*.

This means, in short, that morality must not appeal to other spheres of value, such as the good life or practical expediency, for an external justification or grounding (which, Kant notes, many a confused moral philosopher has believed), since that would undermine the unconditional and categorical nature of morality

---

[7] Forst, *The Right to Justification*, p. 57.

by making it dependent on a particular conception of the good life or whatever is prudent in a given situation. In a word, moral imperatives would become *hypothetical*, and thus not moral at all. To be sure, this might seem to complicate Forst's task, since the question now is how morality can be grounded without appeal to anything outside its own domain. It hardly seems possible that something can 'stand on itself' (the metaphor suggested by term 'grounding')—and if this indeed is the requirement, how can morality deliver its own ground? That is to say, how can we then, as Forst says, even begin to account for 'the normativity of the principle of justification'?[8]

Let us take a step back to clarify this point. Like Habermas, and unlike Honneth, Forst provides a constructivist account (in the metaethical sense) of normativity, according to which different norms are constructed from practical discourses guided by the justificatory criteria appropriate to a given context of justification. However, this account of normativity, including moral normativity, *rests* on the principle of justification, and the problem here is how to account for the normativity of *that* principle in its moral form, without going beyond the moral context itself. Kant faced the same problem with the categorical imperative (the moral law), and to fill this lacuna, he notoriously introduced the elusive term of a 'fact of reason' (*Faktum der Vernunft*).[9] In Kant's moral philosophy, it is our *awareness* of the moral law that is a fact of reason, but it is a peculiar kind of fact in that it has the status of a *reasonable insight*. Accordingly, despite appearances, the fact of reason is supposed to represent an active feat of comprehension of practical reason's own ground *through* practical reason itself. As Forst says, 'we *cognize* and *recognize* the law'.[10]

But what is this peculiar reasonable insight an insight *into*? It is here that Kant responds with reference to our *autonomy*: for Kant, morality is ultimately grounded in the dignity of our own rational nature—and the 'fact of reason' is an insight into our own autonomous selves. According to Forst, however, this answer is unsatisfactory:

> For the self-reflective appeal to *one's own* dignity and the requirement to respect it is not sufficient to explain the specifically moral aspect of the ought. What is missing is the reference to genuinely moral authority to which one owes moral action or responsibility. And without a God, who vouches for the sanctity of the law and the 'humanity in (one's) person' of which Kant speaks, the only possible ground of moral obligation is the *other human being* whose 'humanity' demands unconditional respect, simply because he or she is human.[11]

---

[8] Forst, *The Right to Justification*, p. 51.
[9] Kant, *Kritik der praktischen Vernunft*, p. 56.
[10] Forst, *The Right to Justification*, p. 53.
[11] Forst, *The Right to Justification*, p. 54 [emphasis added].

Forst's answer, therefore, to the question concerning the ground of morality, is the insight into the unconditional value of *other* human beings. Forst insists that this is not only an insight into the value of others as 'justificatory beings' but also as '*finite beings*'—into 'the various risks of human vulnerability and human suffering, bodily and psychological'.[12] In this insight, we thus encounter once again the dialectic between reflection on shared experiences of socially compelled suffering and the demand for reasons—in short, the dialectic between power and autonomy—as a form of moral learning that I have discussed throughout this book. Forst calls this a '*second-order practical insight*, a fundamental insight not only into the "how" but into the "that" of justification, that is, not only into the principle of justification but into the *unconditioned duty of justification* to which it corresponds'.[13]

What are the implications of this refurbished Kantian argument? Some have argued that that Forst's grounding of morality commits him to an untenable moral foundationalism that is at odds both with the more coherentist views that predominate in metaethics in the wake of Rawls's work and the post-metaphysical commitments of the Frankfurt School tradition.[14] Let us explore this question a bit further. The standard assumption in Anglo-American moral philosophy is that one can distinguish between metaethics and moral theory proper and maintain that even though the answers provided in moral theory may ultimately depend on the answers in metaethics, a 'division of labour' can nonetheless be maintained, such that moral theory can go about its business without constantly having to engage in metaethical rear-guard action. But the lesson of Forst's critique of Habermas's half-baked Kantianism is that for those who pursue an account of morality that is at once *deontological* and *constructivist*, things aren't that simple.

As we saw in Chapters 5 and 7, a moral constructivist believes that moral principles, judgments, norms, or even reasons are constructed through a suitably specified procedure, and that it is the fact that they have been constructed by such a procedure that lends them objectivity.[15] The most famous example of such a constructivist procedure is of course Kant's categorical imperative.[16] In Kant's moral philosophy, obligatory moral duties are constructed through application of the universalization requirement of the categorical imperative. As we saw above,

---

[12] Forst, *The Right to Justification*, p. 39.
[13] Forst, *The Right to Justification*, p. 35.
[14] See, for example, Stephen White, 'Does Critical Theory Need Strong Foundations?', *Philosophy and Social Criticism* (41/3), 2015: pp. 207–211.
[15] The *locus classicus* of constructivism is John Rawls, 'Kantian Constructivism in Moral Theory', in *Collected Papers*, ed. by Samuel Freeman (Cambridge MA: Harvard University Press, 2001), his amended account of 'political constructivism', John Rawls, *Political Liberalism. Expanded Edition* (New York: Columbia University Press, 2005), Ch. 3. See also Christine M. Korsgaard, 'Realism and Constructivism in Twentieth Century Moral Philosophy', in *The Constitution of Agency: Essays on Practical Reason and Moral Psychology* (Oxford: Oxford University Press, 2008).
[16] At least many interpreters have thought so. For just such an interpretation, see John Rawls, *Lectures on the History of Moral Philosophy*, ed. by Barbara Herman (Cambridge MA: Harvard University Press, 2000), Lecture VI. For a forceful objection to this interpretation, see Allen W. Wood, *Kantian Ethics* (Cambridge: Cambridge University Press, 2008).

Forst's approach is also constructivist in much this way, although he assigns the role of constructivist procedure to the principle of justification, which he sees as embedded and operative in actual social practice.

Now, as Forst argues, the problem here is that this leaves the normativity of the constructivist procedure unaccounted for, which seems to cast doubt on the 'that' of moral oughts—i.e., it may leave us with the question why we should feel *obligated* by moral judgements or norms, just because they derive from some 'suitably specified procedure'.[17] An account of this 'that' may not amount to an answer to the moral sceptic—as Forst insists it cannot—but it should at the very least tell us something about what makes the outcomes of the constructivist procedure *binding* on us. It is thus important to be clear about what precisely Forst's transcendental justification of morality entails.

As already mentioned, Forst explicitly emphasizes that his account of the ground of morality does not provide 'a "moral skeptic" with a reason to be moral'. Indeed, because such a sceptic is searching for a ground outside the moral domain, Forst stresses that the only possible meaning of the question 'Why be moral? ... if it has any at all, lies in showing how nonsensical it is since it asks for a reason that cannot ground the moral point of view'.[18] Accordingly, a central element of Forst's account of the ground of morality is simply to emphasize the point that—as we might say—'if you don't get it, you just don't get it'. But anyone who has been socialized into the lifeworld as a socially embodied space of reasons, and who is therefore able to competently navigate the moral context of justification, *already has* reached this insight—they *understand* that they *owe others* justifications for norms or actions that affect them, and not because it is a prudent rule for maximizing happiness or some other external standard. According to Forst, it is a *reasonable insight* rather than a 'moral feeling', as Horkheimer would have it, because it is an insight into the nature of moral reasons and their unconditionally and universally binding character.

In fact, Forst's claim that the ground of morality lies in a second-order practical insight into the right to justification seems to me to follow, quite straightforwardly, from the conjunction of three claims: (1) morality is autonomous (it is deontological), (2) a deontological-constructivist account of morality needs a grounding (it needs to account for the normativity of the constructivist principle), and (3) human beings have a basic right to justification. Since the latter claim is—as Thomas Scanlon would say—'a substantive, normative thesis about what reasons we have',[19] we might say that insofar as the substantive thesis (3) is correct, the insight that this is the case should be sufficient for any deontological constructivist to get on board with Forst's second-order practical insight. But this also means that

---

[17] This is what Christine Korsgaard calls 'the normative question' in *The Sources of Normativity*.
[18] Forst, *The Right to Justification*, p. 33.
[19] T.M. Scanlon, *What We Owe To Each Other* (Cambridge MA: Belknap Press, 1998), p. 365.

any disagreement with Forst will take place at the substantive, normative level of the claim that all human beings have a basic right to justification. In other words, Forst's moral foundationalism reduces to the claim that by realizing that others have a right to justification, I also gain a second-order practical insight into the ground of morality, since the insight that others have such a right *is itself an insight into that ground*. I thus fail to see the basis for the worry that Forst is committed to an untenable form of moral foundationalism; rather, Forst's 'grounding' of morality should be seen simply as an elaboration of *what it means to think and act morally*.

However, Forst has also been met with a different sort of critique, which argues that his emerging justification paradigm is not actually a paradigm *of critical theory* but rather a form of 'applied-ethics'.[20] Amy Allen charges Forst with pursuing a strategy of first developing and defending 'a normative philosophical framework that rests on independent—freestanding—grounds and then, in a second step, to apply this theory to the task of criticizing existing social relations'.[21] Allen is highly critical of such an approach, confronting it with a number of rhetorical questions:

> Can an approach such as this do justice to the depth and complexity of power relations, especially as these pertain to the conditions and practices of justification and practical reasoning and the ongoing entanglements of such notions in the subordination of women, queers, racial minorities, and subaltern subjects? Can it illuminate the power investments and normative exclusions on which the conceptions of justification and of practical reason so often seem to rest? Can it make sense of the notion of subjection, understood as a phenomenon of power that shapes and constitutes the space of reasons as such and, in so doing, renders some individuals systematically vulnerable to subordinating forms of identity?[22]

I agree with Allen to the extent that Forst invites this line of critique by focusing his attention on theories of justice and moral theory, and by sometimes speaking of 'practical reason' in a way that seems to abstract from the social practices (and relations of power and domination) within which practical reason is always embodied. But we shall see, Forst has in recent years increasingly turned his attention to developing a conceptual framework for a *critical theory of relations of justification* that connects his normative work with historical and sociological elements. As the cardinal term of his paradigm suggests, the concept of *justification* holds the same paradigmatic significance for Forst as communicative action does for Habermas and recognition for Honneth. Indeed, the concept and practice of justification represents the axis around which Forst seeks to build a critical theory of society, and out of which he seeks to develop a conceptual framework with emphases on such

---

[20] See Raymond Geuss, *Philosophy and Real Politics* (Princeton: Princeton University Press, 2008).
[21] Allen, *The End of Progress*, p. 151.
[22] Allen, *The End of Progress*, p. 152.

descriptive concepts as relations, orders, and narratives of justification, and, crucially, the normative concept of a *basic structure of justification*. I expound these concepts and the relations between them in the following section.[23]

10.3 A Critique of Relations of Justification

In his monumental study, 'Toleration in Conflict' (*Toleranz im Konflikt*) from 2003, Forst develops a two-pronged account of the concept of toleration: One the one hand, he presents a comprehensive 'critical history of argumentation' going back to the early Middle Ages, where the goal is 'to analyse the central arguments which were offered for an attitude or policy of toleration in their sociohistorical and philosophical contexts and to examine them critically, primarily with reference to their systematic content but also with regard to their role in the conflicts of their time'.[24] On the other hand, and on that basis, Forst develops a 'systematic theory of toleration', which takes up and develops one 'route to toleration', namely the one that Forst associates with Pierre Bayle and Immanuel Kant. One of the key findings of the study is that the history of conflicts about toleration emerge as

> the conflictual history of *a dynamic of power and morality*, which already makes sufficiently clear that this is also a history of power and of morality. But, more than that, it is also a history of the state, of law, of freedom, of religion, of autonomy, of the person, of recognition, etc. In short, it represents a multifaceted history of ourselves.[25]

Moreover, he also emphasizes that 'the call for toleration, especially in the political context, is associated from the outset with the language of *justice*, with criticism of intolerance and false toleration which are regarded as unjust and unjustifiable'.[26] The central claim in this regard is that, according to Forst, the concept of toleration is a *normatively dependent concept*, which means that, given the difference and incompatibility between existing conceptions of toleration, 'the concept of toleration ... *cannot* itself answer the question concerning [which one is] the best conception, since each of these conceptions can justifiably claim to be an interpretation of the concept [... The concept of toleration] is indeterminate without other normative principles'.[27] Accordingly, Forst's critical history of argumentation ultimately amounts to a history not only of the concept of toleration,

---

[23] I return to evaluate Allen's critique of Forst as defending an 'applied-ethics' approach in the Conclusion.
[24] Rainer Forst, *Toleration in Conflict. Past and Present* (Cambridge: Cambridge University Press, 2013), p. 13.
[25] Forst, *Toleration in Conflict*, p. 401 [emphasis added].
[26] Forst, *Toleration in Conflict*, p. 449.
[27] Forst, *Toleration in Conflict*, p. 32.

but also of the higher-order principles that must be invoked to adjudicate conflicts concerning the concept of toleration. According to Forst, the higher-order principle that emerges as the only possible normative basis for adjudicating these conflicts is *the principle of justification* itself, and the associated criteria of reciprocity and generality in the moral context of justification.

Much as for the young Horkheimer, Forst's justification paradigm of critical theory thus takes its beginnings with the 'historical agents who are no longer satisfied with the justifications for the normative order to which they are subjected'.[28] Such historical agents 'are always participants in a multiplicity of practices of justification—this is the social-philosophical thesis which [Forst defends] here; all of our thought and actions unfold in particular (social) spaces of reasons and what we call reason is the art of orienting oneself within and between them'.[29] Forst's approach thus amounts to conceiving of the social world as constituted ultimately through practices of justification, and his critical theory of relations of justification seeks to reflectively reconstruct its normative standard from the claims and contestations that historically situated human beings raise against one another.

However, this does not mean that these standards can then, without further ado, be reapplied to the social world from on high, since 'if one regards persons as social and at the same time autonomous beings who are, or should be, able to determine actively the normative structures which bind them', one must observe 'the principle of autonomy according to which it is those who are subjected themselves who should be the subjects, and not merely the objects, of justification in this practice'.[30] Justice must therefore not be understood as a standard that can be applied and realized behind the backs of individual persons, but must be conceived such that a just society is and must be *of their own making*:

> In the political space, which is not demarcated a priori from other social domains and is concerned with the exercise of rule within collectivities, the question of justification always arises in such a way that one must ask who can exercise such rule—if at all—over whom, for what reasons, and in what way.[31]

Forst unfolds this (Lenin-echoing) starting point through a conceptual framework that asks, first and foremost, how individual persons can become the justificatory masters of their own lives—that is, how they might establish a framework within which they will individually and collectively be able to determine their own lives through practices of justification. Moreover, he draws a crucial distinction between *fundamental* and *full* justice: 'The task of fundamental justice is to produce a *basic structure of justification*; the task of maximal justice is to produce a

---

[28] Rainer Forst, *Justification and Critique: Towards a Critical Theory of Politics*, transl. by Ciaran Cronin (Cambridge: Polity Press, 2014), p. 2.
[29] Forst, *Justification and Critique*, p. 2.
[30] Forst, *Justification and Critique*, p. 2–3.
[31] Forst, *Justification and Critique*, pp. 2–3.

fully justified basic structure'.[32] The fundamental requirement of justice is to establish the necessary conditions of possibility for individuals to *be able* to stand on a footing in which all have sufficient 'justificatory power' to participate as equals in establishing the ultimate requirement of justice: a fully justified society, which they have themselves determined. Accordingly, as the first and fundamental requirement of justice, a basic structure of justification can be understood as shorthand for *all those social, economic, political, and psychological conditions necessary for enjoying equal justificatory power*, and a fully justified basic structure as the outcome of autonomous individuals' discursive ordering of their own social and political world.

As we have seen, Forst develops a differentiated account of autonomy as a correlative at the individual level to the idea of a basic structure of justification. Following the different contexts of justification, autonomy differentiates into component domains of moral, ethical, legal, and political autonomy. Citizens of a political community must thus be able to integrate their moral, ethical, legal, and political selves as justificatory authorities in the contexts of moral norms, ethical values, and as subjects and authors of the law. However, as Forst intimates, this differentiated concept of autonomy also presupposes 'the social conditions necessary for the development of the capacity of autonomy and the possibility of its exercise'. Accordingly, '*Social* autonomy thus means that a person has the internal and external means of being an equal and responsible member of the political community, that is, being autonomous in the four senses'.[33] Only when all persons command these internal and external means can we talk of equal justificatory power and a basic structure of justification.

To sum up, Forst not only maintains that 'the core idea of a just order ... consists in the idea that its rulers and institutions of social life be *free of all forms of arbitrary rule or domination*';[34] he also emphasizes that this conception of justice as non-domination requires equally demanding *social and psychological conditions* for its realization. In 'Contexts of Justice' (*Kontexte der Gerechtigkeit*), his first book from 1994 based on his doctoral dissertation, Forst suggests that one might

> interpret the 'contexts of justification' as 'contexts of recognition'; this enables a differentiated view of different forms of the practical *relation-to-self* (recognition of one-self), which at the various levels correspond to relations of *being recognized* by other and of *recognizing others*.[35]

To be sure, Forst emphasizes that this account of contexts of recognition is not what he calls of 'theory-vindicating' importance, but rather 'expletive': 'it

---

[32] Forst, *The Right to Justification*, p. 196.
[33] Forst, *The Right to Justification*, p. 136.
[34] Forst, *The Right to Justification*, p. 189.
[35] Forst, *Contexts of Justice*, p. 276.

supplements and explains the idea of normative contexts and registers phenomena of recognition—and especially phenomena of the lack of recognition—to which a theory of justice must be conceptually sensitive'.[36] That is to say, contrary to what is the case in Honneth's recognition paradigm, the concept of recognition is not of foundational theoretical importance for Forst, but 'recognitional accounts provide an indispensable *sensorium* for experiences of social suffering generally and of injustice more narrowly'.[37] However, notwithstanding this important difference in theoretical emphasis (which I will discuss further below), it is clear that we can understand Forst's account of a basic structure of justification in terms of Honneth's concept of communicative freedom, which, in Forst's vocabulary, becomes a matter of being situated in *relations of mutual justificatory empowerment.*

Taken together, the basic structure of justification, as the fundamental requirement of justice undergirded by the basic right to justification, and the differentiated conception of individual autonomy thus represents the normative dimension of Forst's justificatory paradigm: his formal account of a 'reasonable society', in Horkheimer's terms. This normative dimension in turn calls for 'a comprehensive critique of relations of justification', which must offer

> an explanation of the failure or the lack of effective social and political structures of justification which would be tailored to uncovering and transforming unjustified relations. Historical and social analytical perspectives are essential in this regard.[38]

In fact, Forst draws a distinction that enables us to offer a further specification of the distinction between a traditional and a critical theory of justice that we identified in the original paradigm of the young Horkheimer. This distinction rests, again, on the simultaneously descriptive and normative character of the concept of justification: '[the concept of justification] refers to the justifications of social relations actually offered in a given society and it refers to the relations that could be accepted as justified in light of appropriate reasons'—the former representing the 'facticity' of justifications and the latter the 'validity' of justifications.[39] What I have called a traditional theory of justice is pitched purely at the level of validity; at the level at which justifications for ideal social and political institutions are developed. By contrast, Forst argues that the sphere of critique intervenes at a third level—between 'the world of what holds as a matter of fact' and 'the world of what holds counterfactually', as it were.[40] Indeed, as we saw in Chapter 1, a critical theory of justice does not develop a justification of an ideally just society in the abstract,

---

[36] Forst, *Contexts of Justice*, p. 175.
[37] Forst, *Justification and Critique*, p. 113.
[38] Forst, *Justification and Critique*, p. 8.
[39] Forst, *Justification and Critique*, p. 7.
[40] Rainer Forst, *Normativity and Power: Analyzing Social Orders of Justification*, transl. by Ciaran Cronin (Oxford: Oxford University Press, 2017), p. 24.

but rather turns the 'context-transcending' normative content of existing justifications *against* social reality, thus illuminating the way in which existing social relations and structures of domination *fail* to meet their own socially embedded normative promises, from which a positive outline of a just society can then be developed.

To be sure, this should also make clear that Forst's justification paradigm does not yet amount to a comprehensive critical theory of justice in the sense just specified, and he has yet to offer the kind of normatively guided, comprehensive historical and social-theoretical analysis of modern capitalist society that we find in Habermas's *Theorie des Kommunikativen Handelns* or Honneth's *Das Recht der Freiheit*. For such a theory must not only determine the formal requirements of justice at a normative level—it would also, as Forst himself recognizes, instantiate these requirements in a critical social analysis of actual relations of domination in the existing basic structure of society along a historical and a sociological dimension. These dimensions are in turn necessary conditions for the theory's ability to guide emancipatory practice—the whole *raison d'être* of a critical theory. As Forst acknowledges, the normative claim that fundamental justice *requires* a basic structure of justification does not in itself tell us *how to establish* such a structure. For that task, we need a comprehensive critical theory of society in *all* its dimensions.

To be sure, Forst has recently taken important steps in this direction, by developing a novel conceptualization of power and a descriptive conceptual apparatus of the relations, orders, and narratives of justification in which power congeals. Forst's account of what he (somewhat provocatively) calls *noumenal power* takes its starting point from an insight of Wilfrid Sellars's, which occurs in the course of Sellars's 'pragmatist' attack on epistemological foundationalism—or, in his famous expression, 'the myth of the given'. Sellars's basic claim is that there is no such thing as purely *empirical* descriptions of knowledge: cognition is structured not only by rules of inference, but also by reflexive metajudgements, as well as, crucially, norms of appropriateness, correctness, etc. In other words, cognition is *inherently normative*. This insight into the inherent normativity of cognition leads Sellars to conclude as follows:

> The essential point is that in characterizing an episode or a state as that of *knowing*, we are not giving an empirical description of that episode or state; we are placing it in the logical *space of reasons*, of justifying and being able to justify what one says.[41]

The 'space of reasons' is a noumenal space only in the weak sense that it is just such an inherently normative, rationally structured social space; it is not a 'thing

---

[41] Wilfrid Sellars, *Empiricism and the Philosophy of Mind*, ed. by Robert Brandom (Cambridge, MA: Harvard University Press, 1997), p. 76.

in itself' beyond the boundaries of knowledge. But Forst's innovation is precisely to harvest Sellars's insight for the concept of power. In Forst's paraphrase of Sellars,

> the essential point about power is that in characterizing a situation as an exercise of power, we do not merely give an empirical description of a state of affairs or a social relation; we also, and primarily, have to place it in the space of reasons, or the normative space of freedom and action.[42]

According to Forst, power operates *through* reasons for belief and action: 'to have and to exercise power means to be able—in different degrees—to influence, use, determine, occupy, or even seal off the space of reasons for others'.[43]

But what does it mean to exercise power through reasons—or, perhaps more to the point, what does it mean to say that reasons for belief and action are the *modus operandi* of power? Forst gives examples such as 'a "powerful" speech, a well-founded recommendation, an ideological description of the world, a seduction, an order that is accepted, or a threat that is perceived as real'.[44] But, as Forst is well aware, the perhaps most revisionist implication of noumenal power vis-à-vis ordinary language is that it prevents us from construing the direct use of physical force as a form of power:

> A threat gives the person who is threatened a reason to do something, but as long as a relation of power exists, at least one alternative way of acting is open to the person threatened. Otherwise this person would be a mere object, like a stone or a tree that is being moved. Thus, a case of pure force, where A moves B purely by physical means, by handcuffing him or her and carrying him or her away, is no longer an exercise of power, for the handcuffed person doesn't 'do' anything; rather, something 'is done' to him or her ... At that point, power as a relation between agents turns into brute physical force and violence, and the noumenal character vanishes. The person moved by sheer force is thus completely under the control of the other, as a mere physical object, and so, seen in isolation from noumenal-social contexts, is no longer an agent in the relevant sense ... In contrast to the exercise of physical force or violence, power rests on recognition.[45]

According to Forst, it is thus precisely when human beings act *causally* on each other—i.e., by acting through physical, bodily force—that power ceases to be. Power exists only when human beings relate to one another as agents in relations

---

[42] Forst, *Normativity and Power*, p. 38.
[43] Forst, *Normativity and Power*, p. 42 [emphasis removed].
[44] Forst, *Normativity and Power*, pp. 40–41.
[45] Forst, *Normativity and Power*, p. 41.

of mutual recognition. This claim may seem controversial at first, but by understanding power as operative in the 'realm of freedom', Forst is actually on the same page as a number of seminal theorists of power.[46] It echoes, for example, Thomas Hobbes's striking claim in *Behemoth*, while discussing the basis for the elusive non-coercive power of the Church, that 'the power of the mighty hath no foundation but in the opinion and belief of the people',[47] as well as his famous remark in *Leviathan* that 'reputation of power, is power'.[48] And, of course, Foucault makes the strikingly similar observation that

> a power relationship can only be articulated on the basis of two elements which are each indispensable if it is really to be a power relationship: that 'the other' (the one over whom power is exercised) be thoroughly recognized and maintained to the very end as a person who acts; and that, faced with a relationship of power, a whole field of responses, reactions, results, and possible inventions may open up.[49]

Forst's attempt to conceptualize relations of justification in terms of noumenal power rests on the companion notions of an 'order of justification' and a 'narrative of justification'. These two terms are introduced as follows:

> to have and to exercise power means to be able—in different degrees—to influence, use, determine, occupy, or even seal off the space of reasons for others. This can occur in the context of a single event, such as a powerful speech or an act of deceit, or of a sequence of events or in a general social situation or structure in which certain social relations are regarded as justified, reflexively or not, so that a social order comes to be accepted as an *order of justification*. Relations and orders of power are relations and orders of justification; and power arises and persists where justifications or social relations arise and persist, where they are integrated into certain *narratives of justification*. In the light of such narratives, social relations and institutions and certain ways of thinking and acting appear as justified and legitimate, possibly also as natural or in accordance with God's will.[50]

An *order of justification* refers to the relations within a concrete social and political order, or to that order as a whole, insofar as that order is supported by certain

---

[46] And, indeed, on the same page as Lord Varys, the royal spymaster (and eunuch) from the fantasy-novel-turned-TV-series *A Game of Thrones*, who suggests to Tyrion Lannister (a little person) that 'power resides where men believe it resides; it's a trick, a shadow on the wall, and a very small man can cast a very large shadow'.
[47] Thomas Hobbes, *Behemoth or The Long Parliament* (Chicago: University of Chicago Press, 1989), p. 16.
[48] Thomas Hobbes, *Leviathan* (London: Penguin Books, 1985), p. 150 [nouns decapitalized].
[49] Foucault, 'The Subject and Power', p. 789.
[50] Forst, *Normativity and Power*, p. 42.

justifications, norms, beliefs, and the like. In the present context, the importance of justifications thus derives from their being *vehicles of reasons* and supportive of orders of justification. Forst uses the term *normative order* as near-synonymous with orders of justification, both referring to 'the complex of norms and values, with which the basic structure of a society (or the structure of inter-, supra-, or transnational relations) are legitimated, in particular the exercise of political authority and the distribution of elementary vital and basic goods'.[51]

A *narrative of justification* is understood as 'embodiments of contextual rationality. In them, images, individual stories, rituals, facts, and myths are condensed into powerful grand narratives that serve as a resource for generating a sense of order'.[52] In other words, a narrative of justification represents a historically evolved pool of meaning, values, ideals, and individual and collective identities. As such, the idea of a justification narrative might seem proximate to what Habermas calls the lifeworld, but it is also importantly distinct from this concept, in that Forst explicitly understands a justification narrative as an 'order of power'; its principal modality is precisely the space of reasons in which power unfolds.

This implies that an important aspect of power lies in being able to control the cognitive and imaginative space of others; the art of tapping into and influencing the narratives of justification on which others rely for meaning, identity, and cognitive and practical orientation. Moreover, narratives of justification are also distinct from lifeworlds in not being monoliths; several narratives of justification can coexist and compete with one another within the same lifeworld, presumably integrated into more general and inclusive narratives of justification (along with certain overarching 'grand narratives' of justification, such as 'modernity'). Together, the notions of a narrative of justification and an order of justification represent a view of what we might call the epistemic vis-à-vis the social and political aspects of relations of justification: a narrative of justification is an epistemic framework that informs justifications, whereas an order of justification tends towards the more or less established relations of authority and rule in a society and their supporting justifications.

Against this background, Forst recognizes the existence of multiple *structures* in modern society that have become 'second nature', such as 'the components of an economic structure, from a property regime to a certain organization of production and distribution of goods through a (more or less regulated) market, and so forth'.[53] However, Forst denies that such structures determine our actions causally, emphasizing that a '"second nature" of acting (or "functioning") within certain structures presupposes acceptance of the rules of these structures, as well

---

[51] Rainer Forst and Klaus Günther, 'Die Herausbildung normativer Ordnungen: Zur Idee eines interdisziplinären Forschungsprogramms', *Normative Orders Working Paper* (01/2010), p. 7 [my translation].
[52] Forst, *Normativity and Power*, p. 57.
[53] Forst, *Normativity and Power*, p. 44.

as of certain justifications offered for them, such as ideas about property, cooperation, or efficiency, but also notions of fairness, desert, and the like'. Accordingly, Forst follows Honneth in claiming that 'such structures are not "norm-free"'— they rest on certain narratives of justifications, which may provide good or bad, or even ideological justifications in their favour, and 'even though a social structure can be reduced neither to its narrative foundations nor to a narrow set of such justifications, it does rest on such foundations'.[54]

In *The End of Progress*, Amy Allen argues that Forst's account of noumenal power 'seems to imply an account of power where no one can oppress you without your permission that puts too much responsibility for upholding relations of dominance on those who are subordinated to the power of others'.[55] Accordingly, Allen maintains that when 'used to analyze relations of oppression and domination, this way of conceptualizing power seems to imply that, for example, I am subject to masculine domination only insofar as I recognize it as being justified (whether that justification rests on good or bad reasons)'.[56] But this is a misconstrual of Forst's view. As G.A. Cohen has argued, if I am 'forced *to do*' something, such as when a person attempts to threaten me into a certain action by blackmailing me, I am still, in the relevant sense, *free* not to do what he asks me to do—I retain a choice whether or not to follow his instructions. In Cohen's view, the relevant consideration is that when 'a person is forced to do something he has no *reasonable* or *acceptable* alternative course'.[57] That is, if I choose to follow his instructions, I am indeed compelled to do so, precisely because the alternative is so grim:

> Consider two ways in which Smith, who wants Jones out of the room, might contrive to achieve this aim. Smith might drag Jones over to the door and push him out, there, as we say, *forcing* him out of the room. Or he might get Jones to leave by credibly threatening to shoot him unless he does. Now in the second case, but not the first, it is natural to say that Jones is forced *to leave* the room. Only in the second case is there something that Jones is forced to *do*, since in the first case he does nothing, or nothing relevant: he is just pushed out. And I suggest the contrast is connected with the fact that in the second case Jones has an alternative: he is free to stand fast and be shot.[58]

There is no sense in which Jones must regard the power that Smith exercises over him by threatening to shoot him as *justified*, just as there is no sense in which Allen must necessarily regard masculine domination as justified in order for her

---

[54] Forst, *Normativity and Power*, p. 45.
[55] Allen, *The End of Progress*, p. 148.
[56] Allen, *The End of Progress*, p. 149.
[57] G.A. Cohen, 'Are Disadvantaged Workers Who Take Hazardous Jobs Forced To Take Hazardous Jobs?', in *History, Labour, and Freedom: Themes From Marx* (Oxford: Oxford University Press, 1988), p. 245.
[58] Cohen, 'Are Disadvantaged Workers Who Take Hazardous Jobs Forced To Take Hazardous Jobs?', p. 245.

to be subject to masculine domination. Rather, being subject to power is often precisely a matter of recognizing that several paths are open to me, but that my choice situation has been *unjustifiably engineered* by others in such a way that if I choose a different path to the one that they prefer, I will face certain negative consequences. Of course, I may be deluded about my options, and that delusion may itself be a form of power exercised over me, but it is a caricature of Forst's noumenal view of power to say that I am subject to domination only insofar as I consider such domination justified.

However, I want to argue that Forst's theory of noumenal power *is* vulnerable to a different kind of objection. This vulnerability stems from his claim that structures 'do not "exercise" power as persons do; rather, they rely on and provide opportunities for exercising it'.[59] Indeed, Forst is adamant that we cannot speak of structural domination in the absence of the structure in question enabling some agent or social group to dominate another group or agent: 'a complex social structure of inequality is not produced or controlled by single agents; but that does not mean that powerful agents do not use it for their aims, that they do not do what they can to reproduce and stabilize it and to make sure they benefit from it'. In his view, structural 'power structures action and structural domination expresses and enables the exercise of domination by some over others; and if we want to call that kind of domination, as we should, a form of structural injustice, we must not anonymize what is going on'. According to Forst, if 'the "deprivation" referred to was a simple social or natural accident, one would not call it domination', since doing so 'would be to neglect the question of responsibility for structural injustice, and deprive critical theory of social bite'.[60]

What is most remarkable about these reflections in the present context is, of course, that Forst's rejection of a genuinely structural (or 'systemic'[61]) form of domination—i.e., one that is not regarded as such in virtue of a structure enabling some agents to dominate others, but rather because of its generalized effects on agents—is that it is in manifest contradiction with a central conception of domination of the whole Frankfurt School tradition. Recall the tripartite distinction that I drew in Chapter 7 between three forms of power that we find in this tradition: agential power, structural power, and relational power. I argued that while agential power refers to the capacity of an agent to manipulate or influence another's reasoning (as familiar from Weber's work), and relational power refers to a form of power that is constitutive of the space of reasons as such (as familiar from the 'ontological' conception of power in Foucault's work), structural power refers to the systematic empowering and disempowering effects that structures have upon agents and social groups.

---

[59] Forst, *Normativity and Power*, p. 45.
[60] Rainer Forst, 'Noumenal power revisited: reply to critics', *Journal of Political Power*, (11/3), 2018: pp. 294–321, p. 307.
[61] Dorothea Gädeke, *Politik der Beherrschung: Eine kritische Theorie externer Demokratieförderung* (Berlin: Suhrkamp Verlag, 2017).

While it is true that we can think of class domination as a form of structural power defined as such in virtue of structurally enabling the capitalist class to dominate the proletariat (in accordance with Forst's view), we clearly also find a continuous concern throughout the Frankfurt School tradition with conceptualizing a genuinely structural form of domination: namely, the problem of reification. This is not to say that it is impossible to tell a story about how reification reinforces class domination, but this would be to miss the systematic intention of the concern, I believe. To be sure, reification functionally reinforces the existence of capitalist relations of productions by undermining the class consciousness or self-reflective capacities of agents—i.e., by treating and compelling them to self-identify as objects or clients/consumers—but it is not properly understood as a 'tool' or instrument used by the capitalist class to sustain their domination. Rather, Horkheimer (and Lukács), Adorno, and Habermas all clearly conceive of reification (or systems-colonization) as a genuinely *structural pathology* of the capitalist mode of production.

Forst's concern that conceptually allowing for such 'anonymous' structural forces obscures responsibility for injustice—as well as his suggestion that we would not call 'social or natural accidents' domination—miss their mark, I believe. Indeed, it is *precisely* the notion that forms of structural domination such as reification or systems-colonization systematically impair individual autonomy without any single agent or social group being 'responsible' for this impairment that is so distinctive and unsettling about this recurring theme in the Frankfurt School tradition. Such forms of structural domination are neither intentional impositions nor mere happenstance, but rather 'unconscious' social products, to put it in Lukács's terms; they are the unintended, aggregate macro-consequences of patterns of individual actions, which can, however, be described independently of the micro-level from which they arise.[62] If we relinquish this concept of genuinely structural domination, we would indeed deprive critical theory of 'social bite' by foreclosing its analytical ability to pursue one of the tradition's defining systematic interests: namely, into the 'predominance of social relations over human beings, whose disempowered products they virtually are,'[63] where the societal 'process is realised as a natural occurrence and not under the control of a conscious will.'[64]

10.4 Beyond Proceduralism and Ethical Life

Having expounded the basic tenets of Forst's justification paradigm, I now want to show how his Kantian constructivism steers a middle path between Habermas's

---

[62] Iris Marion Young, *Responsibility for Justice* (Oxford: Oxford University Press, 2013).
[63] Adorno, 'Gesellschaft', p. 827 [emphasis added].
[64] Horkheimer, 'Materialismus und Moral', pp. 116–117.

communicative paradigm and Honneth's recognition paradigm and overcomes their respective impediments to a critical theory of world society. Recall, again, that Habermas's communicative paradigm develops a purely procedural account of discourse ethics, in which the universalization principle is viewed as a second-order rule of moral argumentation, and the discourse principle is seen as legally institutionalized in the form of a system of rights, eliciting the democratic principle. This discourse-theoretical account of the democratic rule of law is then extended to the global context of application, where Habermas calls for the legal institutionalization of the discourse principle in a global multilevel constitutional framework more suitable for the postnational constellation. However, as we saw in Chapter 6, Habermas's focus on re-establishing the institutional conditions of legal and political autonomy remains insufficiently sensitive to the broader social and economic conditions of autonomy. This is a particularly troubling theoretical blind spot in the global context with its vast socioeconomic inequalities and profound asymmetries of power, to which Habermas effectively renders himself theoretically blind. This problem ultimately derives from Habermas's hardnosed proceduralism and his insistence that first-order questions of justice belong to discursive practice, and thus lie beyond the pale of discourse theory.

In contrast to Habermas's purely procedural account of discourse ethics, Forst's Kantian constructivism fuses procedural elements with more substantive concerns of justice, as we have seen. This principled disagreement over 'how far' discourse ethics can penetrate into the moral domain, and whether it allows for the derivation of substantive moral rights and duties, ultimately stems from Habermas's self-imposed limitation to the 'how' of moral justification, whereas Forst insists that a specification of the moral point of view must also provide an account of the 'that' of moral justification. By 'grounding' morality in the right to justification, Forst thus recalibrates the second-order principle of universalization into (also being) a first-order principle of an immediately practical reason. It follows that discourse ethics has licence to abandon the confines of a purely procedural point of view and derive the unconditionally binding moral requirement to establish a *global basic structure of justification*.[65]

In one sense, both Forst and Honneth are considerably better positioned than Habermas, in that they both seek to derive first-order moral principles from a socially embodied moral normativity. However, there are also important differences between Forst's and Honneth's respective paradigms, which ultimately stem from the respective concerns that motivate Forst's theoretical privileging of the concept of justification and Honneth's theoretical privileging of the concept of

---

[65] Of course, beyond his more cautious post-metaphysical predispositions, Habermas's modesty in this regard may also be motivated by a conviction that there is little methodological gain in such an endorsement of an immediate practical reason, since a theory of justice risks decoupling from practice in a way that undermines its ability to offer effective emancipatory advice (Habermas has indeed expressed this concern in private conversation). I address this worry below.

recognition. At the heart of this disagreement lies a dispute concerning which normative criteria are 'doing to the work' in a theory of justice: is it the abstract moral criteria of reciprocity and generality, as Forst contends, or rather the 'social norms and corresponding roles' specified by a 'principle of recognition' in a given sphere of social freedom? This is to some extent, as Forst and Honneth both emphasize, a disagreement that harks back to Kant and Hegel, with Forst maintaining the 'a priori of justification' and Honneth invoking Hegel's 'empty formalism' objection to Forst's Kantian principle of justification, maintaining that 'mutual recognition always precedes discourse'.[66]

To be sure, we might think that the distance between Forst's and Honneth's views is in fact shorter than both are willing to admit. As we have seen, Forst recognizes that contexts of justice and orders of justification can be conceptualized as contexts (and orders) of mutual recognition, in which subjects empower and recognize each other as equals, who have a right to demand and a duty to offer justifications. And as we have also seen, Honneth's mature work places much greater emphasis on the lifeworld as a habitually learned, socially embodied 'space of reasons', and that recognition must be 'motivated by reasons, which we can also try to articulate as necessary', if we are to be able to understand it as expanding the 'domain of the moral'.[67] Indeed, I believe we can to some extent see Honneth and Forst as developing *different but complementary accounts of the social order*, where Honneth focuses to a much greater extent on the social and psychological aspects of relationships of mutual recognition and their corresponding relations-to-self, whereas Forst focuses on the reasons that motivate us to demand and offer recognition and the normative status (the right to justification) that we mutually afford one another in relationships of communicative freedom.

Notwithstanding these theoretical overlaps and disagreements, however, what seems to me decisive in the present context is that Honneth's uncompromising *methodological* commitment to reconstructing the embodied normativity of existing spheres of social freedom runs into trouble when *no such institutions exist*, or when the limited scope of existing institutions of social freedom is itself part of the problem. That is to say, the Hegelian method of normative reconstruction and critique meets its limits precisely when there is no overarching 'culture of freedom'. As we have seen, this problem is particularly crippling in the global context of application, which is characterized precisely by its conspicuous dearth of genuine institutions of social freedom, or perhaps by the presence of institutions of social freedom whose normative content has been stretched so thin that even Honneth recognizes they have come to effectively resemble Habermas's functional subsystems, such as financial and globalized markets. Or—where the limited scope of

---

[66] See Forst, *Justification and Critique*, p. 118; Axel Honneth, 'Rejoinder', in *Axel Honneth: Critical Essays. With a Reply by Axel Honneth*, ed. by Danielle Petherbridge (Leiden: Brill, 2011), p. 416.

[67] Honneth, 'Grounding Recognition: A Rejoinder to Critical Questions', p. 507.

existing institutions of social freedom are in some sense part of the problem, in that a reconstruction of such institutions is fundamentally unable to grasp the forces that frustrate and undermine their promise of social freedom except as a kind of mysterious and external disruptive influence, because those forces are today truly global in nature, and where the only way to tame those forces may be to imaginatively construct *new* institutions of social freedom, to expand or possibly even supplant the old.

By contrast, from a normative point of view, Forst's justification paradigm allows both a *reconstruction* of existing institutions of social freedom and the imaginative *construction* of new social and political institutions, if such institutions are necessary to establish a global basic structure of justification and give reality to every human being's basic right to justification. Accordingly, this crucial methodological difference makes Forst's justification paradigm much better equipped to critically engage with the global context of application, since Forst's idea of a basic structure of justification is able to not only guide the reconstruction of existing institutional relations of mutual justificatory empowerment, but also to require their extension or establishment where such relations do not yet exist. That is to say, if, under present conditions, transnational or even global institutions of social freedom are necessary for realizing an effective basic structure of justification, then we must endeavour to *develop* such institutions in order to accommodate one another's right to justification.

Of course, Honneth may retort here that such normative stipulation is much too removed from the operative moral motivations of existing agents to have any practical purchase in social reality. However, the problem is that if we take this objection as decisive, we at the same time relinquish the possibility of a critical theory of world society. Indeed, even though Honneth is surely right from an empirical point of view that the 'normative constraints' derived from the 'expectations of recognition' that subjects raise against the 'developmental processes in contemporary capitalism' are still largely circumscribed along the territorially demarcated lifeworld borders of nation-states, there seems to be no way of confronting the monumental challenges with which we are today confronted by globalized capitalist modernity unless those constraints and expectations are themselves *given* some kind of transnational or even global institutional form— as Honneth himself recognizes at the end of *Das Recht der Freiheit*, in manifest violation of the self-imposed limitations of his Hegelian method.

The risk of catastrophic climate change; the depths of global poverty and extreme degree of global inequality; the vast increase in refugees and displaced people; the structural pressure exerted on wages, organized labour and democratic politics by economic globalization; the destabilizing and disruptive effects that globally integrated financial markets exercise on politics and various sectors in the real economy, including global food markets; the ever-increasing wealth of the superrich; the gradual undermining of the tax base of both wealthy welfare states and poorer developing nations by global tax evasion and international tax competition; the seemingly unending cycle of global economic instability and crisis; the instantaneous spread of pandemics and infectious disease; the spread of populist authoritarianism across capitalist democracies; the enduring legacy of centuries of European colonialism, imperialism, and racism—the list could go on. The unsettling fact is that these epoch-defining problems all to some extent issue from our fractured and crisis-ridden emergent world society, and they all seem to require *some kind* of transnational or global institutional solutions—and these solutions must be democratically legitimated in a fairly robust sense, if they are not to become instruments of more pernicious forces.[68]

If the Frankfurt School tradition is to engage critically and constructively with these problems—and if it is to hope to retain its relevance and emancipatory aspirations in the twenty-first century—its theoretical and methodological resources must be urgently refocused on the development of a critical theory of global capitalist modernity. Of course, this does not mean that Honneth's reconstructive methodology loses its relevance in contexts where institutions of social freedom *do exist*—far from it. But if, from a Hegelian point of view, Forst's Kantian constructivism might seem throw us back from the domain of democratic *Sittlichkeit* to the more abstract moral domain of *Moralität*, it seems to me that it is in fact the nature of the *at once deeply integrated and fragmented world that we inhabit*, which, to some extent, throws us back on principles of moral and political construction. This metanormative and methodological insight is one, I believe, which forces itself upon us as soon as we engage in sustained reflection on the one context of application that has today become truly inescapable for critical theory: the context of our bourgeoning world society.

10.5 A Critical Theory of Transnational Justice

I have argued that Forst's Kantian constructivism is uniquely suited to serve as the normative foundation for a critical theory of world society. In this final section, I want to expound Forst's own reflections on global justice and see if the way in which he seeks to develop this theory may help us chart the path to developing a comprehensive critical theory of world society. Forst casts these reflections in terms of a 'critical theory of transnational justice', which he develops in sustained engagement with the philosophical literature on global justice. The predominant theorists in this body of literature fall into two opposed camps, while a third camp has more recently emerged that attempts to chart a path between them.[69]

---

[68] Honneth and Fraser, *Redistribution or Recognition*, p. 250.
[69] For a view that is congenial both to Forst's theory and the project of this book, but which places greater emphasis on questions of agency, see Lea Ypi, *Global Justice & Avant-Garde Political Agency* (Oxford: Oxford University Press, 2012).

Firstly, political theorists like John Rawls, Ronald Dworkin, and Thomas Nagel subscribe to what is often called a *political conception of justice*. According to this view, duties of socioeconomic or distributive justice are necessarily dependent on, in Nagel's words, 'a special involvement of agency or the will that is inseparable from membership in a political society'. In this view, the domestic nation-state is the *sole* context of justice proper, because the 'societal rules determining its basic structure are coercively imposed', and it is the only context in which 'we are both putative joint authors of the coercively imposed system, and subject to its norms'.[70] By contrast, theorists such as Thomas Pogge, Charles Beitz, and Simon Caney defend different variations of what is known as *cosmopolitanism*, which might be defined by the claim that 'every human being has a global stature as an ultimate unit of moral concern'.[71] The nature of this 'moral concern' can be understood in substantively different ways, and the 'global stature' can be understood either as interpersonal or as institutionally mediated, but what cosmopolitan positions all share is a commitment to the claim that principles of justice apply globally: that is, they share a commitment to the claim that the global context is a context of justice.

One of the central disagreements in the debate between cosmopolitans and those committed to a political conception turns on the question, *whether there exists a global basic structure*. The 'basic structure of society' is understood here in Rawls's terms, as 'the way in which the major social institutions fit together into one system, and how they assign fundamental rights and duties and shape the division of advantages that arises through social cooperation'.[72] Those committed to the political conception often deny that anything like a global basic structure exists,[73] whereas cosmopolitans tend to argue that a sufficiently developed global basic structure does indeed exist.[74]

The philosophical debate on global justice has been dominated by these two approaches since its inception in the 1970s, but in recent years intermediate positions have emerged that have contributed to a more differentiated and interesting theoretical landscape. One of these positions is the so-called *practice-dependence view*, which holds that principles of justice 'must be grounded in independent judgments about what social practices exist and what kinds of agents participate

---

[70] Thomas Nagel, 'The Problem of Global Justice', *Philosophy & Public Affairs* (33/2), 2005: pp. 113–147, p. 128. See also John Rawls, *The Law of Peoples* (Cambridge MA: Harvard University Press, 2001) and Ronald Dworkin, *Sovereign Virtue*.
[71] Thomas Pogge, *World Poverty and Human Rights* (Cambridge: Polity Press, 2002), p. 169; Simon Caney, *Justice Beyond Borders: A Global Political Theory* (Oxford: Oxford University Press, 2005); Charles R. Beitz, *Political Theory and International Relations* (Princeton: Princeton University Press, 1979).
[72] John Rawls, *Political Liberalism*, p. 258.
[73] Samuel Freeman, 'The Law of Peoples, Social Cooperation, Human Rights, and Distributive Justice', in *Justice and Global Politics: Volume 23*, ed. by Ellen Frankel Paul, Fred D. Miller, and Jeffrey Paul Jr. (Cambridge: Cambridge University Press, 2006).
[74] Beitz, Political Theory and International Relations; Allen Buchanan, 'Rawls's Law of Peoples: Rules for a Vanished Westphalian World', *Ethics* (110/4), July 2000: pp. 697–721.

in them.'[75] Accordingly, practice-dependence theorists hold that principles of justice are indexed to existing social practices, both in terms of their scope and moral content. Evidently, because the practice-dependence view 'tracks' existing social practices, it seems to offer a more differentiated and 'piecemeal' approach to questions of global justice than the simple and rather unfruitful disagreement concerning the existence or non-existence of a full-blown global basic structure that characterizes the stalemate between the political conception and cosmopolitanism.

However, Forst criticizes the most prominent practice-dependence theorists for subscribing to a kind of *practice positivism*, in that these theorists seem to view an established cooperative practice regulated by substantive norms as a necessary condition of application for principles of justice, which in some cases effectively collapses their view into a version of the political conception.[76] More perniciously, an implication of this strategy is also to screen out precisely those practices in which justice is *most needed*—to wit: relations of domination—in favour of those in which individuals and states already 'cooperate' and thus hold themselves to certain established standards and norms.[77] By contrast, Forst's approach starts precisely by identifying existing relations of domination, although the right to justification is 'triggered' wherever relations of power prevail, including, obviously, those that characterize more cooperative practices.[78] This enables Forst to sketch a differentiated account of multiple contexts of justice tracking national, transnational, and global relations of rule and domination, with a certain priority awarded to the nation-state. However, Forst also argues that these relations of domination can only be overcome by establishing a *transnational basic structure of justification*.

To be sure, in the course of developing his ideas he seems to have changed his mind about what precisely such a transnational basic structure of justification involves. The core idea has remained much the same, and this core can be brought out by considering Forst's 'reflexive' justification of democracy and human rights, which represents his version of Habermas's cooriginality thesis. In Forst's view, both democracy and human rights ultimately derive from the right to justification. This view is distinguished from Habermas's—who, recall, maintains that the

---

[75] Aaron James, 'Constructing Justice for Existing Practice: Rawls and the Status Quo', *Philosophy & Public Affairs* (33/3), 2005: pp. 281–316, p. 282. See also Miriam Ronzoni, 'The Global Order: A Case of Background Injustice? A Practice-Dependent Account', *Philosophy & Public Affairs* (37/3), 2009: pp. 229–256; and Andrea Sangiovanni, 'Justice and the Priority of Politics to Morality', *The Journal of Political Philosophy* (16/2), 2008: pp. 137–164.

[76] Andrea Sangiovanni, 'Global Justice, Reciprocity, and the State', *Philosophy & Public Affairs* (35/1), 2007: pp. 3–39. For a similar objection that focuses on James's view, see Malte Frøslee Ibsen, 'Global Justice and Two Conceptions of Practice-Dependence', *Raisons Politiques* (51/3), 2013: pp. 81–96.

[77] Rainer Forst, 'Transnational Justice and Democracy', in *Political Equality in Transnational Democracy*, ed. by Eva Erman and Sofia Näsström (New York: Palgrave MacMillan, 2013), p. 48.

[78] Forst is not completely alone in this approach. Laura Valentini's view is in some respects close to his, although she begins from existing forms of coercion rather than rule and domination. Laura Valentini, *Justice in a Globalized World: A Normative Framework* (Oxford: Oxford University Press, 2011).

universalization principle and the democratic principle are different 'shapes' of the discourse principle, towards which the latter is 'strictly neutral'[79]—precisely by locating a *moral* source, or a morally obligatory 'ultimate ground', of both democracy and rights.

Furthermore, Forst argues that the right to justification branches out into two modes of construction, namely what he, with inspiration from Rawls, calls *moral constructivism* and *political constructivism*. This distinction tracks the distinction between fundamental justice and full justice in the sense that moral constructivism specifies the necessary and sufficient conditions for establishing a basic structure of justification, of which human rights are an essential component part, whereas political constructivism remains the work of *citizens themselves*, who, on the basis of the basic structure of justification, 'have the means to deliberate and decide in common about the social institutions that apply to them and about the interpretation and concrete realization of their rights.'[80] The language of human rights can thus be understood as a historically evolved way of capturing the social and psychological conditions of autonomy (which is, comparatively speaking, arguably a very ambitious conception of human rights), while democracy is understood as

> a political practice of argumentation and reason-giving among free and equal citizens, a practice in which individual and collective perspectives and positions are subject to change through deliberation and in which only those norms, rules, or decisions that result from some form of reason-based agreement among the citizens are accepted as legitimate.[81]

However, when it comes to the *institutionalization* of human rights and the basic structure of justification, Forst seems to have moved from a view in his earlier work that emphasizes the importance of legal institutionalization in concrete political communities towards what he calls a *processual* understanding of democratic self-determination. In his earlier work, Forst suggests that 'the concepts of addressee and author of norms are differentiated within *one* community.'[82] The 'constitution, as the basic legal institution, has the double task of fixing a list of basic rights that citizens of a democratic order ... have to grant and guarantee one another ... and of laying down the principles and rules of a fair deliberative procedure.'[83] Moreover, with regard to the transnational and global contexts, his earlier work emphasizes that whether 'the institutionalization of minimal [i.e. fundamental] justice and the results of justificatory discourses on that basis will lead to a federation of states in a subsidiary "world republic" or to something like a "world state" is hard to predict

---

[79] Habermas, *Between Facts and Norms*, p. 121.
[80] Forst, *Justification and Critique*, p. 65.
[81] Forst, *The Right to Justification*, p. 155.
[82] Forst, *Contexts of Justice*, p. 267.
[83] Forst, *The Right to Justification*, p. 182.

and should not be predetermined'.[84] Yet it is clear that both of these scenarios rest on more or less demanding ways of *constitutionalizing* human rights and the basic structure of justification in the transnational or global context.

In his more recent work, however, he seems to have become less wedded to the idea that a basic structure of justification necessarily requires a concrete and formalized constitutional framework and a determinate political community. This change of mind also seems connected with subtle a change in Forst's view of the very *concept* of democracy. The processual conception of democracy that Forst now espouses seems more institutionally decoupled and less couched in the constitutional and legal terms that are so central to Habermas's communicative paradigm. In his more recent work, he writes: 'The basic structure of justification to which this theory refers aims to create structures of participation and legitimation that can assume and perform the tasks of opening and critique, culminating in the justification and adoption of binding transnational and international norms'.[85] However,

> Democracy as a practice of justice ... must be liberated from the narrow alternative 'world state or world of states' and it is understood as a normative order in which those who are subject to rule or norms should also be the normative authority ... Thus the question of the relevant *demoi* is answered in terms of the existing structures of rule, and the answer to the question of codetermination and the requisite institutional form depends on the degree of subjection.[86]

This seems to be a more fluid and multilayered view of democracy as realized in overlapping *demoi*, where these *demoi* 'track' the given relations of rule and domination to which individuals are subject, rather than the single and fixed *demos* of a constitutional community: 'Justice and democracy are primarily recuperative and processual in nature and are not justified ex nihilo: *demoi* generally take shape through prior social relations that stand in need of justification'.[87] There is here, it seems to me, a much more institutionally free-floating concept of democracy in play than in his earlier work:

> Where privileged actors are forced to surrender their prerogatives because these lose their legitimation when exposed within a system of justification and because counterpower forms—where this occurs—it represents an increase in democracy ... Democracy progresses—often only in modest steps—where nonlegitimized rule, be it political, legal, or economic, is subjected to the justificatory

---

[84] Forst, *The Right to Justification*, p. 265.
[85] Forst, 'Transnational Justice and Democracy', pp. 51–52.
[86] Forst, 'Transnational Justice and Democracy', pp. 52–53.
[87] Forst, 'Transnational Justice and Democracy', pp. 53–54.

authority of those affected. Democracy as a practice is always a matter of *democratization*, of expanding, and equalizing justificatory power ... It is no more confined to long-established institutions and political ways of thinking than are the relations of rule to which we are subjected.[88]

Now, whether this actually represents a change of mind or merely a change of emphasis, the more relevant question is whether a more institutionally embedded conception of democracy is normatively preferable to a more processual and free-floating (i.e. rule- and domination-tracking) understanding, or *vice versa*.[89] To be sure, we may suppose that these two options are not mutually exclusive, but that institutionalized *demoi* simply represent more consolidated democratic practices than those that operate in greater independence of established institutions—and this might indeed be Forst's view. However, if we think of these two options as points on a continuum, it seems to me that the processual notion of democracy is extremely important as a complement to Habermas's one-sided emphasis on top-down global and transnational constitutionalization: indeed, the idea of construing the subjection of any kind of illegitimate power to the justificatory power of affected subjects as democratization serves to conceptually emphasize the decisive importance of precisely those extra-institutional struggles in bourgeoning transnational public spheres that fall into the background of Habermas's later and more institutionally focused work, as well as the ways in which the international state system may *itself* represent a vehicle of domination for marginalized and subaltern states.

---

[88] Forst, 'Transnational Justice and Democracy', p. 54.
[89] For a similar view to Forst's processual view, see James Bohman, Democracy Across Borders: From Dêmos to Dêmoi (Cambridge MA: MIT Press, 2007).

Conclusion
The Tasks of a Critical Theory of World Society

In these concluding pages, I want to take stock of the tasks of a critical theory of world society by assembling the insights reaped through both the reconstructive and the systematic chapters of this book. However, before doing so, I want to dispel a serious worry that may have arisen in the last two chapters of this book. In these chapters, I introduced two emerging paradigms of critical theory as a complement to this book's reconstruction of the Frankfurt School tradition as four paradigms of critical theory, because I believe that through Amy Allen's contextualist paradigm and Rainer Forst's justification paradigm, the shape of a critical theory of world society truly begins to take form.

Although I have taken issue with parts of Allen's critique of Habermas and Honneth and argued that her metanormative contextualism cannot, in some of its central claims, be sustained, I have also argued that a critical theory of world society must embrace Allen's problematizing critique as a reflexive check against ideological misuse and unquestioned biases and blind-sports. To be sure, I have also argued that Allen's problematizing critique is in itself an insufficient methodological approach for a critical theory of world society, and without Forst's Kantian constructivism such a theory will be unable to offer the critique of global injustice, which, for different reasons, escapes both Habermas's proceduralism and Honneth's Hegelianism. It follows that a critical theory of world society must combine and integrate a critique of the global injustices of world society, rooted in Kantian constructivism, with the denaturalizing reflexive check of self-problematizing critique.

However, in the course of this book's discussions of the disagreements between Allen and Habermas, Honneth and Forst, over the possibility of immanent transcendence, the pitfalls of narratives of socio-cultural and moral learning, and the possibility of a universal context of justice, the reader might have concluded that Forst's Kantian constructivism and Allen's self-problematizing critique represent two fundamentally conflicting and mutually exclusive orientations for a critical theory of society. Accordingly, it may therefore seem as if my claim that a critical theory of world society must combine and integrate both of these perspectives is doomed to futility. This would, I believe, be a serious misunderstanding. Indeed, in the following subsection, I want to dispel this suspicion by arguing, first, that both of these approaches can be understood as anchored in one of the central and enduring themes of the Frankfurt School tradition of critical theory—namely, in the dialectic between power and autonomy—and second, that the triadic combination of a constructive, a reconstructive, and a problematizing moment not only captures how the young Horkheimer conceived of the critical enterprise, but also how contemporary critical theorists such as Thomas McCarthy and (perhaps surprisingly) Axel Honneth explicitly define the basic methodological tasks of critical theory.

11.1 Kantian Constructivism and Self-Problematizing Critique: The Dialectic of Power and Autonomy

In Chapter 7, I defined relational power as a conception that sees power as an ontological space of reasons arising in relations of conflict and cooperation between subjects, and which *constitutes* them as subjects in the first place (subjection, in Foucault's term). We identified the germ of such a relational conception of power in the young Horkheimer's claim that critical theory 'understands itself as the theoretical side of the struggle to rid the world of existing misery', according to which critical theory seeks to contribute to a learning process, in which proletarians (or anyone exhibiting a critical attitude) derive insights from reflecting on their suffering and struggles and subsequently apply those insights in emancipatory practice. We found here, in Horkheimer's early work, an indicative account of how subjects constituted through relations of power and domination are nonetheless able to develop some modicum of autonomy: namely, through reflection on their shared experience of socially compelled suffering and the channelling of those reflections into a demand for reasons, which may, when informed by a critical theory of society, form the basis of an emancipatory struggle against forces of social heteronomy.

This basic idea mirrors Horkheimer's view that, from a materialist point of view, the *very concept of justice* may be interpreted as the historical result of certain 'societal forms of life'—including shared experiences of misery, suffering, and privation—for which human beings have 'learned to demand reasons'.[1] Such a concern with the emancipatory potential for moral learning in shared experiences of suffering goes back to his earliest work, such as in the aphorism *'Monadologie'* in *Dämmerung*, where Horkheimer compares the human soul to a house with tiny windows that only allow a grossly distorted view of what goes on outside (i.e., the actual structural make-up of society), to which he adds: 'I only know of one gust of wind, which is able to blow open the windows of the house: that of shared

---

[1] Horkheimer, 'Materialismus und Metaphysik', p. 83; Horkheimer, 'Bemerkungen zur philosophischen Anthropologie', pp. 252–253.

suffering'.[2] Unfortunately, as we know, Horkheimer did not pursue this relational account of the subject-constitutive relationship between the shared experience of suffering in class conflict and the demand for reasons—or between power and autonomy—as a dialectically structured moral learning process in his later work. Instead, under the impression of the rise of fascism, he turned his attention to developing an account of the disempowering effects of structural forces within monopoly capitalism on the individual psyche, which ultimately led him to embrace Adorno's more uncompromisingly negativist views.

However, it is just such a relational account of the dialectic between power and autonomy that we find explicitly thematized as such in Honneth's early work on the struggle for recognition. In this account, which is informed by his reflections on the work of the young Horkheimer, the bridge between the experience of the *denial* of recognition and the practical struggle *for* recognition is supposed to lie precisely in the discursive articulation of affective reactions such as shame, rage, hurt, or indignation, which can contribute to producing the moral knowledge that one has been subject to an *injustice*, with the potential to motivate emancipatory action. According to Honneth,

> whether the cognitive potential inherent in feeling hurt or ashamed becomes a moral-political conviction depends above all on how the affected subject's cultural-political environment is constructed: only if the means of articulation of a social movement are available can the experience of disrespect become a source of motivation for acts of political resistance.[3]

As Honneth argues, shared experiences of suffering and disrespect can translate into a 'moral-political conviction', but only if subjects' 'cultural-political environment' is constituted as a socially embodied space of reasons, which offers the cognitive resources for making sense of suffering and disrespect *as* injustices, can those shared affective experiences be discursively articulated and become the basis for emancipatory demands and struggle, which may overcome those injustices in practice and institutionalize historically acquired moral insights in communicative relations of intersubjective recognition and mutual empowerment.

In this dialectic between socially imposed suffering and reason, between power and autonomy—I want to argue—we find the deep 'anchor' in existing social practice for both the moral universalism of Forst's Kantian constructivism and the epistemic humility of Allen's problematizing critique. On the one hand, the demand for reasons for shared experiences of socially imposed suffering—and the struggle to transform social relations when they cannot be justified—is precisely a recognition of oneself and others as moral subjects with a right to justification,

[2] Max Horkheimer, 'Monadologie', in *Dämmerung: Notitzen in Deutschland*, p. 314.
[3] Honneth, *The Struggle for Recognition*, pp. 138–139.

which simultaneously includes the second-order practical insight into the unconditional value of others as justificatory beings and a common recognition of 'the various risks of human vulnerability and human suffering, bodily and psychological'.[4] The right to justification is itself the outcome of a historical process of moral learning, which is socially and psychologically rooted in shared experiences of suffering and being subjected, with others, to forms of injustice and domination, and this right is, from a normative point of view, the moral ground on which any critique or demand for emancipation rests.

On the other hand, since, on this view, the formation of the autonomous subject is *itself* rooted in dynamics of power and domination—whether through one's culture, social group, or class, or, individually, within the family or in other social relationships—it always bears the imprint of those power relations and risks carrying subjugating norms within itself as stowaway passengers, who can blind the subject to the multiple ways in which he or she is already situated within an opaque social nexus of domination. This compels us, as Allen insists, to turn critique back on the genesis of the autonomous subject in those relationships of power and seek to denaturalize and uncover forms of exclusion and domination at the more subterranean level of subjection, such as the gender or racial norms that introduce domination into the foundations of subjectivity through the earliest affective commitments and the acquisition of language and contribute to stealthily reproduce and sustain a profoundly unjust world society.

As we have seen, this double-sided perspective—the twin tasks of *normative justification* and *critique of ideological justifications*—goes back to the young Horkheimer, who not only defined the very purpose of critical theory as enabling emancipation in practice by outlining the path to a reasonable society, but who also pursued a program of *Ideologiekritik*, which sought to unmask the ways in which the truth content of the *bourgeois* concepts and moral ideas that a critical theory 'takes under its protection' at the same time find distorted expression in *bourgeois* thought. Both of these perspectives—understood here, in the context of a critical theory of world society, as the moral universalism of Kantian constructivism and the epistemic humility of self-problematizing critique—should thus by no means be seen as contradictory but rather as complementary attitudes *methodologically anchored* in the enduring Frankfurt School insight that moral learning is ultimately driven by shared experiences of subjection to socially imposed suffering. These shared experiences in turn engender both the insight that we and others have a right to justification that grounds claims against societal injustice, as well as the ineliminable suspicion that our concepts and moral ideas may be tainted and distorted by the constitutive power relations from which they ultimately adhere.

This argument also enables me to respond to Allen's charge that a critical theory grounded in Forst's Kantian constructivism is not actually a critical theory at all,

---

[4] Forst, *The Right to Justification*, p. 39.

but rather a methodological approach of 'applied ethics', which must remain blind to these more subterranean forms of domination instilled through the very formation of the subject.[5] This charge not only negcts the abomentioned double-sided perspective but also that any critical theory is composed of a historical, a sociological, and a normative dimension, and that what distinguishes a critical theory is not that it does not elaborate its normative dimension, or the exact methodological sequence in which these dimensions are elaborated. Indeed, as we have seen throughout the reconstructive chapters of this book, the normative dimension can be elaborated as much in the young Horkheimer's original paradigm and in Adorno's negativism as in Habermas's, Honneth's, and Forst's respective paradigms – as indeed in Allen's. Rather, what distinguishes a critical theory is the way in which these three dimensions are *methodologically integrated* in a critique of the historical genesis, present, and possible future forms of the basic structure of society that can guide emancipation in practice. As Forst himself recognizes, his Kantian constructivism must be integrated in historical and sociological analyses of the existing social order—and it is ultimately only this normatively driven historical and sociological analysis that at same time 'defines justice in a positive sense, through the outline of a reasonable society',[6] which distinguishes a comprehensive critical theory of society.

As Thomas McCarthy has argued, the contemporary philosophical debate on 'the critique of impure reason' risks splitting into two opposing modes of critique what should rather be understood as different sides of the same critical project: 'On one side are those who, in the wakes of Niezsche and Heidegger, attack Kantian conceptions of reason and the rational subject at their very roots; on the other side are those who, in the wakes of Hegel and Marx, recast them in sociohistorical molds'. However, McCarthy insists that 'a number of deconstructive motifs and techniques, stripped of their totalizing pretensions, could be integrated into a pragmatic approach to communication, where they might serve as antidotes to our deep-seated tendency to hypostatize ideas of reason into realized or realizable states of affairs'.[7] In my view, Allen veers dangerously close to engaging in such 'totalizing pretensions' when she seeks to enlist Foucault and Adorno in a sweeping decolonization of critical theory that decisively rejects the attempt to recast the Kantian conception of reason in left-Hegelian 'sociohistorical' moulds. In McCarthy's words:

---

[5] Allen's further charge in *The End of Progress* that Forst's ostensible moral foundationalism is 'authoritarian' is rhetorically effective but substantively unedifying. Why should the claim that human beings have a right to justification be any more 'authoritarian' than, say, the claim that validity claims are limited by the context in which they are raised? To paraphrase Allen, 'Who, after all, are "we", and how does that "we" go about determining the limits of validity claims?'

[6] Horkheimer, 'Materialismus und Metaphysik', p. 82.

[7] McCarthy, *Ideals and Illusions*, pp. 2–6.

the claims we raise in communicating with consociates are intrinsically related to reasons that can be offered for and against them. The role of warranting and contesting reasons is in turn tied to the ability of accountable subjects to accept and reject them, to assess and revise them, to originate and criticize them. It is just this fact that fades from view in globalizing deconstructionist approaches. Rather than appearing as the *simultaneously dependent and independent moments* of this process that they are, responsible agents get transformed into cultural dopes, nodal points in grids of power, effects of the play of *differance,* and the like. Rational criticism and the learning processes that feed on it appear to be events of entirely local significance or incomprehensible shifts in horizons of meaning.[8]

Instead, *both* constructive and reconstructive engagement with the sociohistorical forms of Kant's 'ideas of reason' *and* a denaturalizing, deconstructive 'antidote' against the sociohistorical forms of Kant's 'transcendental illusions' should be understood as integral to the project of critical theory. Axel Honneth explicitly defends just such a triadic perspective, when he argues that critical theory must unite 'three models of critique' into a 'single program':

The constructive justification of a critical standpoint is to provide a conception of rationality that establishes a systematic connection between social rationality and moral validity. It is then to be reconstructively shown that this potential rationality determines social reality in the form of moral ideals. And these moral ideals, in turn, are to be seen under the genealogical proviso that their original meaning may have socially become unrecognizable.[9]

I have argued that, when faced with a global order, which is the historical result of centuries of imperial expansion, colonial domination, and primitive accumulation, and with a socially embedded space of reasons that carries the imprint of this wretched history in ways that many of us are only—not least through postcolonial critique—beginning to understand, critical theory must self-consciously complement the constitutive theoretical intention of enabling emancipation in practice through constructive and reconstructive critique with a reflexive self-problematizing check or 'proviso' that can dispel the illusions and blind-spots that may have become second nature to us. Neither moral construction or reconstruction, nor self-problematization is alone sufficient; all three must be recognized as ineliminable and necessary elements of any attempt to revitalize the project of the Frankfurt School critical theory in the age of global capitalist modernity.

---

[8] McCarthy, *Ideals and Illusions,* p. 4–5 [emphasis added].
[9] Honneth, *Pathologies of Reason,* p. 53.

11.2 The Critique of Global Capitalist Modernity

In the preceding subsection, I argued that critical theory must integrate a constructive, a reconstructive, and a problematizing element in its critique of world society. I have also argued that this follows, in part, from reflection on the dialectic between power and autonomy that the Frankfurt School tradition of critical theory has consistently understood as the engine of moral learning, and, in part, from reflection on the nature of the theory's global context of application. A critical theory of world society must at once be able to reconstruct the norms embodied in existing institutions of social freedom and to imaginatively construct new or alternative institutions that may be necessary to establish the necessary social, psychological, legal, and political conditions for autonomy in today's unjust world, and it must be able to reflexively scrutinize how the concepts, ideas, and narratives that we use to navigate this world may themselves be vehicles of neocolonial forms of domination in ways that may not be immediately apparent to us. A critical theory of world society must develop such a complex account of possibilities for practical emancipation against the background of a comprehensive, normatively driven analysis of the history and social reality of contemporary global capitalist modernity. Evidently, this is a theoretical project of breathtaking scale and magnitude. How might it be put into practice?

To begin with, we must firmly dispel the notion that a critical theory of world society could be brought to life by any individual philosopher—let alone a European or Western one. Applying critical theory to the global context requires a rethinking of *the kind of intellectual endeavour* that critical theory is. Or rather: it requires a radicalized vindication of the young Horkheimer's vision of critical theory as an interdisciplinary and cooperative, 'continuous dialectical interpenetration and development of philosophical theory and scientific practice'.[10] A critical theory that takes world society as its object must be conceived from the beginning as an inherently *cooperative* effort that must not only be able to integrate insights from across *multiple scientific disciplines*, but which must also encompass different *cultural perspectives* on the shared global infrastructure of world society. It must, in other words, be conceived as an open-ended and intercultural platform for the critique of the pathologies and injustices of global capitalist modernity.

In a sense, this follows directly from the young Horkheimer's insight that philosophy must serve an integrative epistemic function, combining and synthesizing insights from the fragmented human and social sciences into a coherent picture that corresponds to its complex object of study, world 'society as a whole'.[11] We all share certain systematic consequences of living within global capitalist modernity,

---

[10] Horkheimer, 'Die gegenwärtige Lage der Sozialphilosophie und die Aufgaben eines Instituts für Sozialforschung', p. 29.

[11] Max Horkheimer, 'Vorwort [zu Heft 1/2 des 1. Jahrgangs des Zeitschrift für Sozialforschung]', in *Gesammelte Schriften Band 3*, p. 36.

but the specific impact and experience of those consequences differ across cultures and political communities and according to one's resources and place within the profoundly hierarchical and massively unequal global political order. The pathologies and injustices of global capitalist modernity may manifest themselves in very different ways in different lifeworld contexts, even if they often share the same global structural roots, and the norms and values by which to describe and criticize those pathologies and injustices must be negotiated and accommodative of reasonable variations across different lifeworld contexts.

I began this book by arguing that the Frankfurt School tradition of critical theory has hitherto been developed as a critique of Western capitalist modernity, and if critical theory is to remain a vital and relevant tradition of social and political thought and a source of emancipatory guidance, it must today take the form of a critique of global capitalist modernity. Through a reconstruction of the Frankfurt School tradition as a continuous learning process—a history of theory with a systematic intention—I have tried to uncover both the conceptual and methodological obstacles within each paradigm of critical theory for gaining a grasp of world society, and to disclose enduring insights that a critical theory of world society must be able to incorporate. This book has not sought to develop a comprehensive critical theory of world society—indeed, it has argued that such a theory can only be realized as an inherently interdisciplinary, cooperative, and intercultural endeavour—but I have aspired to uncover the normative and methodological perspectives that would allow a historical and sociological critique of the present global order, and the most important tasks that such a critique must take upon itself.

In Chapter 1, I argued that we must understand such a theory as *a critical theory of justice* in Horkheimer's sense: as a theoretical 'demonstration of a contradiction between the principle of *bourgeois* society and its actual existence', which at the same time constructively 'defines justice in a positive sense, through the outline of a reasonable society'.[12] Moreover, although I maintained in Chapter 2 that Horkheimer's original paradigm of critical theory falters on its commitment to historical materialism's stagist view of history, I also argued that a critical theory of world society must integrate a critical political economy of the global economic and political order, in order to grasp its vast inequalities of power and wealth. In Chapter 4, I insisted that a critical theory of world society must go beyond the practical impasse and theoretical cul-de-sacs of Adorno's negativist paradigm, but I also maintained that it must embrace Adorno's concern with the non-identical in at least two ways: in terms of the postcolonial concern with the 'Other' of Western modernity, and in terms of the climatically disastrous ecological dialectic of enlightenment, which is rooted in a very real and historically entrenched

---

[12] Horkheimer, 'Materialismus und Metaphysik', p. 82.

contradiction between society and nature that—Adorno reminds us—we cannot reconcile in theory, but only in practice.

In Chapter 6, I argued that Habermas's analysis of the post-national constellation and proposal for a multilevel constitutional framework demonstrates that the discourse principle must be given a new legal-institutional form more appropriate to the conditions of present-day world society, if democratic politics is to be able regain power over globalized markets, resist systems-colonization of lifeworlds, and pre-empt catastrophic climate change. However, I also argued that Habermas's sole focus on the legal and political conditions of autonomy is insufficient for a critical theory of world society, and that his proceduralism remains at a loss to account for the deep injustices of global capitalist modernity. Finally, I argued that a critical theory of world society must look beyond Habermas's truncated conceptualization of the relationship between society and nature in terms of instrumental action, which falls behind Adorno's advances and reverts to the Prometheanism of the young Horkheimer.

In Chapter 7, I argued that Honneth's work exhibits a broader concern with the social and psychological conditions of autonomy, understood in terms of a communicative conception of freedom as autonomy and a theory of justice as social analysis, and I clarified the agential, structural, and relational conception of power that the central Frankfurt School concern with domination may be understood as incorporating. However, in Chapter 8, I criticized the crippling limitations of Honneth's Hegelian method for a critical theory of world society, which restricts Honneth's recognition paradigm to already-existing institutions of social freedom and forecloses its application to the global context. I also argued that although Honneth has close to nothing to say about the relationship between society and nature, the communicative conception of freedom allows us to appreciate that we must go beyond conceptualizing the social and psychological conditions of individual autonomy to also include the natural conditions of human freedom.

Finally, in Chapters 9 and 10, I argued that a critical theory of world society must be grounded in the moral universalism of the Kantian constructivism defended by Forst, in order to bypass the deadlock between Habermas's proceduralism and Honneth's Hegelianism and develop a critique of the injustices and pathologies of global capitalist modernity, which can in turn allow an imaginative political construction of the transnational or global institutions necessary for human emancipation within and across borders. However, I also argued that a critical theory of world society must integrate the epistemic humility of Allen's problematizing critique, in order to reflexively interrogate its potential complicity in ideological justifications of neocolonial and neoimperialist forms of domination that may have become second nature to us. These are, I submit, the tasks of a critical theory of world society.

11.3 Methodological Holism and the Planetary

I would like to end this book with a short epilogue of sorts—a brief reflection on the implications of the *Anthropocene* for how we conceive of the tasks of a critical theory of world society. Some ecological thinkers and activists may have the impression that anthropogenic climate change or global warming is, in some sense, external to the central and enduring concerns of Frankfurt School critical theory—that it's a kind of afterthought, and the heart's not really in it—and that this may be reflective of the tradition's dated anthropocentric presuppositions. I think that this is certainly true as a description of the personal interests of its recent standard-bearers. Indeed, one hardly gets the impression that Habermas, Honneth, Allen, and Forst have devoted much sustained attention to ecological concerns, given the conspicuous absence of these questions from their work. This is remarkable, of course, not just because the relationship between society and nature was so central to the members of the first generation of the Frankfurt School, but also because the scramble to avert an impending climate disaster on a planetary scale is, unquestionably, the definitive struggle of our time.[13]

However, I also believe that something above and beyond lack of personal interest is at work here. Ever since Horkheimer first formulated the distinction between traditional and critical theory, critical theorists have understood themselves to be concerned with human emancipation from *social* forms of domination, and the natural realm has always been seen as beyond the purview of critical theory. Even in Adorno's work, in which the relationship between society and nature is so central, his concern is not with the implications of that relationship for the natural realm, but rather with its implications for the human self-relation and for relations between humans. In other words: it was never a coincidence that Horkheimer did not invite a biologist or a climate scientist (if such a person had existed in his day) to join his inner circle at the IfS.

I have come to believe that this reflects a serious misunderstanding of the epistemic scope of a critical theory of society—although one that we can perhaps only begin to recognize as such in the Anthropocene, and in the context of a critical theory of world society. In the Introduction, I argued that the Frankfurt School idea of a critical theory is characterized in part by its methodological holism, which takes as its object the 'social totality', or society as such. But this definition is less unambiguous than it may at first seem. As Bruno Latour has argued (see Chapter 6), phenomena such as global warming are characterized precisely by their constitutive transgression of the traditional modern dividing line between nature and society: not only is global warming a product of the human combustion of fossil energy sources; its present and future consequences will also further blur the

---

[13] Nancy Fraser, 'What's Critical about Critical Theory? The Case of Habermas and Gender', *New German Critique* (35), 1985: pp. 97–131.

line between the natural and the social to an extent that it is senseless to insist on its strict maintenance. But if this is true, what are the grounds for restricting the methodological holism of critical theory to the social totality, narrowly conceived?

In fact, in the context of the Anthropocene, a critical theory of world society will be increasingly unable to make sense of anything at all, if it attempts to maintain a strict separation of nature and society and restrict its concern to the latter. How to (or why) abstract from natural processes in the impact of increasing global temperatures and rising sea levels on the likely proliferation of refugees and displaced people across the globe, and in the likely deleterious impact on international relations and the political stability of large parts of the Earth's tropical belt and the Asian subcontinent becoming increasingly uninhabitable? How to (or why) abstract from natural processes in the likely new and intensified social and political conflicts over land and resources and the new constellations of domination and exclusion that such scenarios are likely to engender?

My suggestion here is that, in the Anthropocene, the methodological holism of critical theory will have to be extended beyond the social realm narrowly conceived to include relations between ecosystems and societies—and, in the final analysis, to the *planetary perspective* of the relationship between the Earth system of ecosystems and world society. This does not just require an abandonment of the traditional interdisciplinary restriction of critical theory to an 'interpenetration' of social-scientific and humanistic disciplines and an inclusion of the natural sciences; it is also likely to have profound systematic implications for the theory's whole categorial framework. In Chapter 8, I tried to suggest how we might extend the communicative conception of freedom to include not only social and psychological conditions of autonomy but also natural conditions, and that those natural (or ecological) conditions must be conceived as forming part of the 'objective will' that renders our social and natural environment conducive to a 'liveable life'. To be sure, these brief reflections are not put forth with the intention of ending a conversation, but to open up to one—a conversation about the future of human life on this planet that a critical theory of world society must join.

Bibliography

Abromeit, John. 2011. *Max Horkheimer and the Foundations of the Frankfurt School.* Cambridge: Cambridge University Press.
Adorno, Theodor W. 1966. *Negative Dialektik.* Frankfurt: Suhrkamp Verlag.
Adorno, Theodor W. 1970. 'Zur gesellschaftlichen Lage der Musik'. *Zeitschrift für Sozialforschung* (1/1932), 356–378. München: Kösel-Verlag.
Adorno, Theodor W. 1970. *Ästhetische Theorie.* Frankfurt: Suhrkamp Verlag.
Adorno, Theodor W. 1971. *Erziehung zur Mündigkeit.* Frankfurt: Suhrkamp.
Adorno, Theodor W. 1986. *Gesammelte Schriften Band 20:1. Vermischte Schriften I.* Frankfurt: Suhrkamp Verlag.
Adorno, Theodor W. 1995. *Studien zum autoritären Charakter.* Frankfurt: Suhrkamp Verlag.
Adorno, Theodor W. 2001. *Metaphysics: Concept and Problems.* Translated by Edmund Jephcott. Stanford: Stanford University Press.
Adorno, Theodor W. 2003. *Gesammelte Schriften Band 1: Philosophische Frühschriften.* Frankfurt: Suhrkamp Verlag.
Adorno, Theodor W. 2003. *Kulturkritik und Gesellschaft I: Prismen. Ohne Leitbild. Gesammelte Schriften Band 10.1.* Frankfurt: Suhrkamp Verlag.
Adorno, Theodor W. 2003. *Kulturkritik und Gesellschaft II: Eingriffe und Stichwrote. Gesammelte Schriften Band 10.2.* Frankfurt: Suhrkamp Verlag.
Adorno, Theodor W. 2003. *Minima Moralia: Reflexionen aus dem beschädigten Leben.* Frankfurt: Suhrkamp Verlag.
Adorno, Theodor W. 2003. *Soziologische Schriften I.* Frankfurt: Suhrkamp Verlag.
Adorno, Theodor W. 2006. *Zur Lehre von der Geschichte und der Freiheit.* Frankfurt: Suhrkamp Verlag.
Adorno, Theodor W. 2010. *Probleme der Moralphilosophie.* Frankfurt: Suhrkamp Verlag.
Adorno, Theodor W. 2013. *Erziehung zur Mündigkeit.* Frankfurt: Suhrkamp Verlag.
Adorno, Theodor W. and Max Horkheimer, 2002. *Dialectic of Enlightenment: Philosophical Fragments.* Translated by Edmund Jephcott. Stanford: Stanford University Press.
Allen, Amy. 2008. *The Politics of Our Selves: Power, Autonomy, and Gender in Contemporary Critical Theory.* New York: Columbia University Press.
Allen, Amy. 2015. 'Emancipation without Utopia: Subjection, Modernity, and the Normative Claims of Feminist Critical Theory'. *Hypatia* (30/ 3): pp. 513–529.
Allen, Amy. 2017. *The End of Progress: Decolonizing the Normative Foundations of Critical Theory.* New York: Columbia University Press.
Allen, Amy. 2018. *The Power of Feminist Theory: Domination, Resistance, Solidarity.* New York: Routledge.
Allison, Henry E. 1990. *Kant's Theory of Freedom.* Cambridge: Cambridge University Press.
Anderson, Elizabeth. 1999. 'What Is the Point of Equality?' *Ethics* (109/2): pp. 287–337.
Apel, Karl-Otto. 1998. *Towards a Transformation of Philosophy.* Translated by Glyn Adey and David Fisby. Milwaukee: Marquette University Press.
Atkinson, Anthony B. 2015. *Inequality: What Can Be Done.* Cambridge MA: Harvard University Press.

Austin, J.L. 1962. *How To Do Things With Words*. Oxford: Oxford University Press.
Austin, John. 1995. *The Province of Jurisprudence Determined*. Edited by W.E. Rumble. Cambridge: Cambridge University Press.
Beitz, Charles R. 1979. *Political Theory and International Relations*. Princeton: Princeton University Press.
Benhabib, Seyla. 1986. *Critique, Norm, and Utopia: A Study of the Foundations of Critical Theory*. New York: Columbia University Press.
Benhabib, Seyla. 2009. 'Claiming Rights across Borders: International Human Rights and Democratic Sovereignty'. *American Political Science Review* (103/4): pp. 691–704.
Benjamin, Walter. 1991. *Gesammelte Schriften I: Band I*. Edited by Rolf Tiedemann and Hermann Schweppenhäuser. Frankfurt: Suhrkamp Verlag.
Bennett, Jane. 2010. *Vibrant Matter: A Political Ecology of Things*. Durham: Duke University Press.
Benton, Ted. 1989. 'Marxism and Natural Limits: An Ecological Critique and Reconstruction'. *New Left Review* (1/178): pp. 51–86.
Bhambra, Gurminder K. 2007. *Rethinking Modernity: Postcolonialism and the Sociological Imagination*. New York: Palgrave MacMillan.
Bhargava, Rajeev. 2013. 'Overcoming the Epistemic Injustice of Colonialism'. *Global Policy* (4/4): pp. 413–417.
Bohman, James. 2007. *Democracy Across Borders: From Dêmos to Dêmoi*. Cambridge MA: MIT Press.
Bourdieu, Pierre. 1991. *Language and Symbolic Power*. Edited by John B. Thompson. Cambridge MA: Harvard University Press.
Brunkhorst, Hauke and Peter Krockenberger. 1988. 'Paradigm-core and Theory-dynamics in Critical Social Theory: People and Programs'. *Philosophy & Social Criticism* (24/6): pp. 67–110.
Buchanan, Allen. 2000. 'Rawls's Law of Peoples: Rules for a Vanished Westphalian World'. *Ethics* (110/4): pp. 697–721.
Burkett, Paul. 1999. *Marx and Nature: A Red and Green Perspective*. New York: St. Martin's Press.
Butler, Judith. 2005. *Giving an Account of Oneself*. New York: Fordham University Press.
Caney, Simon. 2005. *Justice Beyond Borders: A Global Political Theory*. Oxford: Oxford University Press.
Chakrabarty, Dipesh. 2000. *Provincializing Europe: Post-Colonial Thought and Historical Difference*. Princeton: Princeton University Press.
Chakrabarty, Dipesh. 2002. *Habitations of Modernity: Essays in the Wake of Subaltern Studies*. Chicago: Chicago University Press.
Chibber, Vivek. 2013. *Postcolonial Theory and the Specter of Capital*. London: Verso Books.
Chomsky, Noam. 1965. *Aspects of the Theory of Syntax*. Cambridge MA: The MIT Press.
Cohen, G.A. 1988. *History, Labour, and Freedom: Themes From Marx*. Oxford: Oxford University Press.
Cohen, G.A. 2000. *Karl Marx's Theory of History: A Defence*. Princeton: Princeton University Press.
Davidson, Donald. 2001. 'Truth and Meaning'. In *Inquiries into Truth and Interpretation*. Oxford: Oxford University Press. 17–36.
Dietsch, Peter. 2015. *Catching Capital: The Ethics of Tax Competition*. Oxford: Oxford University Press.
Dubiel, Helmut. 1978. *Wissenschaftsorganisation und politische Erfahrung: Studien zur frühen Kritischen Theorie*. Frankfurt: Suhrkamp.

Dummett, Michael. 1973. *Frege: Philosophy of Language*. New York: Harper & Row.
Dummett, Michael. 1996. 'What Is a Theory of Meaning? (II)'. In *The Seas of Language*. Oxford: Oxford University Press. 34–93.
Dworkin, Ronald. 1986. *Law's Empire*. Cambridge MA: Harvard University Press.
Evans, Peter B., Dietrich Rueschemeyer, and Theda Skocpol (eds). 1985. *Bringing the State Back In*. Cambridge: Cambridge University Press.
Fanon, Frantz. 2005. *The Wretched of the Earth*. Translated by Richard Philcox. London: Grove Press.
Fassbender, Bardo. 1998. 'The United Nations Charter as Constitution of the International Community'. *Columbia Journal of Transnational Law* (36/3): pp. 529–619.
Focault, Michel. 1992. 'The Subject and Power'. *Critical Inquiry* (8/4): pp. 777–795.
Forst, Rainer. 2002. *Contexts of Justice: Political Philosophy Beyond Liberalism and Communitarianism*. Translated by John M. M. Farrell. Berkeley, CA: University of California Press.
Forst, Rainer. 2012. *The Right to Justification. Elements of a Constructivist Theory of Justice*. Translated by Jeffrey Flynn. New York: Columbia University Press.
Forst, Rainer. 2013. 'Transnational Justice and Democracy'. In *Political Equality in Transnational Democracy*. Edited by Eva Erman and Sofia Näsström. New York: Palgrave MacMillan. 41–59.
Forst, Rainer. 2013. *Toleration in Conflict. Past and Present*. Cambridge: Cambridge University Press.
Forst, Rainer. 2014. *Justification and Critique: Towards a Critical Theory of Politics*. Translated by Ciaran Cronin. Cambridge: Polity Press.
Forst, Rainer. 2017. *Normativity and Power: Analyzing Social Orders of Justification*. Translated by Ciaran Cronin. Oxford: Oxford University Press.
Forst, Rainer. 2018. 'Noumenal power revisited: reply to critics'. *Journal of Political Power* (11/3): pp. 294–321.
Forst, Rainer. 2019. 'The Constitution of Justification: Replies and Comments', in *Constitutionalism Justified: Rainer Forst in Discourse*. Edited by Ester Herlin-Karnell, Matthias Klatt, and Héctor A. Morales Zúñliga. New York: Oxford University Press, 2019. 295–346.
Forst, Rainer. 2019. 'Navigating a World of Conflict and Power: Reply to Critics', in *Justification and Emancipation: The Critical Theory of Rainer Forst*. Edited by Amy Allen and Eduardo Mendieta. University Park, PA: The Pennsylvania State University Press. 157–187.
Forst, Rainer and Klaus Günther. 2010. 'Die Herausbildung normativer Ordnungen: Zur Idee eines interdisziplinären Forschungsprogramms'. *Normative Orders Working Paper* (01/2010).
Foster, John Bellamy. 2000. *Marx's Ecology: Materialism and Nature*. New York: Monthly Review Press.
Foucault, Michel. 1980. *Power/Knowledge: Selected Interviews and other Writings 1972–1977*. Edited by Colin Gordon. New York: Pantheon Books.
Foucault, Michel. 1991. *Discipline and Punish: The Birth of the Prison*. Translated by Alan Sheridan. London: Penguin.
Foucault, Michel. 2007. *Security, Territory, Population. Lectures at the College de France 1977–1978*. Translated by Graham Burchell. New York: Picador.
Foucault, Michel. 2007. *The Politics of Truth*. Edited by Sylvère Lotringer. Cambridge MA: Semiotext(e).
Foucault, Michel. 2008. *The Birth of Biopolitics. Lectures at the College de France 1978–1979*. Translated by Graham Burchell. New York: Picador.

Fraser, Nancy. 1981. 'Foucault on Modern Power: Empirical Insights and Normative Confusions'. *PRAXIS International* (3): pp. 272–287.
Fraser, Nancy. 1985. 'What's Critical about Critical Theory? The Case of Habermas and Gender'. *New German Critique* (35): pp. 97–131.
Freeman, Samuel. 2006. 'The Law of Peoples, Social Cooperation, Human Rights, and Distributive Justice'. In *Justice and Global Politics: Volume 23*. Edited by Ellen Frankel Paul, Fred D. Miller, and Jeffrey Paul Jr. Cambridge: Cambridge University Press.
Freud, Sigmund. 2006. *Werkausgabe in Zwei Bänden. Band 1: Elemente der Psychoanalyse*. Edited by Anna Freud and Ilse Grubrich-Simitis. Frankfurt: Fischer Verlag.
Freud, Sigmund. 2006. *Werkausgabe in Zwei Bänden. Band 2: Anwendungen der Psychoanalyse*. Edited by Anna Freud and Ilse Grubrich-Simitis. Frankfurt: Fischer Verlag.
Freyenhagen, Fabian. 2013. *Adorno's Practical Philosophy: Living Less Wrongly*. Cambridge: Cambridge University Press.
Fricker, Miranda. 2007. *Epistemic Injustice: Power and the Ethics of Knowing*. Oxford: Oxford University Press.
Fromm, Erich. 1970. 'Über die Methode und Aufgabe einer analytischen Sozialpsychologie'. *Zeitschrift für Sozialforschung: Jahrgang 1/1932*. München: Kösel-Verlag.
Fromm, Erich. 1980. *Arbeiter und Angestellte am Vorabend des Dritten Reiches. Eine sozialpsychologische Untersuchung*. Edited by Wolfgang Bonß. Stuttgart: Deutsche Verlags-Anstalt.
Gädeke, Dorothea. 2017. *Politik der Beherrschung: Eine kritische Theorie externer Demokratieförderung*. Berlin: Suhrkamp Verlag.
Gädeke, Dorothea. 2020. 'Does a Mugger Dominate? Episodic Power and the Structural Dimension of Domination'. *Journal of Political Philosophy* (28/2), 2020: pp. 199–221.
Getachew, Adom. 2019. *Worldmaking after Empire: The Rise and Fall of Self-Determination*. Princeton: Princeton University Press.
Geuss, Raymond. 1981. *The Idea of a Critical Theory: Habermas and the Frankfurt School*. Cambridge: Cambridge University Press.
Geuss, Raymond. 1999. *Morality, Culture and History: Essays on German Philosophy*. Cambridge: Cambridge University Press.
Geuss, Raymond. 2008. *Philosophy and Real Politics*. Princeton: Princeton University Press.
Guha, Ranajit. 1983. *Elementary Aspects of Peasant Insurgency in Colonial India*. Delhi: Oxford University Press.
Guha, Ranajit. 1997. *Dominance Without Hegemony: History and Power in Colonial India*. Cambridge MA: Harvard University Press.
Guinan, Joe and Martin O'Neill. 2019. *The Case for Community Wealth Building*. London: Wiley.
Habermas, Jürgen. 1976. *Zur Rekonstruktion des Historischen Materialismus*. Frankfurt: Suhrkamp.
Habermas, Jürgen. 1979. *Communication and the Evolution of Society*. Translated by Thomas McCarthy. Boston, MA: Beacon Press.
Habermas, Jürgen. 1981. *Philosophisch-politische Profile*. Frankfurt: Suhrkamp Verlag.
Habermas, Jürgen. 1984. *Vorstudien und Ergänzungen zur Theorie des Kommunikativen Handelns*. Frankfurt: Suhrkamp Verlag.
Habermas, Jürgen. 1985. 'A Philosophico-Political Profile'. Interview with Perry Anderson and Peter Dews, *New Left Review* (1/151), May-June 1985: pp. 75–105.
Habermas, Jürgen. 1986. *The Theory of Communicative Action: Vol I: Reason and the Rationalization of Society*. Translated by Thomas McCarthy. Cambridge: Polity Press.
Habermas, Jürgen. 1987. *Eine Art Schadensabwicklung. Kleine politische Schriften VI*. Frankfurt: Suhrkamp Verlag.

Habermas, Jürgen. 1987. *Knowledge and Human Interests*. Translated by Jeremy J. Shapiro. Cambridge: Polity Press.
Habermas, Jürgen. 1987. *The Theory of Communicative Action. Vol. II: The Critique of Functionalist Reason*. Translated by Thomas McCarthy. Cambridge: Polity Press.
Habermas, Jürgen. 1988. *Legitimation Crisis*. Translated by Thomas McCarthy. Cambridge: Polity Press.
Habermas, Jürgen. 1988. *Theory and Practice*. Translated by John Viertel. Cambridge: Polity Press.
Habermas, Jürgen. 1989. *The New Conservatism: Cultural Criticism and the Historian's Debate*. Translated by Shierry Weber Nicholsen. Cambridge: Polity Press.
Habermas, Jürgen. 1990. *Moral Consciousness and Communicative Action*. Translated by Christian Lenhardt and Shierry Weber Nicholson. Cambridge: Polity Press.
Habermas, Jürgen. 1990. *The Philosophical Discourse of Modernity. Twelve Lectures*. Translated by Frederick Lawrence. Cambridge: Polity Press.
Habermas, Jürgen. 1992. *Postmetaphysical Thinking: Philosophical Essays*. Translated by William Mark Hohengarten. Cambridge: Polity Press.
Habermas, Jürgen. 1993. 'Concluding Remarks'. In *Habermas and the Public Sphere*. Edited by Craig Calhoun. Cambridge MA: MIT Press. 462–480.
Habermas, Jürgen. 1993. 'Notes on the Developmental History of Horkheimer's Work'. *Theory Culture Society* (10/ 61): pp. 61–77.
Habermas, Jürgen. 1994. *Justification and Application*. Translated by Ciaran Cronin. Cambridge MA: The MIT Press.
Habermas, Jürgen. 1996. *Between Facts and Norms. Contributions to a Discourse Theory of Law and Democracy*. Translated by William Rehg. Cambridge: Polity Press.
Habermas, Jürgen. 1998. *On the Pragmatics of Communication*. Edited by Maeve Cooke. Cambridge MA: MIT Press.
Habermas, Jürgen. 1998. *The Inclusion of the Other: Studies in Political Theory*. Edited and translated by Ciaran Cronin and Pablo de Greiff. Cambridge: Polity Press.
Habermas, Jürgen. 2001. *The Postnational Constellation: Political Essays*. Edited and translated by Max Pensky. Cambridge: Polity Press.
Habermas, Jürgen. 2002. *On The Pragmatics of Social Interaction: Preliminary Studies in the Theory of Communicative Action*. Translated by Barbara Fultner. Cambridge MA: MIT Press.
Habermas, Jürgen. 2003. *Truth and Justification*. Translated by Barbara Fultner. Cambridge, MA: The MIT Press.
Habermas, Jürgen. 2006. *The Divided West*. Cambridge: Polity Press.
Habermas, Jürgen. 2008. *Between Naturalism and Religion*. Translated by Ciaran Cronin. Cambridge: Polity Press.
Habermas, Jürgen. 2009. 'Einleitung'. In *Sprachtheoretische Grundlegung der Soziologie. Philosophische Texte, Band 1*. Frankfurt: Suhrkamp Verlag. 9–28.
Habermas, Jürgen. 2009. *Europe: The Faltering Project*. Translated by Ciaran Cronin. Cambridge: Cambridge University Press.
Habermas, Jürgen. 2012. *Nachmetaphysisches Denken II: Aufsätze und Repliken*. Berlin: Suhrkamp Verlag.
Habermas, Jürgen. 2012. *The Crisis of the European Union: A Response*. Translated by Ciaran Cronin. Cambridge: Polity Press.
Habermas, Jürgen. 2014. 'Democracy in Europe: Why the Development of the European Union into a Transnational Democracy is Necessary and How it is Possible'. *ARENA Working Paper* (13).

Habermas, Jürgen. 2014. *Toward a Rational Society. Student Protest, Science, and Politics*. Cambridge: Polity.
Habermas, Jürgen. 2019. *Auch eine Geschichte der Philosophie. Band I: Die okzidentale Konstellation von Glauben und Wissen*. Berlin: Suhrkamp Verlag.
Hammer, Espen. 2006. *Adorno and the Political*. London: Routledge.
Hart, H.L.A. 1961. *The Concept of Law*. Oxford: Oxford University Press.
Haslanger, Sally. 2012. *Resisting Reality: Social Construction and Social Critique*. Oxford: Oxford University Press.
Hegel, G.W.F. 1970. *Phänomenologie des Geistes. Werke III*. Frankfurt: Suhrkamp Verlag.
Hegel, G.W.F. 1977. *Phenomenology of Spirit*. Translated by A.V. Miller. Oxford: Oxford University Press.
Hegel, G.W.F. 1986. *Frühe Schriften: Werke 1*. Frankfurt: Suhrkamp Verlag.
Hegel, G.W.F. 1986. *Grundlinien der Philosophie des Rechts: Werke 7*. Frankfurt: Suhrkamp Verlag.
Hegel, G.W.F. 1991. *Elements of the Philosophy of Right*. Edited by Allen W. Wood, translated by H.B. Nisbet. Cambridge: Cambridge University Press.
Hegel, G.W.F. 2010. *The Science of Logic*. Cambridge: Cambridge University Press.
Hobbes, Thomas. 1985. *Leviathan*. London: Penguin Books.
Hobbes, Thomas. 1989. *Behemoth or the Long Parliament*. Chicago: University of Chicago Press.
Honneth, Axel. 1991. *The Critique of Power: Reflective Stages in a Critical Social Theory*. Translated by Kenneth Baynes. Cambridge MA: The MIT Press.
Honneth, Axel. 1995. *The Struggle for Recognition: The Moral Grammar of Social Conflicts*. Translated by Joel Anderson. Cambridge: Polity Press.
Honneth, Axel. 2002. 'Grounding Recognition: A Rejoinder to Critical Questions'. *Inquiry: An Interdisciplinary Journal of Philosophy* (45/4): pp. 499–519
Honneth, Axel. 2003. *Unsichtbarkeit: Stationen einer Theorie der Intersubjektivität*. Frankfurt: Suhrkamp Verlag.
Honneth, Axel. 2007. 'Gerechtigkeit und kommunikative Freiheit. Überlegungen im Anschluss an Hegel'. *Eurozine*, (15/1): pp. 1–13.
Honneth, Axel. 2007. *Disrespect. The Normative Foundations of Critical Theory*. Cambridge: Polity Press.
Honneth, Axel. 2009. *Pathologies of Reason: On the Legacy of Critical Theory*. Translated by James Ingram. New York: Columbia University Press.
Honneth, Axel. 2009. *Pathology of Reason: On the Legacy of Critical Theory*. Translated by James Ingram. New York: Columbia University Press.
Honneth, Axel. 2010. *The Pathologies of Individual Freedom; Hegel's Social Theory*. Translated by Ladislaus Löb. Princeton: Princeton University Press.
Honneth, Axel. 2011. 'Rejoinder'. In *Axel Honneth: Critical Essays. With a Reply by Axel Honneth*. Edited by Danielle Petherbridge. Leiden: Brill. 391–421.
Honneth, Axel. 2013. 'Replies'. *Krisis: Journal for Contemporary Philosophy* (1): pp. 37–47.
Honneth, Axel. 2014. 'The Normativity of Ethical Life'. Translated by Felix Koch. *Philosophy and Social Criticism* (40/8): pp. 817–826.
Honneth, Axel. 2014. *Freedom's Right: The Social Foundations of Democratic Ethical Life*. Translated by Joseph Ganahl. New York: Columbia University Press.
Honneth, Axel. 2020. *Die Armut unserer Freiheit*. Berlin: Suhrkamp Verlag.
Honneth, Axel and Nancy Fraser. 2003. *Redistribution or Recognition: A Political-Philosophical Exchange*. New York: Verso Books.
Horkheimer, Max. 1947. *Eclipse of Reason*. New York: Oxford University Press.

Horkheimer, Max. 1987. *Gesammelte Schrriften Band 2: Philosophische Frühschriften 1922–1932*. Frankfurt: Fischer Verlag.
Horkheimer, Max. 1988. *Gesammelte Schriften Band 4: 1936–1941*. Edited by Alfred Schmidt. Frankfurt: S. Fischer Verlag.
Horkheimer, Max. 1989. *Gesammelte Schriften Band 13: Nachgelassene Schriften 1949–1972*. Frankfurt: Fisher Verlag.
Horkheimer, Max. 2002. *Critical Theory: Selected Essays*. Translated by Matthew J. O'Connell et al. New York: Continuum.
Horkheimer, Max. 2009. *Gesammelte Schriften Band 3: Schriften 1931–1936*. Edited by Alfred Schmidt. Frankfurt: Fischer.
Horkheimer, Max, Erich Fromm et al. 1987. *Studien über Authorität und Familie: Forschungsberichte aus dem Institut für Sozialforschung*. Lüneburg: Dietrich zu Klampen Verlag.
Ibsen, Malte Frøslee. 2013. 'Global Justice and Two Conceptions of Practice-Dependence'. *Raisons Politiques* (51/3): pp. 81–96.
Ibsen, Malte Frøslee. 2019. 'The Populist Conjuncture: Legitimation Crisis in the Age of Globalized Capitalism'. *Political Studies* (67/3): pp. 795–811.
Ince, Onur Ulas. 2018. *Colonial Capitalism and the Dilemmas of Liberalism*. Oxford: Oxford University Press.
Iser, Mattias. 2008. *Empörung und Fortschritt: Grundlagen einer kritischen Theorie der Gesellschaft*. Frankfurt: Campus Verlag.
James, Aaron. 2005. 'Constructing Justice for Existing Practice: Rawls and the Status Quo'. *Philosophy & Public Affairs* (33/3): pp. 281–316.
Jay, Martin. 1973. *The Dialectical Imagination: A History of the Frankfurt School and the Institute for Social Research 1923–1950*. London: Heinemann.
Jay, Martin. 1984. *Marxism and Totality. The Adventures of a Concept from Lukács to Habermas*. Berkeley: University of California Press.
Kant, Immanuel. 1996. *Religion and Rational Theology*. Translated by Allen Wood. Cambridge: Cambridge University Press.
Kant, Immanuel. 1998. *The Critique of Pure Reason*. Translated by Paul Guyer and Allen W. Wood. Cambridge: Cambridge University Press.
Kant, Immanuel. 1999. *Grundlegung zur Metaphysik der Sitten*. Hamburg: Felix Meiner Verlag.
Kant, Immanuel. 1999. *Practical Philosophy*. Translated by Mary J. Gregor. Cambridge: Cambridge University Press.
Kant, Immanuel. 2003. *Kritik der praktischen Vernunft*. Hamburg: Felix Meiner Verlag.
Korsgaard, Christine. 1996. *Creating the Kingdom of Ends*. Cambridge: Cambridge University Press.
Korsgaard, Christine. 1996. *The Sources of Normativity*. Cambridge: Cambridge University Press.
Korsgaard, Christine. 2008. *The Constitution of Agency: Essays on Practical Reason and Moral Psychology*. Oxford: Oxford University Press.
Kosskeniemi, Martti. 2001. *The Gentle Civilizer of Nations: The Rise and Fall of International Law 1870–1960*. Cambridge: Cambridge University Press.
Kymlicka, Will and Sue Donaldson. 2011. *Zoopolis: A Political Theory of Animal Rights*. Oxford: Oxford University Press.
Latour, Bruno. 1991. *We Have Never Been Modern*. Cambridge MA: Harvard University Press.
Latour, Bruno. 2017. *Facing Gaia: Eight Lectures on the Climatic Regime*. Translated by Catherine Porter. Cambridge: Polity Press.

Lenin, Vladimir. 1987. *Essential Works of Lenin*. Edited by Henry M. Christman. New York: Dover Publications.
Löwy, Michael. 1997. 'For a Critical Marxism'. *Against the Current* (12/5): pp. 31–35.
Lukács, Georg. 1971. *History and Class Consciousness: Studies in Marxist Dialectics*. Translated by Rodney Livingstone. Cambridge, MA: The MIT Press.
Lukács, George. 1974. *The Theory of the Novel: A Historico-philosophical Essay on the Forms of Great Epic Literature*. London: Merlin Books.
Luxemburg, Rosa. 2003. *The Accumulation of Capital*. Translated by Agnes Schwarzschild. London: Routledge.
Lyotard, Jean-Francois. 1984. *The Postmodern Condition: A Report on Knowledge*. Translated by Geoff Bennington et al. Manchester: Manchester University Press.
Marcuse, Hebert. 1970. 'Der Kampf gegen den Liberalismus in der totalitären Staatsauffassung'. In *Zeitschrift für Sozialforschung: Jahrgang 3/1934*. Published by Max Horkheimer. München: Kösel-Verlag. 161–195.
Marx, Karl. 1978. *The Marx-Engels Reader. Second Edition*. Edited by Robert C. Tucker. New York: W.W. Norton & Company.
Mayer, Arno J. 1975. 'The Lower Middle Class as Historical Problem'. *The Journal of Modern History* (47/3): pp. 409–436.
Mbembe, Achille. 2017. *Critique of Black Reason*. Translated by Laurent Dubois. Durham: Duke University Press.
McCarthy, Thomas. 1978. *The Critical Theory of Jürgen Habermas*. London: Hutchinson & Co.
McCarthy, Thomas. 1991. *Ideals and Illusions: On Reconstruction and Deconstruction in Contemporary Critical Theory*. Cambridge MA: The MIT Press.
McCarthy, Thomas. 2009. *Race, Empire, and the Idea of Human Development*. Cambridge: Cambridge University Press.
McCarthy, Thomas and David Couzens Hoy. 1994. *Critical Theory*. Oxford: Blackwell Publishers.
McDowell, John. 1994. *Mind and World*. Cambridge MA: Harvard University Press.
McDowell, John. 1998. *Mind, Value, and Reality*. Cambridge MA: Harvard University Press.
Milanovic, Branko. 2019. *Capitalism Alone: The Future of the System that Rules the World*. Cambridge MA: Harvard University Press.
Mills, Charles W. 1997. *The Racial Contract*. Ithaca: Cornell University Press.
Morton, Timothy. 2013. *Hyperobjects: Philosophy and Ecology after the End of the World*. Minneapolis: University of Minnesota Press.
Müller-Doohm, Stefan. 2003. *Adorno: Eine Biographie*. Frankfurt: Suhrkamp Verlag.
Müller-Doohm, Stephan. 2014. *Jürgen Habermas: Eine Biographie*. Berlin: Suhrkamp Verlag.
Nagel, Thomas. 2005. 'The Problem of Global Justice'. *Philosophy & Public Affairs* (33/2): pp. 113–147.
Offe, Claus. 2016. *Europe Entrapped*. Cambridge: Polity Press.
Owen, David. 2019. 'Nietzsche and the Frankfurt School'. In *The Routledge Companion to the Frankfurt School*. Edited by Peter E. Gordon, Espen Hammer and Axel Honneth. New York: Routledge. 251–265.
Patten, Alan. 1999. *Hegel's Idea of Freedom*. Oxford: Oxford University Press.
Peters, Bernhard. 1994. 'On Reconstructive Legal and Political Theory'. *Philosophy & Social Criticism* (20/101): pp. 101–134.
Petherbridge, Danielle. 2013. *The Critical Theory of Axel Honneth*. Plymouth: Lexington Books.

Pettit, Philip. 2014. *On the Peoples Terms: A Republican Theory and Model of Democracy*. Cambridge: Cambridge University Press.
Piketty, Thomas. 2014. *Capital in the Twenty-first Century*. Cambridge MA: Harvard University Press.
Pippin, Robert B. 2008. *Hegel's Practical Philosophy: Rational Agency as Ethical Life*. Cambridge: Cambridge University Press.
Pogge, Thomas. 2002. *World Poverty and Human Rights*. Cambridge: Polity Press.
Pollock, Friedrich. 1970. 'Die gegenwärtige Lage des Kapitalismus und die Aussichten einer planwirtschaftlichen Neuordnung'. In *Zeitschrift für Sozialforschung, Vol. 1 (1932)*. München: Kösel-Verlag. 8–27.
Pollock, Friedrich. 1970. 'Is National Socialism a New Order?'. *Zeitschrift für Sozialforschung/Studies in Philosophy and Social Science* 9 (1941): pp. 440–455. München: Kösel-Verlag.
Pollock, Friedrich. 1970. 'State Capitalism'. *Zeitschrift für Sozialforschung/Studies in Philosophy and Social Science* 9 (1941): pp. 200–225. München: Kösel-Verlag.
Popper, Karl, Theodor W. Adorno et al. 1971. *Der Positivismusstreit in der deutschen Soziologie*. Berlin: Luchterhand.
Rawls, John. 1999. *The Law of Peoples*. Cambridge MA: Harvard University Press.
Rawls, John. 2000. *Lectures on the History of Moral Philosophy*. Edited by Barbara Herman. Cambridge MA: Harvard University Press.
Rawls, John. 2001. *Collected Papers*. Edited by Samuel Freeman. Cambridge MA: Harvard University Press.
Rawls, John. 2001. *The Law of Peoples*. Cambridge MA: Harvard University Press.
Rawls, John. 2005. *Political Liberalism. Expanded Edition*. New York: Columbia University Press.
Ronzoni, Miriam. 2009. 'The Global Order: A Case of Background Injustice? A Practice-Dependent Account'. *Philosophy & Public Affairs* (37/3): pp. 229–256.
Rorty, Richard. 1967. 'Introduction: Metaphilosophical Difficulties in Linguistic Philosophy'. In *The Linguistic Turn: Essays in Philosophical Method*. Edited by Richard Rorty. Chicago: Chicago University Press. 1–39.
Rorty, Richard. 2000. 'Response to Jürgen Habermas'. In *Rorty and his Critics*. Edited by Robert Brandom. Oxford: Blackwell Publishing. 56–64.
Saar, Martin. 2010. 'Power and critique'. *Journal of Power* (3/1): pp. 7–20.
Saar, Martin. 2013. *Die Immanenz der Macht: Politische Theorie nach Spinoza*. Berlin: Suhrkamp Verlag.
Said, Edward W. 2003. *Orientalism*. London: Penguin Books.
Saito, Kohei. 2017. *Karl Marx's Ecosocialism: Capitalism, Nature, and the Unfinished Critique of Political Economy*. New York: Monthly Review Press.
Sangiovanni, Andrea. 2007. 'Global Justice, Reciprocity, and the State'. *Philosophy & Public Affairs* (35/1): pp. 3–39.
Sangiovanni, Andrea. 2008. 'Justice and the Priority of Politics to Morality'. *The Journal of Political Philosophy* (16/2): pp. 137–164.
Scanlon, T.M. 1998. *What We Owe To Each Other*. Cambridge MA: Belknap Press.
Scheffler, Samuel. 2003. 'What Is Egalitarianism?'. *Philosophy and Public Affairs* (31/1): pp. 5–39.
Searle, John. 1969. *Speech Acts: An Essay in the Philosophy of Language*. Cambridge: Cambridge University Press.
Sellars, Wilfrid. 1997. *Empiricism and the Philosophy of Mind*. Edited by Robert Brandom. Cambridge, MA: Harvard University Press.
Singer, Peter. 1975. *Animal Liberation: A New Ethics for our Treatment of Animals*. New York: Harper Collins.

Slobodian, Quinn. 2018. *Globalists: The End of Empire and the Birth of Neoliberalism.* Cambridge MA: Harvard University Press.
Smith, Adam. 2007. *An Inquiry into the Nature and Causes of The Wealth of Nations.* Petersfield: Harriman House.
Specter, Matthew G. 2010. *Habermas: An Intellectual Biography.* Cambridge: Cambridge University Press.
Spencer, Robert. 2010. 'Thoughts from Abroad: Theodor Adorno as Post-Colonial Theorist'. *Culture, Theory and Critique* (51/3): pp. 207–221.
Spivak, Gayatri Chakravorty. 1988. 'Can the Subaltern Speak?'. In *Marxism and the Interpretation of Culture.* Edited by Cary Nelson and Lawrence Grossberg. London: MacMillan. 271–313
Stahl, Titus. 2013. *Immanente Kritik: Elemente einer Theorie sozialer Praktiken.* Frankfurt: Campus.
Stiglitz, Joseph E. 2002. *Globalization and Its Discontents.* New York: Norton.
Straumann, Tobias. 2020. *1931: Debt, Crisis, and the Rise of Hitler.* Oxford: Oxford University Press.
Theunissen, Michael. 1978. *Sein und Schein. Die kritische Funktion der Hegelschen Logik.* Frankfurt: Surhkamp Verlag.
Tooze, Adam. 2007. *The Wages of Destruction: The Making and Breaking of the Nazi Economy.* London: Penguin Books.
Tully, James. 2008. *Public Philosophy in a New Key: Volume II: Imperialism and Civic Freedom.* Cambridge: Cambridge University Press.
Valentini, Laura. 2011. *Justice in a Globalized World: A Normative Framework.* Oxford: Oxford University Press.
Warren, Rosie (ed). 2017. *The Debate on* Postcolonial Theory and the Specter of Capital. London: Verso Books.
Max Weber, 1946. *From Max Weber.* Edited by H.H. Gerth and C. Wright Mills. New York: Oxford University Press.
Weber, Max. 1992. *The Protestant Ethic and the Spirit of Capitalism.* Translated by Talcott Parsons. London: Routledge.
Weber, Max. 2001. *The Protestant Ethic and the Spirit of Capitalism.* Translated by Talcott Parsons. London: Routledge.
Wellmer, Albrecht. 1986. *Ethik und Dialog. Elemente des moralischen Urteils bei Kant und in der Diskursethik.* Frankfurt: Suhrkamp Verlag.
Whitbook, Joel. 1979. 'The Problem of Nature in Habermas'. *Telos: Critical Theory of the Contemporary* (40/41): pp. 41–69.
White, Stephen. 2015. 'Does Critical Theory Need Strong Foundations?' *Philosophy & Social Criticism* (41/3): pp. 207–211.
Wiggershaus, Ralf. 1998. *Die Frankfurter Schule: Geschichte, Theoretische Entwicklung, Politische Bedeutung.* München: Deutscher Taschenbuch Verlag.
Wittgenstein, Ludwig. 2009. *Philosophical Investigations, rev. 4th ed.* Translated by G.E.M. Anscombe, P.M.S. Hacker and Joachim Schulte. Chichester: Wiley-Blackwell.
Wood, Allan W. 1972. 'The Marxian Critique of Justice'. *Philosophy & Public Affairs* (1/3): pp. 244–282.
Wood, Allen. 1990. *Hegel's Ethical Thought.* Cambridge: Cambridge University Press.
Wood, Allen W. 2008. *Kantian Ethics.* Cambridge: Cambridge University Press.
Young, Iris Marion. 2013. *Responsibility for Justice.* Oxford: Oxford University Press.
Ypi, Lea. 2012. *Global Justice & Avant-Garde Political Agency.* Oxford: Oxford University Press.

Index

Abendroth, Wolfgang 150–1, 198–9
administered world, the 107–10, 186, 220, 237, 301
Adorno, Theodor W.
  the administered world 107–10
  as anti-system thinker 82, 87–8
  autonomous art 115
  biography of 85–6, 142–3
  collapses the world into Europe 130
  constellations 89
  the culture industry 114–16
  the dialectic of freedom 120–1
  ecological dialectic of enlightenment 132–5
  and Edward Said 136–8
  ego-strength and -weakness 111–12
  ethics of resistance to social heteronomy 124–5
  Eurocentrism of 129
  the exchange principle 109, 122
  expressive totality 129–30
  false consciousness 112
  freedom of the will 122–3
  on global implications of his thought 128
  against idealism's constitutive subject 95–6
  ideology 112–14
  on the irrationality of social reality 88, 109–10
  and Michel Foucault 135–6
  mimesis 125
  Mündigkeit 118–20
  negative dialectics 92–8
  negativism 90–2
  the non-identical 95, 97–8, 115, 125, 132
  permanent catastrophe 132–3
  on philosophy 87–90
  social heteronomy 208
  on social research 106–7, 140
  the standpoint of redemption 140
  and the student movement 142–3
  the universal system of delusion 112–14
Allen, Amy
  critique of Forst's approach as applied-ethics 321, 345–6
  critique of Habermas's modernism 214
  critique of Honneth's modernism 286–7
  critique of noumenal power 330
  immanent transcendence 302

  metanormative contextualism 301–2, 308–9
  on the necessity of decolonizing critical theory 304–5
  progress as fact *vs.* progress as imperative 289
  self-problematizing critique 306, 309–10
  subjection 300–1
  subordinating gender norms 301
  synthesis of Frankfurt School critical theory and poststructuralism 295
  three different modes of genealogy 305–6
Anderson, Elizabeth 63
Anthropocene, the 3, 351–2
Apel, Karl-Otto 189–90, 317
Auschwitz 98–100, 116
  as negative sign in history 116–17, 128–9
Austin, J.L. 159–60
autonomy, freedom as 12–14, 59–61, 256–61
  and communicative conception of freedom 260–1
  legal-political *vs.* socioeconomic conditions of 212
  natural conditions of 292–3
  as socially effective capacity/achievement 13, 121, 189, 213, 316, 324
  undermined by globalization 209

basic structure of society, the 10–13, 35, 37, 54, 191, 199, 293, 337
  global 57, 337
Beitz, Charles 337
Benhabib, Seyla
  on identity 72
  on jurisgenerativity of law 211
Benjamin, Jessica 241
Benjamin, Walter 28, 89, 114
Bennett, Jane 133–5
Bhambra, Gurminder K. 214

Caney, Simon 337
Chakrabarty, Dipesh
  historicism and stagist view of history 68, 286
  on the mimetic self-representation of postcolonial subjects 138

Chomsky, Noam 157
class consciousness
  as empirical problem 46–7, 51–5
  Lukács's theory of 45–6
Cohen, G.A. 41–2, 330
communicative action 164–5
constructivism
  Kantian 316–21, 332–6, 346
  moral 264, 278–9, 319–21
  moral *vs.* political 339
contextualism, metanormative 301–4, 308–10
cosmopolitanism 2, 205–8, 211–12, 337
critical theory 6–16, 37–40
  emerging paradigms of 296
  historical dimension 7–10
  methodological holism of 3–4
  and nature 351–2
  normative dimension 12–14
  paradigm of 6–7
  practical criterion of validity 14–17
  sociological dimension 10–12
  as theory of justice 61–5, 251–2, 325–6
  and traditional theory 35–9, 64, 325, 351
  of world society 5–6, 23, 71, 73, 127, 129, 132, 135, 138, 140–1, 213–14, 217, 283–5, 291, 332–6, 342, 348–51
critique
  immanent 92, 163, 263
  self-problematizing 306, 309–10
culture industry, the 114–16

Darwall, Stephen 241
Davidson, Donald 158
democracy 58–9, 146–7, 192–9, 273–7, 340
  crisis of 74
Dialectic of Enlightenment, the 99–104, 170
  enlightenment reverts into myth 102
  myth as already enlightenment 103
  as a work of negative dialectics 104
discourse principle 188–9, 195, 197, 204, 209, 278–9
domination 9–12, 14, 15–16, 53–5, 72–3, 96, 104, 110–11, 136–7, 153, 231, 235–9, 288, 297, 305–8, 324, 326, 330–2, 338, 345, 351
  as autonomy-impairment 63, 260
  German words for 101–2
  and justice 324
  structural 9, 101–2, 150, 187, 237, 331–2
Dummett, Michael 158–9
Durkheim, Emile 269
Dworkin, Ronald 193, 337

ecological dialectic of enlightenment 132–5
Eco-Marxism 75–6

emancipatory interest 153–4
Enlightenment and critical theory 16, 64, 119
Eurocentrism 4–5
  Adorno 129, 141
  Habermas 214–15, 216
  Honneth 284–6
European Union, the 73–4, 145, 206–7, 211, 290

formal pragmatics 153–63
  as philosophical foundation of critical theory 164
Forst, Rainer
  democracy 339–41
  dimensions of autonomy 314
  fundamental *vs.* full justice 323–4
  global justice 336–41
  grounding of morality 316–21
  human rights 339–40
  justice as non-domination 324
  moral *vs.* political constructivism 339
  noumenal power 326–32
  orders *vs.* narratives of justification 328–9
  practice-dependence 338
  the principle of justification 314–15
  the right to justification 313–16
  structural power 329–32
  synthesis with analytical political theory on justice 296
  toleration 322–3
Forsthoff, Ernst 150–1
Foucault, Michel
  and Adorno 135–6
  and the domain of the social 233
  on enlightenment 119
  genealogy 306
  and methodological nominalism 4, 139
Frankfurt School, the
  as history of Western capitalist modernity 22–3
  as Left-Hegelian 12–13, 16, 139, 252, 260, 263, 305, 346
  and the rise of Donald J. Trump 74
  and three conceptions of power 235–9
Fraser, Nancy 246, 295
freedom
  communicative 13, 15, 56, 252–61, 278, 325, 334
  legal 264
  moral 265
  and nature 292–3
  social 265
Frege, Gottlob 158
Freud, Sigmund
  on the Oedipus complex 54, 300

structural model of the psyche 53
Fromm, Erich
  theory of social psychology 52-5

gay marriage 287-9
Getachew, Adom 307-8
globalization 2, 4, 73, 146, 200-5, 212-13, 225, 271-3, 276-7, 283-5, 307, 335
Guha, Ranajit 70

Habermas, Jürgen
  autonomization of the self 300
  biography of 149-51
  cognitive interests 153-4
  the colonization thesis 184-7
  communicative action *vs.* discourse 164-5
  communicative reason 161-2
  communicative *vs.* instrumental action 173
  the constitutionalization of international law 204
  democratic principle, the 195
  developmental logic *vs.* dynamics 174-5
  disagreement with Forst over constructivism 316-17
  discourse ethics 188-92
  discourse principle, the 188-9, 195, 197, 204, 209
  discourse theory of law and democracy 192-9
  on domesticating (liberalism) *vs.* constituting (republicanism) legitimate power 210
  early admission of Eurocentrism 215
  emancipation as utopian-end state *vs.* process 171
  formal pragmatics 156-63
  on four problems in Horkheimer's and Adorno's work 145-6, 169, 194, 199
  globalization and the postnational constellation 200-4
  global modernity as common infrastructure 216-17
  ideal speech situation 165-8
  internal *vs.* external sociological perspective 178, 192-3
  interpretation of Hegel's Jena writings 233, 239
  intersubjective paradigm of reason 169-70
  as the "last Marxist" 219-22
  the linguistification of the sacred 176
  multilevel global constitutional framework 205-8
  multiple modernities 216
  philosophical grounding of critical theory 163-4
  proceduralism 213
  the public sphere 197
  the rationalization of the lifeworld 175-7
  rational reconstruction 156
  recasting of critique of reason as social theory 151-4
  and recognition 239-40
  reconstruction *vs.* critique 155
  reformism 220
  relapse into Prometheanism 217-19
  relation to Forst's work 333
  steering media 182-3
  system of rights 196, 199
  system *vs.* lifeworld 177-84
  theory of social evolution 172-8
  two-track model of deliberative politics 197
  validity claims 161-2
Haslanger, Sally 70
Hegel, Georg Wilhelm Friedrich
  communicative conception of freedom 258-60
  critique of Kant's moral philosophy 256-8
  dialectics 92-4
  Rechtsphilosophie 94, 251-2
heteronomy, social 108, 123, 181, 300, 343
  and the colonization thesis 184-6
  resistance to 124-6
Historical Materialism 40-2
  teleological structure of 68, 163
Honneth, Axel
  account of morality 244-5
  autonomy as master-value of modernity 261-2
  biography of 227
  democratic will-formation as a sphere of social freedom 273-7
  disaggregated view of moral learning 287-8
  the domain of the social 228-31
  globalization as external force of disruption 284
  Hegelian account of moral normativity 278-80
  justice 243-4, 278
  legal freedom 264
  the market economy as sphere of social freedom 268-73
  moral freedom 265
  moral progress 249-50
  normative reconstruction 262-3
  ontological status of recognition 283-4
  personal relations as sphere of social freedom 267-8
  reconstructive critique 263-4
  relation to Forst's work 333-5
  second-order *vs.* first-order norms 264

Honneth, Axel (*Continued*)
  social freedom 265
  social pathologies of freedom 265-6
  the struggle for recognition 239-46
  theory of recognition as account of normative constraints on capitalist development 246, 285
  three forms of disrespect 243-4
  three models of critique 347
  three patterns of recognition 240-2
  on three problems in Horkheimer's, Adorno's and Habermas's work 224-5, 228-9
Horkheimer, Max
  account of sadomasochistic personality 54-5
  biography of 27-9, 77-9
  critical theory as a theory of justice 61-3
  democracy 58
  and Donald J. Trump 73-4
  false consciousness 52
  fascism 55
  and global claim to validity 67
  human suffering 33-5
  ideal of a reasonable society 56-61
  Ideologiekritik 32
  interpretation of historical materialism 46-7
  Kant and freedom as autonomy 59-61
  materialism as interdisciplinary theory of society 30-2
  monopoly capitalism 49-55
  Prometheanism 76-7
  relational conception of justice 63-5
  stagist view of history 68-71
  traditional *vs.* critical theory 35-40
  on truth 32-3
  two phases of his thought 29-30, 35, 39, 51
human rights 196, 205-6, 208-11, 338-40

ideal speech situation 165-8
Ideologiekritik 31, 59, 170, 345
ideology 62, 96, 112-16, 154, 185, 345
Institut für Sozialforschung (Institute for Social Research)
  history of 27
  Studies on Authority and Family 53-5
  The Worker and Employee Survey 51-3
instrumental action 152, 173, 175, 218, 292

justice
  and communicative freedom 225-6, 278
  as demand for reasons 63-4, 343
  distributive *vs.* relational 62-4, 278
  fundamental *vs.* full 323-4
  global 206-8, 213-14, 336-41
  global epistemic injustice 138, 210
  as non-domination 324
  vs. proceduralism 190-1, 213-14
  and recognition 232, 243-4, 280
  and utopia 140

Kant, Immanuel
  categorical imperative 255
  cosmopolitan right 2, 205
  critique of reason 151, 153
  enlightenment 100, 119
  freedom as autonomy 59-61, 256
  moral philosophy 254-6, 318
  transcendental idealism 253-4
  world republic *vs.* voluntary league of nations 204-5

Latour, Bruno 133-5, 218, 293, 351
learning process 5-6, 16, 63-4, 83, 145, 169, 171, 174-5, 177, 204, 217, 224, 238, 243, 249-50, 258, 286-9, 305, 343-5, 349.
Lenin, Vladimir 16, 49, 71-2
lifeworld 178-81, 185-6
  as power-free 229-30
  rationalization of 175-7
Lukács, György
  on Adorno in the Grand Hotel Abyss 81
  class consciousness 45-6
  reification 42-4, 96
Lyotard, Jean-François 4, 139

Marcuse, Herbert 22
Marshall, T.H. 241
Marx, Karl
  commodity fetishism 42-3
  the contradictions of capitalism 49
  the creation of surplus value 48
  and critical theory 37-9, 152
  the falling rate of profit 49
  freedom 56
  freedom and nature 75
  world trade 131
mass media 276
materialism
  as interdisciplinary research programme 30
  as post-metaphysical philosophy 31-3
McCarthy, Thomas 32, 58, 153, 295, 346-7
McDowell, John 247-9
Mead, George Herbert Mead 241, 249, 300
mimesis 103, 125, 292
monopoly capitalism 48-55
moral universalism 57, 311, 345-6
Morton, Timothy 218-19
Mündigkeit 118-21, 124, 186, 199, 250

Nagel, Thomas 337
negative dialectics 92–9, 104, 112, 122, 171, 263
New International Economic Order 307
new materialism 133–5
Nietzsche, Friedrich 61, 306
non-identical, the 95, 97–8, 115, 125, 132

Odyssey, the 102
Orientalism 136–8
ownership, deconcentration of 273

pathology, social 187–9, 265–6, 332
Pettit, Philip 63
Piketty, Thomas 73
Pippin, Robert 280–2
Pogge, Thomas 337
political economy 73
Pollock, Friedrich
    as background for *Dialectic of Enlightenment* 104
    on monopoly capitalism 49–50
Popper, Karl 104–5
populism, right-wing 73–5
Positivismusstreit, der 104–5, 140
postmodernism 4, 138–9, 233
power
    administrative 182–3, 196
    agential 234–5
    and autonomy 344–5
    communicative 196–7
    noumenal 326–32
    relational 234–5, 343
    structural 234–5
    as subjection 300–1, 345
    three conceptions of 234–9
    and validity 301–4
practice-dependence 337–8
progress, moral 216, 249–50, 268, 270–1, 277, 279, 284–9, 305
Prometheanism 75–6, 217–19, 292

Rawls, John 2, 9–10, 174, 196, 296, 315, 337, 339
reason
    communicative 161–2
    instrumental 100–1, 170
    practical 213
    rationalisation as learning process 16
    as socially embodied 7–9
reasonable society 56–62, 88, 221–2, 236, 260, 263, 293, 325, 345–6
recognition
    and moral progress 249
    ontological status of 283
    and reason 248
    reception *vs.* attribution 247
    three patterns of 240–1
reification 42–5, 57, 96, 108, 181, 184, 186–7, 332

Said, Edward 136–8
Scheffler, Samuel 63
Searle, John 159
Singer, Peter 133
social, domain of the 228–31
Spivak, Gayatri Chakravorty 139
state capitalism 79, 131–2
Strawson, Peter 244
Subaltern Studies Group 70
subsystems, functional 181–4
    colonization of the lifeworld 184–7
    as norm-free 230
suffering
    human and justice 63–4, 343–4
    theoretical significance of 33–5

Theunissen, Michael 252
traditional theory 35–7

Weber, Max
    disenchantment 101
    social rationalization 43–4
Weimar republic 27–9
Western Marxism 28
will, freedom of 123, 134
Wittgenstein, Ludwig 159
world society 2–3, 17, 23, 34, 67–71, 127, 130–1, 200–17, 283–91, 297–8, 304, 307–10, 335–41, 348–50
    as placeholder concept 5

Zeitschrift für Sozialforschung 28